D1602607

PANDEMIC PLANNING

PANDEMIC PLANNING

Edited by

J. Eric Dietz
David R. Black

CRC Press
Taylor & Francis Group
Boca Raton London New York

CRC Press is an imprint of the
Taylor & Francis Group, an **informa** business

This book focuses on innovations and new ways to address catastrophic problems. This does not mean the old methods should be eliminated or abandoned, but carefully reviewed for efficient mitigation of the problem. The methods described are based on research and experience attained from university research and Pandemic Influenza grant in 2008, Engineering the Degradation of Healthcare Systems in Pandemic Influenza, and 2009, Pandemic Influenza Exercise Preparedness Program: An Extended Analysis of the 2008 Pan Flu Tabletop and Functional Exercise Program that were awarded to Purdue University. It is important to recognize that the methods described are not a panacea for a pandemic. The information provided is a foundation upon which individuals and organizations can build. The intention of the book is for readers to use the information given to enhance practical responses of emergency response.

CRC Press
Taylor & Francis Group
6000 Broken Sound Parkway NW, Suite 300
Boca Raton, FL 33487-2742

© 2012 by Taylor & Francis Group, LLC
CRC Press is an imprint of Taylor & Francis Group, an Informa business

No claim to original U.S. Government works

Printed in the United States of America on acid-free paper
Version Date: 20120213

International Standard Book Number: 978-1-4398-5765-6 (Hardback)

Visit the Taylor & Francis Web site at
http://www.taylorandfrancis.com

and the CRC Press Web site at
http://www.crcpress.com

Dedication

The editors would like to thank our families for a near endless stream of support throughout research and military careers. We would like to thank our colleagues for support that has led to this book. We especially appreciate the authors who have contributed time and expertise toward our common goal of improving our national readiness.

Contents

Foreword

The impact of an influenza pandemic can be measured in a variety of ways: 50 million deaths in 1918 and 1919, hundreds of millions of individual cases of sickness in 1957, and an estimated three to four trillion dollars lost in global productivity in 2009.

By their very nature, the characteristics and outcomes of future pandemics are extremely difficult to predict. This uncertainty, however, should not be viewed as a reason to avoid planning, but rather as a motivator to emphasize the necessity of thorough, complete, and flexible plans for the inevitable pandemics of the future. By improving the readiness of your organization to operate during a pandemic, the likelihood is increased that you will be able to respond quickly and appropriately to future events.

Preparedness requires cooperation and collaboration on multiple levels. Individuals should protect themselves and their families; employers should enact policy changes to avoid the spread of illness in the workplace and in schools; healthcare providers and governmental bodies should exercise to test themselves and their communities. True preparedness requires multilevel commitments across geographic and organizational borders.

Pandemics result in urgent needs and demands, and resources will be limited. To be effective during the real event requires us to train and exercise the necessary skills and create plans before the crisis. It is imperative to develop and implement clear metrics for both individual and organizational performance.

The ultimate purpose of planning and preparing for a pandemic is twofold: (a) to decrease the morbidity and mortality rates of the illness, and (b) to improve recovery time so that economic and social activities can be resumed at their normal levels. Additionally, by actively engaging your organization in preparedness improvement, efficiency and effectiveness of normal day-to-day operations can be enhanced.

The journey of preparedness is never-ending. There is no perfect pandemic plan for any one individual, company, school, region, or government. The goal of researching, analyzing, and modifying pandemic plans is to increase the likelihood that your organization can and will respond efficiently and appropriately in the actual time of crisis.

No matter where you find yourself on your journey of preparedness, it is the hope of the endorsers, authors, and editors of this book that you find the text useful in guiding you toward an improved level of preparedness.

Judy Monroe, MD, FAAFP, is the director of the Office for State, Tribal, Local and Territorial Support (OSTLTS) and deputy director for the Centers for Disease Control and Prevention (CDC). Before her current role, she was the state health commissioner for Indiana and served in the National Health Service Corps as a family practice physician in rural Tennessee. Additionally, she has been a faculty member in the Department of Family Medicine at Indiana University and directed the Family Medicine Residency Program at St. Vincent Hospital in Indianapolis. She served as a member of the Indiana Health Information Exchange Board of Directors, chaired the Association of State and Territorial Health Officials (ASTHO) Preparedness Policy Committee and was president of ASTHO. During her tenure as state health commissioner for Indiana, one of her primary areas of focus was preparedness. Partnering with Purdue University, she led the Indiana Public Health System Quality Improvement Project (PHSQIP), designed to increase local public health capacity, improve infrastructure, and strengthen overall public health system performance.

Acknowledgments

The editors would like to thank Julie Shaffner for her commitment to this volume in editing, communicating with authors, monitoring submissions and shortfalls, and providing an important chapter to this book that presents a major data collection problem. We also are indebted to her for support in the formulation of the concept and focus of this book.

Editors

David R. (Randy) Black, PhD, MPH, HSPP, CHES, CPPE, FASHA, FSBM, FAAHB, and FAAHE, is a distinguished scholar and the professor of public health and co-director of the Homeland Security Institute, Purdue University. He is a fellow of five different health organizations and has received forty federal, national, and state awards or recognitions for his contributions to public health. He has participated in the publication of eight books and twenty-five book chapters. He has published more than 150 peer-reviewed manuscripts and participated in 180 presentations and another fifty invited presentations. He completed his doctoral degree at Stanford University in psychology and a postdoctoral fellowship at the Stanford Heart Disease Prevention Program and Laboratory for the Study of Behavioral Medicine at the Stanford School of Medicine. Later, he accepted a faculty appointment at the University of Nebraska Medical Center. He remained there for four years and held a faculty appointment in the College of Pharmacy where he taught communication skills and statistics and in the Department of Preventive and Stress Medicine as well as in the Department of Psychology. His next faculty appointment was at Purdue University where he has been since 1984. He completed his master of public health degree in residence at San Diego State University while still a faculty member at Purdue University. He is a full professor of public health and holds adjunct appointments in health sciences, nutrition sciences, and nursing. The major focus of his teaching has been behavioral epidemiology, public health and prevention, design and analysis of health promotion programs, and service delivery of program interventions.

Dr. Black is a retired colonel who served for 37½ years and an Iraq veteran. He has received many military awards including the Legion of Merit. He has commanded units ranging in size from company to brigade. He has been commandant of the Indiana Military Academy and is a graduate of the US Army War College. Dr. Black was a part of the State Partnership for Peace Program and helped cold war countries such as Slovakia set up military operations to promote peace and not war and to offer national protection at affordable costs.

The combination of his public health and military education and training was a natural segue to pandemic influenza. Professor Black is the co-director of Purdue

Homeland Security Institute (PHSI). PHSI presented him the Meritorious Service Award in recognition and appreciation of meritorious service and research excellence. The relationship between public health and homeland security has been symbiotic among administrative units, faculty, and students. Examples of multidisciplinary projects encompass statewide pandemic training exercises and assessments of agency disaster plans; development of simulations to demonstrate the spread of influenza within a school; provision of simple recommendations and "minimal" interventions to prevent, protect, and control the spread of influenza; and promotion of population-based delivery systems, social-media monitoring and survey methods, and military leadership models for public health and disaster preparedness.

J. Eric Dietz, PhD, PE, is the director of the Purdue Homeland Security Institute and associate professor of computer and information technology at Purdue University. Dr. Dietz's research interests include optimization of emergency response, homeland security and defense, energy security, and engaging veterans in higher education. As a director in Purdue's Discovery Park, Dr. Dietz is responsible for the catalysis of Purdue's homeland security research enterprise, increasing the impact of Purdue on society, and organizing large multidisciplinary projects within Purdue.

Prior to his current responsibilities, Dr. Dietz was on loan from Purdue to Indiana's governor as the founding executive director for the Indiana Department of Homeland Security, a new state agency responsible for planning and response and assuming the responsibility for the safety and security of 6.2 million Indiana residents. His duties included reorganization of five state agencies into functional divisions responsible for the development of plans, training, and exercises to improve the emergency response for Indiana governmental functions. Dr. Dietz also led the Governor's Counterterrorism and Security Council, a multiagency organization guiding Indiana's homeland security policy. The comprehensive emergency management command and control systems developed by Dr. Dietz were tested by seven presidential declared disasters and emergencies including Indiana's task force response to Hurricane Katrina. Under his leadership, Indiana added new statutory programs and funding that enhanced statewide emergency services. Dr. Dietz leadership brought a long-sought objective to the fire service in the Indiana State Fire Training System to offer standardized training to more than 26,000 Indiana first responders. Dr. Dietz led the formation of the Indiana Intelligence Fusion Center to coordinate all crimes and terrorism law enforcement intelligence. Eric also established a state disaster fund which provided process and funding to support individuals and local government following disasters. Dr. Dietz was a board member for several national and regional boards which included the Central United States Earthquake Consortium, the Certified Emergency Manager Commission, Homeland Security Consortium, the National Weather Service Storm Ready program, Federal Emergency Management Agency Region 5 Advisory Council, and National Emergency Managers Association.

Retiring as a lieutenant colonel from the US Army in 2004, Dr. Dietz led a number of army acquisition programs throughout his twenty-two-year military career including power systems, chemical sensors, and command and control systems. Balancing a career between tactical and research responsibilities, Dr. Dietz was able to effectively lead military as well as the civilian workforce in projects of technical sophistication between detections systems to command and control systems. A professional engineer in Indiana, he earned BS and MS degrees in chemical engineering from Rose-Hulman Institute of Technology and a PhD from Purdue.

Contributors

Tim Baldwin, MA, is a program associate for counterterrorism training and research at Westminster Institute in Washington, DC. Mr. Baldwin completed a graduate degree in strategic intelligence studies at the Institute of World Politics in Washington, DC in 2011. Prior to living in the Washington, DC area, Mr. Baldwin worked for the Purdue Homeland Security Institute and Purdue Office of Planning and Preparedness where he worked closely with campus, local, and state emergency management leaders on various aspects of exercise design, continuity of operations plans, critical infrastructure, threat assessments, and campus emergency preparedness. Mr. Baldwin was also part of a team that focused on pandemic influenza preparedness for hospitals and county officials throughout the State of Indiana. Mr. Baldwin is a graduate of the Krannert School of Management at Purdue University (2008) where he studied business management and sociology.

Andrew Branum, MS, consultant with Booz Allen Hamilton, graduated from Purdue University in West Lafayette, Indiana, with a bachelor's degree in economics and a master's degree in technology. While an undergraduate student, Mr. Branum worked with the Indiana Department of Homeland Security on projects in the State Emergency Operations Center during a governor-declared state of emergency. Mr. Branum also worked with the Purdue Homeland Security Institute on several projects including pandemic influenza exercise planning, emergency management planning, and local and state coordination and response. He currently works at Booz Allen Hamilton in McLean, Virginia, where he works closely with the Department of Homeland Security and the critical infrastructure sectors to improve national and organizational cyber security strategy and response.

Martha Burns, BS, is an industrial engineer who is currently the director of lifelong learning at the Purdue School of Veterinary Medicine. She is responsible for all aspects of continuing education, including online education courses, workshops, and the annual Purdue Veterinary Medicine Fall Conference. She previously worked as assistant director of engagement and education for Purdue University, Visual Analytics for Command, Control and Interoperability Environments (VACCINE) and the Purdue Homeland Security Institute where she developed educational initiatives for K-12 programs through undergraduate and graduate level work, to professional training programs, and preparedness exercises. Ms. Burns received her AS in industrial engineering from Purdue University in West Lafayette, Indiana.

John F. Burr, PhD, is a continuous term lecturer in the Krannert School of Management at Purdue University. His teaching includes both strategic management and entrepreneurship. Dr. Burr has been with Purdue University since 2001 when he began to pursue his PhD while working full time in Purdue's Discovery Park as an IT manager. In 2009, Dr. Burr took a visiting assistant professor position with Consumer Sciences and Retailing teaching selling and sales management before joining Krannert.

Prior to returning to Purdue, Dr. Burr had a ten-year career with DuPont. While at DuPont he held multiple positions and in his last position he was business manager for implementation of a new business model in the Corian® division where he also spent a number of years as marketing manager. At DuPont he held roles ranging from sales to international business strategy consulting. During this period he worked in approximately thirty different countries and consulted with brands including Teflon®, Lycra®, and Dacron®, and business units ranging from engineering polymers to crop protection to packaging.

His degrees include a PhD in strategic management with a minor in finance, a master's in science in industrial administration, and a bachelor of science in mechanical engineering technology.

Steven Cain, BS, project director, Extension Disaster Education Network Homeland Security; president, Indiana Voluntary Organizations Active in Disaster, and member of the board of national VOAD, has been a major player in three national USDA team awards for disaster education: *Award for Superior Service* in 1988, *Group Honor Award for Excellence* in 2002, and *The Partnership Team Award for Efficient Use of Resources* in 2009. In 2002, he was named the national leader for the EDEN Homeland Security project. In 2005, he was selected as an agroterrorism consultant to the National Academies of Science. In 2009, he was elected president of Indiana Voluntary Organizations Active in Disaster. He is now involved in forming community organizations active in disaster around the state of Indiana.

He has published thousands of articles nationally. In the 1970s and 1980s, Cain was an agricultural journalist. Since 1987 he has been a communication specialist for Purdue Extension. From 1989 to 2003, he was a contributing writer to *World Book's Science Yearbook*. In 1997 and 1998, he hosted the nationally televised Science and Technology Report for DirectTV's Channel Earth. In the 1990s, Cain was a volunteer communication consultant in Bulgaria, Croatia, Estonia, Russia, and Uganda.

Bert Chapman, MSLS, is government information, political science, and economics librarian and professor of library science at Purdue University. He has written four books on conducting foreign and national security policy research including *Geopolitics: A Guide to the Issues* (Santa Barbara, CA: Praeger, 2011) and *Military Doctrine: A Reference Handbook* (Santa Barbara, CA: Praeger Security International, 2009). His research interests include literature on foreign policy, intelligence, national security policy, and various historical and political science topics emphasizing the use of government information resources. He has authored many scholarly articles on these topics.

Alok R. Chaturvedi, PhD, is a professor in Purdue University's Krannert Graduate School of Management and the founder, chairman, and CEO of Simulex Inc., a modeling and simulation company located in Purdue Technology Park. He served as the technical lead for the US Department of Defense's Sentient World Simulation project. Dr. Chaturvedi is the founding director of Purdue Homeland Security Institute and has also served as an adjunct research staff member at the Institute for Defense Analyses (IDA), Alexandria, Virginia—a leading think tank on national and homeland securities matters. He received his PhD in management information systems and computer science from the University of Wisconsin at Milwaukee. He is an accomplished scholar and thinker and has published extensively in major journals and conference proceedings. Over the last two decades, Dr. Chaturvedi has developed the synthetic environment for analysis and simulation (SEAS). SEAS is widely used by *Fortune 500* companies, local, and state governments, and the US Department of Defense for experimentations, planning, analysis, operations, and shaping for complex problems. Since 2007, Dr. Chaturvedi has worked closely with Indiana's Department of Education and Family and Social Services Administration (FSSA) to devise innovative intervention strategies to improve underprivileged students' achievement potential. The National Training Simulations Association (NTSA) recognized SEAS as the best simulation for analysis in all of the Department of Defense for the year 2005. Dr. Chaturvedi is the principal investigator (PI) and the project director for several major grants from the National Science Foundation, Indiana 21st Century Research and Technology Fund, Office of Naval Research, Defense Acquisition University, and several *Fortune 500* companies. He has been involved with several government task forces on important public policy and national security matters. Professor Chaturvedi was named in Federal 100 by *Federal Computer Weekly* and was awarded the "Sagamore of the Wabash" by the Governor of Indiana, the highest civilian award for his service to the State.

Bryan J. Damis, MPH, is program manager for the Society for Public Health Education (SOPHE) in Washington, DC. He received his master's in public health from Florida State University. He also has a BS in geography from James Madison University. Prior to that, Bryan spent three and a half years as a senior analyst in public health preparedness at the National Association of County and City Health Officials (NACCHO).

Anne L. Drabczyk, PhD, is director of the Advanced Practice Centers Program for the National Association of County and City Health Officials in Washington, DC. Dr. Drabczyk holds a PhD in public health from Walden University, and is a Central Michigan University alumnus with a master's degree in public health administration, and a bachelor's degree in community health education and psychology. Dr. Drabczyk earned certification in Appreciative Inquiry from the Weatherhead School of Business at Case Western Reserve University, and uses the research method in her consultation with clients. Dr. Drabczyk has worked in the field of public health for more than 30 years, including executive positions in government, profit and non-profit organizations, and as a tenured-track assistant university professor. Dr. Drabczyk has extensive speaking and peer-reviewed publications on her research related to strength-based organizational values, leadership accountability, community capacity building, and resilience. She serves on the editorial board of the peer-reviewed journal *Journal of Homeland Security and Emergency Management*.

Steven Dunlop, MBA, is the managing director of the Indiana Advance Electric Vehicle Training Consortium. He has spent the last twelve years at Purdue working on a variety of education and software development projects primarily in design and delivery systems. These cover projects for the K–16 and private sector markets. During this time, Mr. Dunlap has held roles as project director, managing director for the Envision Center for Data Perceptualization, and his current role as managing director, Indiana Advance Electric Vehicle Training Consortium. Mr. Dunlap has also taught a variety of classes within the College of Technology and holds a courtesy appointment within the school. Prior to his efforts at Purdue, Mr. Dunlap worked in a variety of roles in the private sector including time spent as CFO for a national company which included overseeing the operations and software development teams.

Paul Etkind, PhD, is the lead program analyst for immunizations and epidemiology as well as the acting senior director of infectious diseases at the National Association of County and City Health Officials (NACCHO) in Washington, DC. Dr. Etkind holds a BA in biology from Clark University, and an MPH and DrPH from Yale University's School of Epidemiology and Public Health. Dr. Etkind has worked in public health practice for more than 30 years as an epidemiologist and director at the state and local health department levels. His portfolio also includes public health preparedness planning and training. Dr. Etkind has extensive speaking and teaching experience at the undergraduate and graduate levels and he is also an author of articles in peer-reviewed journals. He also served on the board and was chair of the National Coalition of STD Directors, and was on the board of the Massachusetts Public Health Museum.

V. Scott Fisher, MPH, is currently serving as director of preparedness programs for several of NACCHO's public health preparedness projects, including Project Public Health Ready and Public Health Law and Preparedness. Prior to serving as director of preparedness programs, Mr. Fisher held the positions of senior analyst and program associate for various projects in public health performance standards and community health assessment. Mr. Fisher received his master's in public health from the George Washington University School of Public Health, with a concentration in epidemiology. He also holds a bachelor of science degree from the University of Pittsburgh, with a major in biology. Prior to joining NACCHO, Mr. Fisher was a research fellow at the National Institutes of Health.

William A. Foley, Jr., PhD, is on the faculty of Indiana University's School of Public and Environmental Affairs teaching national security, homeland security, and public safety. Dr. Foley is also a contractor for the US Department of Homeland Security (DHS) for the National Level Exercise (NLE) 2009 in DC and works with the 2011 NLE. Previously, Dr. Foley was the chief of operational plans for the Indiana Department of Homeland Security (IDHS) and served as the plans chief (Indiana) for Ardent Sentry/Northern Edge. On the National Roles and Responsibilities Committee, he served on the team that wrote the National Response Framework. Through 2005, Dr. Foley was director of Strategic Leadership at the US Army War College. He also served as chief of operations for Homeland Security, US Army Forces Command (FORSCOM), and was prior WMD Branch Chief. For US Northern Command (NORTHCOM), he served as the Joint Forces Land Component Command (JFLCC) FORSCOM Operations Shift Chief and helped write the WMD piece of the 2003 National Defense Authorization Act. Serving on the Initial Integrated Concept Team for all Homeland Defense Doctrine and Homeland Security doctrine, Dr. Foley contributed to the first seven publications post 9/11. He retired from the US Army as a full colonel, serving 36 years (21 active and 15 reserve) and receiving 17 individual awards, three badges, and four unit commendations. Dr. Foley earned his PhD from Indiana University Bloomington, which included PhD courses at Harvard University, where he also served on the faculty in American history.

David Hankins, MBA, is the senior project manager at the Purdue Homeland Security Institute (PHSI), Purdue University. Colonel Hankins retired from the U. S. Air Force in 2002. He then joined the Purdue Homeland Security Institute (PHSI) team in April 2005 and serves as their senior project manager. As such, he has played major roles in numerous PHSI projects including being the lead planner for the 2006 tabletop and full-scale emergency response exercises completed for the Indiana Department of Homeland Security. He was also the lead planner for PHSI efforts with the Indiana State Department of Health (ISDH) for health preparedness and response exercises between 2007 and 2010. The 2007 exercises were aimed primarily at developing "self-contained" exercise packages that counties/districts could then use to further their preparedness. In 2008, he led the team that developed and delivered ten tabletop exercises, ten functional exercises, and a state agency tabletop exercise for pandemic influenza. The tabletop and functional exercises were completed for each of Indiana's Homeland Security districts using distance-based tools that allowed us to direct the exercises from Purdue University. In 2009–10, he was the lead planner for on-site pandemic influenza tabletop exercises tailored for five Indiana districts with nine counties participating in a hospital pandemic readiness exercise.

Jack Herrmann, MS, is the senior advisor and chief for public health preparedness for the National Association of County and City Health Officials (NACCHO). In this role, he serves as the organization's chief public health preparedness liaison to local, state, and federal partner agencies and oversees the organization's portfolio aimed at enhancing and strengthening the preparedness and response capabilities of local health departments. Mr. Herrmann currently serves on a variety of workgroups and committees addressing preparedness policy issues at the national level. He is also the planning committee chairperson of the annual Public Health Preparedness Summit, a national conference bringing together professionals across the public health enterprise. Mr. Herrmann has extensive experience in disaster management and response and has been deployed to numerous disaster relief operations with the American Red Cross since 1994. He received his master's degree from the University of Rochester and a bachelor's degree from St. John Fisher College in Rochester, New York. He is a national certified counselor (NCC) and a licensed mental health counselor in the state of New York.

Jefferson F. Howells, BS, is the assistant project director for the Purdue University Campus Emergency Preparedness and Planning Office. Mr. Howell uses his 20 years of multidiscipline public safety experience to proactively prepare campus stakeholders to prevent, prepare, respond, and recover from campus emergencies. Mr. Howell holds simultaneous project responsibilities on both the West Lafayette and Calumet campuses facilitating *All-Hazards* emergency preparedness awareness and academic/operational continuity planning by the direct management of two Department of Education Emergency Management for Higher Education Grants; "Secure Purdue" for the main campus and "Secure Purdue Calumet" for the regional urban campus located in the greater Chicago area of northwest Indiana. As a certified fire service instructor, Mr. Howell campus responsibilities also include the preparation and delivery of National Incident Management System (NIMS) Incident Command System (ICS) training courses for students, faculty, and staff, coupled with discussion and scenario-based exercises for operational validation and active engagement in the emergency preparedness, response, and recovery process.

Mr. Howell's public safety experience includes career fire service, emergency medical services, airport rescue fighting, hazardous materials technician response, and campus emergency management disciplines.

Chih-Hui Hsieh, BS, is a research associate in the SEAS lab at the Krannert School of Management, Purdue University, and has been with them for more than eight years. She received her undergraduate degree in computer science from Purdue University in 2000. She has extensive research experience with SEAS, epidemiological modeling, agent-based programming, and simulation modeling in the areas of MIS, economics, business, and homeland security. Chih-Hui also played a key part in the measured response exercises of 2002, 2003, 2004, and 2005 where she configured and developed software interface modules using SEAS architecture. Her areas of interest include simulation modeling, graphics design, and 2D/3D visualization.

Patrick Kuhlman, BS, is an engineer in the technical department of Weas Engineering. Prior to Weas Engineering, he worked at the Purdue Homeland Security Institute where he developed models and tools used with pandemic preparedness exercises for state government agencies, local government agencies, and hospitals in Indiana. He is currently completing a master of science degree in engineering with a focus on healthcare systems from Purdue University and previously received a bachelor of science in biomedical engineering degree from Purdue University.

Kara E. Leonard, MPH, is currently pursuing her DrPH in health administration at the University of Texas School of Public Health in Houston, Texas. She currently works as a project coordinator for the UTSPH on a CDC-funded grant in partnership with MD Anderson Cancer Center. During her master's program, Ms. Leonard worked at the Purdue Homeland Security Institute, where she worked on pandemic preparedness projects for Indiana schools and hospitals. She received her master's in public health with a focus in community health from Purdue University, and her bachelor of science in health sciences from Purdue University.

Abby Lillpop, BS, is a communication specialist for the Extension Disaster Education Network (EDEN), and has been with Purdue University since January of 2010. EDEN is a collaborative multistate effort by extension services across the country to improve the delivery of services to citizens affected by disasters. Ms. Lillpop serves as a consultant to nearly 300 campus and county-based specialists and educators regarding marketing strategies and communication efforts and disaster education issues. A graduate of Purdue University, Ms. Lillpop earned a bachelor of science degree in agricultural communication in 2008.

Virginia Morgan, EdD, is an Administrator III, Outreach Programs, Extension Specialist IV, with the Alabama Cooperative Extension System, Auburn University. While working for a North Carolina-based mass merchandise company, she held several positions, ranging from point-of-sale trainer to order distribution manager. She returned to school and, in 1992, received an Ed D in human resource development from Vanderbilt University. Later that year, she moved to Auburn and joined the Alabama Cooperative Extension System (ACES) as an extension specialist and coordinator of the visual resources unit. In 1999 she was named co-leader of extension communications, while continuing her earlier assignment. In 2007, she changed roles to become extension's lead person for disaster education, assume greater responsibility for Alabama's role in eXtension, and collaborate with the assistant director for program development.

Dr. Morgan became the Alabama representative to EDEN (Extension Disaster Education Network) in 2003. In 2006, she was elected to serve as secretary to the EDEN executive committee, and in 2007, assumed managerial/administrative responsibilities for the Disaster Issues Community of Practice—the EDEN-supported eXtension CoP. In 2010, she became EDEN chair. She was the 2005-2006 president of the Association for Communication Excellence in Agriculture, Natural Resources, and Life and Human Sciences (ACE). During her 18 years with ACE, she has also served as committee chair for the development fund and nominating committees, and as a member of two ad hoc committees. Throughout her tenure with Extension, she has conducted numerous workshops on presentation skills, interpersonal communication skills, instructional design, learning styles, and ethics in the workplace. In addition, she wrote "Public Speaking," a chapter in the *Communicator's Handbook*, third and fourth editions.

William Newgent, AA, has been fire chief of the Greencastle Fire Department since he was appointed in 2000. He has served the Greencastle Fire Department for 20 years. In addition to his duties as chief, he also serves as chairperson of the Indiana District 7 Training Council; board member and past president of the Indiana Fire Chief's Association; and in 2005, Chief Newgent was appointed by the governor to the Indiana Public Safety Commission (IPSC).

Kevin Ply, AS, is in his nineteenth year and is now chief of the Purdue University Fire Department. Chief Ply has nearly 25 years' experience in the fire service. He serves on the board of directors of the Indiana Fire Chief's Association, and as a fire instructor and an emergency medical technician (EMT). Chief Ply has completed numerous fire training programs across the country including those at the National Fire Academy, the Nevada Test site, and Texas A&M. He is the president of the Tippecanoe County Fire Chiefs Association and is a board member of the Tippecanoe County Fire Association.

Randy R. Rapp, D Mgt, PE, CCE, CPC, AIC, is an associate professor of building construction management technology at Purdue University and leads the industry-funded disaster restoration and reconstruction management concentration. He has practical experience with both natural and manmade disasters and has directed assorted programs in government and commercial contexts. While with Kellogg, Brown & Root (KBR), he managed project controls and operations for Hurricane Katrina and logistics for Hurricane Wilma. He was also the project controls manager and deputy program general manager for the Restore Iraqi Oil program. In earlier years as a US Army engineer, he directed operations and support activities from construction project sites to the engineer district executive office, and also served as an action officer for NATO (logistics and engineering) and in the Pentagon (R&D and procurement prioritization). He co-authored *Introduction to Engineering Construction Inspection* (2004), contributes to the redevelopment of the certified restorer credential for the Restoration Industry Association, and chaired the Government Affairs Committee of the Institute for Inspection, Cleaning, and Restoration Certification (IICRC). He wrote *Disaster Recovery Project Management: Bringing Order from Chaos* (Purdue University Press, 2011).

Connor D. Scott, BA, emergency management planner with the Baltimore City Office of Emergency Management, served as a firefighter and emergency medical technician in suburban Philadelphia, Pennsylvania, from 2000-2010, and reached the rank of emergency medical services (EMS) lieutenant. In that role, he coordinated patient care and emergency management at the scenes of numerous emergency incidents and planned events. Mr. Scott graduated from Temple University in Philadelphia with a bachelor's degree in political science and public administration, and also worked as a technician on the critical care transport team at Temple University Hospital. He currently works for the Mayor's Office of Emergency Management in Baltimore, Maryland. Mr. Scott manages the city preparedness exercise program, develops emergency plans, and responds to significant emergencies within the city.

Julie E. Shaffner, MS, MPH, is the manager of Obesity Prevention Initiatives at the Illinois Chapter of the American Academy of Pediatrics (ICAAP). Prior to ICAAP, she worked at the Purdue Homeland Security Institute, where she developed and delivered pandemic preparedness projects for Indiana schools and hospitals. She received her master's in public health, with a focus in community health from Purdue University, her master of science, with a focus on Biomechanics, from Purdue University, and her bachelor of science in kinesiology from The College of William and Mary.

Will Shelby has a bachelor's degree from Southern Utah University. He is a history major with psychology and Spanish minors. He will graduate summa cum laude and attend graduate school at Purdue University. He is the president of Phi Alpha

Theta, the history honor society for universities. He has worked at PHSI for three years, working on emergency planning for pandemic influenza, an active shooter scenario, and the city of Chicago Regional Preparedness Grant.

Jennifer A. Smock, MPH, is a program analyst with the National Association of County and City Officials. Since May 2010, Ms. Smock has been employed by the National Association of County and City Officials (NACCHO) working on Project Public Health Ready (PPHR). PPHR is a competency-based training and recognition program that assesses preparedness and assists local health departments in responding to emergencies. She provides technical assistance to local health departments across the nation to aid in the achievement of PPHR recognition. Prior to NACCHO, she worked at Purdue Homeland Security Institute (PHSI). At PHSI her main project included developing CDC-funded pandemic tabletop exercises (TTXs). Additionally, she worked for the Purdue Campus Emergency Preparedness and Planning Office. Her main project was to produce the Purdue Infectious Disease Plan. Jennifer received her bachelor of science in health science and master of public health degree from Purdue University.

Introduction

Considerations

Public health has been making profound impacts on life expectancy and the quality of life of people in the United States For example, according to the Centers for Disease Control and Prevention (2011), there has been a 25-year increase in life expectancy in the United States due to public health advances. Public health also has played a major role in meeting other major challenges such as preparation for potential bioterrorism and natural disasters and responding to communicable diseases such as meningitis, tuberculosis, and influenza.

Definitions and Terms

Distinction among Pandemic, Epidemic, and Outbreak

We offer this part of the introduction to reinforce a particular issue in preparing for, responding to, and recovering from a pandemic. Common planning principles are needed, but common terms of doctrine are necessary to ensure understanding of technical terms. One of the most misused terms is pandemic.

Pandemic, epidemic, and outbreak are used in place of one another and as synonyms, which is incorrect. Misuse of terms is common and easy to find on the web. Searches have produced a plethora of examples included in the following box:

SOME EXAMPLES OF MISUSED TERMINOLOGY

- Multistate outbreaks of human *Salmonella*
- Avian influenza outbreaks among poultry occur worldwide from time to time
- 2006 mumps outbreak in 8 states
- 1951 England and Wales, Canada, and the United States influenza epidemic
- Regional pandemic influenza preparedness and response

Table 0.1 Classifying terms of outbreaks, epidemics, and pandemics

Classifying Terms		
Term	Distribution	Criteria
Outbreak	Localized (confined)	Two or more cases (foodborne, waterborne)
Epidemic	Community State Region	Number of observed cases is greater than expected
Pandemic	Country Continent World	Number of observed cases is greater than expected

To be correct, the planning that has occurred nationally should be referred to as pandemic plans for the nation. Pandemic plans are used to develop epidemic plans at the state level. At the state level, plans may be made for outbreaks. Outbreaks are localized and may occur in such specific locations as schools, hotels, campuses, and contaminated food sources at a local restaurant. Notice in all instances that the number of observed illnesses has been greater than expected. Black, Smock, and Ardaugh (2011) provide visuals in Table 0.1 and Figure 0.1 to help make the distinction in terms clearer. The large oblong represents the nation, and the two smaller ones represent the state level (Table 0.1).

The only way to make sure that a pandemic has occurred is to compare the number ill with endemic state or usual occurrence (steady state or baseline) of the disease. The endemic state can be at a low level as shown in Figure 0.2 or at a high

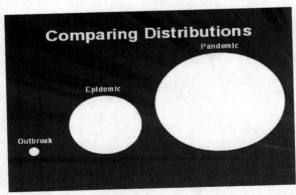

Figure 0.1   Compares outbreaks versus epidemics versus pandemics.

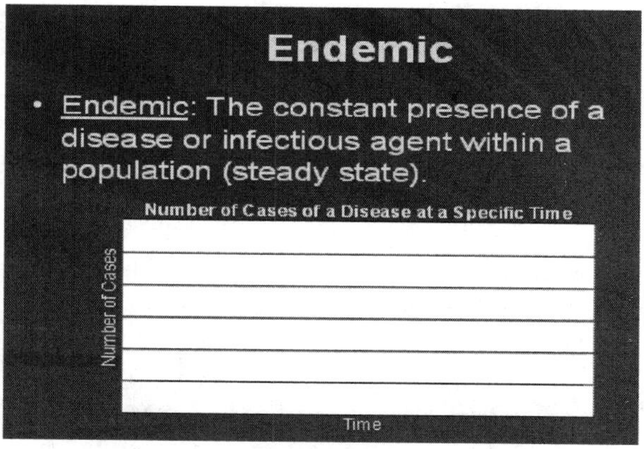

Figure 0.2 Illustration of a low occurrence disease during summer months.

level known as hyperendemic. Examples of a disease that might be hyperendemic would be AIDS/STD/STIs. Figure 0.2 shows a low occurrence disease such as influenza during summer months.

- *Disaster*: A natural or manmade event impacting people, property, agriculture, or industry. The impact of a disaster is mostly negative and permanent in change. A number of similar terms might describe disasters of various levels of severity including crisis, disruption, event, outage, interruption, or catastrophe. The term disaster can apply to manmade or natural events depending on the origin of the disaster including a pandemic.
- *Incident Command*: A tool for systematizing command, control, and communications that provides a framework for coordination throughout levels of government and between various government agencies (Branum, Dietz and Black, 2010).
- *National Incident Management System*: National Incident Management System (NIMS) provides standardization to the incident management including processes, protocols, and procedures common to federal, state, tribal, and local responders of all types who use the system to manage coordination and provide response as needed for disasters (US Department of Homeland Security, 2008).
- *Pandemic Disease Distribution*: Pandemic disease distribution from a source or sources that exceed(s) the regional distribution of elevated disease over a larger geographic area such as a country, continent, or the entire globe (Black, Smock, and Ardaugh, 2011).

Book Perspective

The federal government, including the US Department of Homeland (2011) Security and US Department of Health and Human Services (2011), has identified the prevention of and preparation for a pandemic influenza as a national priority. Though pandemic influenza may be an illness at the forefront, the lack of specific yet flexible guidelines for action will hinder the response efforts of local, state, and federal agencies. We have sought to capture lessons learned from three years of pandemic preparedness exercises including a 2008 exercise that involved healthcare providers, first responders, and key policy decision-makers. This effort, as a research and evidence-based book, guides strategic plan development by government and various organizations. By working with national research leaders across campuses and community stakeholders, our collaborating authors are able to discuss preparedness across a variety of institutional levels and take into consideration issues and concerns that may arise throughout the process. This could include using social media such as Twitter to broadcast information to more people or relying more on public health than medicine since public health strategies are a more efficient method of mitigation. However, the purpose of this book is not to tell individuals exactly what needs to be done to lessen the effects of a pandemic. The purpose of this book is to describe the *processes* necessary for the efficient and effective preparation, prevention, response, and recovery from a pandemic threat.

Goals and Objectives

The primary goal of this book is to provide readers with an understanding of the threat of pandemic illness, emphasizing the importance of preparedness and rigorous planning on community, state, and regional levels. Knowledge gained through the practice and completion of tabletop exercises with community and campus partners provides an inherent strength in the recommendations and guidelines presented in this book. Solutions to common strategic, ethical, and practical challenges to pandemic preparedness are included.

Learning Objectives:

- Summarize current threat of pandemics, specifically how they relate to homeland security and emergency management in terms of preparation, mitigation, response, and recovery.
- Explain issues of leadership and management structure based on historical, theoretical, and practical models and their roles in pandemic preparedness and management.
- Describe the utilization of a computer simulation model and data visualization to strengthen the necessity of prevention and control measures within a community.
- Introduce the principles of marketing and explain how they promote pandemic preparedness for a community.
- Discuss lessons learned from pandemic influenza exercises conducted with regional hospitals and show how those lessons can be applied to other institutions.

- Provide a detailed description of planning, conducting, and evaluating useful, applicable, and specific planning exercises.
- Describe government resources available to assist with the planning for and monitoring of a pandemic influenza.
- Analyze economic and logistic concerns that arise during a pandemic to provide a realistic expectation of levels of support.

Pandemic Planning Strategy

We intend this book to help students and practitioners understand pandemic response based on principles learned from centuries of security operation. These events include public health related events, but also events that mandate improvements to our security or safety. Black (2002) provides "A Strategic Plan for Winning the War in Public Health" that is needed to establish a systemic framework for planning, training healthcare providers and government officials with insight into processes, and distribution of resources needed to manage a pandemic event.

Our model of public health systems, community designs, and military organization or systems are examples of societal improvements that meet specific needs. Each of these systems is managed to minimize cost while maximizing the effectiveness of public investment. The systems are guided by the development of planning strategies that guide strategic, operational, and tactical decisions for the appropriate systems. The US Department of Defense derives guidance and decisions from the *Quadrennial Defense Review* (2011). The US Department of Homeland Security does the same from the *Quadrennial Homeland Security Review* (2010). In December 2009 under section 2802 of the Public Health Service Act, the US Department of Health and Human Services published a similar document, the *National Health Security Strategy* (2010). As the first draft of this document, a comment request began to refine the process and applicability.

This book seeks to develop the concepts and resources informed by our experience in national defense and homeland security planning processes and guided by our experience in research on pandemic issues. In total, the principles, as derived from military planning methods and intended to focus on objectives and manage scarce resources, are needed in some capacity to manage what would be our most challenging situation during a pandemic in modern medical care. While our health systems confront resource challenges daily, we struggle to develop methods for efficient application of limited public health resources (Black, 2002). Our international travel and interactions would allow a new pandemic to occur with speed perhaps unlike previous pandemic events.

Our contributors provide resources, principles for planning and public health fundamentals relevant to pandemic preparation, response, and recovery that impact our national health readiness. As with military planning, we seek to maneuver from our greatest risk while improving surveillance to discover a pandemic event as close to the outbreak stage as possible and respond with resources to limit the effect. This approach also requires that our plans include the public to improve our resistance to a pandemic by accepting vaccination, developing programs to improve health resilience, and improving our basic skills such as hand washing, isolation of our sick, and reduction of contact with disease spreading fomites.

We also expect that the concepts developed can contribute toward training a new generation of health leaders in our academic institutions as well as in postgraduate professional training that will apply the National Health Security Strategy and a series of related principles to win the war in public health.

Applications of Incident Command

The planning and implementation of pandemic strategies would be incomplete without acknowledging the incident command process. The principles of incident command are another focus of this book intended to help readers develop the understanding of staffing and organization needs for pandemic response. Incident command is a tool for systematizing command, control, and communications that provides a framework for coordination throughout levels of government and between various government agencies. This framework can have many suitable formulations that are consistent with the NIMS as required by federal agencies' mandated use. We present research with the effectiveness of NIMS as applied to pandemic exercises and our analysis in developing the right organization and health teams. A local government may make different organization decisions and different staff decisions consistent with NIMS to meet state or local needs. The Federal Emergency Management Agency (FEMA) also has developed a series of online training programs to meet NIMS requirements and reinforce acceptance of the program. The most important aspect of NIMS compliance is the flexibility in managing the process while incorporating common threads so other levels of government and agencies can interface at all levels to maintain effective coordination. Our collaborators offer insights intended to help readers make appropriate decisions based on local priorities, strengths, weaknesses, and available resources.

FEMA describes mitigation as the long-term, community-based strategy for reducing the disaster impact by lessening the losses suffered by subsequent disasters, therefore breaking the cycle and limiting the severity of damage. Commonly, damages include loss, reconstruction, and restoration. Proper application of mitigation ensures that our communities become more resilient with each challenging event. Pandemic planning can follow this same mitigation philosophy by ensuring pandemic preparation using incident command and focusing on actions that can reduce the impact of the common influenza seasons. We also can treat pandemic readiness as a means of reducing our national risk for a bioterrorism event since the surveillance system, response programs, equipment, and plans consider the possibility of other disasters for our public.

This book is intended to support the planning that may prevent the level of the next instance of disease that might lead to a pandemic. As a reaction before and after the 2009 event of H1N1Influenza A, many communities, states, and nations have developed or improved pandemic plans. These jurisdictions might more precisely have developed plans to react to and prevent an outbreak at the community level or epidemic at the state level. The ultimate level of disease spread is pandemic, which would require a global, continental, or national coordinated reaction and response. This book discusses concepts for planning for the various jurisdictions and refers to these as pandemic plans consistent with the titles commonly used.

REFERENCES

Black, D. R. 2002. A strategic plan for winning the war in public health. *American Journal of Health Education*, 3, 265–275. [Scholar of the year award presentqtion at the annual meeting of the American Association for Health Association (April 2002), San Diego, CA.

Branum, A., Dietz, E., and Black, D. R. 2010. An evaluation of local incident command system personnel in a pandemic influenza. *Journal of Emergency Management* 8(5): 39–46.

Black, D. R., Smock, J. A., and Ardaugh, B. 2011. *The foundations of epidemiology*, 5th ed. Oshtemo, MI: Center for Social Problem Solving Measurement.

Centers for Disease Control and Prevention. 2011. Justification of estimates for Appropriation Committee. www.cdc.gov/fmo/topic/.../appropriations.../FY2012_CDC_CJ_Final. Pdf

Federal Emergency Management Agency. 2004. *Are you ready? Guide.* http://www.ready.gov/are-you-ready-guide (Accessed November 29, 2011.)

US Department of Defense. 2011. *Quadrennial defense review.* http://www.defense.gov/qdr/ (Accessed November 29, 2011.)

US Department of Health and Human Services. 2010. *National health security strategy.* http://www.hhs.gov/news/press/2010pres/01/20100107a.html (Accessed November 29, 2011.)

US Department of Health and Human Services. 2011. *HHS pandemic influenza plan.* http://www.hhs.gov/pandemicflu/plan/ (Accessed November 29, 2011.)

US Department of Homeland Security. 2008. *National incident management system.* Washington, DC: Government Printing Office.

US Department of Homeland Security. 2010. *Quadrennial homeland security review.* http://www.dhs.gov/xabout/gc_1208534155450.shtm. (Accessed November 29, 2011.)

US Department of Homeland Security. 2011. FLU.gov. http://www.pandemicflu.gov/ (Accessed November 29, 2011.)

Chapter 1

Resources Available to Assist with Planning and Monitoring a Pandemic

Bert Chapman

Contents

Abstract

Numerous publicly accessible information resources are available from US federal and state and foreign and international government organizations for examining the multiple factors involved in governmental policymaking responses to public health emergencies. These resources cover environmental, foreign policy, legal, legislative, public health, national security, political, and regulatory aspects of governmental responses to pandemics. This chapter will describe these resources and how to access them so readers can gain a heightened understanding of governmental pandemic policymaking activities.

Keywords: Government Information Resources, Governmental Policymaking, Public Health and Policy, Law, Legislation, and Regulation

The US Government has been concerned with pandemics since at least the 1918-1919 influenza pandemic after World War I killed an estimated 675,000 Americans. The government and other sources have produced a significant documentary corpus quantifying and assessing this event's epidemiological impact on the US (US Department of Health and Human Services nd; US Public Health Service 1919; Crosby 2003.) There are numerous US Government information resources providing information on governmental responses to pandemics covering multiple legal, regulatory, and policymaking aspects of all the US Government and the multiple agencies involved in pandemic policymaking. These resources cover the executive, judicial, and legislative branches and reflect the complicated and political bureaucratic and jurisdictional factors involved in early twenty-first century federal government epidemiology policymaking (Etheridge 1992; US Department of Homeland Security 2006; US Congress, House Committee on Homeland Security 2009a; US Government Accountability Office 2009).

This chapter will provide a detailed listing of US Government resources on responses to epidemics and pandemics with the vast majority of these being freely accessible on the Internet. It will be broken into three distinct sections covering legal and regulatory resources, executive branch resources, and congressional resources (including congressional support agencies). It also will cover US state governments, international government organizations, and foreign national government information resources.

US Government Legal Resources

Public laws are passed by Congress and signed by the President to fulfill governmental policymaking needs (US Government Printing Office 2009). Laws are passed in numerical order by two-year congressional sessions and are available online from the 104th Congress (1995 to 1996 to the present) at www.gpoaccess.gov/plaws/. For instance, the controversial healthcare legislation enacted in 2010 is classified as Public Law 111-148 (referring to it being the 148th public law enacted by the 111th Congress) during 2009-2010 and its short title is the Patient Protection and Affordable Care Act.

US GOVERNMENT LEGAL RESOURCES

- Legal/Regulatory Resources
- Public Laws
- US Code
- Code of Federal Regulations
- Federal Register
- List of Sections Affected
- Unified Agenda
- Regulations.gov

The text of this and other laws contains changes to existing sections of federal law, information about funding various agencies will receive to implement the law's provisions, and criminal penalties for violating act provisions. It also features dates when certain requirements must be met, the names of agencies implementing these requirements, and reports these agencies are required to file with Congress concerning implementation of these acts. The conclusion of each of these laws includes legislative history information, such as congressional bill number, a report number citation for the congressional committee report describing congressional intent for the legislation, when the legislation was debated in the Congressional Record, including debate transcript and recorded votes, and whether the President made any public statement when signing this legislation into law. These legislative history resources are accessible from 1995-present at www.gpoaccess.gov/serialset/creports/ and www.gpoaccess.gov/crecord/.

Once laws are passed, they are codified by the US House of Representatives Office of Legal Revision Council into the *US Code (USC)*. This contains the complete text of all US laws broken up into 50 different titles or subject areas. These have been revised completely every six years since 1926 and are updated annually to reflect their current status (US Government Printing Office 2010a). Possible sections of the *USC* where pandemic-related statutes may be located include Title 21 dealing with food and drugs, and Title 42 dealing with public health and welfare. Within each *US Code* title there are chapters and sections providing further organizational breakdowns for these laws. For instance, Chapter 6A of Title 42 covers public health service legislation and Section 247d-1 within Title 42 Chapter 6A features the current legal text covering tracking federally purchased influenza vaccine during an influenza pandemic and should be cited as 42 USC 247d-1[US Government Printing Office. 2009. *Public and Private Laws: About*, 1. <www.gpoaccess.gov/plaws/about.html> (accessed February 21, 2011)] [42 *USC* 247d-1].

Once laws are passed by Congress and signed by the President, federal agencies are charged with drafting regulations to enforce these laws and this field of legal activity is called administrative law. There are several information resources available to track these regulations and their changing status published by the National Archives and Records Administration. The *Code of Federal Regulations (CFR)* www.gpoaccess.gov/cfr/ contains the complete text of federal regulations. It is broken up into 50 different titles or subject areas and published annually on a rotating basis throughout the year. Title 42 of the *CFR* covers public health and part 73.3 of this title (cited as 42 CFR 73.3) lists agents and toxins such as botulinum neurotoxins and ricin, which the Department of Health and Human Services has determined have the potential to severely threaten public health and safety. The end of individual *CFR* sections such as 42 CFR 73.3 features a regulatory history of when these items were first published in the *Federal Register* that may date back as far as 1936, amendments to that initial listing, and their *Federal Register* publication dates (Bowers 1990; US Office of Management and Budget nd; US National Archives and Records Administration 2010).

The *Federal Register* is published Monday through Friday each week, excluding federal holidays, and includes the text of proposed and newly adopted federal regulations, announcements of agency meetings, and the text of presidential executive orders. This publication has been produced since 1936 and is online from 1994 to the present at www.gpoaccess.gov/fr/. Entries are arranged alphabetically by agencies and describe the newly approved or proposed federal regulation including its text, list the *US Code* citation giving agencies the authority to issue the regulation, including the date the regulation takes effect, and list the names and contact information for official(s) at the agency responsible for enforcing this regulation. An example of a relevant regulation on pandemic vaccines was published in the March 5, 2010, *Federal Register* beginning on p. 10268 and continuing through p. 10272 and should be cited as 75 FR 10268-10272. The *Federal Register* and Title 3 of the *CFR* also include presidential executive orders (EO), which are presidentially signed documents having the force of law without going through the congressional legislative process. Presidential EOs are numbered consecutively and presidents can reverse executive orders issued by their predecessors. An example of a recent EO is 13546 "Optimizing the Security of Biological Select Agents and Toxins in the United States" published in the July 8, 2010, *Federal Register* on pp. 39439-39442 (Federal Register 2010a; Federal Register 2010b).

List of Sections Affected (LSA) www.gpoaccess.gov/lsa/ is published monthly and tracks and describes changes in federal regulations between publication of the annual *CFR* volumes and the *Federal Register* (US Government Printing Office 2010a). An entry in the July 2010 *LSA* on p. 52 refers to "42 CFR 423.600(a) amended" and lists it as being on p. 65363 of the *Federal Register* between October 1, 2009, and July 30, 2010. This particular *CFR* citation refers to "Medicare Prescription Drug Benefits" and the amendment or change can be found on p. 65363 in the December 9, 2009, *Federal Register*.

The *Unified Agenda* is published in the *Federal Register* twice annually and lists regulatory actions executive branch and independent agencies are taking, have recently taken, or are considering (US Government Printing Office 2010c p. 9). The December 20, 2010, *Federal Register* is the most recent *Unified Agenda* and pp.

21782-21805 from the April 26, 2010, edition of this work feature the Department of Health and Human Services Regulatory Agenda with Centers for Disease Control (CDC) Notice 128 "Control of Communicable Disease: Foreign Quarantine" on p. 21788 having descriptive details and agency contract information (US Government Printing Office 2008.)

The website http://regulations.gov/ allows individuals and organizations to submit comments on proposed regulations for possible revision or reversal. Users can see comments submitted by other individuals and organizations and submit their own comments, which are read by officials at the responsible agencies and can influence agencies and their regulatory policymaking (Warren 2004; US Congress, House Committee on the Judiciary, Subcommittee on Commercial and Administrative Law 2007; Priest 2009).

US Government Executive Branch Resources

Flu.gov features the collaborative efforts of multiple government agencies, including the Department of Health and Human Services, to deal with influenza and other pandemic occurrences. Its features include textual and audiovisual information geared toward individuals and families including webcasts such as Mixing Tamiflu with Sweet Liquids; information on getting seasonal flu shots; practical guidance for flu vaccination, prevention/protection, and control; and interventions including recommendations for caregivers, seniors, travelers, and public service announcements.

The flu.gov website also features detailed pandemic response resources for healthcare professionals and organizations, including businesses; educational institutions; school and transportation planners; and local, state, federal, and international government organization planning. Specific government strategic planning documents are here, including National Strategy for Pandemic Influenza (2005); HHS Pandemic Influenza Plan (2005); Community Strategy for Pandemic Influenza Mitigation (2007); H1N1 Flu: A Guide for Community and Faith-Based

US GOVERNMENT EXECUTIVE BRANCH RESOURCES

- Flu.gov
- Army Public Health Command
- Avian Influenza Action Group
- Avian Influenza-US Department of Agriculture
- Department of Defense
- Pandemic Influenza Watchboard
- Force Health Protection and Readiness
- Environmental Protection Agency Homeland Security
- Department of Health and Human Services

- Centers for Disease Control and Prevention
- National Library of Medicine
- Department of Homeland Security
- Homeland Security Digital Library
- Ready.gov
- Ignet.gov
- Medical Countermeasures
- Transportation Pandemic Resources

Organizations (2009); The Public Health Emergency Medical Countermeasures Enterprise Review (2010).

A companion website www.medicalcountermeasures.gov/ seeks to enhance communication between federal agencies and public stakeholders to improve national public health emergency preparedness. It also gives registered external stakeholders the opportunity to discuss products that deter, identify, and treat potential threats with appropriate government policymakers (Medicalcountermeasures.gov 2010).

Army Public Health Command

The US Army Public Health Command (AHPHC) is being formed as a collaborative venture between the army's Center for Health Promotion and Veterinary Medicine and Veterinary Medical Command to provide a unified public health command, which was expected to achieve operational status on October 1, 2011. This organization's missions include promoting health and preventing disease, injury, and disability for soldier retirees, army civilian employees, and producing effective execution of all-spectrum veterinary service for the army and Defense Department. Personnel within AHPHC include preventive and occupational medicine physicians, epidemiologists, food safety and quality assurance experts, chemists, toxicologists, and other personnel (US Army Public Health Command 2010).

Resources at this unit's provisional website http://phc.amedd.army.mil/ include H1N1 influenza information resources and links to relevant resources such as the Occupational Safety and Health Administration Guide, Guidance on Preparing Workplaces for an Influenza Pandemic (2007); H1N1 Surveillance Questionnaire (nd); ERGM Algorithmic Treatment for Testing and Treatment of Suspected H1N1 Influenza (2009).

Avian Influenza Action Group

This group (www.state.gov/g/avianflu/) is part of the State Department's Undersecretary for Democracy and Global Affairs and it collaborates with other

US Government agencies to develop international strategies to prepare for, prevent, and contain avian flu. It seeks to achieve its objectives through bilateral contact and multilateral forums; improving surveillance and laboratory capacity; strengthening coordination between human and animal health sectors; and enhancing coordination with concerned countries (US Congress, House Committee on International Relations 2006; US Department of State, Avian Influenza Action Group, nd).

Accessible information resources here dating back to 2001 include Office of Medical Services Supplements to the Department of State Pandemic Influenza Plan (2007); North American Plan for Avian and Pandemic Influenza (2007); Avian and Pandemic Influenza: The Global Response (2008); Fact Sheet: 2009-H1N1, Pandemic Influenza, and H5N1 (2009).

Avian Influenza—US Department of Agriculture

Accessible at website www.usda.gov/wps/portal/usda/usdahome?navtype= SU&navid=AVIAN_INFLUENZA, this site features Agriculture Department avian flu resources from agencies such as the Animal and Plant Health Inspection Service, Agricultural Research Service, and Food Safety and Inspection Service. Information resources include information on reporting sick farm birds to appropriate authorities; a glossary of relevant terms, including pathogenicity; fact sheets such as Avian Influenza Diagnostics and Testing (2008); and publications such as Avian Influenza Protecting US Agriculture: Imports of Legal Birds and Bird Products (2007); United States Animal Health Report (2008).

Department of Defense (DOD) Resources

The DOD is concerned about the vulnerability of military personnel and civilian employees to pandemics and has established a number of programs and information resources to address these concerns. The DOD Pandemic Influenza Watchboard http://fhpr.osd.mil/aiWatchboard site emphasizes DOD's mission in an influenza pandemic as preserving US combat capabilities and readiness and supporting US Government efforts to save lives, reduce human suffering, and slow the spread of infection (Miller 2004; US Government Accountability Office 2007; Ememark 2009; US Department of Defense, Pandemic Influenza Watchboard 2010).

Information resources here include H1N1 Frequently Asked Questions (2009); Influenza Preparedness on the Pentagon Reservation and in Washington Headquarters Services (WHS)-Managed Lease Facilities (2009); and Public Health Emergency Management within the Department of Defense (2010).

Force Health Protection and Readiness

The website http://fhp.osd.mil/ is part of the Military Health System Partnership for Health and it seeks to safeguard the health and well-being of service members and their families by promoting and sustaining healthy forces; preventing injuries and illness and protecting personnel from health hazards; and providing optimum medical and rehabilitative care for personnel globally (US Department of Defense, Force Health Protection and Readiness 2010).

Accessible information resources include reports and factsheets such as Handling of Human Remains from Natural Disasters (nd); A Soldier's Guide to Staying Healthy in Afghanistan and Pakistan (nd), Department of Defense in-Theater Medical Tracking and Health Surveillance (2005); Barracks Layout to Prevent Disease Transmission (2007); and Agreement to Participate in Anthrax Vaccine Immunization Program (2009).

This website also provides links to other relevant military health websites, including the Anthrax Vaccine Immunization Program (www.anthrax.mil/), Armed Forces Health Surveillance Center (www.afhsc.mil/), Defense Medical Readiness Training Institute (www.dmrti.army.mil/), and Vaccine Health Care Centers Network (www.vhcinfo.org/).

Environmental Protection Agency Homeland Security

The Environmental Protection Agency (EPA) serves as the US Government's principal environmental policymaking agency and is responsible for protecting human health along with the natural environment (US National Archives and Records Administration 2009). EPA's homeland security programs (www.epa.gov/nhsrc/) were formed on September 24, 2002, giving EPA key federal agency responsibility for protecting the water sector from terrorist attacks and decontaminating indoor and outdoor areas from such attacks which may involve biological, chemical, and radiological agents (US Environmental Protection Agency 2009).

Its water protection research focuses on protection and prevention, including developing mechanisms for addressing vulnerabilities in drinking water and wastewater systems; developing tools and methodologies to detect, confirm, and measure contamination events; developing responses to these events; and engaging in research seeking to enhance water infrastructure and contaminated water treatment and decontamination. Decontamination research programs evaluate and measure the performance of commercially available technologies and their detection capabilities; predicting contaminant dispersion and how it might affect humans and machines; and developing scientific measurement standards for determining the extent of contamination and ways of effectively removing and remediating this damage (US Environmental Protection Agency 2010).

Information resources on this website include the text of relevant Homeland Security Presidential Directives (HSPD) from the George W. Bush and Barack Obama administrations directing agency homeland security policymaking, including HSPD 7 Critical Infrastructure Identification, Protection, and Prioritization (2003); HSPD 9 Defense of United States Agriculture and Food (2004); and HSPD 10 Biodefense for the 21st Century (2004). Available research reports include Highly Pathogenic Avian Influenza H5N1 Virus Persistence Testing and Evaluation of Liquid Decontamination Technologies (2009); Systematic Evaluation of the Efficacy of Chlorine Dioxide in Decontamination of Building Interior Surfaces Contaminated with Anthrax Spores (2010); Sensor Network Design for Drinking Water Contamination Warning Systems (2010).

Department of Health and Human Services

The Department of Health and Human Services (HHS) serves as the federal government's principal healthcare policy agency and its website, www.hhs.gov/, provides access to a wide variety of health policy information resources, including those dealing with pandemics (US National Archives and Records Administration 2009).

The Centers for Disease Control and Prevention (CDC)

The CDC (www.cdc.gov/) is headquartered in Atlanta, GA, and is responsible for collaborating to create the expertise, personnel, and tools enabling individuals and communities to protect their health through health promotion, disease prevention, and preparedness for new health threats (US Centers for Disease Control 2010; Pendergrast 2010). CDC's website provides a variety of information resources, including detailed descriptions of its global health programs, such as global disease detection, border infectious disease surveillance, and migration and quarantine program activities.

A detailed A to Z subject index provides access to authoritative medical information on topics such as anthrax vaccination, antibiotic and antimicrobial resistance, health hoaxes and rumors, influenza, and terrorism. CDC and its component organizations, such as the National Center for Health Statistics (NCHS), www.cdc.gov/nchs/, provide numerous reports and journals. These include *Where to Write for Vital Records*, which lists state contacts for birth and death records, the annual *Health United States* (1975-present) which documents health trends and developments; *National Vital Statistics Reports* (1998-present); *Morbidity and Mortality Weekly Reports* (1982-present), which includes its *Surveillance Summaries* supplement; and *Emerging Infectious Diseases* (1995-present). CDC publications are essential resources for those studying governmental pandemic policymaking.

National Library of Medicine

The National Library of Medicine (NLM), www.nlm.nih.gov/, is part of the National Institutes of Health (NIH) and is the United States' leading medical information source. It is responsible for providing library search and bibliographic services, such as the MEDLINE medical journal literature database and the Toxicology Data Network (TOXNET) database, covering environmental health, hazardous chemicals, toxic releases, and toxicology to public and private agencies, individuals, institutions, and organizations (US National Archives and Records Administration 2009; Miles 1982).

- NLM's website provides information resources organized for the public, healthcare professionals, researchers, librarians, and publishers. Examples of NLM resources include:
- Clinical Trials, www.clinicaltrials.gov/, which provides information on federally and privately supported clinical trials conducted in the US and internationally which can be searched by condition, drug intervention, location, and sponsor
- Household Products Database, http://householdproducts.nlm.nih.gov/, providing information from materials safety data sheets on the chemical ingredients and health effects of more than 10,000 consumer brand products broken down by categories, such as auto products, inside the home, lawn care, and pesticides
- PubMed, www.pubmed.gov/, which is a version of MEDLINE geared toward the general public, featuring more than 20 million citations to and abstracts of biomedical literature from medical and life science journals and online books with some of these including full-text article content
- Toxnet, http://toxnet.nlm.nih.gov/. Toxnet resources include the hazardous substances data bank, emphasizing the toxicology of more than 5,000 potentially hazardous chemicals, including their toxicity data, emergency handling procedures, industrial hygiene, environmental fate, human exposure, detection methods, and regulatory requirements
  - the EPA's integrated risk information system (IRIS), contains carcinogenic and non-carcinogenic health-related information on more than 500 chemicals which have been risk assessed by EPA scientists
  - the EPA's genetic toxicology (GENE-TOX) database containing genetic toxicology results for more than 3,200 chemicals
- HAZMAP Occupational Exposure to Hazardous Agents providing information about 1,595 chemicals and biological agents and their potential impacts on workplace environments, along with 224 occupational diseases and their symptoms associated with hazardous job tasks (US National Library of Medicine 2010)

Department of Homeland Security (DHS)

DHS (www.dhs.gov/) was established by the 2002 Homeland Security Act and began operations on January 24, 2003. Its missions include leading a unified national effort to protect America by preventing and deterring terrorist attacks, protecting against and responding to national threats and hazards, ensuring safe and secure borders, welcoming legal immigrants and visitors, and promoting the free flow of commerce (US Government Manual 2009, Maxwell 2004; Ball 2005; Borja 2008).

- DHS organizational components include several directorates with the following organizational responsibilities, such as the:
- Federal Emergency Management Agency (FEMA), whose responsibilities include preparing and directing responses and recovery efforts to national incidents, whether caused by humans or nature
- National preparedness and response programs which safeguard critical information systems, borders, seaports, bridges, and highways by cooperating with state, local, and private sector partners to identify threats, determine vulnerabilities, and properly target resources to areas of greatest risk
- The Science and Technology Directorate, which provides federal, state, and local officials with technological homeland protection capabilities, including developing and deploying systems to prevent, detect, and mitigate the consequences of weapons of mass destruction attacks; developing equipment, protocols, and training procedures for responding to and recovering from these attacks; and enhancing governmental capabilities to execute their homeland security functions; and establishing certified laboratories and technical standards to evaluate homeland security and emergency responder technologies to meet statutory certification requirements (US National Archives and Records Administration 2009); US Homeland Security Advisory Council 2008; US Congress, House Committee on Homeland Security 2009b; Berrick 2009)
- Reports and other general DHS information resources include departmental Performance and Accountability Reports (2003-present); Science and Technology Strategic Plan (2007); Department of Homeland Security Strategic Plan 2008-2013 (2008); National Response Framework (2008); National Emergency Communications Plan (2008); the text of laws and executive orders, such as Medical Countermeasures Following a Biological Attack (2009); statistics from DHS agencies, including the Office of Immigration Statistics; and training materials for emergency responders.

Homeland Security Digital Library (HSDL)

HSDL (www.hsdl.org/) is the nation's largest open-source database of homeland security policy, strategy, and organizational management, and is a collaborative venture between DHS' National Preparedness Directorate and the Naval Postgraduate School. It contains more than 77,000 documents from federal, state, and local government agencies, professional organizations, public policy research institutions, and international government organizations that are selected by HSDL subject specialists. Most resources are publicly accessible, but some materials are restricted to registered officials and practitioners (US Naval Postgraduate School Center for Homeland Defense and Security 2010).

Site contents include national homeland security policy planning documents, including executive orders, laws, and presidential directives from the White House and DHS from 1947 to the present; research reports and theses from the Congressional Research Service (CRS), Government Accountability Office (GAO), and Naval Postgraduate School. Additional materials include topic-based websites providing access to sources on agroterrorism, fusion centers, mass evacuation, and pandemic influenza; links to biweekly assembled critical releases of homeland security related reports from diverse organizations; and links to HSDL-recommended homeland security websites on topics such as emergency management, public health, and state government homeland security offices.

Examples of publicly accessible DHSL resources include North American Plan for Avian and Pandemic Influenza (2007); Non-Pharmaceutical Disease Mitigation Strategies: Schools (2007); At-Risk Populations and Pandemic Influenza: Planning Guidance for State, Territorial, Tribal, and Local Health Departments (2008); The 2008 American Preparedness Project: Why Parents May Not Heed Evacuation Orders & What Emergency Planners, Families, and Schools Need to Know (2008); and the National Archives and Records Administration web exhibit and documents collection, The Deadly Virus: The Influenza Epidemic of 1918 (nd).

Ready.gov

This DHS-produced website seeks to provide information to individuals, families, and businesses to be prepared in case natural or human-caused disasters produce breakdowns in governmental and private sector emergency response or critical infrastructure systems. Materials here include guidance on setting up emergency kits with recommendations for food and water supplies; having batteries and a battery-powered radio; first aid supplies; protective equipment, such as dust masks and filter fans; maintaining lists of medicines; medical insurance documents, medical supplies, and medical contact information; and a personal support information listing other individuals who will know where and how you can be reached if an emergency occurs.

Available publications include Family Emergency Plan (nd); Are You Ready?: An In-Depth Guide to Citizen Preparedness (2004); Emergency Supply List (n.d.); and Every Business Should Have a Plan (2004).

Ignet.gov

This website (www.ignet.gov/) is a web portal to the federal inspector general community. Federal inspector general offices were established by the 1978 Inspector General Act. Their officials, who are presidentially appointed and require Senate confirmation, and their staffs are responsible for evaluating the management performance of programs administered by their agencies, preventing abuse, fraud, and waste, and have the legal authority to issue criminal penalties if fraud is committed in these programs by agency employees or private-sector contractors (Friedes 1992; Council of Inspectors General on Integrity and Efficiency 2010).

Examples of useful agency inspector general (IG) reports on pandemic matters include those produced by HHS (http://oig.hhs.gov/) and DHS (http://www.dhs.gov/xoig/). IGs prepare semiannual reports documenting their overall investigative and evaluative activity of agency programs and regularly audit programs administered by their respective agencies. Examples of relevant reports from the HHS and OIG inspectors general include *State and Local Bioterrorism Preparedness* (2002); Public Health Laboratory Testing to Detect and Report Biological Threats (2008); FEMA Response to Formaldehyde in Trailers (2009); 2009 H1N1 School-Located Vaccine Program Implementation (2010); and Customs and Border Protection (CBPs) to Detect Biological and Chemical Threats in Maritime Containers (2010).

Medical Countermeasures

- This interagency mechanism (www.medicalcountermeasures.gov/) consists of agencies such as the Department of Veterans Affairs and HHS agencies such as the CDC, Food and Drug Administration (FDA), NIH, and the Office of the Assistant Secretary for Preparedness and Response. Its mission seeks to facilitate communication between federal agencies and public stakeholders to enhance national public health emergency preparedness by:
- Facilitating communication and improving transparency on public health emergency medical countermeasures by interacting with industry and research and development community stakeholders
- Giving external stakeholders a single US Government access point to discuss products capable of treating, identifying, and reducing harm from such threats
- Facilitating information flow between government and stakeholders in the research and development community to provide current information on governmental initiatives and events (US Department of Public Health Services, Public Health Emergency 2011)
- Accessible resources through this website include press releases and announcements (August 2008-present), which often feature information about available grants, information about federal procurement

opportunities through the FedBizOpps database (www.fbo.gov/), federal acquisition regulations (www.acquisition.gov/) information about historical and forthcoming medical countermeasures meetings sponsored by participating agencies; and links to the websites of related government advisory committees, such as the Food and Drug Administration's Vaccines and Related Biological Products Advisory Committee (www.fda.gov/cber/ advisory/vrbp/vrbpmain.htm) and the National Science Advisory Board for Biosecurity (http://oda.ob.nih.gov/biosecurity/).

Transportation Pandemic Resources

Transportation sectors and overall economic activity would be affected by a pandemic restricting and curtailing the ability of automotive, aviation, rail, and shipping transportation modes to deliver supplies to their intended recipients (US Congress, House Committee on Transportation and Infrastructure, Subcommittee on Aviation 2005; Turnbull 2008; Stambaugh, et al. 2008; Flu.gov 2011; World Health Organization 2010). The Pandemic Influenza website contains a number of resources devoted to how transport sectors would need to respond to a pandemic (accessible at www.flu.gov/professional/transport/). General guidance is provided by agencies such as the CDC as to how the airline and travel industries would cope with an H1N1 outbreak in documents such as Interim Guidance for Cruise Ships during the 2009-10 Influenza Season (2010). Additional resources include airline industry guidance documents, such as Interim Guidance for Airline Flight Crews and Passengers Meeting Persons Arriving from Areas with Avian Influenza (2010); the Transportation Department's National Aviation Resource Manual for Quarantinable Diseases (2006); Interim Guidance for Cargo Trucking Preview for the Prevention of Pandemic Influenza (nd); Interim Guidance for Cleaning Transit Stations during an Influenza Pandemic (nd); and the CDC's quarantine and isolation website www.cdc.gov/quarantine/ featuring the text of relevant federal quarantine laws and regulations and the location of US quarantine stations.

Additional pandemic resources provided by the Department of Transportation (DOT) include www.ems.gov/ which is hosted by DOT's National Transportation Highway Safety Administration. This resource contains links to other federal agencies with emergency medical service (EMS) responsibilities, state EMS laws, and reports, including Preparing for Pandemic Influenza: Recommendations for Protocol Development for 9-1-1 Personnel and Public Safety Answering Points (PSAPS) (2007); EMS Pandemic Influenza Guidelines for Statewide Adoption (2007); EMS Workforce for the 21st Century: A National Assessment (2008); and National Emergency Medical Services Education Standards (2009).

Congressional Resources

Congressional resources are valuable materials for learning about governmental pandemic and public health policymaking. These resources include congressional bills, congressional committee hearings, committee legislative reports, and information resources produced by congressional oversight agencies. Congress is responsible for approving new laws or revising existing government laws, funding government programs, and conducting oversight of government program performance (Zwirn 1988; US Congress, House Committee on Science 2006; US Congress, House Committee on Homeland Security 2009; US Centers for Disease Control 2010).

CONGRESSIONAL RESOURCES

- Congressional Bills
- Congressional Committee Reports
- Congressional Committee Hearings
- House and Senate Appropriations Committees
- House Energy and Commerce Committee
- House Homeland Security Committee
- House Oversight and Government Reform Committee
- Senate Health, Education, Labor, and Pensions Committee
- Senate Homeland Security and Governmental Affairs Committee
- Congressional Budget Office
- Congressional Research Service
- Government Accountability Office

Congressional Bills

Congressional bills are legislation in its rawest form. Bills are written by members of Congress, their professional staff, and the professional staff on various committees. They are introduced on the House and Senate floors, assigned a number for the congressional session they are in, and are referred to one or more appropriate committees for potential future action. Most bills introduced in a congressional session do not become law; many of them go through different linguistic versions and amendments; and they also go through a number of quality control procedures to ensure their accuracy and currency. If legislation does not pass during a two-year congressional session, it dies and must be reintroduced during a subsequent two-year congressional session and will likely have a different bill number (Zwirn 1988).

Formal legislation begins with the letters H.R. and a number to designate its introduction in the House of Representatives, and an S and a number to designate its introduction in the Senate. For instance, H.R. 3798 was introduced in the House of Representatives on October 13, 2009, by Rep. Steve Israel (D-NY) during the 111th Congress' first session. The bill's short title is the School Protection Act of 2009, and it sought to provide grants to train elementary and secondary school nurses to respond to pandemic influenza in school buildings or grounds, and it was referred to the House Committee on Energy and Commerce. Congressional bills will contain information on what the legislation is supposed to accomplish, how much money is to be spent carrying out the law, reports agencies may have to file with Congress to implement this legislation, and criminal penalties for violating this legislation. This bill will ultimately have to be approved by the House and Senate before being signed by the President and becoming law or being vetoed by the President and returning to Congress for potential veto override and renewed consideration. An example of a Senate bill during this congressional session is S. 2809 introduced on December 10, 2009, by Sen. David Pryor (D-AR). The bill's short title is the Defense Against Infectious Diseases Act of 2009 and it was referred to the Senate Health, Education, Labor, and Pensions Committee (Sullivan 2007).

Online information about bill versions, linguistic changes, and legislative history from 1993 to the present can be found at www.gpoaccess.gov/bills/ with bills from the 110th Congress (2007-2008) on being digitally authenticated by the US Government Printing Office (GPO). This resource also makes it possible to track the status of bills and translate the glossary of esoteric terms (e.g., (rh) Reported in House) used to describe bills' status. You can also use this site to find when bills were debated in the House and Senate as chronicled in the *Congressional Record* (www.gpoaccess.gov/crecord/) and determine how individual lawmakers voted on legislation in which Congress held roll call votes. The *Congressional Record* also includes the text of speeches legislators made on the House or Senate floors or had inserted into the transcript of the record (Springer 1986).

Congressional Committee Reports

Congressional committee reports are critical sources for documenting a law's legislative history and for determining congressional legislative intent. Legislation reaching the House and Senate floor must be accompanied by committee reports from both bodies which match word-for-word and numerically. If these reports do not match, the congressional leadership will appoint a conference committee, consisting of leaders from the relevant congressional committees, to attempt to resolve the different versions of these committee reports. If this reconciliation process is successful, a conference committee report will be adopted by this committee which must be approved by the full House and Senate before being submitted to the President for signature into law (Longley and Oleszek 1989; Oleszek 2004).

Committee reports are accessible from 1995 to the present at www.gpoaccess. gov/serialset/creports/. These reports are numbered numerically for the congressional session and the legislative chamber they were approved in and in numerical order. For instance, House Report 111-562 is the Disaster Response, Recovery, and Mitigation Enhancement Act of 2009 accompanying H.R. 3377 during the 111th Congress (2009-2010). This report was submitted by the House Transportation and Infrastructure Committee and its chair Rep. James Oberstar (D-MN) on July 22, 2010, and is 69 pages long. This report tells what Congress intends for this legislation to accomplish, describes committee hearings and recorded votes held during its development and evolution, contains a Congressional Budget Office (CBO) estimate of how much the legislation will cost, and may contain the text of additional or dissenting comments on this legislation from committee members. An example of a recent Senate Committee report is Senate Report 111-103 the Emergency Management Assistance Compact Grant Reauthorization Act of 2009 accompanying S. 1288 during the 111th Congress. This report was issued by the Senate Homeland Security and Governmental Affairs Committee and its chair Sen. Joe Lieberman (ID-CT) on December 9, 2009, is seven pages long, and contains similar kinds of information to the aforementioned House Committee report. Because a committee has passed a report on legislation does not mean that this document has been approved by the Congress or signed by the President. Nevertheless, these reports are important for determining congressional legislative intent and committee report numbers, including conference committee report numbers, and are cited in the concluding legislative history sections of most passed public laws (Library of Congress, Congressional Research Service 1983; Koempel 2007).

Congressional Committee Hearings

Congressional committee hearings are crucial sources for learning about federal programs dealing with pandemics and other policymaking activities. The US Constitution gives Congress the power of the purse and Article 1 Section 9 of this document says:

> No Money shall be drawn from the Treasury, but in Consequence of Appropriations made by Law; and a regular Statement and Account of the Receipts and Expenditures of all public Money shall be published from time to time (US Congress, Senate Committee on Appropriations 2005).

Congressional committees, their members, and professional staff have enormous power over government programs, including the ability to fund these programs, determine individual program resource allocations, conduct oversight of their performance, create new or revise existing laws, direct the compilation of reports and statistics on these programs, and have the legal authority to subpoena and swear in witnesses from government and non-government agencies to testify about these programs (Lindsay 1990; Bianco 2000; Taylor 2001; Canon, Nelson, and Stewart III 2002).

House and Senate Appropriations Committees

Funding for government programs must be raised in the House of Representatives according to the US Constitution [US Constitution, Article 1, Section 7]. This is done through the House Appropriations Committee (http://appropriations.house.gov/) and through the Senate Appropriations Committee (http://appropriations.senate.gov/) once legislation reaches the Senate. Serving on one of the appropriations committees is highly coveted by many representatives and senators because of the financial disbursing power they possess. Their membership consists of 58 representatives and 30 senators during the 112th Congress (2011-2012) (Marshall, Prins, and Rohde 1999; Handy and Strahan 2004). Funding for governmental programs occurs during the budget process cycle which occurs at various points throughout the year. The process ultimately results in the passage of 12 annual appropriations bills which constitute the budget for federal government agencies and individual programs. The budget is administered by these agencies which submit their upcoming requests to the Office of Management and Budget (OMB) as the presidential administration's representative who then submits them to Congress. Over the next several months, agency heads will testify before the appropriations committees and their subcommittees by presenting highly detailed programmatic budget requests. They will seek to gain legislative allies for their request and negotiate desired funding levels (US Congress, Senate Committee on Appropriations 2005; Library of Congress THOMAS 2010).

Within the House and Senate appropriations committees there are departmental subcommittees who are officially charged with guiding agency budget requests through the congressional budgetary process. Where public health and pandemic program funding are concerned, the most crucial appropriations committee subcommittees are Labor, Health and Human Services, Education, and Related Agencies and Homeland Security in the House and their two Senate appropriations committee subcommittee counterparts covering the same agencies and groups of agencies. These committee websites and their subcommittee websites will list the names of current members and contain some information about their activities. However, to access transcripts of their hearings (including agency budget requests), you will need to access the US Government Printing Office's Federal Digital Systems (FDSYS), www.fdsys.gov/, and select the congressional hearings link to access appropriations committee hearings transcripts from 1995 to the present.

Examples of recent accessible relevant House and Senate appropriations committee hearings addressing pandemic matters include Department of Homeland Security Appropriations for 2010: Part 2 (2009); Departments of Labor, Health and Human Services, Education, and Related Appropriations for 2010: Part 6 (2009); Public Health Response to Swine Flu (2009); and Biological Threats: Is the Current US Vaccine Production System Prepared? (2009). Congressional committee website content will reflect the legislative and political priorities of the parties currently controlling them, but will also feature links to minority party viewpoints on issues within the committee's jurisdiction.

House Energy and Commerce Committee

The House Energy and Commerce Committee (http://energycommerce.house. gov/) was originally established in 1795 and has jurisdiction over a variety of US economic sectors, including energy regulation, medical research, public health, and telecommunications and consists of 54 members during the 112th Congress (King 1994; Chapman, 2004; Library of Congress THOMAS. 2010). This committee and its multiple subcommittees, covering topics such as commerce, trade, consumer protection, communications, technology, the Internet, health, and oversight and investigations, engage in a rigorous oversight and investigative program of federal and private sector management performance in these multiple economic sectors.

Committee website contents include information about ongoing investigations, news about committee hearings and legislative markups, and archived hearings from 2001 to the present, with some of these being video webcasts. Examples of relevant committee hearings include Germs, Viruses, and Secrets: The Silent Proliferation of Bio-Laboratories in the United States (2007); FDA's Foreign Drug Inspection Program: Weaknesses Place Americans at Risk (2008); Federal Oversight of High-Containment Biolaboratories (2009); Promoting the Development of Antibiotics and Ensuring Judicious Use in Humans (2010); and Antibiotic Resistance and the Threat to Public Health (2010).

House Homeland Security Committee

The House Homeland Security Committee (2010) was established in 2002 in the aftermath of the 9/11 terrorist attacks and became a permanent standing House committee on January 4, 2005, with responsibility for overseeing the Department of Homeland Security (US Congress, House Committee on Homeland Security, 2009b, 2010). The committee has 33 members during the 112th Congress and its subcommittees cover topics such as transportation security and infrastructure protection, emergency communications, preparedness and response, intelligence, information sharing, terrorism risk assessment and emerging threats, cybersecurity, science, and technology.

Examples of recent hearings by this committee include Can Bioshield Effectively Procure Medical Countermeasures That Safeguard the Nation? (2007); Examining the Training of First Responders in Rural Communities (2008); Post-Katrina Emergency Management Reform Act (PKEMRA) Implementation: An Examination of FEMA's Preparedness and Response Mission (2009); and Interoperable Emergency Communications: Does the National Broadband Plan Meet the Needs of First Responders? (2010).

House Oversight and Government Reform Committee

This committee (http://oversight.house.gov/) was originally established in 1816 and its modern focus includes overseeing the federal civil service; District of Columbia governance; the overall economic efficiency and management of governmental operations and activities; relationships between federal, state, and local governments; and executive branch governmental reorganizations (Chapman 2004). During the 112th Congress this committee had 40 members and its subcommittees cover domestic policy, the federal workforce, government management, organization and procurement, information policy, and national security and foreign affairs. Examples of recent public health and homeland security hearings held by the House Oversight and Government Reform Committee include Healthcare-Associated Infections: A Preventable Epidemic (2008); The Administration's Flu Vaccine Program: Health, Safety, and Distribution (2009); and Viral Hepatitis: The Secret Epidemic (2010).

Senate Health, Education, Labor, and Pensions Committee

The Senate Health, Education, Labor, and Pensions Committee (HELP) (http://help.senate.gov/) has jurisdiction over most Department of Health and Human Services programs, health insurance, and emerging threats and patterns in the healthcare industry. Along with other Senate committees, it is constitutionally responsible for confirming presidential appointments such as the Secretary of Health and Human Services and it consists of 22 members during the 112th Congress (US Congress, Senate Committee on Health, Education, Labor, and Pensions 2010).

The committee's website includes information about recent historical and ongoing activities, including legislation being considered. Examples of recent hearings it has held include Meeting the Global Challenge of AIDS, TB, and Malaria (2008); Access to Prevention and Public Health for High-Risk Populations (2009); and Treating Rare and Neglected Pediatric Diseases: Promoting the Development of New Treatments and Cures (2010).

Senate Homeland Security and Governmental Affairs Committee

The Senate Homeland Security and Governmental Affairs Committee (http://hsgac.senate.gov/) dates back to the nineteenth century and in 1921 was charged with evaluating expenditures in executive branch agencies. It later was known as the Committee on Government Operations, became the Committee on Governmental Affairs in 1978, and received its current name in 2005. Its primary jurisdictional responsibility is the Department of Homeland Security, but it also covers the federal civil service and similar subjects to the House Oversight and Government Reform

Committee and has 17 members during the 112th Congress (US Congress, Senate Committee on Homeland Security and Governmental Affairs 2010).

Recent hearings produced by this committee include Pandemic Flu: Closing the Gaps (2009); Protecting Our Employees: Pandemic Influenza Preparedness and the Federal Workforce (2010); and A Review of Disaster Medical Preparedness: Improving Coordination and Collaboration in the Delivery of Medical Assistance During Disaster (2010).

Congressional Budget Office

The Congressional Budget Office (CBO) (www.cbo.gov/) was established in 1974 by the Congressional Budget Act to give Congress an enhanced overview of the federal budget and the ability to make overall spending and taxing decisions with an idea of how these decisions impact federal budget deficits and surpluses. CBO also carries out multiyear cost projections for legislation reported by congressional committees, and prepares annual reports on the federal budget and periodic reports on the budgetary implications of federal programs. Plus, the 1995 Unfunded Mandates Reform Act requires CBO to tell congressional authorizing committees if reported legislation has financial impacts on state, local, and tribal governments as well as the private sector (US National Archives and Records Administration 2009; Joyce 2011).

Works produced by CBO include regular periodicals such as The Budget and Economic Outlook: Fiscal Years 2010 to 2020 (2010) and Analysis of the President's Budgetary Proposals for Fiscal Year 2011 (2010) and topical reports on the budgetary impact of federal programs, including Homeland Security and the Private Sector (2004); A Potential Influenza Pandemic: An Update on Possible Macroeconomic Effects and Policy Issues (2006); US Policy Regarding Pandemic Influenza Vaccines (2008); and The Budgetary Effects of Expanding Government Support for Preventive Care and Wellness Services (2009).

Congressional Research Service

The Congressional Research Service (CRS) is a branch of the Library of Congress established in 1914 to serve congressional legislative needs by providing members, their professional staff, and committee staff with objective analyses of public policy issues falling within congressional jurisdictional oversight. CRS received its current name in 1970 and its five interdisciplinary research divisions—American Law; Domestic Social Policy; Foreign Affairs, Defense, and Trade; Government and Finance; and Resources, Science, and Industry—prepare analyses of public policy issues as Congress requests (Library of Congress, Congressional Research Service nd; Everette 2002).

CRS does not have a publicly accessible website for a variety of political reasons, but Internet access to its reports is provided by some public policy research organizations and academic groups, such as www.opencrs.com/, the Federation of American Scientists www.fas.org/sgp/crs/ and the University of North Texas Library http://digital.library.unt.edu/explore/collections/CRSR/. CRS reports can also be acquired by individuals requesting them from their congressional representatives or senators (Gude 1985; Liptak 2005).

Examples of CRS reports dealing with pandemics or emergency management issues include *Influenza Antiviral Drugs and Patent Law Issues* (2005); US and International Responses to the Global Spread of Avian Flu: Issues for Congress (2006); Federal and State Quarantine and Isolation Authority (2006); The 2009 Influenza Pandemic: An Overview (2009); and Immigration Laws and Health-Related Grounds for Exclusion (2009). CRS reports are extremely valuable resources for examining current legislative developments in public policy issues.

Government Accountability Office

The Government Accountability Office (GAO), www.gao.gov/, received its current name in 2004 and was established in 1921 as the General Accounting Office. It assists Congress in its oversight responsibilities by investigating federal government expenditure of taxpayer dollars. GAO's work involves evaluating government policy and program performance; auditing agency operations to determine if federal funds are being spent appropriately, effectively, and efficiently; investigating allegations of illegal and improper activities; issuing legal decisions and opinions; releasing more than 1,000 reports per year; and testifying before congressional oversight committees on agency program performance matters. These reports provide detailed analyses of these programs and feature comments from the agency or agencies whose programs are being reviewed which may often diverge sharply from GAO's assessment (US National Archives and Records Administration 2009; Trask 1991).

Examples of the rich variety of GAO's corpus of work in public health and emergency management program analysis includes Influenza Pandemic: HHS Needs to Continue Its Actions and Finalize Guidance for Pharmaceutical Interventions (2008); Influenza Pandemic: Monitoring and Assessing the Status of the National Pandemic Implementation Plan Needs Improvement (2009); Influenza Pandemic: Key Securities Markets are Making Progress, but Agencies Could Do More to Address Potential Internet Congestion and Encourage Readiness (2009); Biosurveillance: Efforts to Develop a Biosurveillance Capability Need a National Strategy and a Designated Leader (2010).

US State Government Information Sources

State governments are also significant producers of information on preparing for and responding to pandemics. Most of this information will be generated by state health and emergency management departments. Other state agencies, including state legislatures and state court systems, will also be involved in producing relevant information resources. The text of state laws or state codes can generally be found on state legislature websites, and the text of state regulations, often called administrative codes, can also be found on these websites. Relevant state bills and information on their status and cost can be found on state legislature websites and through state legislative research agency websites (Smith et al. 2003).

International and Foreign Government Pandemic Resources

Concern over controlling and defeating pandemics is an integral part of the missions of international government organizations and foreign national health policy agencies. Some of these will now be profiled. The national governments section will emphasize health departments, but truly comprehensive study of foreign national government pandemic response policies should also examine information resources produced by homeland security, quarantine, and emergency management agencies, and legislative/parliamentary institutions and their oversight committees and support organizations emphasizing budgetary and scientific and technology matters.

INTERNATIONAL AND FOREIGN GOVERNMENT PANDEMIC RESOURCES

- World Health Organization
- European Union Public Health
- Pan American Health Organization
- Argentina Ministry of Health
- Australia Department of Health and Ageing
- Brazil Ministry of Health
- Canada—Health Canada
- China Ministry of Health
- Germany—German Federal Health Ministry
- India Ministry of Health and Family Welfare
- Israel Ministry of Health
- Japan Ministry of Health, Labour, and Welfare
- South Africa Department of Health
- United Kingdom Department of Health

World Health Organization

The World Health Organization (WHO), www.who.int/, established in 1948, is a United Nations affiliated organization located in Geneva, Switzerland. The 193 member countries produce health guidelines and standards, help countries address public health matters, and support and promote health research (World Health Organization 2007; Siddiqi 1995).

WHO activities are carried out through regional liaison offices in Africa, the Americas, Southeast Asia, Europe, the eastern Mediterranean, and western Pacific. Its website describes its programmatic activities in areas such as avian influenza, blood transfusion safety, disease outbreak news, drug resistance, foodborne disease surveillance, global alert and response, global foodborne infections, immunization surveillance assessment, and monitoring, and water sanitation and health. Statistical resources provided include a *Global Health Atlas* and the *Global Health Observatory,* providing statistics for WHO member countries. Representative publications include the annual *World Health Report* (1995-present); *International Health and Travel* (2010); *Bulletin of the World Health Organization* (1947-present); and *Weekly Epidemiological Record* (1926-present).

European Union Public Health

Information on European Union (EU) public health activities can be found at http://europa.eu/pol/health/index_en.htm This resource provides information about EU public health activities and emphasizes the need to cooperate against potential threats, such as bioterrorism and influenza epidemics, as well as developing common standards on safe food labeling and nutrition, the safety of blood, medical equipment, and organs, and common air and water quality standards (European Union 2010; European Commission, Directorate-General for Research 2008; Mossialos et al. 2010).

Resources on this website include the text of EU health-related laws and legislation with examples such as On Cooperation in the European Union on Preparedness and Response to Biological and Chemical Agent Attacks (Health Security) 2003; Regulation (EC) No 851/2004 of the European Parliament and of the Council Establishing A European Centre for Disease Prevention and Control (2004); Together for Health: A Strategic Approach for the EU 2008-2013 (2007); and Council Recommendations on Patient Safety, Including the Prevention and Control of Healthcare Associated Infections (2009).

Pan American Health Organization

The Pan American Health Organization (PAHO), www.paho.org/, is a regional WHO affiliate located in Washington, DC, consisting of most western hemisphere countries seeking to improve health and living standards within these countries (Pan American Health Organization 2010; Howard-Jones 1981).

Topics addressed on PAHO's website include antimicrobial resistance, biological terrorism, chemical terrorism, disasters and preparedness, emerging and reemerging diseases, Pandemic (H1N1) 2009, and vaccine preventable diseases. Examples of PAHO publications include Major Trends in Health Legislation in the English-Speaking Caribbean 2001-2005 (2006); and Response to Pandemic (H1N1) 2009 in the Americas: Lessons and Challenges (2009); epidemiological alerts for diseases such as cholera, dengue, malaria, and West Nile Virus 2003-present; and links to member countries' influenza response websites.

The following list of foreign national government resources represents a variety of geographic regions, governmental policymaking practices, and national public health concerns on possible responses to pandemics.

Argentina Ministry of Health

This agency (www.msal.gov.ar/) is responsible for developing and implementing Argentine national health policies in areas as diverse as manufacturing, distributing, and marketing medicinal products; developing and updating health statistics and related information resources; reducing morbidity and other healthcare risks; and coordinating preventive medicine and responses to public health emergencies (Argentina, Ministry of Health 2006; Lin 2007; and Austrailia Department of Health and Aging, 2006; Argentina, Ministry of Social Welfare, National Secretary of Public Health 1973).

Information resources on this ministry's website include statistical reports, such as Dengue Epidemiological Alert (2009-present); Surveillance of Acute Respiratory Infections in Argentina (May 6, 2010-present); Pandemic Influenza H1N1 (2009-2010); recent issues of the newsletter *Epidemiological Alert*; and technical reports such as Manual of Rules and Procedures of Supervision and Control of Notifiable Diseases (2007).

Australia Department of Health and Ageing

Australia's national health department (www.health.gov.au/) was established in 1921 and received its current name in 2001. Its institutional objectives include improving individual, state, territorial, and national healthcare quality, along with responding to disease threats, national emergencies, and large-scale health incidents (Australia, Department of Health and Ageing, 2010).

Information resources produced by this agency include the text of laws they administer; departmental annual reports (1997-1998 to present); International Surveillance Reports (2007-present); descriptions of department communicable disease activities; articles from the scholarly journal *Communicable Diseases Intelligence* (1996-present); and reports such as Australian Health Management

Plan for Pandemic Influenza: B: The Strategy for Responding to an Influenza Pandemic (2008).

Brazil Ministry of Health

This agency (www.saude.gov.br/) serves as Brazil's national health system and its current institutional structure dates from 1988. Ministry responsibilities include providing the full spectrum of outpatient care: surveilling food and drug registration, promoting vaccinations, and taking preventive actions and health surveillance to protect Brazilians against emerging epidemiological threats such as pandemics (Brazil, Ministry of Health 2010; Tuyen, 1997).

Information resources provided by this ministry include details about activities and programs, the text of constitutional provisions, laws, health-related legislation, a health standards database, links to state health department websites, and other materials.

Canada—Health Canada

Health Canada (www.hc-sc.gc.ca/) is the Canadian government's healthcare policymaking agency. Its responsibilities include promoting high-quality health for Canadians, conducting ongoing consultations with them on the best ways to meet their healthcare needs, communicating disease prevention information to protect Canadians from avoidable risks, and encouraging them to increase their health quality through healthy dieting and exercising (Health Canada 2009; Curtis and MacMinn 2008; Bernier 2003).

Accessible information resources include descriptions of this agency's organizational components covering hazardous materials and medicines, the text of advisories, recalls and warnings, and documents such as It's Your Health: Preparing for an Influenza Pandemic (2006); The Canadian Pandemic Influenza Plan for the Health Sector (2006); Influenza Pandemic: Psychosocial Care Planning (2007); Lessons Learned: Health Canada's Response to the 2008 Listeriosis Outbreak (2009); and Government of Canada and Cowessess First Nation Highlight Cooperation on Pandemic Planning and Preparedness (2009).

China Ministry of Health

This agency (www.moh.gov.cn/) is responsible for developing China's national health and drug policy, food safety systems, developing disease prevention and control planning and implementation strategies, conducting monitoring and early warning for public health emergencies, and various other aspects of governmental health policy (Ministry of Health of the People's Republic of China 2008; Leung and Furth 2010).

Resources provided on this agency's website include translated press releases and policy documents and statistics such as 2009 Central Government Subsidies for Local Endemic Diseases Control Project Briefing (2010); National Influenza Surveillance Program (2010); and National Patriotic Sanitation on Carrying Out The Monitoring of Rural Drinking Water Quality Control and Capacity Assessment Notice (2010).

Germany—The German Federal Health Ministry

The German Federal Health Ministry (www.bmgesundheit.de/) has multifaceted institutional responsibilities, including drafting health laws and regulations, disease prevention, distributing and monitoring the quality and safety of medical devices, preventing infection, ensuring blood supply safety, and cooperating with European and international health policymaking entities (Germany, Federal Ministry of Health 2010; Knox 1993).

Materials provided here include the names of key policymaking officials, the texts of current laws and regulations, and proposed legislation, some of which is translated into English; statistics covering areas such as health monitoring and reports including Health in Germany (2006) and Expenditure in Euros Per Inhabitant Per Year for Self-Medication (2006).

India Ministry of Health and Family Welfare

This ministry (http://mohfw.nic.in/) is India's healthcare policymaking agency encompassing a multiple spectrum of health activities, including emergency response (India Ministry of Health and Family Welfare 2010; Jeffrey 1988; Gupta and Rani 2004). English language resources provided here include links to ministry component websites, such as the Central Bureau of Health Intelligence, Directorate General of Health Services and National Centre for Disease Control, the text of recently enacted legislation and governmental regulations as published in the India Gazette, and publications such as departmental Annual Reports 1992-present; Mortality Statistics in India (2006); and National Health Profile of India (2007 and 2009).

Israel Ministry of Health

Israel's Ministry of Health (www.health.gov.il/) serves as this country's healthcare policymaking agency and provides a variety of resources on its scientific, medical, and emergency response activities (Israel, Ministry of Health 2010; Nun, Berlowitz, and Shani 2005). Resources available through this ministry's website include descriptive information on organization components such as Emergency and Disaster Management Division and Epidemiology Division, details about severe acute respiratory syndrome (SARS), and publications such as Assessment and Evaluation of Readiness (2005), Influenza Activity Weekly Reports (2008-present), and Weekly Epidemiological Report (2000-present).

Japan Ministry of Health, Labour, and Welfare

This agency (www.mhlw.go.jp/) serves as Japan's healthcare policymaking agency and its health entities cover topics such as disease control, environmental health, infection, and water (Japan, Ministry of Health, Labour, and Welfare 2010?; Powell and Anesaki 1990). Relevant pandemic information resources provided here include the text of English-language titles of conference reports such as Severe Acute Respiratory Syndrome (SARS) Action Plan (2003); Pandemic Influenza Preparedness Action Plan of the Japanese Government (2007); and regular vital statistics reports on births, deaths, epidemiology, and mortality.

South Africa Department of Health

South Africa's Department of Health (www.doh.gov.za/) aspires to increase national healthcare access and quality, promote preventive and promotional health, work with all affected stakeholders, and enhance the efficiency of that country's health-care delivery system (South Africa, Department of Health 2010; Shisana 2003; Van Rensberg and Benatar 2004). This website provides departmental organizational structure information, descriptions of its efforts to contact HIV/AIDS and other sexually transmitted diseases, along with cholera and malaria, and press releases from 1995 to the present.

Statistical resources include South Africa Demographic and Health Survey (2003) and The Burden of Cryptococcosis in South Africa (2008). Additional information resources include the text of laws, regulations, and proposed legislation, and assorted training and policy documents including Infection Prevention and Control Training Module (2007) Monitoring and Evaluation Framework for the HIV & AIDS and STI's National Strategic Plan 2007-2011 (2009); and An Overview of Health and Health Care in South Africa 1994-2010: Priorities, Progress and Prospects for New Gains (2010).

United Kingdom Department of Health

This agency (www.doh.gov.uk/) serves as the United Kingdom's healthcare agency and its objectives include promoting personal health and delivering the best possible and most effective health care (United Kingdom, Department of Health 2010; Baggott 1994). Information resources provided on the departmental website include listings of organizational components, such as the Performance Committee; the names of leading officials; topically oriented resources on influenza; the text of relevant laws; and circular policy documents containing specific action requirements by domestic health authorities, including Better Blood Transfusion: Safe and Appropriate Use of Blood (2007).

Statistical publications include Referral to Treatment Waiting Time Statistics (2007-present) and Inpatient and Outpatient Waiting Time Statistics (2009-present) with local hospital facility breakdowns. Additional noteworthy publications include Urgent and Emergency Care Bulletin (2002-present) and Pandemic Flu: A National Framework for Responding to an Influenza Pandemic (2007).

References

Argentina. Ministry of Health. 2006. *Functions and objectives, 1-2.* www.msal.gov/htm/site/instit_des/_func.asp (accessed September 10, 2010).

Argentina. Ministry of Social Welfare, National Secretary of Public Health. *Public Health in the Argentine Republic*, 1973. Buenos Aires: Ministry of Social Welfare, National Secretary of Public Health.

Australia. Department of Health and Ageing. 2010. *History of the department*, 1. www.health.gov.au/internet/main/publishing.nsf/Content/health-history.htm (accessed September 10, 2010).

Australia. Department of Health and Ageing. 2006. *Our Role: Overview.* 1. www.health.gov.au/internet/main/publishing.nsf/Conent/health-overview.htm (accessed September 10, 2010).

Baggott, R. 1994. *Health and health care in Britain.* New York: St. Martin's Press.

Ball, H. 2005. *US homeland security: A reference handbook.* Santa Barbara, CA: ABC-CLIO.

Bernier, J. 2003. *Disease, medicine, and society in Canada: A historical overview.* Ottawa: Canadian Historical Association.

Berrick, C. A. 2009. *Homeland security: DHS' progress and challenges in key areas of maritime, aviation, and cybersecurity.* Washington, DC: GAO.

Bianco, W. T., ed. 2000. *Congress on display, Congress at work.* Ann Arbor: University of Michigan Press.

Borja, E. C. 2008. *Brief documentary history of the Department of Homeland Security.* Washington, DC: US Department of Homeland Security History Office.

Bowers, J. R. 1990. *Regulating the regulators: An introduction to the legislative oversight of administrative rulemaking.* New York: Praeger.

Brazil. Ministry of Health. 2010. *What is the unified health system: Presentation*, 1. http://portal.saude.br/portal/saude/cidadao/area.cfm?id_area=1395 (accessed September 10, 2010).

Canon, D. T., Nelson, G., and C. Stewart III. 2002. *Committees in the US Congress, 1789-1946.* Washington, DC: CQ Press.

Chapman, B. 2004. *Researching national security and intelligence policy.* Washington, DC: CQ Press.

Council of Inspectors General on Integrity and Efficiency. 2010. 1. www.ignet.gov/ (accessed August 26, 2010).

Crosby, A. W. 2003. *America's forgotten pandemic: The influenza of 1918.* Cambridge: Cambridge University Press.

Curtis, L. J. and W. J. MacMinn. 2008. Health care utilization in Canada: Twenty-five years of evidence. *Canadian Public Policy* 34 (1): 65-87.

Ememark, C. 2009. Regional health and global security: The Asian cradle of pandemic influenza. In *Security Politics in the Asia-Pacific: A regional-global nexus,* ed. W. T. Tow, 284-298. Cambridge, UK: Cambridge University Press.

Etheridge, E. W. 1992. *Sentinel for health: A history of the Centers for Disease Control.* Berkeley: University of California Press.

European Commission Directorate-General for Research. 2008. *Emerging epidemics research*. Luxembourg: Office for Official Publications of the European Communities.

European Union. 2010. *Public health*, 1-2. http://europa.eu/pol/health/index_en.htm (accessed September 8, 2010).

Everette, C. J. 2002. *Orientation guide for congressional interns and volunteers*. Washington, DC: Library of Congress, Congressional Research Service.

Federal Register. 2010(a). *Pandemic influenza vaccines enrollment*. 75 (43): 10268-10272.

Federal Register. 2010(b). Executive Order 13546 of July 2, 2010: *Optimizing the security of biological select agents and toxins in the United States*. 75 (130) (July 8, 2010): 39439-39442.42 USC 247d-1.

Flu.gov (2011), Transportation Planning, 1; www.flu.gov/professional/transport/; accessed November 9, 2011.

Friedes, T. 1992. Inspector General reports as instruments of government accountability. *Government Information Quarterly* 9 (1): 53-66.

Germany. Federal Ministry of Health. 2010. *A Portrait*, 1-2. www.bmg.bund.de/cln_151/nn_1192800/DE/Ministerium/Aufgaben/aufgaben_node.html?_nnn=true (accessed September 10, 2010).

Gude, G. 1985. Congressional Research Service: Research and information arm of Congress. *Government Information Quarterly*, 2 (1): 5-11.

Gupta, M. D. and M. Rani. 2004. *India's public health system: How well does it function at the national level?* Washington, DC: World Bank.

Handy, S. K. and R. Strahan. 2004. Staff politics in the Republican House: The case of the Appropriations Committee. *Congress and the Presidency* 31 (1): 1-19.

Health Canada. 2009, 1-2. www.hc-sc.gc.ca/ahc-asc/index-eng.php (accessed September 10, 2010.

Howard-Jones, N. 1981. *The Pan-American Health Organization: Origins and evolution*. Geneva: World Health Organization.

India. Ministry of Health and Family Welfare. 2010. http://mohfw.nic.in (accessed September 13, 2010).

Interim guidance to assist flight deck and cabin crew in identifying passengers who may have swine influenza. 2009. Atlanta: CDC.

Israel Ministry of Health. 2010. www.health.gov.il/ (accessed September 13, 2010).

Japan. Ministry of Health Labour, and Welfare. 2010? Health Department. www.mhlw.go.jp/bunya/kenkou/index.html (accessed September 13, 2010).

Jeffrey, R. 1988. *The politics of health in India*. Berkeley: University of California Press.

Joyce, P. G. 2011. *The Congressional Budget Office: Honest numbers, power, and policymaking*. Washington, DC: Georgetown University Press, forthcoming.

King, D.C. 1994. The nature of congressional committee jurisdictions. *American Political Science Review* 88 (1): 48-62.

Knox, R. A. 1993. *Germany: One nation with health care for all*. New York: Faulkner & Gray.

Koempel, M. L. 2007. *Homeland security: Compendium of recommendations relevant to House committee organization and analysis of considerations for the House, and 109th and 110th Congresses epilogue*. Washington, DC: Library of Congress, Congressional Research Service.

Leung, A. K. C and C. Furth., eds. 2010. *Health and hygiene in Chinese East Asia: Policies and publics in the long twentieth century*. Durham, NC: Duke University Press.

Library of Congress. Congressional Research Service. nd.. *About CRS*, 1-3. www.loc.gov/crsinfo/whatcrs.html (accessed September 7, 2010).

Library of Congress. Congressional Research Service. 1983. *Congressional foresight: History, recent experiences, and implementation strategies: A report.* Washington, DC: GPO, Congressional Research Service.

Library of Congress THOMAS. 2010. Status of appropriations legislation for fiscal year 2010. http://thomas.loc.gov/home/approp/app10.html (accessed February 21, 2011).

Lin, V. 2007. *Public health in Australia: The organised effort.* Crows Nest, NSW: Allen & Unwin.

Lindsay, J. M. 1990. Congressional oversight of the Department of Defense: Reconsidering the conventional wisdom. *Armed Forces and Society* 17(1): 7-33.

Liptak, D. A. 2005. Congressional research service reports revealed. *Online* 29 (6): 23-26.

Longley, L. D. and W. J. Oleszek. 1989. *Bicameral politics: Conference committees in Congress.* New Haven: Yale University Press.

Marshall, B. W., Prins, B.C., and D. W. Rohde. 1999. Fighting fire with water: Partisan procedural strategies and the Senate Appropriations Committee. *Congress and the Presidency* 26 (2): 113-132.

Maxwell, B., ed. 2004, *Homeland security: A documentary history.* Washington, DC: CQ Press.

Medicalcountermeasures.gov. 2010. *About us,* 1. www.medicalcountermeasures.gov/ AboutUs.aspx (accessed August 19, 2010).

Miles, W. D. 1982. *A history of the National Library of Medicine: The nation's treasury of medical knowledge.* Washington, DC: National Library of Medicine.

Miller, R. I. 2004. *The impact of quarantine on military operations.* Maxwell Air Force Base, AL: Air University/USAF Counterproliferation Center.

Ministry of Health of the People's Republic of China. 2008. Agency profile, 1-6. <www.moh.gov.cn/publicfiles/business/htmlfiles/zwgkzt/piggk/200804/621,htm> (accessed September 10, 2010).

Mossialos, E., Permanand, G., Baeten, R. and T. Hervey. eds. 2010. *Health systems governance in Europe: The role of European Union law and policy.* Cambridge: Cambridge University Press.

Nun, G. B., Berlowitz, Y., and M. Shani. 2005. *Health system in Israel.* Tel Aviv: Ministry of Defense.

Oleszek, W. J. 2004. *Congressional procedures and the policy process.* Washington, DC: CQ Press.

Pan-American Health Organization. 2010. About Paho, 1-2. http://new.paho.org/hq/index.php?option=com_content&task=view&id=91&ltemid=220 (accessed September 8, 2010).

Pendergrast, M. 2010. *Inside the outbreaks: The elite medical detectives of the epidemic intelligence service.* Boston: Houghton Mifflin Harcourt.

Powell, M. and M. Anesaki. 1990. *Health care in Japan.* New York: Routledge.

Priest, S. H. 2009. Risk communication for nanobiotechnology: To whom, about what, and why? *Journal of Law, Medicine, and Ethics* 37 (4): 759-769.

Shisana, O. 2003. *The impact of HIV/AIDS on the health sector: National survey of health personnel, ambulatory, and hospitalised patients and health facilities.* Pretoria: National Department of Health.

Siddiqi, J. 1995. *World health and politics: The World Health Organization and the UN system.* Columbia, SC: University of South Carolina Press.

Smith, L. L., Barkley, D. C., Cornwall, D. D., Johnson, E. W., and J. L. Malcomb. 2003. *Tapping state government information sources.* Westport, CT: Greenwood Press.

South Africa. Department of Health. 2010. *Mission and vision.* www.doh.gov.za/about (accessed September 14, 2010).

Springer, M. M. 1986. The Congressional Record: Substantially a verbatim report? *Government Publications Review* 13 (3): 371-378.

Stambaugh, H., Sensinig, D., Casagrande, R., Flagg S., and B. Gerrity. 2008. *Quarantine facilities for arriving air travelers: Identification of planning needs and costs.* Washington, DC: Transportation Research Board.

Sullivan, J. V. 2007. *How our laws are made.* House Document 110-49. Washington, DC: GPO.

Trask, R. R. 1991. *GAO history, 1921-1991.* Washington, DC: GAO.

Turnbull, K. F. rapporteur. 2008. *Inter-Agency aviation industry collaboration in planning for pandemic outbreaks: Summary of a workshop.* Washington, DC: Transportation Research Board.

Tuyen, J. M. 1997. *Brazil: A country study.* 5th ed. Washington, DC: Federal Research Division, Library of Congress.

UK Department of Health. 2010. About Us; 1. www.dhs.gov.uk/health/aboutus/; (accessed November 9, 2011).

US Army Public Health Command (Provisional). 2010; 1. http://phc.amedd.army.mil/ (accessed February 21, 2011).

US Centers for Disease Control and Prevention. 2010. *CDC organization*; 1. www.cdc.gov/ about/organization/cio.html (accessed August 20, 2010).

US Congress. House Committee on Homeland Security. 2010. *Homeland Security Committee overview;* 1. http://hsc.house.gov/about/ (accessed September 3, 2010).

US Congress. House Committee on Homeland Security. 2009a. *Beyond readiness: An examination of the current status and future outlook of the national response to pandemic influenza.* Washington, DC: GPO.

US Congress. House Committee on Homeland Security. 2009b. *The challenge of aligning programs, personnel, and resources to achieve border security.* Washington, DC: GPO.

US Congress. House Committee on International Relations. 2006. *Avian flu: Addressing the global threat.* Washington, DC: GPO.

US Congress. House Committee on the Judiciary. Subcommittee on Commercial and Administrative Law. 2007. *Interim report on the administrative law, process and procedure project for the 21st century.* Washington, DC: GPO.

US Congress. House Committee on Science. 2006. *Scientific and technical advice for the US Congress.* Washington, DC: GPO.

US Congress. House Committee on Transportation and Infrastructure. Subcommittee on Aviation. 2005. *Efforts to prevent pandemics by air travel.* Washington, DC: GPO.

US Congress. Senate Committee on Appropriations. 2005. *A history of the Senate Committee on Appropriations and the appropriations process.* Washington, DC: GPO.

US Congress. Senate Committee on Health, Education, Labor, and Pensions. 2010. http:// help.senate.gov/ (accessed September 3, 2010).

US Congress. Senate Committee on Homeland Security and Governmental Affairs. 2010. About the committee, 1. http://hsgac.senate.gov/public/index.cfm?Fuse Action=AboutCommittee.History. US Constitution. Article 1, Section 7. (accessed November 9, 2011).

US Department of Defense Pandemic Influenza Watchboard. (2010); 1-2. http://fhpr.osd. mil/aiWatchboard (accessed August 19, 2010).

US Department of Health and Human Services. nd. The great pandemic: The United States in 1918-1919: The Legacy of the Pandemic; 1. http://1918.pandemicflu.gov/the_pandemic/04.htm (accessed September 3, 2010).

US Department of Homeland Security. 2006. *Pandemic influenza preparedness, response, and recovery guide for critical infrastructure and key resources.* Washington, DC: US Department of Homeland Security.

US Department of State. nd. *Avian influenza action group;* 1. www.state.gov/g/avianflu/ (accessed August 19, 2010).

US Environmental Protection Agency. Homeland Security Research. 2009. *Basic information: Overview;* 1. www.epa.gov/nhsrc/basicinfo.html (accessed August 20, 2010).

US Environmental Protection Agency. Homeland Security Research. 2010. *Indoor and outdoor decontamination research.* 1-2. www.epa.gov/nhsrc/aboutdecon.html (accessed August 20, 2010).

US Environmental Protection Agency. Homeland Security Research. 2010. *Water security research;* 1-2. www.epa.gov/nhsrc/aboutwater.html (accessed August 20, 2010).

US Government Accountability Office. 2007. *Influenza pandemic: DOD combatant commands preparedness efforts could benefit from more clearly defined roles, resources, and risk mitigation.* Washington, DC: GAO.

US Government Accountability Office. 2009. *Influenza pandemic: Monitoring and assessing the status of the national pandemic implementation plan needs improvement.* Washington, DC: GAO.

US Government Printing Office. 2008. *Unified agenda: About;* 1. www.gpoaccess.gov/ua/ (accessed August 18, 2010).

US Government Printing Office. 2009. *Public and private laws: About,* 1. www.gpoaccess.gov/plaws/about.html (accessed February 21, 2011).

US Government Printing Office. 2010. List of CFR sections affected (LSA): About; 1. www.gpoaccess.gov/lsa/about.html (accessed August 18, 2010).

US Government Printing Office. 2010. *US code main page,* 1. www.gpoaccess.gov/uscode/ (accessed August 18, 2010).

US Homeland Security Advisory Council. 2008. *Top ten challenges facing the next Secretary of Homeland Security.* Washington, DC: US Department of Homeland Security.

US National Archives and Records Administration. 2009. *United States government manual, 2009-2010.* Washington, DC: GPO.

US National Archives and Records Administration. 2010. *Code of federal regulations: About;* 1. www.gpoaccess.gov.cfr/about.html (accessed February 21, 2011).

US National Library of Medicine. 2010. *Factsheet: Toxnet: Toxicology Data Network;* 1-2. www.nlm.nih.gov/pubs/factsheets/toxnetfs.html (accessed August 25, 2010).

US Naval Postgraduate School Center for Homeland Defense and Security. 2010. *About the Homeland Security Digital Library;* 1. www.hsdl.org/?about (accessed August 26, 2010).

US Office of Management and Budget. Office of Information and Regulatory Affairs. 2010. Reginfo.gov. (accessed February 21, 2011).

US Public Health Service. 1919. *Annual report of the Surgeon General of the Public Health Service of the United States for fiscal year 1919.* House Document 66-436. Washington, DC: GPO.

Van Rensberg, H. C. J. and S. R. Benatar. eds. 2004. *Health and health care in South Africa.* Pretoria: Van Schaik.

Warren, K. F. 2004. *Administrative law in the political system.* Boulder, CO: Westview Press.

Welcome to the Force Health Protection & Readiness Website. 2010. 1. http://fhp.osd.mil/ (accessed August 19, 2010).

Working for health: An introduction to the World Health Organization. 2007; 2, 4; www.who.int/about/brochure_en.pdf (accessed September 8, 2010).

World Health Organization. 2010. *International travel and health.* www.who.int/en/ (accessed August 31, 2010).

Zwirn, J. 1988. *Congressional publications and proceedings: Research on legislation, budget, and treaties.* 2nd ed. Englewood, CO: Libraries Unlimited, Inc.

Chapter 2

Classic Military War Principles Applied to Pandemic Preparation

Will Shelby, J. Eric Dietz, and David R. Black

Contents

Abstract

Sun Tzu and Carl von Clausewitz, as two classical developers of military theory, provide insights into the challenges of "fighting" pandemic influenza. Sun Tzu's *The Art of War* was written as early as the sixth century BC and Clausewitz wrote his book in the nineteenth century (Giles 2007; Howard and Paret 1984). Yet these books and the principles described are still applicable to modern military tactics as well as to a host of other disciplines. A novel strain of H1N1 Influenza A caused concern worldwide in 2009. Many countries took precautions, but most could improve their pandemic preparation. An exploration of military principles and application could uncover new methods to establish priorities for the public health and increase efficiency by reducing demands on resources and managing shortages. This chapter attempts to develop principles based on classical military strategy that support planning success for pandemic influenza and the amelioration of disaster preparedness operations by formally recognizing parallels to the military and incorporating concepts and terms.

Keywords: Influenza, Pandemic Influenza, Sun Tzu, Carl von Clausewitz, H1N1 Influenza A, Military Principles, Strategic Planning

Rationale

A pandemic is similar to other natural disaster events in the difficulty of minimizing impact through mitigation. This chapter uses classic military principles to assuage the impact of pandemic influenza. The principles applied are those of Sun Tzu's *The Art of War* (Giles 2007), circa 550 to 320 BC, and Carl von Clausewitz's *On War* (circa, 1831). These highly regarded principles of warfare provide opportunities for developing similar principles for managing a pandemic. Sun Tzu's *The Art of War* was studied by military leaders such as Eisenhower and Bradley at the US Army War College, and in popular culture by people such as athletic coaches (Associated Press 2005; Wilcoxon 2010). David R. Black applied principles of Carl von Clausewitz's *On War* to public health (Black 2002).

This chapter applies classical military principles of Sun Tzu and Carl von Clausewitz to emergency planning for pandemic influenza at the tactical level. The principles are used to recommend an organizational structure based on the incident command system and the command staff, including incident commander, liaison officer, information officer, safety officer, and general staff in the following sections: Logistics, Finance and Administration, Planning, Intelligence, and Operations (Quick Series 2008; Emergency Management Institute 2010).

One reason for the application of military principles is the ongoing concern about influenza as a public health challenge because of the recent novel H1N1 influenza A strain, which became a pandemic in 2009. Fortunately, H1N1 case fatality rates were below expectation because fewer people died than from seasonal flu (Flu.gov 2011; Worldwide Statistics of the H1N1 Influenza A Pandemic 2011). However, concern arose due to the novelty of the H1N1 flu strain and its potential to mutate, which exacerbated the public health challenge (National Health Service, 2010).

A pandemic progresses through six phases, according to the World Health Organization (WHO 2010). Phases 1 to 3 exist when no or very few human infections are present, though these phases might include many animal infections. Phase 4 is confirmation of human-to-human transmission. Phases 5 and 6 entail widespread infection of a disease in a single country or multiple countries. Until Phase 6, the influenza event would be classified simply as an elevation above endemic levels and as an epidemic with greater incidence and broader transmission disease.

In the past, it was more difficult for a disease to spread to multiple countries. However, modern global travel has increased the likelihood of a pandemic due to the fact that people worldwide are exposed to a disease, each other, and a variety of vectors (Arguin, Marano, and Freedman 2009). Created is the necessity to implement a response system that elicits cooperation among agencies and results in efficient solutions. This interagency and multidisciplinary response demands a common series of strategy and tactics for managing pandemics. Many organizations have used military principles to solve problems in other areas, including public health. Black (2002) suggested using military terms, such as center of gravity, ends, ways and means, and instruments of power to focus on "winning" the war in public health. The Centers for Disease Control and Prevention (CDC) and the WHO also use terms similar to the military, which encourage health leaders to manage multiple health challenges of a pandemic with urgency. The CDC discusses the need to "fight the flu" (CDC 2011) and the need to "combat pandemic influenza" (Booz, Allen, Hamilton 2011; Howard County Health Department 2011). The WHO discusses global alert and response for pandemic preparedness and readiness in terms of consequence, detection, and preparation (World Health Organization 2011). In 2005, the WHO published strategic actions for pandemic readiness which included: (a) reduce opportunities for human infection; (b) strengthen the early warning system; (c) contain or delay spread at the source; (d) reduce morbidity, mortality, and social disruption; and (e) conduct research to guide response measures (WHO 2005).

Method

Military principles of war are applied to public health and disaster preparedness. Public health leaders, like military leaders, can be required to organize and maneuver tactically against a relatively unknown adversary, while maintaining the public trust and responding with the best possible use of government and private resources. What is lacking is a common set of strategic principles for preparation and response. Proposed are five principles for adaptation from historical military study. Those principles are:

Leadership – As a response to a large geographic area, pandemic response must have a single direction proven to be rational and clear to the public.

Logistics – Pandemic logistical resources include personnel, supplies, and funding, which combine into the available resources that must be decisively concentrated for impacting an effective and timely emergency response. Pandemic is an event of global shortage of numerous key resources over a broad geographic area of human suffering. Shortages will create needs for key resource management and creativity to solve problems with minimal available resources.

Surveillance – The broad geographical area for a pandemic demands that surveillance systems be developed to monitor resources, civil order, and spread of disease as well as allocation of resources throughout the pandemic uncertainty and shortage so that informed decisions can be communicated to the public.

Simplicity – One of the principles that should guide a plan is minimal intervention, which states that if there are two situations that lead to the same conclusion, then the simpler of the two is to be chosen (cf. Black 2002). In public health, this concept of simplicity or parsimony also is known as Occam's Razor (Last 2001). The complexity of the problems in pandemic will be large. Pandemic plans must be simple and clear, allowing for understanding at all governmental levels, including the public and private sectors to ensure that the plan is implementable.

Objective – Success derived in pandemic planning is from a clear, understandable, and obtainable set of goals leading to an objective to be communicated throughout government levels, and understood and accepted by the public.

These five principles are used by Sun Tzu, whose writings date to the sixth century, and Carl von Clausewitz, whose writings date to the nineteenth century. Sun Tzu and Clausewitz use different theories to develop an understanding of warfare. Sun Tzu and Clausewitz each seek to find overarching principles that provide guidance to military leaders. These overarching principles seek to explain military operations with concepts that are familiar to the leaders of their day by comparing military operations to the physical understanding of the environment. These concepts attempted to simplify the complexity of military systems and leadership techniques needed to succeed on the battlefield with careful use of available resources.

There have been many interpretations and translations of Sun Tzu, including the translation by Giles (2007). Presented in Table 2.1 are Sun Tzu's 13 principles.

Table 2.1 Sun Tzu's principles adapted to provide principles for pandemic influenza preparation

Sun Tzu		Pandemic Influenza Principles
Principles	Brief Definition	
Maneuvering	Taking advantage of decisive terrain	Objective
Army on the March	Moving to engage the enemy in new territory	
Energy	Building momentum for army	Logistics
Attack by Fire	Using weapons and environment as weapon	
Waging War	Winning with efficiency and limited cost	
Variations in Tactics	Taking gain of army's flexibility for protection	Leadership
Attack by Stratagem	Strengthening army by unity and coordination	
Tactical Dispositions	Positioning army for strength and opportunity	
Weak Points and Strong	Taking advantage of strength differences	Surveillance
Laying Plans	Computing the chances of victory with careful consideration	
Use of Spies	Developing adequate information for success	
Terrain	Reviewing the battlefield for strengths and weaknesses	Simplicity
Nine Situations	Categorizing situations in common situations	

We mapped Sun Tsu's 13 proposed principles to our five proposed pandemic principle categories presented in Table 2.1. Sun Tzu discussed maneuver and army on the march, which can be equated to the development of the first principle necessary for pandemic preparation: objective. The second principle, logistics, includes Sun Tzu's concept for managing energy, attack by fire, and waging war since a pandemic is largely a logistics problem of managed shortages. Beyond social distancing, the main public health weapon is vaccination and antiviral medical treatments, both logistical challenges. Leadership, the third principle, equates to variations in tactics, attack by stratagem, and tactical dispositions as proposed by Sun Tzu. For a pandemic, these principles of Sun Tzu are largely challenges by public health leaders in communicating the challenges, tactics, and distribution of assets or dispositions. Next is surveillance, which Sun Tzu might consider determining weak and strong points, developing plans, and using spies or intelligence operations. The importance of surveillance to a pandemic is the need to find diseases above endemic levels as early as possible and reacting to limit disease transmission. The last principle, simplicity, combines the Sun Tzu ideas for use of the terrain and the nine different situations. Simplicity's importance in a pandemic is to ensure that effective communications and coordination are possible in a rapidly changing, complex, and resource-constrained environment.

To apply the principles of Sun Tzu to pandemics, there must be a change in focus from enemy organizations to natural events. Like military operations, pandemic response must organize command, manage resources, economize efforts, and develop simple plans. Developing intelligence and maneuvering to gain information about a pandemic must be derived from diverse global sources of information based on the natural transmission of disease, monitoring of disease changes, and assembling the mass of data to determine endemic levels of disease as well as intelligence on effective methods for treating disease.

Carl von Clausewitz's publication, *On War,* also has been translated. One translation is by Howard and Paret (1984). Clausewitz uses critical analysis of military science to study application of military power in attack and defense. He also discusses the difference between strategy and tactics in addition to introducing the concepts of center of gravity, military superiority, ends, ways and means, and culmination or the achievement of military objectives at the tactical and strategic levels. In Table 2.2 are 11 terms and brief definitions attributed to Clausewitz.

Clausewitz discussed offense and defense, military and political considerations, and operational strategy that we associate with the first principle, objective. The second principle, logistics, includes the Clausewitz concept for engagement; limited or total campaigns of attrition that are essentially logistical problems of managed shortages for the campaign or plan duration. Pandemic resources include personnel, supplies such as vaccination, healthcare systems such as ventilators and disposable supplies including gloves and masks. Other resources are process or conceptual, such as social distancing or effective hand washing. All logistical challenges are similar to those historically seen during military campaigns that influenced Sun Tzu and Clausewitz. Leadership, the third principle, equates to Clausewitz's concepts for the art and science of war or the art and science of leading a public health response to a pandemic. Clausewitz also would describe military genius as the intuitive and trained knowledge needed to lead

Table 2.2 Clausewitz principles of war adapted to provide principles for pandemic influenza preparation

Clausewitz		Pandemic Influenza Principles
Principle	**Brief Definition**	
The Offensive/ The Defensive	Seizing the objective in offensive battle at a time and place of choosing/ Preservation of the army through the superiority of defense until transiting to attack	Objective
Military and Political	Use of military power to wage total war which can gain public favor and military power and war is a policy	
Operational Strategy	Military battles to achieve the end of military conflict by military, political, and social means	
Engagement – Limited or Total	Engagements fit the need toward ultimate war objective	Logistics
Campaign of Attrition	Culmination point of battle is impacted by wearing down opponent and available resources	
Strategy	Art of war/Moral forces	Leadership
Tactics	Science of war/Quantified elements and critical analysis	
Military Genius	Importance of leadership and character in an unpredictable venture	
Intelligence	Tactical intelligence in warfare can be imprecise, contradictory or wrong; "Fog of War;" political intelligence is important	Surveillance
Center of Gravity	Strategic and operation hubs of power and movement that the military depends on	Simplicity
Use of Terrain	Political objectives seized through locations that promote offense/defense	

people during great challenge. For a pandemic, the military genius principles of Clausewitz include the skillful management by public health leaders in communicating the challenges, system demands on resources, and technology available to respond. The second most important principle, surveillance, equates to the Clausewitz principle of intelligence. The last principle, simplicity, combines Clausewitz' concepts of center of gravity and use of terrain. Simplicity's importance in a pandemic is to ensure effective communication of challenges (center of gravity) and effective coordination of resources or terrain in the resource-constrained pandemic environment.

Application

Using the proposed principles, we applied these to pandemic response and the national incident management system (NIMS) staffing recommendations. After the September 11 attacks, homeland security presidential directive 5 (HSPD-5) created the system in order to minimize the damage of future disasters in the United States. The purpose of HSPD-5 was, "To enhance the ability of the United States to manage domestic incidents by establishing a single, comprehensive national incident management system" (HSPD-5, 2003, p. 3). NIMS seeks to allow local, state, and federal agencies to mitigate hazards in the quickest and most efficient manner. The response system within NIMS is the incident command system (ICS). ICS integrates personnel and equipment from different organizations into a single structure, allows multi-agency cooperation, and establishes common practices for response (Quick Series 2008). Incident command identifies staff organization and functions that would be responsible for applying the principles that we propose. The principles are divided into the nine positions of incident command, explaining what each position should consider to enhance the effects of its efforts based on the principles taken from Sun Tzu and Carl von Clausewitz.

Command Staff

Incident Commander

No position in incident command better exemplifies leadership than the command staff. The staff is responsible for the overall response to an emergency. The incident commander is the person leading a coordinated response and who has overall responsibility for leading the response. Many factors affect the selection of the incident commander. Branum, Dietz, and Black (2010) discussed factors impacting this selection. As an outbreak progresses toward an epidemic or pandemic, local leaders must select the best individuals to provide leadership to the response. The commander should be fully knowledgeable of the ICS, but also able to apply the principles outlined in this chapter (Quick Series 2008). The commander could be

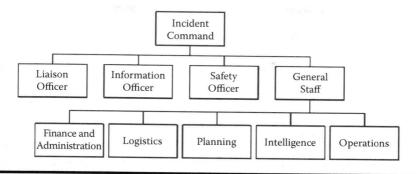

Figure 2.1 Proposed incident command structure based on the proposed pandemic principles.

a first responder, emergency manager, or a public health official (see Figure 2.1 for a general pandemic ICS). Different situations call for different commanders. The incident commander must manage the development of the response principles stated above. However, a person may not be the most qualified just because of the experience she/he has in public health. In order to be the most qualified, an incident commander also needs proper training in emergency management concepts and have the capability to lead.

There are three main types of command to consider for response to a pandemic: normal command, specialized command, and unified command (Branum, Dietz, and Black 2010). One of the three types will be chosen depending on the situation. Each has its own strengths and weaknesses. Normal command personnel typically have the most experience and, therefore, are most able to make quick decisions, but may lack specialized knowledge. Specialized command personnel may have the appropriate knowledge base, but also may lack experience or knowledge of incident command. Unified command personnel, even if they are able to cooperate well, may lack specialized knowledge or ICS knowledge. One method of command is not better than the other. The best type of command is the one that works while operating within the pandemic principles and can incorporate the necessary knowledge and leadership (Branum, Dietz, and Black 2010).

Important qualities for command are leadership, effective communication, the ability to maintain composure, and adaptability. A commander should be well acquainted with his/her general staff: the directors of Logistics, Finance and Administration, Planning, Intelligence, and Operations (Emergency Management Institute 2010). Each of these positions manages the pandemic principles for the incident commander, and is critical to mitigating the damage from a disaster (Moynihan 2008).

Once the incident commander decides the plan of action, she/he needs to be able to communicate the plan effectively so orders are clearly understood. "A general who misunderstands an order or who bungles it places your undertaking in the greatest jeopardy" (Luvaas 1999 p. 273). At the Battle of Gettysburg during the Civil War, General Robert E. Lee told Lieutenant General Richard S. Ewell to take Cemetery Hill and Culp's Hill "if practicable." Ewell decided not to attack Cemetery Hill. General Lee was too vague with his orders. Therefore, his general did not obey. This miscommunication could have cost him the battle (Schwartz 2002). A plan can fail for multiple reasons, but miscommunication should not be one of them.

Adaptability is another important quality of an incident commander. Plans always change because they are plans, not absolutes. It is the job of the incident commander to make sure that as plans change, the original purpose remains: to protect the public. By changing the plans, an incident commander could increase the efficiency of a plan or save more people. "He who can modify his tactics in relation to his opponent and thereby succeed in winning may be called a heaven-born captain" (Giles 2007 p. 17).

After leadership, simplicity guides the development of the plan with close coordination of the commander; in particular, as a planning function. The incident commander must ensure the simplicity of the plan and he/she and staff must manage simplicity. The incident commander also must be able to manage the planning process and ensure that plans are as simple as possible while ensuring decisions are timely. Although it would be preferable to ponder a decision, sometimes decisions require immediacy. A good incident commander will balance decision making between urgency and precision. Clausewitz explains:

> "If the mind is to emerge unscathed from this relentless struggle with the unforeseen, two qualities are indispensable: first, an intellect that, even in the darkest hour, retains some glimmerings of the inner light which leads to truth; and second, the courage to follow this faint light wherever it may lead... We repeat again: strength of character does not consist solely in having powerful feelings, but in maintaining one's balance in spite of them" (Howard and Paret 1984, pp. 102 and 107).

By maintaining composure, the incident commander will help others remain calm. However, she/he does not have to do everything alone. The command staff play crucial supporting roles, including maintaining relationships with all organizations involved, compiling and releasing up-to-date information, and ensuring the safety of all personnel.

Liaison Officer

In the past, local, state, and federal agencies did not work well together. During the terrorist attacks of September 11, 2001, this was a problem because the multiple agencies working at Ground Zero had great difficulty sharing information, which ultimately caused confusion and inefficiency among response agencies. According to the September 11 Commission Final Report (Report of National Commission on Terrorist Attacks upon the United States 2004):

> "Information that was critical to informed decision-making was not shared among agencies. FDNY chiefs in leadership roles that morning have told us that their decision-making capability was hampered by a lack of information from NYPD aviation. At 9:51 A.M., a helicopter pilot cautioned that 'large pieces' of the South Tower appeared to be about to fall and could pose a danger to those below. Immediately after the tower's collapse, a helicopter pilot radioed that news. This transmission was followed by communications at 10:08, 10:15, and 10:22 that called into question the condition of the North Tower. The FDNY chiefs would have benefited greatly had they been able to communicate with personnel in a helicopter" (p. 321).

The ICS has provided improvements. It is one of the key tools for expanding the leadership principle. People from multiple agencies can work together to share information regardless of their title or position (Quick Series 2008). The liaison officer is the person who connects agencies and groups so that a job is not repeated and to improve communication. If resources are coordinated, then the duplication of necessary missions is minimized.

Information Officer

> "As a rule most men would rather believe bad news than good, and rather tend to exaggerate the bad news. The dangers that are reported may soon, like waves, subside; but like waves they keep recurring, without apparent reason. The commander must trust his judgment and stand like a rock on which the waves break in vain...." (Howard and Paret, 1984, p. 117).

During pandemic influenza, another key leadership function is the management of the media, which can make the situation seem worse than actual (Brainard 2009). Therefore, it is very important to release media statements on a predetermined schedule that accurately depict the situation. Order is necessary regardless of the situation so that people will not become enraged and chaotic. To minimize the risk of chaos, many nations were constantly releasing information about the H1N1 influenza virus during the pandemic. Specifically, the United Kingdom posted a page on their National Health Service website that gave accurate information about the virus. The US also posted accurate information on the Centers for Disease Control and Prevention website. The facts stated were clear on their website (CDC 2010; National Health Service 2010). It also would be helpful to release information about cleaning products and non-prescription medicines that may help relieve symptoms. This information should be available on government and health websites, in the news, and even on product websites. An incident commander must make sure that information sent out on his/her behalf is timely and accurate.

Safety Officer

The safety officer provides another key leadership role for the incident commander and ensures that people are following proper safety procedures, identifies dangerous situations that can occur during the pandemic, and can override authority for an operation if deemed unsafe (Irwin 2008). Militaries have been acting in a similar manner since the time of Sun Tzu. Generals view the battlefield prior to the battle for possible disadvantages and hazards. Generals would make many calculations to determine if a situation was favorable for success or not (Giles 2007). A good general would halt an advance if the conditions would destroy the army much like a safety officer would call off an operation if it was deemed unsafe. However, in both cases, it is sometimes necessary to execute an operation regardless of safety, if a certain part of an operation need is essential. In this last scenario, the safety officer ensures damages that occur are minimized.

General Staff

The remaining general staff functions support the incident command, but are also responsible for implementing principles as well.

Finance and Administration

According to Giles (2007):

> "In the operations of war, where there are in the field a thousand swift chariots, as many heavy chariots, and a hundred thousand mail-clad soldiers, with provisions enough to carry them a thousand *li*, the expenditure at home and at the front, including entertainment of guests, small items such as glue and paint, and sums spent on chariots and armor, will reach the total of a thousand ounces of silver per day. Such is the cost of raising an army of 100,000 men" (p. 6).

The Finance and Administration section, a vital part of the logistics principle, deals with money or administration, including funds and compensation for damages (US Financial Services Sector 2007). Money is important in any situation. If there is no funding, there is no plan and no logistics. There may be a plan to mitigate a pandemic, but if that plan is too expensive, then it is useless. Plans tend to vary so much due to this issue. A big city like Los Angeles can afford to use more money on an emergency plan than a rural, sparsely populated city in Montana. Finance and Administration are there to ensure that a plan is financially sound for the area that is going to use it (Quick Series 2008).

Knowing funding sources is an important part of handling finances. If a group finds something useful for containing a pandemic, but is void of money in the process, then implementation is impossible. Therefore, it is important to secure funding before determining a plan. There are government grants awarded to municipalities and universities so that a local area would be able to formulate a plan. Funding can come in other ways such as through the Federal Emergency Management Agency (FEMA) or private organizations. If an area needs help from the private sector, advance arrangements are possible so the plan can be developed (Quick Series 2008).

Logistics

"In order to carry out an attack, we must have means available. The material... should always be kept in readiness" (Giles 2007, p. 36).

The logistics section manages the remaining part of this principle and is responsible for providing facilities, people, and supplies for a situation. The responsibility of logistics is to ensure distribution of people and supplies to the proper place at the right time (Irwin 2008). If there are not enough supplies, negotiations need to occur before an event to stockpile supplies or expedite delivery prior to a pandemic. The private sector can help gather supplies. If a privately owned company is willing to donate supplies, such as stockpiled antivirals, an ambulance, or manpower, then a memorandum of understanding is important between the local government and the private companies in the event of an emergency (Quick Series 2008).

Supplies should be available, distributed, and packaged for delivery where and when needed. Factors to consider in the planning of distribution of people and supplies are traffic, terrain, mode of transportation, and security (Howard and Paret 1984). In large metropolitan areas, traffic can halt distribution of resources, especially if there is no sequencing to distribution (e.g., such as Ground Zero during and after the September 11 attacks, Emergency Management Institute, 2010). Terrain and mode of transportation also may vary in different locations. For example, in Colorado it may be necessary to airlift supplies to certain areas in the mountains, while a ship would be prime transportation to move supplies to Key West, if the only bridge were destroyed. Security in an area might be a problem, if citizens are extremely concerned about the pandemic and are willing to do anything to get supplies. Consideration should be given to all of these factors before any action to be sure that the supplies arrive on time at a designated location.

Planning

"The art of war teaches us to rely not on the likelihood of the enemy's not coming, but on our own readiness to receive him; not on the chance of his not attacking, but rather on the fact that we have made our position unassailable" (Giles 2007, p. 22).

Planning is crucial to containing a pandemic and to the principles of being objective and parsimonious. When we say objective, it is easy to discern what is meant. There are measurable actions needed to successfully thwart a pandemic. Simple means to solve the problem with least amount of effort needed so that resources are not misused. As stated earlier, minimal intervention states that if there are two possible solutions, the simpler one should be used. This concept is paramount when creating a plan. Planning should start prior to a pandemic. There should be routine planning, simulating (through computer models), testing with readiness drills, and updating during the pandemic. Peacetime planning is a key component to success on the battlefield. Prussia prepared extensively for war and succeeded even though the Prussian army was usually smaller in comparison to any of their enemies (Luvaas 1999).

There are many ways to respond to a pandemic, epidemic, or outbreak. One plan of action would be to quarantine and distribute antiviral drugs, and vaccines. Another plan would be to quarantine and vaccinate without antivirals. There also are prevention measures to use, such as wearing masks, encouraging routine hand washing, and travel restrictions (Aledort et al. 2007). Plans can include using multiple methods or even doing nothing because very few people will die. Black (2002) suggested that plans should have limited, but *salient* objectives as opposed to a plan with a plethora of objectives, as these simple methods may be able to save just as many lives as more complicated methods. Keeping things simple avoids redundancy and increases the potential of the number of people who can be helped. Too many objectives will spread supplies thin and make a plan less efficient. "He who attempts to defend too much defends nothing" (Luvaas 1999, p. 120). Regardless of the plan developed, the pandemic plan needs to be detailed so that an objective is clear and measurable. When objectives are executed, the responsible parties must understand what has to be performed and exactly how it fits in the plan (Howard and Paret 1984). For example, planning to vaccinate would not be enough. It is important to explain which people are in priority groups for vaccination, such as healthcare workers, special populations such as those over 65, etc., and where and when to distribute the vaccination.

Review barriers that would invalidate the plan or may cause it to fail. Implementing the plan in segments or in total may help identify insufficiencies (Luvaas 1999). Modify the plan, when barriers are identified. A plan will never be perfect because it is a plan, and not a mirror of reality. Quick adaption is requisite and the plan should provide a creditable means for problem solving and decision making. A plan for influenza may need to be applied and adapted for a bioterrorism attack, an industrial chemical release, a tornado, and evacuating a hospital. The plan may need to be modified or rescaled on whether it is an outbreak, epidemic, or pandemic.

Intensity of service may need alteration depending on the phase of the catastrophic event. No two pandemic influenza events are exactly alike, as history has demonstrated. Normal influenza affects certain high-risk groups, such as people older than 65 and young children, but recent pandemics, such as the 1918 pandemic, affected young and healthy adults as well (Taubenberger and Morens 2006). Influenza has propagated or multimodal peaks because influenza occurs in "waves" (cf. Black, Smock, and Ardaugh 2011). As influenza spreads, herd immunity develops. O'Connor (1991) defines herd immunity as the collective immunity of the population or "herd" that provides resistance because of the ultimate immunity of a large proportion of the population. The result is greater resistance, and fewer susceptible. Eventually, the pandemic will return to the "endemic state" or the level prior to the pandemic. Surveillance of the disease is necessary to monitor resurgence. According to Howard and Paret (1984), "He must always keep an eye on his opponent so that he does not, if the latter has taken up a sharp sword, approach him armed only with an ornamental rapier" (p. 99).

Intelligence

Surveillance is necessary to gather new information about a disease. Whether intelligence warrants its own section during an incident, or it is part of another section, accurate information is vital to success. Gathering timely information may help to avert the disease and implement primary prevention strategies. Social media may help because a recent study showed that tweets from Twitter provided a two-week earlier warning than relying on traditional surveillance (Ginsberg et al. 2009).

In military terminology, intelligence is divided between advance warning and research. Advance warning is the part of intelligence that searches for an imminent pandemic, and plans accordingly to prevent or minimize damage. It is important to observe, to avoid being unprepared. Susceptibility is always an issue that influences vulnerability/lack of resistance to disease and priorities. It is important to trace the influenza pandemic to the index or first case. As in the military, individuals in the intelligence area collect information concerning disease spread, speed of movement, disease transmission, and support the development of products that can provide answers to questions about the pandemic, epidemic influenza or outbreaks in a way that is intended to hold the disease at the lowest level possible. It is important to identify the origin for the information acquired (Black, Smock, and Ardaugh 2011).

The research intelligence and planning section should be linked. Researchers gather information to add data about the potential threats, magnitude, and killing power (case fatality rate). During peacetime planning, Frederick the Great would dispatch his generals to other countries to learn how other armies functioned. He found that other armies were more efficient than the Prussians in areas such as cavalry units and artillery. He learned and applied their tactics to his own army (Luvaas 1999). Much like Frederick the Great, those in influenza intelligence would benefit from identifying strategies or best practices from various agencies and countries. For example, the United Kingdom suggested that people should establish a system of "flu friends" that would be able to help the person during illness. By establishing flu friends, the United Kingdom hoped to contain the spread of the H1N1 virus (Information about Flu Friends 2009). The United States and other countries might adopt a similar method due to efficacy.

Operations

Objective and simplicity are vital to responding properly to a disaster. Validation of a plan is essential: "Simulated disorder postulates perfect discipline; simulated fear postulates courage; simulated weakness postulates strength" (Giles 2007, p. 14). Simulations are one way to test a pandemic plan. The incident command team uses objectives to focus on a reasonable task to accomplish during the resource and demand challenges of a pandemic. Simulations provide experience and identify weaknesses. There are different types of simulations: computer models, tabletop exercises, and full-scale exercises. Computer models are basic, but are implementable anytime, including during a disaster. However, simulations based on assumptions and statistical models can result in error and need validation. Both simulations and tabletop exercises can provide information, although different information. A tabletop exercise requires that participants meet and respond to a pandemic with certain parameters and generate individual section and consolidated solutions. Assessed are ways to reduce stress and time constraints. Full- or partial-scale exercises test the capabilities of a plan (Levi et al. 2002). They attempt to emulate an actual emergency as much as possible, including using real personnel and equipment (Potash Corp. 2008). A full-scale or functional exercise, although costly, prepares the emergency response team to manage the threat better than a computer simulation or partial tabletop exercise. The plan undoubtedly will need modification.

Operations would mobilize based on a test plan and be a "quick strike force." As Sun Tzu puts it, "Let your rapidity be that of the wind, your compactness that of the forest" (Giles 2007, p. 19). Containment of a pandemic influenza may not be immediate. Intermediate, systematic, sequential, thoughtful objectives will provide time needed for the containment of the pandemic. Any time spent in not following a well thought-out plan is wasteful. "Freelancing" makes it difficult to execute a plan. The hours spent in developing a plan are sacrificed and lead to opportunities for chaos. During the September 11 attack, many ambulances, fire trucks, and law enforcement agencies were not dispatched to Ground Zero. The official dispatched vehicles had difficulty reaching their designation because freelance vehicles blocked passage routes and clogged streets (Quick Series 2008). Before initiating a task, the crew needs to check in with incident command for purposes of command, control, and coordination.

An After Action Report (AAR) is requisite for a system of continuous improvement. An AAR is a document that chronicles execution, improvements, and how to be fully prepared in the future (Ross et al. 2008). Subsequently, updating of the plan is next. The revised plan should be tested and modified further. Planning is a continuous process and the only option for efficiently containing a pandemic (Luvaas 1999).

Discussion

- Sun Tzu and Clausewitz are famous historical military strategists. Their concepts are still salient and applicable today. Today's military strategists continue to study, learn, and use Sun Tzu and Clausewitz's books to teach strategy to contemporary military officers. By learning classical principles and learning from history, the evolution of warfare and effectiveness of strategy becomes more understandable. Most of the structure and operations of prevention, protection, and control of a pandemic are based on military organizational principles and concepts. This chapter attempts to point out the similarities in order to increase efficiency and effectiveness. Awareness and knowledge of these concepts and relationships should help ameliorate operations. These concepts will be needed to manage the eventual challenge of a pandemic:
- Objective
- Logistics
- Leadership
- Surveillance
- Simplicity

A pandemic, by definition, is a large event that can cause massive casualties and will be a significant challenge for the response team. In the tradition of the military, it is imperative to focus on a series of achievable and responsive tasks, and update and train according to modified pandemic response plans. The communication required for the planning also will likely ensure public support once high demands and limited resources are understood and put into perspective.

Validation of these principles, while well understood and tested by centuries of military operations, is warranted. Improvement must be the hallmark of disaster preparedness. There is no luxury of satisfaction of past successes. The saying that follows seems to characterize history of disaster preparedness well:

> "If you know the enemy and know yourself, you need not fear the result of a hundred battles. If you know yourself but not the enemy, for every

victory gained you will also suffer a defeat. If you know neither the enemy nor yourself, you will succumb in every battle" (Giles 2007, p. 9).

References

Aledort, J. E., Lurie, N., Wasserman, J., and S. A. Bozzette. 2007. Non-pharmaceutical public health interventions for pandemic influenza: An evaluation of the evidence base. *BMC Public Health* 7, doi: 10.1186/1471-2458-7-208.

Arguin, P. M., Marano, N., and D. O. Freedman. 2009. Globally mobile populations and the spread of emerging pathogens. *Emerging Infectious Disease* 15 doi: 10.3201/eid1511.091426, 1713-1714.

Associated Press. (2005, February 4). Put crafty Belichick's patriot games down to the fine art of war. *Sydney Morning Herald*. http://www.smh.com.au/news/Sport/Put-crafty-Belichicks-patriot-games-down-to-the-fine-art-of-war/2005/02/03/1107409980481.html (accessed July 9, 2011).

Black, D. R. 2002. A strategic plan for winning the war in public health. *American Journal of Health Education* 33(5): 267-275.

Black, D. R., Smock, J. A., and B. Ardaugh. 2011. *The foundations of epidemiology*. 5th ed. Oshtemo, MI: Center for Problem-Solving Measurement.

Booz, Allen, Hamilton. 2011. Delivering results that endure. http://www.boozallen.com/media/file/lab-capacity-planning-case-study.pdf (accessed July 9, 2011).

Brainard, C. 2009. Media hype swine flu report. *Columbia Journalism Review*, August 26. http://www.cjr.org/the_observatory/media_hypes_swine_flu_report.php (accessed July 9, 2011).

Branum, A., Dietz, J. E., and D. R. Black. 2010. An evaluation of local incident command system personnel in a pandemic influenza. *Journal of Emergency Management* 8(5): 39-46. doi: 10.5055/jem.2010.0031.

Centers for Disease Control and Prevention (CDC). 2010. H1N1 Flu (Swine Flu). http://cdc.gov/h1n1flu/ (accessed July 9, 2011).

Centers for Disease Control and Prevention (CDC). 2011. Seasonal flu information for business and employers. http://www.cdc.gov/flu/business/index.htm (accessed July 9, 2011).

Emergency Management Institute. 2010. IS-200 ICS for single resources and single action plans. http://training.fema.gov/EMILMS/IS200A/index.htm. (accessed July 9, 2011).

"Flu friends" in the U.K. bring tamiflu as virus spreads (Update 1 published July 24, 2009). http://www.bloomberg.com/apps/news?pid=newsarchive&sid=af3AuLkU00Ao

Flu.gov. *Seasonal flu*. http://www.flu.gov/individualfamily/about/seasonalflu/index.html (accessed July 9, 2011).

Flucount.org. Worldwide statistics of the H1N1 influenza A pandemic. http://www.flucount.org/ (accessed July 9, 2011).

Germann, T. C., Kadau, K., Longini Jr., I. M., and C. A. Macken. 2006. Mitigation strategies for pandemic influenza in the United States. *Proceedings of the National Academy of Sciences of the United States of America* 103: 5935-5940. doi: 10.1073/pnas.0601266103.

Ginsberg, J., Mohebbi, M. H., Patel, R. S., Brammer, L., Smolinski, M. S., and L. Brilliant. 2009. Detecting influenza epidemics using search engine query data. *Nature* 457: 1012-1015 doi: 0.1038/nature07634.

Howard County Health Department. 2011. *Pandemic influenza*. http://www.co.ho.md.us/health/healthmain/infectioncontrol/ep_pandemicflu.htm (accessed July 9, 2011).

Irwin, R. L. 2008. The incident command system. In *Disaster response: Principles in preparation and cooperation online edition.* http://orgmail2.coe-dmha.org/dr/DisasterResponse. nsf/section/07?opendocument (accessed July 9, 2011).

Last, J. M.,ed. 2001. *A dictionary of epidemiology.* 4th ed. New York: Oxford.

Levi, L., Michaelson, M., Admi, H., Bregman, D., and R. Bar-Nahor. 2002. National strategy for mass casualty situations and its effects on the hospital. *Prehospital and Disaster Medicine* 17:(1): 12-16.

Luvaas, J., ed.1999. *Frederick the Great on the art of war.* New York: Da Capo.

Monroe, J. A. 2009. *Pandemic influenza plan.* http://www.in.gov/isdh/files/PandemicInfluenzaPlan.pdf (accessed July 9, 2011).

Moynihan, D. P. 2008. Combining structural forms in the search for policy tools: Incident command systems in US crisis management. *Governance: An International Journal of Policy, Administration, and Institutions* 21: 205-229.

National Commission on Terrorist Attacks upon the United States. 2004. *The 9/11 Commission Report.* New York: W.W. Norton & Company.

National Health Service. 2009, June 30. *Information about flu friends.* http://www.reading.gov.uk/adviceandbenefits/emergencyplanning/Category.asp?cat=1911(accessed July 9, 2011).

National Health Service. 2010. *Swine flu — Questions & answers.* http://www.nhs.uk/Conditions/Pandemic-flu/Pages/QA.aspx (accessed July 9, 2011).

O'Connor, W. T. 1991. Herd immunity and the HIV epidemic. *Prevention Medicine* 20: 329-342.

Office of the President, Homeland Security Presidential Directive 5. February 2003, 3.

Osterholm, M. T. 2005. Preparing for the next pandemic. *The New England Journal of Medicine* 352: 1849-1852.

Potash Corp. 2008. *Training.* http://www.dhs.gov/xlibrary/assets/chemsec-Industry-Practices-towards-Performance-Standards-Deborah-Allen-OK.pdf (accessed July 9, 2011).

Quick Series. 2008. *Incident command system (ICS) for higher education.* Ft. Lauderdale: Quick Series Publication.

Ross, M., Candice, K. K., Smith, A., Smith, R., Ryan, L. W., and S. Humphreys. 2008. Analysis of after-action reporting by deployed nurses. *Military Medicine* 173: 210-216. http://web.ebscohost.com.proxy.li.suu.edu:2048/ehost/detail?vid=4&hid=13&sid=6034d6bf-e529-4d29-b86c-3e2adc2f7958%40sessionmgr4&bdata=JnNpdGU9ZWhvc3QtbGl2ZQ%3d%3d#db=c8h&AN=2009810093 (accessed July 9, 2011).

Schwartz, P. 2002. *Lieutenant General Robert S. Ewell.* http://schwartz.eng.auburn.edu/ACW/lrtmap.docs/ewell.html (accessed July 9, 2011).

Sun Tzu. 2007. *The art of war.* Giles, L., ed. Ann Arbor, MI: Borders Classics.

Taubenberger, J. K. and D. M. Morens. 2006. 1918 influenza: The mother of all pandemics. *Emerging Infectious Diseases* 12(1): 15-22.

von Clausewitz, C. 1984. *On war.* Howard, M. and P. Paret, eds. Princeton, NJ: Princeton UP.

Wilcoxon, G. L. 2010. *Sun Tzu: Theorist for the twenty-first century.* (Strategy Research Project, US Army War College). http://www.hsdl.org/?view&doc=136936&coll=limited.

World Health Organization. 2005. Responding to the avian influenza pandemic threat: Recommended strategic actions. http://www.who.int/csr/resources/publications/influenza/WHO_CDS_CSR_GIP_05_8-EN.pdf (accessed July 9, 2011).

World Health Organization. 2010. Current WHO phase of pandemic alert. http://www.who.int/csr/disease/avian_influenza/phase/en/ (accessed July 9, 2011).

World Health Organization. 2010. *WHO pandemic preparedness.* http://www.who.int/csr/disease/influenza/pandemic/en/ (accessed July 9, 2011).

Chapter 3

Local Leadership in Pandemic Influenza

Andrew Branum, J. Eric Dietz, and David R. Black

Contents

Abstract

This chapter focuses on the lessons learned from two statewide pandemic influenza exercises conducted for the State of Indiana in 2008 and 2009 by the Purdue Homeland Security Institute. It discusses those lessons learned under the framework of the importance of local leadership in emergency response during pandemic influenza. The exercises tested various organizations and their levels of preparedness and response, while leaders from local law enforcement, emergency management, public health, and hospital administration gathered to exercise their existing emergency plans. In 2008, the scope of the test included all county and local response teams statewide. The most important lesson learned pertained to the organizational structure of leadership and the design and staffing of a county's incident command influenced the level of effectiveness during the exercise activities. In 2009, hospitals and healthcare facilities participated in tabletop exercises focused on a response to high levels of at-need patients and the ability to implement altered standards of care. Aspects important to success were staff education, problem solving, and for all leaders to be present during the planning stages to prepare for the actual response. An important finding in both exercises was that local leaders do need to be involved in the planning and preparedness part of emergency response, which is contrary to the premise that local emergency management is the most crucial aspect to emergency response. Local leadership continues to be a key aspect of response effectiveness.

Keywords: H1N1, Incident Command System, Leadership, Public Health, Emergency Response, Pandemic Influenza

Perhaps past director of the US Department of Health and Human Services Michael Leavitt said it best when he stated, "Pandemics are global in nature but their effects are always local." In many widespread emergencies, local or state governments may look to the federal government for assistance and resources. In a pandemic influenza, however, all levels of government will be challenged with the event that causes numerous requests for assistance and services combined with an event that challenges government to maintain normal services. Localities will have to respond on their own. This chapter will discuss this response by showing the importance of local leadership during a pandemic. The 2008 and 2009 tabletop exercises conducted by the Purdue Homeland Security Institute not only tested hospital and public health leadership, but analyses show that county leadership can make a difference in managing the outcome of a pandemic episode. While subsequent chapters will address these tabletop exercises, this chapter will focus on the lessons learned regarding key aspects of leadership. In a 12-week pandemic wave, leadership from across county agencies will be needed in a unified government response, and perhaps more importantly, in preparation and planning.

Introduction

While research prior to the 2009-2010 H1N1 pandemic influenza discusses many conditions of uncertainty, some of that uncertainty is over. Emergency responders and leaders at all levels prepared for and responded to the H1N1 pandemic in a strong way. Though the recent pandemic did not stress responders to the degree a larger pandemic has and could, it required localities to exercise their capabilities and implement existing pandemic plans. Leadership was brought to the forefront as hospitals stockpiled supplies and worked with staff on issues previously overlooked. Local politicians and health departments worked with media outlets to create status updates and educational announcements to alert local populations on current events. Emergency management agencies helped their localities plan for the worst, and in some circumstances, coordinated the entirety of events during both pandemic waves.

The US Government Accountability Office (GAO) 2009) discussed the GAO's themes for a pandemic strategy: "The strategy was built around six key themes... While all of these themes are interrelated, our earlier work underscored the importance of leadership, authority, and coordination, a theme that touches on all aspects of preparing for, responding to, and recovering from an influenza pandemic" (GAO-09-334). To have an effective pandemic response plan, leadership must be involved at the beginning of the planning, not just at the beginning of the pandemic. From creating the plan, to practicing the plan, to implementation, leaders must drive preparedness and response. An earlier GAO Report (US Government Accountability Office 2007) speaks to only a few of the difficulties of preparing for a pandemic influenza:

> "...the leadership roles and responsibilities prescribed under the [National Response Plan] need to operate somewhat differently because of the characteristics of a pandemic that distinguish it from other emergency incidents. For example, because a pandemic influenza is likely to occur in successive waves, planning has to consider how to sustain response mechanisms for several months to over a year—issues that are not clearly addressed in the Plan" (GAO-07-1257T).

One of the continued difficulties of pandemic preparedness will be to define who the leaders are and what their roles should be. Hospital officials, emergency management agency officials, emergency responders, health department officials, and politicians are all expected to play a significant role in response. Many times, their roles and responsibilities overlap. The 2009–2010 H1N1 Pandemic Influenza Event After Action Report for the State of New Mexico states the recognized that without clear organization, response operations were frustrated when there was difficulty in determining who was in charge (New Mexico Department of Health 2010). The 2009 GAO report also discusses national level coordination issues within the Department of Health and Human Services and Department of Homeland Security responding to pandemic influenza (GAO-09-334). While leadership at the national level may need to be continuously addressed to address changing policy issues, the training and education issues most likely leading to improving pandemic response as verified with scientific research will begin and be accomplished at the local level.

French and Raymond (2009) recognized the inherent importance of localities in pandemic response: "While national strategy for pandemic preparedness will focus on showing the entry of the virus into the United States, local government officials will be responsible for implementing plans that address public health interventions and maintenance of the infrastructure of the community." A 2006 article written on two expert panel findings discussing pandemic response found that one of the most important pandemic health directives would be to train local leaders on various aspects of pandemic response, including communication and the use of subject matter experts (Reissman, Watson, and Klomp 2006). Even the National Response Framework states that: "State and local governments are closest to those impacted by incidents, and have always had the lead in response and recovery" (US Department of Homeland Security 2008). It must be continually emphasized that while preparing our national leaders for a pandemic response will be critical, the most important preparations will occur at the local level.

Pandemic Influenza Exercises

In 2008 and 2009, the Purdue Homeland Security Institute (PHSI) conducted exercises throughout Indiana for the Indiana State Department of Health to test county preparedness for a pandemic influenza. The exercises in 2008 involved local leaders in 68 Indiana counties from various impacted agencies; those in 2009 focused on hospitals, healthcare facilities, and emergency management technicians in six counties. Although the two exercises were distinct in scope and objectives, one thing they had in common: local coordination.

A national survey found that coordination between local hospitals and emergency partners still needs improvement (Braun, Wineman, and Finn 2006). A 2008 article states that, "Emergency Management Agencies (EMAs) are generally delegated responsibility for local emergency management, while health departments have responsibility for public health issues, and hospitals remain independent organizational actors, meaning that any coordination is dependent on the ability of local sector leaders to cooperate with each other and define roles on a local level" (Avery, Lawley, and Garrett 2008). Local leaders must realize that a pandemic influenza will not affect just one aspect of a community alone. Key challenges that exist for hospitals, a player at the forefront of a pandemic response, such as security, staffing, and supply shortages, will tax a hospital's ability to care for the infected. This will require leadership personnel outside of a healthcare facility to take responsibility in situations assumed to belong to hospitals.

Leadership agencies and officials will not work separately during a pandemic though. Hospitals, emergency management agencies, and public health officials will not be effective, no matter how clearly responsibilities and roles are defined, without working together. In a 2000 bioterrorism exercise in Colorado, after-exercise commentary expressed the difficulties of communication during these times: "Although lines of authority were clear, much time was spent in consultation and debate through scheduled bridge calls. Many persons joined these calls, and decision making became inefficient, although not impossible" (Hoffman and Norton 2000).

PHSI 2009 Tabletop Exercise

The 2009 PHSI Tabletop Exercises (TTX) tested hospitals' existing plans for a pandemic emergency. Four hospitals from four counties participated along with a community healthcare facility and an emergency transportation provider from two other counties. While leaders from the respective county health department and emergency management agencies participated, the leaders from county hospitals and healthcare facilities were targeted most in the exercises. Many of the hospital leaders developed the plans and participated in the exercise planning meetings, yet even more players participated in the exercise, providing a glimpse at how leaders would implement the plans and how they would relate that information to hospital staff.

For each of the participating county healthcare facilities, actual leaders during the exercise differed. For many of the participating counties, the official most directly involved in writing the plan took the lead. For some participants, this was a president or director of the hospital. For another, it was the director of nursing. Staffing was identified within the plans and in pre-exercise planning as one of the most important challenges in a pandemic. The directors of nursing provided the most knowledge on this issue for their organization.

One key objective throughout the exercise involved focusing on hospital supplies. As the exercise scenarios showed an increasing amount of inpatients, many of the leaders chose to order more supplies, or implement altered standards for supply use for their organization. One county in particular, had those officials in charge of hospital finances and supplies in attendance at the exercise. They provided different perspectives to the problem, along with different solutions; they also were focused on long-term financial stability of the hospital, not just ordering large amounts of supplies. It is important to note that while it may be difficult to engage all parties in the planning stage, if plans are created by only a select few individuals, the most effective solutions for that specific healthcare facility may be overlooked and ineffectively implemented during a response.

The largest topic of discussion during the exercises was "altered standards of care," or when the healthcare facilities would begin to either reduce the services they provided or change the standards of care each patient is provided. The importance of leader participation during the planning, exercising, and response phases of a pandemic was stated earlier. If leaders are called upon to make critical decisions during a response, it is crucial that they be involved in the planning stages to define the protocols they, or someone acting in their place, will use. Although during the exercise, it was the nursing leaders who were deciding when to alter standards, in a real-life scenario it may be hospital executives (for a private hospital) or county and local leadership (for a public hospital).

A 2006 Indiana Pandemic Influenza State Summit After Action Report identified important altered standards of care resources still needed. Included was the item of who was to actually make those decisions. Like with any emergency preparedness exercise, it is important that the actual decision makers be present. These leaders must, however, be present during the planning stages, and in the case of this exercise, the stage in which the actual plan was written. Key personnel make tough decisions during rapid exercise scenarios, yet the learning process can be rendered moot if actual decisions would be poles apart with different leaders in place in a pandemic.

Upon completion of the exercises, participants completed evaluation reports. Many of these reports expressed the need for staff education on the plans. Though leaders had worked to create the most in-depth and effective plans for their healthcare facilities, at times they had neglected to fully educate their staff on the actual policies that would be in place. Other leaders recognized that at times, they had neglected to take input from their staff when creating the plans. Though leaders will be called on to make swift and difficult decisions, these decisions cannot be made in a vacuum.

For this exercise, participants in the exercise planning decided to leave communication out of the key exercise objectives due to time constraints. They felt as though this was something that had been previously addressed and well covered. However, communication continuously came up in discussion. Who would communicate changes to the public? How would hospitals communicate to staff? Without memoranda of understanding (MOUs) in place, or even simple communication during planning stages, how would a hospital communicate its need for local resources? Most participants recognized a need for increased security personnel levels. If local and county law enforcement is already stressed from other organizational needs, where would the hospital get personnel and who would communicate with these sources? Key leaders realized that no matter how much a problem is addressed, continuous exercise and planning must occur. Perhaps detailed plans build stronger mechanisms for communication during emergencies. Bringing leaders together in order to exercise these plans will provide an actual arena for them to make decisions together.

Hoffman and Norton (2000) recognize the importance of having multiple leaders in a pandemic: "...activities cannot depend on the direction of one or two key persons...other skilled, informed persons must be able to assume leadership roles." In this exercise, one of the activities required of the main leaders was not to participate in the last part of the exercise, during which players were to assume they were in one of the more difficult time periods of the pandemic influenza wave. Either because of sickness or death, these leaders—the most knowledgeable on operations and pandemic waves—were not available to help their exercise teams. Though the teams were able to put the next most trusted leaders in command, it showed the necessity of not over depending on a few leaders for all response actions. Leaders must realize that they may not be available in times of emergency response and must prepare themselves and others for this possibility in the planning stage.

PHSI 2008 Tabletop Exercise

The 2008 PHSI tabletop exercise allowed local leaders across 68 counties to test their existing pandemic plans and response mechanisms. Gaining a broader view of local pandemic response than the 2009 exercise, participants of the 2008 exercise saw that a pandemic emergency does not involve one hospital alone. In a 2006 meeting of senior government, hospital, and public officials, a key challenge found was "Some key preparedness tasks cannot be accomplished by hospitals individually" (Toner, Waldhorn, and Maldin 2006). A 2009 Pandemic Response Toolkit published by the United States Agency for International Development tells local officials in authority to plan for a 40% reduction in workforce; this reduction would lead to an immediate need for local officials to implement any existing continuity of operation plans, allowing for critical infrastructure and essential functions to continue. This problem clearly extends beyond the realm of a hospital and will require the full support of local emergency management.

The national incident management system (NIMS), loosely defined as an approach to guide all players in the prevention, protection, response, and recovery of an emergency, states that states should use an incident command system (ICS). ICS is an all-hazards incident management approach to coordinate emergencies. Players in the 2008 tabletop exercise, regardless of their ICS knowledge, recognized its importance. The first inject, or task, in the pre-exercise tasks of the counties participating in the tabletop exercise was to establish the personnel who would fill the county ICS in a pandemic emergency. Branum, Dietz, and Black (2010) researched the counties' use of the ICS and the correlation it had with their performance in the exercise. The following segment summarizes their findings.

Although 68 counties participated in the exercise, only 52 completed the ICS task. These 52 provided an ICS chart along with the designated personnel who would staff each position and were the only counties studied in the research by Branum and colleagues. The counties participated in 18 injects throughout the duration of the exercise. At the end of the exercise, all participants completed evaluation reports. Their research found that these 52 counties used three distinctly different ICS types in the exercise, and determined the effectiveness of these three types by comparing their inject completion percentages and evaluation reports.

Analyses of the data provided the researchers a case to create definitions for the three different ICS types: normal, specialized, and unified. Normal command consisted of county personnel who would respond to any county-wide emergency, regardless of its nature. Specialized command consisted of local health department and hospital personnel, where local leadership considered the nature of the emergency, and utilized personnel felt to be most capable of understanding the emergency's effects. Unified command consisted of a blend of many county leaders, from emergency responder, emergency management, and public health agencies. Between the three different ICS types there was nearly an equal number, with 21 counties using a specialized command, 16 using a normal command, and 15 using a unified command.

While the research found that the counties using normal command structures performed better when completing the injects (followed by unified and specialized), the analyses did not state that normal command was the best structure type of an ICS. A performance metric was not built into the exercise itself. Inherent to an exercise, the purpose was to test plans and abilities, not necessarily the degree to which it was completed. Within (Branum, Dietz, and Black 2010) research, performance was determined as to whether a county was able to finish an inject or not. Counties using a normal command completed nearly 96% of the injects, while specialized command completed 88.4%.

Actual exercise injects were from the identification of a proper public information officer, to allocation of county strategic national stockpile (SNS), to the determination of need from the National Guard. While some of the injects were pandemic influenza specific, several of them could be considered for any local emergency. Specialized command structures most often failed to complete those injects dealing with the critical infrastructure concerns of a county. The research found this correlation to be with personnel; the other structures used personnel familiar with broad-ranging local emergencies and who had experience. Specialized command personnel may have been new to these concerns.

By examining participant evaluation report comments for each of the three command types, it was found that the participants themselves indirectly provided insight into each of the three commands. These insights allowed the researchers to conclude that regardless of the command structure chosen, certain considerations should be taken into account for the best response mechanism in the county. Normal command had strengths in experience and personnel. These persons were used to working together and had broad knowledge of local resources, which would prove crucial in a 12-week pandemic wave. This command type, however, lacked the technical expertise that a pandemic may require regarding public health and hospital needs. Specialized command types contained personnel with this knowledge and expertise. Unified commands had a strength in agency cooperation because they themselves were created as a composite of multiple agencies. Where the other two command types at times lacked an ability to bring multiple parties to the table, for a unified command, the parties were already there.

Conclusion

Through exercise planning and an actual pandemic event, leaders now realize the local needs and impact during pandemic response will be local, and local coordination is crucial to response. Evaluation of data shows that local officials must evaluate the needs and resources of a jurisdiction before creating plans and selecting response leaders. The 2009 exercise of local hospitals and public health officials showed that at the early stages of a pandemic wave, these may be the lead responders. The sick and those who believe they are sick will be arriving at hospitals in large numbers, while looking to public health officials for guidance and care. But as a pandemic progresses, a community's needs may change. The essential operations of a community will need to be addressed as more and more people are too sick for work. Who will make sure public sewer systems are running? Who will make sure generators are available if electricity goes out? Who will take food to those who are home sick when hospitals are too full to take another patient? Hospital and public health leaders may be in command early, but county emergency management agencies may play the most crucial role in a lengthy crisis.

In a Pandemic Influenza Leadership Forum, US Department of Health and Human Services Secretary Michael Leavitt stated, "Local leadership is the key. There needs to be preparedness at every level. There is a part for everyone in preparing for a pandemic—from stockpiling necessities to adopting good public health habits. Every county, every business, every school, every church, every household needs a plan. But people won't plan unless urged to repeatedly by leaders they know and respect" (US Department of Health and Human Services 2007). A pandemic influenza will require a leadership team uniquely suited to respond to the demands of a lengthy emergency. Leaders from all facets of a community will be looked upon to lead, communicate, and make tough decisions during the pandemic. However, in order to prepare for the best response, leaders must be involved in the planning.

References

Avery, G., Lawley, M., and S. Garrett. 2008. Planning for pandemic influenza: Lessons from the experiences of thirteen Indiana counties. *Journal of Homeland Security and Emergency Management* 5(1): Art. 29.

Branum, A., Dietz, E., and R. Black. 2010. An evaluation of local incident command system personnel in a pandemic influenza. *Journal of Emergency Management* 8(5): 39-46.

Braun, B., Wineman, N., and N. Finn. 2006. Integrating hospitals into community emergency preparedness planning. *Annals of Internal Medicine* 144(11): 799-811.

French, P. and E. Raymond. 2009. Pandemic influenza planning: An extraordinary ethical dilemma for local government officials. *Public Administration Review* 69(5): 823-830.

Hoffman, R. and J. Norton. 2000. Commentary: Lessons learned from a full-scale bioterrorism exercise. *Emerging Infectious Diseases* 6(6): 652-653.

New Mexico Department of Health. 2010. After Action Report. https://nmhealth.org/H1N1/documents/NMDOH_H1N1_AAR-IP_Master_Final_073010_Web_version_08162010.pdf. (accessed October 1, 2010).

Reissman, D., Watson, P., and R. Klomp. 2006. Pandemic influenza preparedness: Adaptive responses to an evolving challenge. *Journal of Homeland Security and Emergency Management* 3(2): Art. 13.

Toner, E., Waldhorn, R., and B. Maldin. 2006. Hospital preparedness for pandemic influenza. *Biosecurity and Bioterrorism: Biodefense Strategy, Practice, and Science* 4(2): 207-213.

US Department of Health and Human Services. 2007. http://www.hhs.gov/news/speech/2007/sp20070613a.html. Remarks as delivered at the Pandemic Influenza Leadership Forum, Washington, DC. (accessed August 15, 2010).

US Department of Homeland Security. 2008. National Response Framework. *FEMA Publication*, p. 682.

US Government Accountability Office. Influenza pandemic: Opportunities exist to clarify federal leadership roles and improve pandemic planning. GAO-07-1257T. September 26, 2007.

US Government Accountability Office. Influenza pandemic: Sustaining focus on the nation's planning and preparedness efforts. GAO-09-334. February 26, 2009.

Acknowledgment

The 2008 and 2009 exercises were sponsored on contract from the Indiana State Department of Health.

Chapter 4

Developing a Systematic Pandemic Influenza Program for Preparing a State

William A. Foley, Jr.

Contents

Abstract

From a planning perspective, this chapter discusses how to effectively mitigate the spread of an extensive viral infection on a large scale, which requires timely, sensible, and highly sound planning. The focus is on state level planning under the federal model for developing good operational plans. The chapter clarifies terminology, such as "epidemic" rather than "pandemic," as the preferred term for a local or state response. However, after that is explained, "pandemic," which is the common and more frequently used name and in the chapter's title, is referenced thereafter in quotation marks. After the introduction, this study presents a brief history of "pandemic influenza," how a state prepares to develop a plan, agreements and trigger points which must be decided, the planning process itself, the operational plan with its important template for local use, and conclusions. Tracing a common operating picture from the federal, to the state, and to the city/county levels for "pandemic influenza," planning is the first theme. How to incorporate continuity of government and continuity of operations into a plan, in the face of a rapidly spreading "pandemic," is the second one. Last, how to deliver from the state to the county level, one workable document called an Operational Plan (OPLAN) with a county template for local use, is the last theme. That template gives counties a "pandemic influenza" model for planning that is the same as states and regions use, which they can directly apply locally. Thus this planning process saves lives during a "pandemic."

Keywords: Pandemic Planning, Preparedness, State Level, Homeland Security

> Commencing in 1918....Influenza killed more people in a year than the Black Death of the Middle Ages killed in a century; it killed more people in twenty-four weeks than AIDS killed in twenty-four years." And it killed many millions more in its World War I outbreak, than the War itself (Barry, 2005, p. 5).

Introduction

"Pandemic influenza" has produced horrible and tragic results in the United States, as well as worldwide. Vulnerable rural populations in the past have suffered from unknown pathogens, and larger and denser urban populations even more so. Thus mitigation planning for a state with a reasonably large population requires exceptional collaboration, plus some very extensive and systematic work, to produce an effective plan. Using Indiana as a model, this chapter discusses preparing a state for a "pandemic influenza." How to create a workable plan involving state homeland security, state public health, the federal sector and the private sector within a state is the focus of this chapter. In summary, all of the above agencies and sectors effectively collaborated and cooperated to produce an outstanding outcome. First, though some terminology needs to be clarified.

Three terms from public health, specifically epidemiology, are frequently used interchangeably or as synonyms to describe distributions of morbidity (e.g., influenza or other diseases). These three terms are pandemic, epidemic, and outbreak. If all the terms meant the same thing, then only one term would be used and the other two could be discarded. As in any field such as homeland security and public health, it is important to use terms correctly because each term has precise meanings, which are used to plan suitable actions. For example, at the state level, the most appropriate term is epidemic influenza where "the number of observed cases in a community, state, or region is greater than the expected number of cases." Conversely, pandemic influenza is the proper term at federal or national level where "the number of cases observed is greater than the expected number of cases." Different from an epidemic, a pandemic affects large geographic areas, such as an entire "country, continent, or portions of the world." An outbreak is localized and confined to restaurants, schools, hotels, etc., and as in the other two instances, the observed must be greater than the expected or endemic state (baseline). Sadly, pandemic influenza or pan flu planning became the catchall phrase for mitigating dangerous or deadly influenzas at all levels of government. When the government develops plans for a pandemic, each state must translate these principles and refine them for its state and develop an epidemic and/or outbreak plan. In other words, states or regions or even particular institutions and facilities should have their own epidemic plan. References to pandemic in almost all instances in this chapter should really read epidemic, but will be left as pandemic as this is what the literature unfortunately called it. However, pandemic will be in quotations, to indicate that epidemic is the correct term to use (Black, Smock, and Ardaugh 2011, slides 55–83).

Indiana serves as a good model because the state was nationally recognized for creating inventive programs to combat this dreaded disease. Nationally, the Center for Infectious Disease Research and Policy (CIDRP) cited the Indiana State Department of Health's (ISDH) pandemic influenza "tool kit," designed for the local public health director's use with county level health constituents, as a best practice and adopted its format as a model. A video simulation online initiated by ISDH was accepted in Midwestern public health circles as a best practice for training healthcare providers and mental health caseworkers regarding influenza pandemic. And the Indiana Department of Homeland Security's (IDHS) five-paragraph, three-phased operational plan (OPLAN) for "pandemic influenza" (pan flu) along with its county template and 15 state emergency support functions specific to pan flu, were accepted and endorsed by the Department of Homeland Security's (DHS) Federal Emergency Management Agency (FEMA) Region V Regional Interagency Steering Committee (RISC). This was in June 2006, and it was applauded as a FEMA V state best practice. The latter was published for the RISC and distributed region-wide in a fine study compiled by the Department of Emergency Management of the State of Minnesota (Minnesota Division of Homeland Security and Emergency Management 2007, p. 2). Other accolades followed for the IDHS plan and this chapter discusses those top practices.

Under the national response framework, the key phases of disaster mitigation are "prepare," "respond," and "recover," but for "pandemic influenza" prepare—plan, prevent, and protect—is the most critical. Without proper preparation, situational awareness, then mitigation, control can be lost and rather quickly. Along with the Department of Homeland Security's (DHS) Federal Emergency Management Agency's (FEMA) Region V in Chicago, Indiana's preparation is analyzed using the efforts of the Indiana Department of Homeland Security to support the Indiana State Department of Public Health, and other major emergency management agencies. Private sector involvements for battling the effects of pandemic influenza are discussed as well.

Initially, a brief discussion explains the history of Indiana's experience with pandemic influenza. Following that, the composition and development of the plan is elaborated upon; then its implementation is examined. Last, the product itself and its consequences are discussed.

"Pan Flu" Strikes in the Recent Past

Pandemic flu is exceptionally dangerous, has haunted and infected humans for ages, and Indiana's population has been no exception. The most recent, serious, worldwide pandemic, which was extremely lethal, took place in 1918, killing from 60 to 100 million across the globe and 695,000 in the US. In Indiana, it struck at once in the fall of 1918, infecting 350,000 Hoosiers, and killing 10,243 citizens, including nearly 1,000 in Indianapolis in a short period of time (Wheeler 2006). Then as now, no comprehensive "cure" existed and only different forms of "mitigation" were available. Consequently, the key was to be prepared.

When pandemic influenza struck the US in the fall of 1918, the first and third "waves" of the illness were weak, while the second wave horribly assailed its victims. In 1918, striking during the height of American involvement in World War I, the initial onslaught of pan flu arrived in the US that April, and the third surge occurred from December 1918 through March 1919. But the second lethal wave struck with chilling ferocity in October and November of 1918, unfortunately killing babies and the elderly, but also uniquely healthy young adults. In Indiana, Dr. John Hurty (then the Indiana state department of health commissioner), attempted everything, from ordering "Public No Spitting Laws;" to woolen masks for everyone; to open air hospitals; to suspension of public gatherings in schools, churches, saloons, and early movies; to isolation of the infected, but nothing except the latter worked. In rural Indiana, many families tried "homespun" rumors and remedies like placing a young captured, live deer in the bedroom of their children to ward off the influenza; to temporarily burying their children in cloves up to their necks; to wearing garlic necklaces, which were all designed to ward off the sickness. Masks at that time were woolen and had no effect on the deadly pathogens, as no one then knew it was a virus, which was not discovered until 1953. As the virus mutated and spread, the lungs would scar, internal bleeding occurred, the bladder filled with blood and fatal pneumonia quickly followed. Larger cities like Philadelphia often burned 7,500 bodies daily, but rural Indiana fared much better during the great pandemic. This was chiefly due to both the isolation of the state and the geographic isolation of its population (Wheeler 2006).

Since then, other waves of different kinds of flu have spread across the United States with varying degrees of severity. The 1943 swine, 1957 Asian, and 1968 Hong Kong influenza viruses visited America. One common theme prevailed as all these occurred in times of either high troop deployment or war. Global mobility and encounters have spread disease over many past centuries (Aaltonen 2009).

Preparing to Develop a Plan

The sequence of developing a systematic plan was initiated by determining the desired outcome, and then using backward planning from that outcome to build a framework for plan development. In setting this up, a synchronization matrix of key tasks that needed to be accomplished along a planning timeline, was developed in reverse sequence. The timeline commenced with the execution of the plan and worked backward to the start of planning. In-between planning goals were matched to dates to ensure it was completed when needed (Department of the Army 2001, pp.6–1 through 6–7). Last, the "Homeland Security tool kit," which provided a number of publications offering federal planning guidance, was carefully utilized."

As early as December 21, 2003, Indiana readied itself to start pandemic influenza planning. A catastrophic incident response working group of senior planners met to discuss courses of action (COAs) for all-hazards threats, including pandemic influenza. No significant response or recovery plans existed then, save for a large collection of state "how to do it" manuals and county comprehensive emergency management plans (CEMPs), all kept in a library in the then Indiana Department of Emergency Management, now the Indiana Department of Homeland Security. Those early CEMPs were not operational plans, but rather descriptions of what to do in separate incidents by type (Dietz, Wojtalewicz, and Mack 2006). It also was recognized that the healthcare and public health missions were the central issues for controlling disease of any kind in what was then termed "crisis and consequence management," and plans were quickly needed. It was further recognized that the public judges governmental success or failure in a serious disease outbreak based on its perception of fast and effective government response. Plans must provide the right response; at the right time and place; they must effectively train and exercise the responders; and plans must be designed to anticipate local needs, because every disaster is local (Dietz, Wojtalewicz, and Mack 2006).

However, it was not until March 2006 that Indiana began the comprehensive pandemic planning process in earnest. The overall goal then was to build a successful preparation and response cycle that had as an implied task prepositioned locations for dispensing mitigation drugs fully known and readily available. These would be locally supported by the state's two largest agencies. This was kicked off by a major conference involving the Indiana Department of Homeland Security and the Indiana State Department of Health. Key emergency management personnel from allied state agencies were invited, and the Indiana Economic Development Corporation and the Indiana Chamber of Commerce covered the private sector. The conference's opening statement proclaimed, "The purpose is to share information … concerning the state's plan for responding to and coping with a future outbreak of influenza" (Dietz, Wojtalewicz, and Mack 2006).

Basic assumptions were drawn, facts presented, and issues were addressed. It was determined that an H5N1 avian influenza of a highly pathologic variety could result in an approximately 50% human mortality rate. In its best case scenario, only a 15% illness rate would be the consequence. On average, a 35% infection rate would not be uncommon, yet any of these consequences would be catastrophic in a state of more than six million residents (D'Araujo nd). As well, it was noted that an influenza epidemic could be resistant to most antivirals and the influenza might strike the state in more than one wave of disease. The estimated impact on Indiana was based on "FluSurge" software, and simulations and modeling from the Department of Health and Human Services (HHS) through the Centers for Disease Control (CDC). It was asserted that the duration of any given transmission period and resultant illnesses might last from six to eight weeks, causing extreme shortages of hospital beds, ventilators, antivirals, and other necessary items, supplies, and a logistical nightmare (Department of Health and Human Services, CDC, 2007, pp. 1-3).

It was critically noted that among the ill would be healthcare workers, first responders (fire, law enforcement, and emergency medical services), and second responders—health and hospital personnel and emergency support function workers, including public works, emergency management, homeland security, transportation, and volunteer agencies). Additionally, it was stressed that the situation could worsen rapidly, causing significant social and economic disruption, particularly within the six larger cities of the state.

Thus, with the little planning that had been completed previously, pandemic influenza became the responsibility of the IDHS and ISDH "tiger teams," identified as groups of key individuals to initiate the process. Tasks were assigned and follow-up meetings were initially conducted within IDHS' Homeland Security Team (HST)—a body encompassing all state emergency support functions (ESFs) agencies, plus other interested agencies. The planning process began in late April 2006, and the federal "tool kit" of homeland security and public health information was readily used, along with the two state agency directors' guidance.

Developed over time and simultaneously with Indiana's plan, this federal tool kit provided direction and format to the state for framing its plan. It was particularly helpful in developing the operational or homeland security support side to and for public health's effort in locating and organizing the critical dispensing sites.

In May 2006, *The National Strategy for Pandemic Influenza: Implementation Plan* was released by the federal Homeland Security Council, a body that parallels the National Security Council, where the number two and three cabinet level secretaries concentrate on domestic response. *The Implementation Plan* provided excellent planning direction for Indiana (Homeland Security Council 2006, pp. 1-5). Additionally and specifically *Pandemic Planning Status for Response* was drafted by the Department of Homeland Security's Coast Guard Rear Admiral Mary E. Landry and shared with the states (Landry nd). This publication helped states prioritize the sequence of tasks. Following that, the *National Preparedness Guidelines* of the federal government were reviewed. Originally promulgated as part of Homeland Security Presidential Directive 8, Annex 1, 2003, and then revised in 2007, the *Guidelines* addressed four aspects for preparedness and planning.

They provided a national preparedness vision, which stated that America must be "a nation prepared with coordinated capabilities to prevent, protect against, respond to, and recover from all hazards in a way that balances risk with resources against need." Following that and as a separate publication, the *Fifteen National Planning Scenarios* pinpoint and discuss the 15 "highest consequence threat scenarios," including pandemic influenza. From those scenarios, 1,600 unique tasks were listed in a universal task list which, if performed effectively and on time, could help mitigate the effects of a disaster prompting faster recovery. Last, a target capabilities list discussed 37 critical capabilities which "communities, the private sector and all levels of government" must accomplish to respond effectively to disasters. Figure 4.1 shows "The Guidelines" version of the planning cycle which was applied at the state level (Department of Homeland Security 2007, pp. iii, 22).

All guidance for epidemic influenza planning from the tool kit then was translated into *State Planning Guidance* by the collaborative efforts of the state homeland security community and the state public health community. The key focus was how the state could best serve its citizens to honor the social contract it has with them, in times of endemic outbreak. That planning called for a comprehensive and integrated plan, with assigned roles and responsibilities, producing a tiered and integrated template. The template was for pandemic influenza mitigation, which counties and local communities could use. The latter, along with effective points of dispensing were absolutely critical pieces of the architecture.

This template constituted the heart of the plan, providing local government with a guide that set planning priorities and established response criteria. If the 92 county emergency management agencies and their matching 93 local health departments could not utilize it, the template was worthless. It became the state's

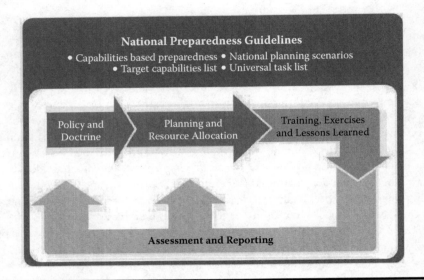

Figure 4.1 National Preparedness Guidelines.

main effort for the communities regarding epidemic flu planning. The template's overall outcome was a public health preparedness operational plan for all 10 Indiana emergency management and public health districts and the respective 92 counties, which established a common model or template that could be adapted to local use. The state enumerated its goals and how it supports the 10 districts and 92 counties and each was then asked to send back to the state their parallel plan. Thus with a common operating picture, the results would show unity of effort for all jurisdictions with enumerated federal, state, and local levels of responsibility. Emphasis was placed on the medical stockpiles to be dispensed at specific, known locations where citizens could receive appropriate medicines and personal protective equipment (PPE). These sites, called points of dispensing (PODs), were locations that merged the support of the 92 emergency management agencies with the needs of the 93 local health departments to assist more than six million Hoosiers.

Additionally, from discussions and agreements reached in Homeland Security Team meetings, it was established which state agencies would serve as "lead, coordinating, and supporting state agencies." How that would be woven into the seamless plan was key. Tricky, specific problems were tackled as was the all-important continuing education during a pandemic and how best to assist special needs populations. Additionally, how to execute social distancing at government work sites and how shifting and staffing there would be accomplished was another difficult issue. Keeping government functioning was both a continuity of government (COG) and continuity of operations (COOP) issue and plans were written addressing that. Then plans for the private sector were drafted concerning the same matters. These systematic plans were then phased in for timely execution and sensible goal attainment, by the homeland security team (HST). Last, it was recognized that preparations must be inserted to accept mass casualties. The roles and responsibilities of state agencies, using rational response framework phases of "prepare, respond, and recover" included mass casualty planning.

For this kind of natural disaster, the state also mirrored some of the *National Strategy for Homeland Security*, and afterward published its own *Indiana Strategy for Homeland Security*. Running through several drafts by January 2008, the *Indiana Strategy* included the visions, strategic goals, missions, and enumerated specific information for disaster mitigation including pandemic influenza. Updated annually, eight strategic goals were published which included the state's target capabilities listed within (Dietz and Mack, 2008, pp. 25–53). Costs plus funding sources also were presented in this document.

Additionally, the *National Response Plan* transitioned into the *National Response Framework* commencing February 2007 and the state developed its own *Indiana State Response Plan* (Framework 2007). That *State Response Plan* consisted of three main segments: the base overview discussion; the operational plans (five of them in number); and the roles of state agencies within the 15 state emergency support functions (ESFs) keyed to each operational plan. Pandemic influenza was the first, and *The Indiana State Response Plan* detailed how, among other things, resources will be pushed through the 10 districts and 92 counties to victims. The director of the Indiana Department of Homeland Security (IDHS) took the 15 separate national planning scenarios and determined that those 15 actually fell into five broad, all-hazards categories: natural disasters, biological outbreaks, radiological catastrophes, chemical issues, and cyber complications. If five good, systematic, model plans were drawn up, each could cover its respective five plans in an all-hazards way, and 15 separate operational plans could give way to five only. Consequently, one plan respectively could become the cornerstone of a grouping of five plans in the same family. Accordingly, those 15 national planning scenarios (NPSs) were grouped in the *State Response Plan* into five broad classifications of disasters: natural hazards (for Indiana—the New Madrid Seismic Zone), biological (here pan flu), radiological (improvised nuclear device due to a major homeland defense exercise planned in Indianapolis in 2007), chemical (VX nerve agent because of stores of that agent at Newport, Indiana), and cyber (communications). This blending was an important piece, as for example, a good pandemic influenza plan with only slight modification could accommodate plague, food contamination, foot and mouth disease and anthrax, and other NPSs of the biological disease grouping. This process permitted the state to focus on both the most likely to happen and most dangerous scenarios readily, by writing only five major all-hazards plans rather than 15 (State Response Plan, 2006, pp. 9–15). Figure 4.2 shows how this was accomplished. As a consequence, these five plans served as the *State Response Plan's* operational section. The process of effectively accomplishing this follows. The decision to blend fifteen National Planning Scenarios into five all-hazards plans was made by Dr. Eric Dietz, Director, Indiana Department of Homeland Security; Indiana Department of Homeland Security. (2006)

Operations Plans (OPLANs)

- 15 National planning scenarios
  - Nuclear detonation –10-kiloton improvised nuclear device
  - Biological attack – aerosol anthrax
  - Biological disease outbreak – pandemia influenza
  - Biological attack – plague
  - Chemical attack – blister agent
  - Chemical attack – toxia industrial chemicals
  - Chemical attack – nerve agent
  - Chemical attack – chlorine tank explosion
  - Natural disaster – major earthquake
  - Natural disaster – major hurricane
  - Radiological attack – radiological dispersal devices
  - Explosives attack – bombing using improvised explosive devices
  - Biological attack – food contamination
  - Biological attack – foreign animal disease (foot and mouth disease)
  - Cyber attack

- IDHS Planning efforts focused on five scenarios most likely to affect Indiana – blends in 15 NPS

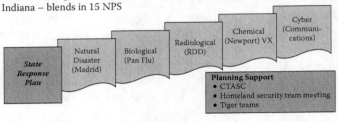

Figure 4.2 Pandemic planning operations plan.

Agreements and Trigger Points

Meetings between Indiana's two chief agencies involved with pandemic influenza planning, homeland security and the state department of health, produced benchmark agreements on cooperation, then on action points or trigger points needed for execution. It was universally concluded these needed to be agreed upon before the planning cycle was initiated. Trigger points would be mutually approved where events require or cause needed actions to take place. Assisted by ideas from the Department of Homeland Security (DHS), the Department of Health and Human Services (HHS), the Federal Emergency Management Agency (FEMA), and the Centers for Disease Control and Prevention (CDC), a list of key questions that had to be answered was created. Through FEMA Region V in Chicago the state of Minnesota's Emergency Management Department also contributed some ideas (State Department Health, 2007, pp. 1-20).

The first issue was to address the agreements that must develop. It was agreed the Indiana Department of Homeland Security would serve as the state coordinating agency (SCA) for all-hazards disaster response, including pandemic influenza. This was an important benchmark that had to be agreed upon before other real trigger points could be established.

Another IDHS benchmark was to begin with avian influenza, operating under a three-phased operations plan (entitled the Pan Flu OPLAN) similar to the Federal Department of Homeland Security and the Federal Emergency Management Agency plan. The public health plan began with a human-to-human transmission phase (anywhere in the world) and abided by the six phases of the World Health Organization (WHO), as approved by the Department of Health and Human Services (HHS) and the Centers for Disease Control (CDC). ISDH also would field its own comprehensive pandemic influenza plan which integrated these WHO phases. Happily, both Indiana departments followed the guidelines of the *National Strategy for Pandemic Influenza Implementation Plan* from the Homeland Security Council (May 2006), through their respective DHS and HHS organizational structures. Both departments worked together through the state, then down to the district and further to the county levels with unparalleled cooperation.

The trigger points for collaborative state action during an avian influenza epidemic were easier to determine. It was decided that trigger points differ slightly by state agency view and by influenza type, but common ground could be found. Common ground would be where all agreed events required action by both first- and second-level responders.

Trigger points specifically for IDHS occur when an infected bird enters the state, dies, and spreads a high pathogen H5N1 to other wild or domestic fowl or animals. That implies potential danger exists to humans via avian influenza, and a series of actions would be taken by the state Department of Natural Resources (DNR) (in surveillance) and by the Board of Animal Health (BOAH) (in bird quarantine and euthanasia), if required. IDHS' second trigger point would be when H5N1 spreads from birds to humans; and a third would be human-to-human transmission along with a morphed virus. Public health readily recognized that action was immediately necessary when human-to-human transmission took place anywhere in the world. All the following were necessary—conduct increased surveillance, public awareness, education, monitoring, school surveillance, and airport surveillance. Both state agencies agreed they would merge their respective actions when any form of influenza spreads from birds to humans within the state itself. This became a continuous process then, where homeland security and public health worked together on continuous trigger points.

Departmental cooperation was connected directly to trigger points. To do so, roles and responsibilities had to be determined. First, the Indiana Board of Animal Health (BOAH) would handle the agriculture piece for avian influenza for the state. Beyond that, a chain of command was set. It went from IDHS and ISDH under the *National Strategy for Pandemic Influenza Implementation Plan*, through FEMA V and CDC, respectively, to DHS and HHSs. Simultaneously, it went to the governor and the director of public health, then back through the director of homeland security and director of public health, to the 10 state districts (and District Planning Councils), to the 92 parallel county emergency management agencies (EMAs) and 93 county local health departments (LHDs). Accordingly, IDHS as the lead coordinating state agency, and ISDH as the primary state agency needed close cooperation and liaison.

It also was determined that non-pharmaceutical intervention trigger points were needed as key resources for critical infrastructure. It was recommended schools be closed last due to educational requirements, but they would be carefully monitored by ISDH through syndromic surveillance. It was further and roundly agreed they would be closed before the arrival of a pandemic.

The sequence for school closure would be by virtue of a declaration of a public health emergency from the commissioner of public health (a doctor of medicine), the governor would follow with a declaration of a state of emergency, and the state response plan would then be placed into effect, with all schools closed. But the authority still remained local and with the school corporations, both public and private, leaving many issues to be ironed out. A policy process for school closure and a communication plan for this decision were developed. The state superintendent of public instruction asked each school system in the state to plan for a pandemic. Local health departments met with school districts to assist in their planning. Defining and refining a statewide policy on the closure of schools to include defining authority and responsibilities, trigger points, duration of closure, plans to reopen, and social consequences of implementing school closures was a must. As a trigger point, Indiana would follow the CDC guidance for school closure as outlined in the *Interim Pre-Pandemic Planning Guidance* published in February 2007 and revised in February 2009. Depending upon how rapidly the virus spread, schools might be closed in increments throughout the state or entire school systems might be closed simultaneously. There was complete agreement that schools would be closed prior to the arrival of a pandemic. Lists of individuals with the authorities, roles, and responsibilities to officially declare schools closed and authorize their reopening were pinpointed. Assisted by their emergency management agency counterparts and local health officers, they had the authority to close and eventually reopen schools within their jurisdiction. The state health commissioner had the authority to close all schools in the state and clear them for reopening. By law, the state health commissioner's directives supersede local authorities.

At any time, closure could be announced through official homeland security channels as well as through the media, Indiana Health Alert Network, and notices on the state websites. Online distance education and educational drop-off sites, where books and lessons could be distributed and collected with minimal contact, were also to be established, covering major testing requirements also. Each school system in the state could choose to offer continuing education. Trigger points for closing significant public venues, such as sports, civic, social, and other gatherings, were established using the same policies as those developed for the schools. This applied to public transportation, with syndromic surveillance being key, then a gradual shut-down would occur as needed. Trigger points for staffing the various emergency operations centers were resolved, and plans were laid out to form common operating pictures (COPs) between levels of government for disaster management. The latter included when continuity of government (COG) and continuity of operations (COOP) plans would be placed into effect and how this would be done. Trigger points for activating or updating the state's websites were agreed upon and websites established and updated.

Further points of action were decided upon for state assistance to business and for assisting the private sector in activating their plans for this kind of event. Private sector concepts were developed on how this would be executed. These were written by the Indiana State Chamber of Commerce, the Indiana Economic Development Corporation, and the Indiana Office of Community and Rural Affairs, plus through ISDH's business collaboration partnership. Universities and colleges in the state developed policies and procedures and shared those with the state agencies.

Last, caution was addressed between the IDHS and ISDH working on this because it was realized rather that Indiana's trigger points might activate rapidly and even all at once. "Pandemic influenza" could come quickly to this state. Chicago's airports, particularly O'Hare International Airport, have a huge Asian air transportation footprint affecting northern Indiana. The Indianapolis International Airport does heavy freight commerce with Canada, Mexico, and the Caribbean through FEDEX. CDC monitors these sites. Moreover, global avian wild bird pathways extend across the length of Indiana and a huge federal interstate highway system of five major national roads blankets the state, adding heavy interstate trucking traffic. Additionally, Interstate 69, halting now in Indianapolis and known as the "North American Free Trade Area" highway, when completed, will pass through all of Indiana reaching from east-central Canada to central Mexico Archer, et al., Paper: Priorities, Policies, and Proceedings, pp. 13–17).

The Planning Process

First, characteristics of a successful plan were needed. The plan had to synchronize capabilities to needs. How to do things needed to be spelled out, and last, the plan should draw a "roadmap" for execution of all-hazards operational response. Further, characteristics of a successful operation plan included that the plan implement higher level mission guidance while also providing intent, tasks, activities, constraints, and coordinating information for successful mission completion from the state. Good plans focus on the mission to be completed while clearly providing the necessary mission completion guidance. A well-drawn-up plan spells out urgent factors needed for success up front, along with the details, all in a standard, recognizable, clear, and simple language. Plan development must take into consideration the best efforts of the multi-agency deliberate planning process, and the results were officially called an operational plan (OPLAN), which came with a local template version for use at the county level. Using the national planning and operations system (NPOS) as a guide, which the Department of Homeland Security borrowed from the Department of Defense, the Indiana systematic planning sequence commenced in May 2006.

Table 4.1 Annexes

Annex A Command and Control and Task Forces	Annex B Intelligence
Annex C Resources	Annex D Public Information
Annex E Medical Mass Casualities	Annex F State Legal Authorities
Annex G Education	Annex H Communications
Annex I Strategic National Stockpile	Annex J Mass Care and Mass Shelter
Annex K Evacuation	Annex L Law Enforcement Authorities
Annex M Mortuary	Annex N Damage and Debris Management
Annex O Training	Annex P Exercise
Annex Q Definitions	Annex R Reporting and Situational Reports

Overall, three phases were established: prepare, respond, and recover. Tasks as mentioned previously from the federal *Universal Task Lists* were woven into these phases, along with what duties state agencies must perform. Critically and by phase, representatives from lead state agencies, coordinating state agencies, and supporting state agencies were appointed to help draft this. Annexes would cover in more detail what the OPLANs did not, adding additional data in certain emergency support functions and tasks. The state annexes were patterned after the federal *Catastrophic Incident Supplemental Annexes* (see Table 4.1).

For "pandemic influenza" planning, states must establish memoranda of agreement on how to utilize key resources and equipment, and for positioning critical personnel to accept antivirals. Further emergency management assistance compacts (EMACs), under the National Emergency Management Association (NEMA) framework within DHS-FEMA Region V, were written to share personnel and resources among Midwestern states should a pandemic occur. Admittedly though, by the nature of pandemics, it was recognized chances were slim that these would ever be executed, as generally in pandemics a medical surge already is blanketing an entire FEMA region.

The planning cycle itself was inaugurated to include the following tasks: establish responsibilities, build a timeline, draw a synchronization matrix, develop priorities for planning (mission essential task list), plan relationships (with other agencies), and use interim progress reviews (IPRs) to monitor progress.

The deliberate planning process was used to write the plan and consisted of six phases. Phase 1 included plan initiation. Planning tasks were assigned and resources for planning identified. Groundwork for planning was laid. Phase 2 is concept development, which highlights factors that significantly affect mission accomplishment. Data are collected and analyzed, and as the mission statement is written, subordinate tasks are assigned and courses of action determined. Phase 3 is concept review where the concept is reviewed and approved. Phase 4 is plan development, where the plan is drafted as an operational plan (OPLAN). Here resource shortfalls are identified. Courses of action are tested and one is selected that is the best. Phase 5 is the plan review and approval. Phase 6 includes all the major supporting annexes where appropriate (Department of Defense 2006, pp. III-19 to III-41).

The last three phases (plan development, plan review, and supporting annexes) required the most time. By their nature, operational plans (OPLANs) must be fully collaborative state agency documents. Often, gaining approval for a course of action takes the most significant amount of time. Each task is essential to mission accomplishment and had to be carefully delineated in the OPLAN, both as specified tasks and implied tasks. Then all of this had to be placed into three sequential phases consisting of prepare, respond, and recover. Next, all key agencies involved had to agree. When it came to select and approve the preferred course of action, careful negotiation was required. The 15 primary state ESF agencies, often joined by as many as 37 other city-county ones, had to approve as well.

Further, the plan had to meet the common-sense test. The plan overall had to be acceptable, complete, feasible, workable, and easy to communicate and implement. The objective was that successful plans could be easily used by the local health department (LHD) and emergency management agencies (EMAs) (Department of Defense 2006, pp. III-28 to III-32).

The operational plans were collectively written in extended brainstorming sessions of the state homeland security team (HST) (Indiana Department of Homeland Security 2006). Realizing the seriousness of the situation, in a series of lengthy HST meetings at the Indiana Government Center South (IGCS), the plan was hammered out in less than six weeks, in spite of demanding HST member schedules. Because the leadership was good, completing the plan went quickly and Governor Mitch Daniels and Lieutenant Governor Rebecca Skillman helped nudge a few state agencies in the right direction. Public Health sent some of their best planners and most knowledgeable healthcare providers and practitioners. The State Homeland Security Department did the same and leadership from Dr. Eric Dietz of the Indiana Department of Homeland Security and Dr. Judy Monroe of the Indiana State Department of Health was consistently excellent. Butcher block paper, computers, cameras, and recording devices captured the main ingredients and ideas of the plan as discussed and laid out. All kept in mind rather the admonition that "We have not had a Pandemic since 1968, and we have one in the United States about every 40 years...and we are due...overdue." Determining constraints (limitations) and restraints (curbs on actions) were the last things completed (Monroe 2006). This was summer 2006, and this was serious business. Compelling arguments for worst-case scenarios often interrupted discussions adding to the importance and validity of the plan as crafted.

Formatting the OPLAN

The arrangement or format of the operational plan consisted of the standard five-paragraph operational plan (OPLAN), adopted from the American military by the Department of Homeland Security (Department of the Army 1993, pp. 1-5, 4-6, 6-1). Regarding phasing, it should be noted that these OPLANs can be written in two ways: the first incorporates phasing "prepare, respond and recover" with all three phases in one document. The second way is to have one individual OPLAN for each phase of prepare, respond, and recover. To provide more detail, the original state OPLAN was written in the latter fashion, but for simplicity, the county template was written as the former.

Yet any OPLAN, regardless of how it is formatted, consists of five segments called paragraphs. Paragraph 1 is the situation, where a clear statement appears of what kind of an event is being confronted and the circumstances. "Who" serves as the lead state agency (the Indiana Department of Homeland Security) and supporting whom (the Indiana Department of Health) are both noted in this first paragraph.

Paragraph 2 consists of the mission statement, which clearly explains what has to be completed, when it needs to be accomplished, and where all this will be enacted. A clearly written mission statement is paramount to having a successful plan.

Paragraph 3 is the most important and contains detailed information about the execution of the mission. It clarifies for the last time why this is taking place and how this will happen. "How" encompasses the means to accomplish the operation, and is discussed in four areas: 1) The director's intent (what is critical); 2) the concept of the operation (how it will be done); 3) phasing (either prepare, respond, and recover); and 4) tasks to supporting agencies (which include coordinating instructions).

Paragraph 4 covers support, which does not include actions of lead, coordinating, or supporting state agencies, but rather what resources are needed to support the mission to foster success. This paragraph highlights from where those materials or items will come.

Paragraph 5, called "command and signal," encompasses the chain of authority or responsibility for the operation, where those in charge are located, and how they can be reached electronically or by radio communications. Under the incident command system (ICS), this is generally known, and under the national incident management system (NIMS), the levels of the disaster and kinds of equipment needed are clear. The particulars of communications often are not well known and those are specified in this paragraph. A media plan, plus the safety plan, can also be placed here.

The OPLAN

As previously mentioned, the original state OPLAN (Foley, Pappas and Wojitalewicz 2006) was written with each phase (prepare, respond, and recover) constituting separate documents. The county template is Enclosure 1 with all phases as one document. Both are in their original formats as issued on June 15, 2006, at the beginning of the "pandemic flu" operational plan execution. Discussing these in detail and what they accomplished comprises the remainder of this chapter (Indiana OPLAN, Pan Flu 2006).

In the state OPLAN, blending the public health and the homeland security response through one seamless effort in three phases was critical. Homeland Security remained the "lead state agency" and Public Health served as the coordinating or executing state agency.

Phase 1 was Prepare: Plan, Protect, and Prevent. Prepare meant warning citizens; being prepared to euthanize huge flocks of domestic fowl, if needed; and preparing points of dispensing (PODs) for humans. As mentioned, because public health and homeland security differed somewhat on how to address "pandemic influenza" OPLAN phases, the mutually agreed upon trigger points for when action would take place were written into the three phases of the OPLAN. Counties, after receiving the template, were expected to establish their own plans based on it. When a bird died in Indiana and was identified as having Type A high pathogenic H5N1, Phase 1 opened for homeland security. Infected birds fly through the Aleutians to Alaska, and then south to the United States and eventually Indiana. In Phase 1, the Board of Animal Health (BOAH) played a large role with assistance from the Department of Natural Resources (DNR) and the Indiana Department of Environmental Management (IDEM). BOAH would coordinate investigations, conduct surveillance, and epidemiologic activities on suspected wild and domestic fowl populations to include domestic poultry, ducks, and geese to determine the severity of an epidemic. Agricultural security emergency response teams (ASERTs) in the affected counties would be activated to identify, locate, test, and isolate infected fowl and animal populations. Animal testing and facility monitoring would be conducted and warnings to animal owners given. The Indiana Department of Environmental Management would, in conjunction with BOAH, prepare for the euthanasia of large flocks of domestic fowl if need be.

In Phase 1, the Department of Public Health concurrently would be preparing its hundreds of points of dispensing to receive antivirals and mitigation drugs, plus personal protective equipment (PPE). As well in Phase 1, the websites of public health and homeland security agencies would inform the citizens of what personal and collective actions they could take to mitigate this potential epidemic, and where sites for dispensing antivirals were located. Symptoms of the influenza would be made broadly known to the public. People traveling from infected areas of the world, who could bring the disease here, most likely from Asian-based air routes from O'Hare International Airport in Chicago, would be monitored. Phase

1 consisted of syndromic surveillance of both birds and humans thought to be high risk in bringing the influenza to the state. Last, homeland security also in this phase planned with the state Department of Transportation, the Indiana state police, and the Indiana National Guard to ensure its distribution and dispensing system was in place for the mitigation drugs. In essence, trucks would deliver antivirals to PODs, escorted by state police to ensure they got there safely and were assisted where appropriate by the Indiana National Guard and local law enforcement.

Response, which is Phase 2 of the "pandemic influenza" operational plan, started when avian and/or animal influenza was transmitted to humans. Normally each response phase has three sub-phases: regain command and control, stage for life-saving, and life-saving. With "pandemic influenza" it is different because influenza comes in waves. Some of response phase thus overlapped into the early stage of recovery phase.

In Phase 2, transmission to human beings in Indiana has taken place resulting in an H5N1 highly pathological virus characterized as highly dangerous. The duration of the increased transmission period and resultant illnesses would be from six to eight weeks, but could be as long as 10 to 12 weeks.

Thus response phase required maintaining continuous trigger point surveillance between IDHS and ISDH while increasing public awareness, plus the full activation of the points of dispensing and the numerous prepared public information messages. Shifting additional responsibility to the Department of Public Health would take place in the response phase. Based on the situation, ISDH will employ courses of action articulated in their pandemic influenza plan, and the governor would issue a statement of public health emergency based upon the recommendation of the ISDH state health commissioner. The State Department of Administration would execute continuity of government (COG) and continuity of operations (COOP) plans in this phase. Agencies were asked to update rosters of essential personnel and contact information. Policies to address work responsibilities for ill, but essential, employees and contractors were written. Social distancing guidelines were prepared for those still at work, and other protocols were executed such as hand washing and respiratory etiquette. If domestic and/or wild fowl euthanasia took place, IDEM would address mass disposal and decontamination issues. As well, IDEM would protect state drinking water and the wastewater infrastructure. The Indiana state police would provide law enforcement support to state agencies as needed and assist local law enforcement at selected ISDH resource distribution locations, while providing support and escorts for the distribution of basic and essential supplies such as food, water, and medical supplies as needed to appropriate sites. In this phase also, the state Department of Education would publicize and initiate necessary school and school event closures with selected school districts and/or superintendents. In Phase 2, plans to initiate distance-learning procedures, while preparing selected schools so they also can be used as mass care facilities, would be executed.

Phase 3, Recovery, has two sub-phases: short-term and long-term recovery. Tasks in short-term recovery overlapped the response phase because "pan flu" comes in waves and over time. In Phase 3, human-to-human transmission of influenza has occurred and disruption of services and activities has started. All Indiana's COP and COOP plans are in effect and it is expected the "pandemic" will cause economic hardship on residents and severe economic disruption to the state.

Symptoms and infections may vary between the different waves but absenteeism will eventually include those who are ill with "pandemic influenza," then increase numerically as those caring for sick household members grow. Concerned that they may have influenza, some workers will stay home to avoid contaminating healthy workers. Most will stay home because they are sick. The numbers of well persons who remain at home to care for children due to school or daycare closure will increase as will the actual ill with other infections or diseases. Those in bereavement due to the loss of life of family members or significant others will grow as well.

Utilizing points of dispensing (PODs) were written into Response Phase 2 and also Recovery Phase 3. It was decided by the nature of "pandemic influenza" that both phases could provide appropriate guidance for second and third responders. Each county may have from one to 100 PODs, depending on population, and PODs are set to known locations, with easy access, and established with basic medical dispensing capabilities and offer some semblance of protection, should there be a rush or riot to get antivirals. Schools, heated fairgrounds buildings, and sites near shopping centers were most commonly selected. Hospitals were avoided as PODs as the general public, hoping to receive an antiviral or PPE item, need not burden hospitals with that kind of a problem.

Also in Phase 3 of the OPLAN, the timing of "pandemic influenza" and the probable effects on the workforce were analyzed. The "facts and assumptions" section discussed a serious situation. At that time it was thought a serious "pandemic influenza" outbreak would activate the strategic national stockpile and energize its regional stockpiles into action. With one of those nearby, antivirals would be distributed to the vulnerable and special needs populations, then to first- and second-responders, and finally to the general population as a whole. The Indiana Department of Homeland Security spelled out what it would do to support public health. ISDH wrote into their separate plan guidelines for the issues below and published them. Those were: social distancing, hand washing, respiratory etiquette, signs, symptoms, and transmission routes of infection, treatment guidelines, infection control procedures, school closure issues, cancellation of public mass gatherings, mental health support, procedures for sending specimens to the ISDH laboratory, antiviral prioritization and distribution policy, hospital resource availability, vaccine prioritization and distribution (when vaccine is available), altered standards of care, and requirements to provide daily status reports to IDHS.

Plans of 20 other state agencies were consolidated into final response and recovery phases, and what emergency operations centers (EOCs) would be open and who would be in charge of those agency EOC operations was discussed.

ENCLOSURE 1. COUNTY TEMPLATE

Pan Flu OPLAN (Template) (Includes Phases 1, 2, and 3 of the State Plan, in one County Annex) Annex _____ to (County Name) Emergency Response Plan (County /Local Agency Title/Name can be inserted in areas marked in bold)

I. SITUATION
    A. References: Indiana State Department of Health website – www.isdh.in.gov
    B. (County Name) local health department influenza plan (accessed via hyperlink)
    C. (County Name) Emergency Management Agency is designated as the incident command and shall coordinate county support.
    D. Definitions:
        1. Phase 1 – Avian and/or animal influenza of a subtype causing high avian/animal mortality has been identified in US wildlife flocks, domestic birds, domestic farm animals, or other wildlife. Indiana initiates selected response plans and procedures.
        2. Phase 2 – Avian and/or animal influenza has been transmitted to humans; disruption of services may occur. Indiana's continuity of operations plans are initiated.
        3. Phase 3 – Human-to-human transmission of influenza has occurred; disruption of services and activities is likely. Indiana's continuity of operations plan (COOP) is initiated.

Phase 1
    E. Phase 1 is the arrival of an infected bird(s) in Indiana.
    F. Overall, the following scenario describes the fundamental situation involving avian flu arriving in Indiana via infected birds, spreading from infected birds to humans, and being transferred from one human to another in Indiana, and as this reaches endemic proportions nationally, simultaneously worldwide viral infections rates soar resulting in a global pandemic influenza. Mitigating this in Indiana is divided into three phases, paralleling the above scenario.
    G. Overall, commencing in Asia, influenza A virus subtype H5N1, with a bird strain of H5N1 called Highly Pathogenic Avian Influenza (HPAI) A, currently persists as a problem in wild and domestic birds in several countries and can be dangerous to humans. Slowly this is spreading.
    H. Overall, a virus transmission from birds to humans, then humans to humans is of very serious concern. In limited numbers this

has already begun, since the fall of 2003, and the World Health Organization (WHO) using six phases, states globally we are in the third phase of this progression.

I. If this comes to the United States and subsequently Indiana, it is likely infected birds could come through the Aleutians to Alaska, and then south to the United States and eventually Indiana, or people traveling from infected areas could bring it here, most likely from Asian-based air routes coming into O'Hare International Airport in Chicago and spreading to District 1 through Lake County.

J. Variations of this flu infected human populations in 1918-1919, 1957-1958, and in 1968, with the 1918 pandemic killing 60 to 100 million worldwide, including 695,000 Americans. In Indiana 10,243 Hoosiers died, including 1,000 residents of Indianapolis.

K. Currently, there are no reports of the progression of HPAI through H5N1 to any further morphing, found in Indiana, but this OPLAN is designed to mitigate that should it happen.

L. Refer to www.fluinfo.in.gov for more information.

M. IDHS is designated as the lead state agency for the pan flu for all three phases. A primary state agency (PSA-that agency coordinating for the lead state agency) and supporting state agencies (those assisting the primary state agency) are designated for each phase as well.

Phase 2

N. General references are the Indiana State Department of Health website – www.isdh.in.gov; National Strategy for Pandemic Influenza, Implementation Plan (May 2006) http://www.whitehouse.gov/homeland/pandemic-influenza-implementation.html ; Agency specific continuity of operations plans (COOP) or www.fluinfo.in.gov for more information on avian/animal influenza.

O. Transmission to human beings in Indiana has taken place resulting in an H5N1 virus that has been characterized as highly dangerous.

P. The duration of the increased transmission period and resultant illnesses would likely range from six to eight weeks to up to 10 to 12 weeks.

Q. Efforts to mitigate this from becoming an outbreak are initiated.

R. IDHS is designated as the lead state agency for all three phases. A primary state agency (PSA-that agency coordinating for the lead state agency) and supporting state agencies (those assisting the primary state agency) are designated for each phase as well.

Phase 3

S. References are the Indiana State Department of Health website – www.isdh.in.gov; National Strategy for Pandemic Influenza, Implementation Plan (May 2006) http://www.whitehouse.gov/homeland/pandemic-influenza-implementation.html Agency specific continuity of operations plans (COOP); or www.fluinfo.in.gov for more information.

T. H5N1 virus has been initiated in humans, morphs, and spreads, both in the United States and worldwide, into a pandemic influenza.

U. The duration of the increased transmission period and resultant illnesses would likely range from six to eight weeks to up to 10 to 12 weeks, with anticipated shortages of hospital beds, ventilators, antivirals, and other necessary supplies.

V. Among the ill would be healthcare workers, first responders (fire, law enforcement, emergency medical services), and emergency support function personnel (public works, emergency management, transportation). The situation would result in significant social and economic disruption.

W. IDHS is designated as the lead state agency for the pan flu for all three phases. A primary state agency (PSA-that agency coordinating for the lead state agency) and supporting state agencies (those assisting the primary state agency) are designated for each phase as well.

II. MISSION: Selected County Agencies respond to the arrival, transfer, and outbreak of pan flu in a manner that protects the health of Indiana citizens and safeguards the state's agriculture and economy.

III. EXECUTION: Concept of Operations

A. (County Name) Animal Control will be designated as the lead response agency for a Phase 1 outbreak of avian/animal borne influenza. (County Name) Board of Health will be designated the lead response agency for Phase 2, with support from (County Name) Animal Control. (County Name) Board of Health will be designated as the lead response agency for a Phase 3 response.

B. Tasks to selected county agencies or subordinate elements:

1. County EMAs in conjunction with the county Board of Health provide information on social distancing which refers to methods to reduce the frequency and closeness of contact between people, to include:

    a. Keep distance from those coughing or sneezing by at least three feet.

    b. Avoid meeting people face to face; use the telephone and Internet for communications as much as possible.

    c. Avoid unnecessary travel, crowded places, public transportation, and crowded restaurants

And EMAs will coordinate training requirements for:

1. Assessing hazards and consequences: Recognize, identify, analyze, confirm, and evaluate the immediate consequences of an incident.
2. Response functions A.2; sequence #1 through 1.5 – establish procedures for the immediate incident scene.
3. HAZWOPER 29 CFR 1910.120(q), awareness level training 229 CFR 1910.1030 (g) (2) (i) Bloodborne Pathogens; Information and Training

    d. Written exposure control plans

    e. Using engineering controls to isolate or remove bloodborne pathogen hazards from the workplace

    f. Emplacing and enforcing administrative work practice controls to include hand washing, sharps disposal, lab specimen packaging, laundry handling, and contaminated material cleaning.

    g. Providing personal protective clothing and training in its usage

2. County Animal Control – ESF # 11

    a. Phase 1 – Be prepared to coordinate and interface with state BOAH and ASERTs to perform investigative, surveillance, or epidemiologic activities on suspected domestic animal populations; identify, locate, test, and quarantine affected animal populations.

    b. Phase 2 – Identify locations from which the influenza passed from avian to human. Establish contact with county Board of Health and county EOC. Provide regular status reports.

    c. Phase 3 – Monitor.

3. County Board of Health (ISDH) – ESF # 8

    a. Phases 1, 2 & 3 – Be prepared to employ one or more courses of action articulated in the county level public health pan flu response plan (refer to the county website for a copy of this plan).

4. Indiana Department of Environmental Management (IDEM) (County level) – ESF # 3 & 10
   a. Phase 1 through 3 – Be prepared to address mass disposal issues of infected wild or domestic animals with the county EMA director(s). Be prepared to activate variances temporarily suspending environmental regulations (provide reg code # and other pertinent info) to expedite mass disposal.
5. County Law Enforcement – ESF # 13
   a. Phases 1 through 3 – Be prepared to provide law enforcement support to county agencies.
   b. Be prepared to assist county Board of Health resource distribution locations TBD.
   c. Be prepared to support distribution of basic and essential supplies – food, water, medical supplies.
   d. Be prepared to provide escort services for convoys carrying resources for distribution.
   e. Be prepared to provide dignitary protection to selected members of the county government.
   f. Be prepared to provide site security and traffic/parking control at the county governmental center and campus grounds area; provide security at the county EOC.
6. County Agents – ESF # 11
   a. Phases 1, 2, 3 – Be prepared to provide support to BOAH
7. Office of the County Auditor
   a. Phases 1, 2, 3 – Establish a budget account to support this OPLAN
8. School District Superintendents
   a. Phase 2 & 3 – Be prepared to address school and school event closure issues with selected schools and districts. Be prepared to initiate distance learning procedures.
   b. Phase 3 – Identify closed schools that can be used as mass care and staging facilities.
   c. Be prepared to adjust dates, time, and location of critical testing, e.g., ISTEP, SAT.
9. County Department of Administration – ESF 7
   a. Phase 2 – Initiate expedited procurement procedures to identify, locate and distribute needed personal protective equipment (PPE). Establish a PPE distribution point for selected agencies.
   b. Phase 2 & 3 – Be prepared to have selected personnel perform the following:

c. Cleaning and disinfecting ingress/egress points at city/county government centers and other locations. Ensure adequate stockpile of disinfection agents, supplies, and PPE.

10. County Budget Agency
    a. Phase 1 through 3 – Be prepared to support selected county agencies.
    b. Be prepared to provide finance and administration staff to the county EOC.

11. County Chambers of Commerce, Rotary Clubs, Faith-Based Organizations
    a. Lead agencies for emergency support function (ESF) # 14 – Long-Term Community Recovery and Mitigation.
    b. Interface with the private sector and provide feedback to the county EMA director concerning the private sector's ability to perform continuity of operations for selected critical infrastructures – water, gas, electric, and food.

12. County Department of Personnel
    a. Phase 1 – Be prepared to implement flex-hour scheduling and other personnel issues for state employees and selected contractors.
    b. Other workforce-related issues need to be addressed here.
    c. Be prepared to assist with the expedited establishment and filling of XX number of positions at no later than XX hours following this tasking.

13. County Highway Department – ESF 1
    a. On order personnel, resources, and equipment to support this plan.

14. Intelligence
    a. GIS – Regular support.
    b. All incoming field observations that include location will be promptly forwarded to the GIS staff in the EOC.
    c. The EOC GIS staff will task local agencies for data, services and subject matter expertise to maintain an updated common operating picture and to best reflect the real world situation at the incident location.
    d. If the county's mobile incident command vehicle is mobilized, locational data will be reported to the GIS staff in that vehicle for incorporation into the common operating picture.

C. Coordinating Instructions

1. All supporting agencies listed in this OPLAN will follow their internal standard operating procedures and respective emergency support functions in order to accomplish the mission.

IV. SUPPORT
  A. Logistics
    1. County EOC will coordinate support as needed.
    2. Personal Protective Equipment
      a. Phase 2 – Each county agency shall draw from their pan flu stockpile of PPE and provide the following item: individual deployment kits – N 95 masks, surgical gloves, disinfectant, and information sheets.
  B. Finance/Administration
    1. In all phases, ensure proper budget and personnel are available.

V. INCIDENT COMMAND
  A. Command
    1. The County EOC is located at: _____.
  B. Signal
    1. Hoosier SAFE-T
  C. Public Information
    1. Phase 1 through 3 – Until further notice, Joint Information Center (JIC) will issue a statement concerning the incident daily at XXXX hours from the JIC location which is: _____.
    2. Phase 1 through 3 – JIC media conferences will be scheduled daily at XXXX hours.
    3. Incident website:
    4. Incident email:
    5. County PIO will provide TV news updates as needed.
    6. Agency emergency support functions (ESFs) for OPLAN with the ESF Coordinator for each listed.
       # 1 Transportation – County Highway Department
       # 2 Communications – County EMA
       # 3 Public Works and Engineering – County Public Works
       # 4 Firefighting _____
       # 5 Emergency Management – EMA
       # 6 Mass Care/Housing/Human Services – County EMA or American Red Cross
       # 7 Resource Support – EMA

> \# 8   Public Health and Medical Services – county Board of Public Health or local
> \# 9   Urban search and rescue _____.
> \# 10 Hazardous Materials Response – county/city fire departments or local IDEM
> \# 11 Agriculture/Natural Resources – county animal control
> \# 12 Energy – REMC or CINERGY
> \# 13 Public Safety and Security – county sheriff/city police
> \# 14 Long-Term Recovery – chambers of commerce
> \# 15 External Affairs – county PIO

Finally, annexes spelled out specified information not covered in the OPLAN, which gave greater guidance to the concept of support. They appear in Table 4.1. The OPLAN was sent to the 92 county emergency management directors as a package in mid-June 2006. The information contained a copy of the Indiana Historical Society's lecture explaining past spread of influenza pan flu in this state, a letter of instruction from the chief of staff of the Indiana Department of Homeland Security on what to do, a timeline, and a template for the counties to facilitate their local plan. It asked them to use the template included here.

This template blended all three phases of the pan flu OPLAN into one singular document, formatted as an OPLAN, but allowed counties to pattern their local OPLAN after the state model. It requested they meet with their respective county councils, local health departments, and all 15 emergency support functions holders at the local level to draft a local OPLAN. As an electronic template, each county needed only fill in their agency responses, and their five paragraphs of information using the same electronic template, and return it to the state by a certain date. Thus the template was a usable, "living" document that formed a common operating picture (COP) from the local level to the state agencies, telling in the same format and same language what would be done to mitigate "pandemic influenza." This, along with an aggressive public education program at the behest of the state homeland security organization and state public health staff provided extensive preparedness to the state. Coupled with the extensive strategic national stockpile program of the federal government and state implementation, it provided a good blend of government assistance to support citizens. It was now time to implement.

Through the 10 districts of the state, on June 16, 2006, everything was sent to the 92 counties, and using the template, asking them to return to the state their county plan by September 30, 2006. It was expected each county plan would include all the essential concepts of operations and support, on how each county would serve its citizens. This then was a workable and comprehensive formula. The plans at the local level included law enforcement, fire, emergency medical support, hospitals, public health, nonprofit, faith-based community organizations, schools, institutions of higher education, and other healthcare organizations and volunteer entities.

In June 2006, Indiana's program was introduced at the Regional Interagency Steering Committee (RISC) of DHS FEMA Region V in Chicago and also discussed there in September 2007; in both instances it was warmly received. At these meetings, from the six states of DHS FEMA Region V ranging from state police, Coast Guard, postal inspectors, to state nursing organizations, emergency management personnel, public health organizations, to the defense Coordinating Element, all wanted copies of the Indiana template and ideas about the concept; what the process entailed. In April 2007 in Minneapolis, this idea was also discussed by state representatives at the National Governor's Association, Center for Best Practices, Regional Workshop on Pandemic Preparedness in the States (Minnesota HSEM 2007 and FEMA V. RISC 2006).

A number of exercises have been conducted to test these plans both at state and local levels. Ten district tabletop exercises were conducted in 2006. These exercises included first responders, schools, businesses, hospitals, faith-based community, nonprofit organizations, institutions of higher education, and other healthcare organizations/entities. Functional exercises at the county level also were conducted and those tested the strategic national stockpile delivery. A statewide tabletop exercise was conducted in October 2006 and a statewide school closure exercise was completed in February 2007. Other exercises followed to test this plan through 2008. Numerous local exercises also have been conducted along with an ongoing training and awareness program. Since implementation, local public health departments conducted 290 town hall meetings around the state and the Indiana Department of Homeland Security conducted a statewide epidemic tabletop exercise that brought all the state and local agencies together.

The real test came on April 26, 2009, when seasonal and H1N1 influenza antivirals were to be distributed through the strategic national stockpile network. Seventeen large semi-tractor trailers were used and the entire system was exercised. In one day, all appropriate PODs were filled at the right time with the right mix of medicines and people. Rated at 100 percent effective, the preparedness, response and recovery plan as developed, designed, implemented, and evaluated was shown to be successful in protecting the citizens of the state. Originally accomplished in only six months and perfected in less than two years, this represented what operative planning can accomplish. Julian Huxley once wrote that there are two parts of duty, "one to ourselves…and an additional one…to others to be fulfilled in service to the community and in promoting the welfare of the generations to come." This effort met that standard (Frank 1999, p. 225).

References

Aaltonen, P. Pandemic influenza. Lecture presented at Indiana University-Purdue University Indianapolis, IN, April 21, 2009.

Archer, J., Lewis, P., Foley, W., and D. Barrabee. 2007. Paper: Priorities, policies and procedures. Indiana Department of Homeland Security, Indiana State Department of Health, and the Indiana Department of Education.

Black, D. R., Smock, J. A., and B. Ardaugh. 2011. *The foundations of epidemiology.* 5th ed. Oshtemo, MI: Center for Social Problem Solving Measurement.

Barry, J. M. 2005. *The Great Influenza: The story of the deadliest plague in history.* New York: Penguin Books Inc.

D'Araujo, J. R. nd. Department of Homeland Security, Federal Emergency Management Agency, *FEMA Recovery Policy RP95xx.xx: Emergency assistance for human influenza pandemic.* Washington, DC: United States Government Printing Office.

Department of the Army. 1993. *Field Manual 100-5: Operations.* Washington, DC: United States Government Printing Office.

Department of the Army. 2001. *Field Manual 3-0: Operations.* Washington, DC: United States Government Printing Office.

Department of Defense. 2006. *Joint Publication 5-0: Joint Operational Planning.* Washington, DC: United States Government Printing Office.

Department of Health and Human Services, Centers for Disease Control. 2007. *CDC's Division of Strategic National Stockpile, Emergency MedKit Evaluation Study Summary, Background, Key Results, and Next Steps.* Washington, DC: United States Government Printing Office.

Department of Homeland Security. 2007. *National preparedness guidelines.* Washington, DC: United States Government Printing Office.

Department of Homeland Security, Federal Emergency Management Agency. 2006. Regional Interagency Steering Committee Meetings, Chicago; and National Governors Association (2007, April 9, 10, 11). NGA Center for Best Practices, Regional Pandemic Preparedness Workshop, Minneapolis.

Dietz, E. and D. Mack. 2008. Indiana Strategy for Homeland Security. Indiana Department of Homeland Security. Indianapolis, IN: Indiana Department of Administration Printing.

Dietz, E., Monroe, J., and S. Pappas. 2006. Planning and Preparing for the Worst Case Scenario. Indiana Department of Homeland Security. Indianapolis, IN: Indiana Department of Administration Printing.

Dietz, E., Monroe, J., and S. Pappas. 2006. Follow up to Indiana's Pandemic Flu Summit. Indiana Department of Homeland Security. Indianapolis, IN: Indiana Department of Administration Printing.

Dietz, E., Wojtalewicz, C., and D. Mack. 2006. Pan flu timeline and strategic planning branch assignments. Indiana Department of Homeland Security.

Foley, W. and S. Pappas. 2006. Indiana Department of Homeland Security. OPLAN 1, Biological Disease Outbreak—Pandemic Influenza—Phases 1, 2, and 3 to the Indiana State Response Plan (SRP)—Avian/Animal Influenza. Indiana Department of Homeland Security.

Foley, W. and C. Wojtalewicz. 2006. *Indiana State Response Plan.* Indianapolis, IN: Indiana Department of Administration Printing Office.

Frank, L. R. 1999. *Random House and Webster's Quotationary.* New York: Random House.

Homeland Security Council. 2005. *National Strategy for Pandemic Influenza*. Washington, DC: United States Government Printing Office.

Homeland Security Council. 2006. *National Strategy for Pandemic Influenza: Implementation Plan*. Washington, DC: United States Government Printing Office.

Indiana Department of Homeland Security. Homeland Security Team Meetings, May through September 2006.

Landry, M. nd. Pandemic planning status for response—Department of Homeland Security. Washington: DC: United States Government Printing Office.

Minnesota Division of Homeland Security and Emergency Management. 2007. *Highly pathogenic avian influenza and pandemic influenza: State by state comparison.* Wheeler, J. 2006. The 1918 influenza pandemic: Stories then and lessons for now. Lecture presented at the Indiana Historical Society, Indianapolis.

Monroe, J. 2006. Comments presented at the Homeland Security Team Meeting, Indianapolis, IN, June 11.

Chapter 5

Pandemic Planning for Local Health Departments

Jennifer A. Smock, Jack Herrmann,
V. Scott Fisher, and Bryan J. Damis

Contents

Abstract

The public health initiatives encapsulated in the Public Health Service Act, Public Health Security and Bioterrorism Preparedness and Response Act, and the Pandemic and All-Hazards Preparedness Act (PAHPA) enacted by Congress have helped to establish an infrastructure to build upon public health preparedness efforts at the local, state, and federal levels. These laws facilitated the enhancement of the capacity to detect and respond effectively to significant public health threats. One of the more significant preparedness initiatives pertains to planning for and responding to an influenza pandemic. Within the development of a pandemic plan, much consideration needs to be focused within the areas of communication, mass prophylaxis and immunization, quarantine, isolation, social distancing, and volunteer management. To ensure continual improvement and identify vulnerabilities, plans must be tested with well-designed exercises. The 2009-2010 H1N1 pandemic event gave local health departments (LHDs) the opportunity to implement their pandemic plans within their communities on a large scale. Similar to an exercise, the real event unveiled strengths and improvement needs at the local level. This chapter provides considerations on how to develop and exercise pandemic plans along with providing the lessons learned from the 2009-2010 H1N1 pandemic based on experiences in the field. Through continuous improvement of pandemic plans, LHDs will ultimately empower communities to be more resilient during the next pandemic event.

Keywords: Local Health Department, Pandemic Influenza, H1N1, Communication, Mass Prophylaxis, Immunization, Quarantine and Isolation, Non-Pharmaceutical Interventions, Volunteer Management, Tabletop Exercise

The planning and response role of US local health departments (LHDs) has evolved significantly during the past decade. In 1998, the Institute of Medicine (IOM) concluded that public health was in disarray and attempted to better define the mission and objectives of governmental public health, including LHDs, in its report *The Future of Public Health* (IOM 1998). Although this report set the foundation for the development of the essential public health services framework that continues to serve as the backbone for public health, it lacked a particular focus on preparedness.

In 2000, Congress amended the Public Health Service Act to address public health threats and emergencies. The Public Health Service Act outlined the broad powers provided to the US Secretary of Health in responding to a public health emergency. The law mandated the development of capacities for federal, state, and local public health to detect and respond effectively to significant public health threats, including major outbreaks of infectious disease, pathogens resistant to anti-microbial agents, and acts of bioterrorism. However, the law lacked the details and funding necessary to increase the public health preparedness capacity of LHDs.

It was not until the terrorist attacks of 2001 that the federal government and subsequently state health departments (SHDs) and LHDs greatly expanded their commitment to public health preparedness. In 2002, Congress passed the Public Health Security and Bioterrorism Preparedness and Response Act. The law required the establishment of the assistant secretary of public health emergencies within the US Department of Health and Human Services and established the strategic national stockpile. Additionally, the law authorized grants for SHD and LHD preparedness capacity, which the Centers for Disease Control and Prevention (CDC) continues to coordinate through the public health emergency preparedness (PHEP) cooperative agreement program (CDC 2011). This was the first national effort that required grant recipients (SHDs and LHDs) to develop, exercise, and evaluate public health emergency preparedness and response plans.

In 2006, Congress enacted the Pandemic and All-Hazards Preparedness Act (PAHPA) that required the development of plans for responding to a pandemic influenza. PAHPA granted the Health and Human Services (HHS) secretary with the operational control of all federal assets during medical and public health emergencies (except armed services), and consolidated medical surge capabilities in HHS. The act created the position of assistant secretary for preparedness and response (ASPR), established national health security strategy, and the Biomedical Advanced Research and Development Authority (BARDA), a program focused on the research and development of life-saving counter measures. Additionally, PAHPA promoted an all-hazards approach to preparedness, encouraged the development of core public health preparedness and medical response training, and addressed challenges with recruiting and deploying voluntary medical personnel. It also established a mechanism to develop and procure medical countermeasures, and developed strategies for at-risk populations. The role and organization of LHDs vary across the United States and have important implications in the development of public health emergency response plans. Based on the *2008 National Profile of Local Health Departments* developed by the National Association of County and City Health Officials (NACCHO), approximately 2,800 LHDs serve a variety of jurisdiction types with populations from less than 1,000 to more than 9 million (NACCHO National Profile of Local Health Departments 2008). According to this survey, 71% of LHDs serve a county or combined city-county jurisdiction, yet many LHDs are associated with cities, towns, multi-town, multi-county, or other regional entities within a state. The data also supports the increased emphasis on preparedness planning efforts by LHDs following the 9/11 terrorist attacks and subsequent preparedness legislation and funding. After 9/11, 89% of LHDs had written or updated a pandemic influenza preparedness plan, 86% had participated in a drill or exercise to test their plans, and 85% had conducted staff training on emergency preparedness (NACCHO 2008).

Despite the encouraging data regarding public health preparedness efforts within LHDs, more work is required to meet the expectations of Congress and the public to be fully prepared to respond effectively to any public health hazard. This starts with the ability to develop, exercise, and evaluate preparedness and response plans. This chapter describes the components essential to a preparedness plan, the importance of testing and updating these plans, and lessons learned through responding to real-life challenges, such as the 2009-2010 H1N1 influenza pandemic.

Developing a Plan

The nature of a pandemic influenza event (and other disease epidemics) is unique because SHDs and LHDs are at the forefront of the response. In other types of emergency response, entities such as emergency management agencies, fire and emergency medical services (EMS), law enforcement, or other first responders take the lead role, with LHDs usually in a supportive role. During the H1N1 pandemic of 2009-2010, LHDs took the lead on prevention and mitigation efforts and were a key focus of the media. Planning for an influenza pandemic and the subsequent response is a vital part of the preparedness cycle to prevent, respond, and recover from disasters and public health emergencies. Inherent within this cycle are different types of planning considerations that must be considered and documented at the state and local level. However, when it comes to the actual event, LHDs are considered first responders and the culmination of all the planning is a coordinated response effort within a community.

Every year, LHDs plan for and respond to seasonal influenza. During each fall and winter in the northern hemisphere, the flu season begins and efforts are coordinated to educate the public and establish clinics and other venues to vaccinate risk groups and others throughout the community. While these efforts may form the core of pandemic influenza planning for LHDs, they are at an endemic state. Surveillance activities and the communication of threats to the public are part of the day-to-day activities that become enhanced in light of a pandemic. New planning considerations and new partners in response need to be incorporated into a LHD's pandemic influenza plan. As public health professionals further consider the societal and economic impacts of a severe pandemic, the planning considerations become broader and more critical. This challenges LHDs to develop innovative ways to combat the threat on many fronts. This section will highlight the broader areas of planning and response efforts in which LHDs participate while facing a pandemic, and integrate the lessons that were learned through the real-life challenges of responding to the 2009-2010 H1N1 pandemic.

Communication

While important messages regarding influenza are common each year (hand washing, cough etiquette, etc.), it becomes necessary for LHDs to consider and plan for their emergency risk communication during a pandemic. This is a coordinated approach to communicating messages to the public (and to partners in response) that is not only an important piece of a pandemic influenza plan, but is useful for all-hazards and emergencies that a health department may confront. When constructing a communications plan, an LHD must consider several factors. First, LHDs need to identify those who will need to be notified just prior to and during a pandemic, including public, private, and other health and medical partners critical to the response. When partners are identified, the LHD must test the modes by which communication will take place. Redundancy and links to other communication networks are critical. While the construction of a thorough and well-tested communication plan is vital to the health department's response during a pandemic such as H1N1, it is equally important to note they are generally constructed with an all-hazards approach to public health preparedness. This includes ensuring contact lists are up-to-date, current templates for press releases are available and assessed with a behavioral health lens, key staff are trained as trusted spokespersons, and communication outreach is provided to vulnerable populations.

In a July 2009 public opinion poll conducted by the Harvard School of Public Health, more than 60% of the Americans surveyed were not concerned about their personal risk for getting sick from the H1N1 virus. In contrast, 59% of those surveyed believed it was "very or somewhat likely" that there would be widespread cases of the H1N1 virus, with more people getting sick during the fall or winter (The President and Fellows of Harvard College 2010). Educating the public about precautions they can take to protect themselves and their family during an influenza pandemic can be particularly difficult. Public health officials must balance the act of providing the public with enough information to make informed decisions about how to respond during an emergency, but not to the point that it creates confusion or panic.

During the 2009-2010 H1N1 pandemic, public health officials found themselves tasked with a variety of communication challenges. The epidemiology of the virus suggested that a variety of demographic groups may be more at risk for morbidity and mortality associated with the virus than those impacted by the traditional seasonal influenza (CDC 2010a). Health departments across the country needed to embark on mass communication campaigns to target at-risk audiences. Radio, print, and television media public service announcements appeared to be the most common approach to informing the public about the effects of the virus and how to obtain the influenza vaccine. Some communities took more novel approaches with the use of telephone technology, which provided an automated message to residents of a community with the dates, times, and locations of the closest mass vaccine clinic. Other communities partnered with their local supermarket chain to provide flu information near cashier check-outs and a checklist of flu remedies that could be purchased in supermarkets.

Mass Prophylaxis and Immunization

During a pandemic response, LHDs activate the operational portion of their mass prophylaxis and immunization plans. Important protocols for an immunization plan include the management and tracking of personnel and resources, vaccination procedures (e.g., development and testing of points of dispensing [POD] sites and other dispensing modalities), and monitoring adverse reactions (i.e., post-event tracking).

In response to the 2009-2010 H1N1 pandemic, PODs were established nationwide in various new ways. One of the most popular new POD set-ups was the "drive-thru" model, in which individuals drive up to a designated community site and are administered a flu shot without leaving their vehicle. NACCHO, in collaboration with the Louisville Metro Department of Public Health and Wellness in Kentucky and the Orange County Department of Health in Florida, has developed guidance for the drive-thru POD model (NACCHO 2010). Using this model, health department staff could quickly and efficiently accommodate a large number of patients, and thus relieve potential surge on hospitals, health clinics, and community-based medical practices.

Another critical element of mass prophylaxis activity at the local public health level is the planning for and activation of assets received from the strategic national stockpile (SNS). The SNS is the nation's cache of medicine and medical supplies to protect the public in a public health emergency (CDC 2010c). While the distribution of the SNS cache is a coordinated effort from the federal to state level, LHDs must construct plans to dispense these life-saving medications and supplies at the community level. These plans include the delineation of responsibilities for receipt and distribution of SNS assets from their state. Additionally, plans should include legal authorities or other memoranda of understanding outlining the health department's license to suspend normal activities to accomplish mass prophylaxis functions, and a system for tracking the prophylaxis of first responders who will treat the public during a pandemic or other event.

Quarantine, Isolation, and Social Distancing

While a certain level of social distancing is predicated by the aforementioned risk communication to the public (e.g., staying home if you are ill), LHDs must construct plans for quarantine, isolation, and other non-pharmaceutical interventions (NPIs), such as social distancing of the public in the event of a pandemic. LHDs use quarantine, isolation, and NPIs to mitigate the spread of disease within the population. By using these community mitigation strategies, the spread of the virus is contained, resulting in a decrease in morbidity and mortality in the population (CDC 2010b).

Isolation and quarantine of the public often involves intricate planning on many levels. Legal authorities need to be developed, as actions to isolate or quarantine must be legally defined not only for individuals of the general public, but for facilities, animals, and food products as well. To prevent or mitigate the spread of an emerging infectious disease, NPIs, such as school closures or the cancellation of large community events, require additional consideration. Laws differ in localities on who has the authority to close educational institutions and cancel public events.

If proper provisions are not made in advance to address and resolve these issues, considerable time and effort may be taken during the emergency, posing potentially lethal consequences.

Furthermore, consideration must be given to those needing access to care and medical services for reasons not related to the pandemic. The coordination of public health and medical services becomes a critical juncture for planning at LHDs and can involve a number of medical partners. These services are not only directed at the physical well-being of the public, but also the mental health of the community. Individuals under isolation and quarantine will face many challenges to their mental health with the prospect of illness and death around them. Health department responsibilities include delivery of stress management strategies to the public and development of a coordinated approach to providing mental health services to individuals in isolation or quarantine as well as those providing their care.

Volunteer Management and Response

Volunteers can be a vital resource during disasters and public health emergencies. The key to their success is the robust and thorough planning for the identification of these resources, adequate vetting of their professional credentials, appropriate training to the needs of the event, and resolving any potential issues that pose risk and liability for the organization.

A declining public health workforce has required local and SHDs to consider using volunteers to help them carry out their public health mission during disasters and other public health emergencies (NACCHO 2010). During an influenza pandemic, it is commonly understood that the ability to protect the nation's health will be challenged by the pervasive nature of the virus. Hospital workers, emergency medical technicians, physicians, nurses, and others performing critical roles during a public health emergency will find themselves ill or needing to tend to ailing loved ones. Without the resources to backfill their positions, critical life-saving functions will not be offered, amplifying the morbidity and mortality associated with the pandemic. During the 2009–2010 H1N1 pandemic, the public health and health-care system was faced with a surge in the number of people in hospital emergency rooms, walk-in clinics, and private physician offices. This system also was faced with the challenge of considering how to vaccinate a large segment of the population against the virus. Many health departments turned to volunteer organizations in their communities.

Concern over the lack of uniform liability protection for volunteers was frequently voiced in discussions with local and state public health officials during the H1N1 crisis. The absence of such protection inhibited health departments from recruiting the volunteer resources necessary to implement life-saving medical countermeasures. Following the most recent pandemic, many health departments nationwide are exploring novel approaches to ensure such liability protections are in place. One example includes "deputizing" volunteers as official health department staff during a disaster so they can benefit from the agency's liability protection coverage. Other public health representatives are working with elected officials to introduce or modify existing state and local laws and statutes to include volunteer liability protection. Such issues are not easily resolved and warrant adequate planning to put the necessary protections in place for the next disaster. Health departments engaged in pandemic planning should clarify with their agency's legal counsel, the implications of their state and local laws, and the provisions necessary to resolve these issues.

Despite these issues, during the 2009-2010 H1N1 pandemic, the mobilization of volunteers became a critical and often celebrated aspect to the response efforts of LHDs. Trained volunteers were used to dispense vaccines in PODs and in other facets of the response, such as providing education to the public, and other non-medical support roles. One of the most noteworthy volunteer programs during the H1N1 response was the Medical Reserve Corps (MRC).

A nationally based volunteer program, MRC was established in the aftermath of 9/11 and has been a major volunteer resource for many health departments nationwide. To date, more than 900 MRC units have been formed in local communities across the United States. Many of them are housed in LHDs, emergency management agencies, faith-based organizations, and a variety of other institutions. Largely composed of both medical and non-medical personnel, these dedicated volunteer units are engaged in a variety of disaster-related activities. Because of their success, many communities are finding additional ways to use this highly skilled volunteer workforce (e.g., health fairs, educating the public on disease management, etc.) to enhance and protect the public's health. LHDs enhanced the 2009-2010 H1N1 pandemic response efforts through the use of MRC volunteers.

During the 2009-2010 H1N1 pandemic, one California MRC unit partnered with its LHD and a community-based nonprofit group to vaccinate a segment of its community's population. The nonprofit partner group was established to provide free, volunteer medical care for the community's most vulnerable individuals. During the influenza pandemic, the MRC volunteer unit and the nonprofit partner worked hand-in-hand at a local H1N1 vaccination clinic to immunize the community's veterans and homeless populations. In preparation to fulfill this critical role, the LHD trained these volunteers and assigned them various duties based upon their medical qualifications. The partnership was successful from many perspectives. It allowed the health department to carry out its critical public health mission by offering a venue for at-risk individuals to receive a life-saving vaccine and it created a sustainable partnership that can be mobilized for future pandemics and other public health emergencies.

Another LHD used its MRC volunteers to conduct a POD clinic at a large arena during a national sporting event. Volunteers provided the vaccine to the public attending the event and to arena employees. The event was advertised through local media outlets and through a partnership with the national sports team. Even the team's mascot participated by walking around the arena sporting a bandage on his arm.

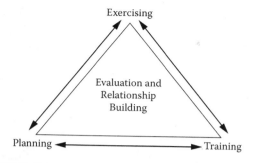

Figure 5.1 The Preparedness Cycle.

Some communities used their MRC assets to augment local laboratory capacity. One county health department utilized MRC volunteers to receive and process H1N1 laboratory specimens, thereby keeping up with the surge from hospitals, clinics, and private physician offices.

Developing a Pandemic Influenza Exercise

Developing a plan is not a one-time project; it is a dynamic process that requires attention and effort over time. This process is in constant transition between planning, exercising, and training as depicted in Figure 5.1. Through this cycle, the plan strengthens, thus continuously increasing the specificity of the pandemic exercise objectives over time. Additionally, it is crucial to continue this process as staff transitions and other relationships at the state and local level are acquired and educated. Progressing through this cycle will ultimately help a pandemic influenza plan become a living, breathing document during an emergency response.

In 2009, the CDC funded pandemic tabletop exercises in nine Indiana counties. The exercises involved a wide range of participants including LHDs, healthcare facilities, EMS, state and local police, the Indiana Department of Homeland Security (IDHS), the Indiana State Department of Health (ISDH), and the CDC. These exercises were recognized as a success at the local, state, and federal level. Several best practices gathered from the 2009 pandemic tabletop exercises were identified.

Building the Exercise

The ultimate purpose of an exercise is to identify and learn from the gaps within emergency preparedness plans. Therefore, it is highly recommended that an external, objective agency be appointed to develop an exercise to evaluate the pandemic plan. This outside perspective is crucial to identifying gaps within the pandemic plan and building an exercise scenario that will magnify those vulnerabilities. In addition, it is recommended that a core planning team, consisting of a few local emergency preparedness representatives, meet with the agency several times prior to the pandemic exercise to assist in its development. The planning team is responsible for ensuring the consulting agency obtains a clear understanding of the structure of authority, the population served, and community resources. More importantly, the planning team needs to have a role in shaping the evaluated objectives and the scenarios that will be used to evaluate the objectives. It is also advisable that the planning team identify three to five objectives that are specific, measurable, achievable, realistic, and time-bound (SMART) (CDC 2009b). This allows an adequate and realistic timeframe to fully work through each objective. A pandemic exercise exceeding more than five objectives runs the risk of participants rushing through the scenarios and missing potential lessons learned.

Identifying Exercise Participants

There are many benefits to exercising a pandemic plan. A high-quality exercise will consist of scenarios that present the opportunity for participants to work as a group to solve problems outside the realm of the current pandemic plan. This allows the group to perform out-of-the-box thinking to facilitate the enhancement of the plans when vulnerabilities are apparent. This "group-think" may aid in identifying additional resources within the community and strengthening partnerships.

Representatives from agencies that have an identified role within the pandemic plan should participate in the exercise. This may include healthcare facilities, EMS, police, fire, school districts, higher education facilities, the American Red Cross, MRC unit, and any other partners documented in the plan. The exercise allows participants to function in their given roles and responsibilities and can clarify the roles and responsibilities of other partners during a pandemic. Additionally, a representative from the state department of health is highly recommended. Throughout the scenario, participants will encounter several legal and liability issues as a result of their proposed actions. State representation will allow the state to directly speak to identified concerns arising during the scenario.

Constructing an Improvement Plan

The improvement plan is one of the most important outcomes of an exercise. It documents the gaps within each objective and offers solutions on how to resolve these vulnerabilities. To construct an effective improvement plan, it must consist of goals derived from the exercise objective evaluations, reasonable completion dates for each goal, a designated agency to carry out the goal, a direct point of contact, and a training plan for staff once the plans have been enhanced. Not documenting any one of these areas in the improvement plan will risk unresolved gaps that were identified in the plan during the exercise.

After successfully exercising, planning, and training staff, the cycle begins again, by increasing the specificity of the pandemic exercise objectives. Continuous movement through the cycle will ultimately result in a more resilient community during a real pandemic event.

Conclusion

The federal initiatives enacted by Congress have increased preparedness efforts at the local level (NACCHO 2008), and the 2009-2010 H1N1 pandemic event gave LHDs the opportunity to exercise these plans. Although H1N1 was considered a mild pandemic (CDC, 2009a), it is paramount to enhance pandemic preparedness plans by incorporating the lessons learned from the real-world event and continuing the plan-train-exercise cycle. By continuing this cycle, LHDs will be more effective in responding to public health emergencies and ultimately will build a more resilient community during the next pandemic event.

References

Centers for Disease Control and Prevention. 2009a. *2009 H1N1 ("swine flu") flu and you.* http://www.cdc.gov/h1n1flu/qa.htm. Accessed Dec. 16, 2009.

Centers for Disease Control and Prevention. 2009b. *Writing SMART objectives. Evaluation brief.* http://www.cdc.gov/healthyyouth/evaluation/pdf/brief3b.pdf. Accessed Nov. 8, 2010.

Centers for Disease Control and Prevention. 2010a. *2009 H1N1 vaccination recommendations.* http://www.cdc.gov/h1n1flu/vaccination/acip.htm. Accessed Jan. 16, 2010.

Centers for Disease Control and Prevention. 2010b. *History of quarantine.* http://emergency.cdc.gov/preparedness/quarantine. Accessed Sept. 23, 2010.

Centers for Disease Control and Prevention. 2010c. *Strategic national stockpile.* http://www.bt.cdc.gov/stockpile. Accessed Sept. 23, 2010.

Centers for Disease Control and Prevention. 2011. *Funding guidance and technical assistance to states.* http://www.bt.cdc.gov/cdcpreparedness/coopagreement/index.asp. Accessed April 16, 2011.

Dausey, D. J., Aledort, J. E., and N. Lurie. 2006. *Tabletop exercises for pandemic influenza preparedness in local public health agencies.* Santa Monica, CA: RAND Corporation. http://www.rand.org/pubs/technical_reports/2006/RAND_TR319.pdf. Accessed Nov. 8, 2010.

Institute of Medicine. 1998. *The future of public health.* Washington, DC: National Academy Press.

National Association of County and City Health Officials. 2008. *National Profile of Local Health Departments. Washington, DC: National Association of Country and City Health Officials; 2009.* http://www.naccho.org/topics/infrastructure/profile/resources/2008reports/upload/NACCHO 2008 ProfileReport post-to-website-2.pdf. Accessed Nov. 10, 2009.

National Association of County and City Health Officials. 2010. *Drive-thru point of dispensing guide.* Washington, DC. http://www.naccho.org/topics/emergency/SNS/loader.cfm?csModule=security/getfile&PageID=211986. Accessed Nov. 20, 2011.

National Association of County and City Health Officials. 2010. *Local health department job losses and program cuts: Finding from January/February 2010 survey.* Washington, DC. http://www.naccho.org/topics/infrastructure/Ihdbudget/upload/Job-Losses-and-Program-Cuts-5-10pdf. Accessed Nov. 20, 2011.

The President and Fellows of Harvard College. 2010. *National survey finds six in ten Americans believe serious outbreak of influenza A (H1N1) likely in fall/winter.* Boston, MA: Harvard School of Public Health. http://www.hsph.harvard.edu/news/press-releases/2009-releases/national-survey-americans-influenza-a-h1n1-outbreak-fall-winter.html. Accessed Sept. 23, 2010.

Showronski, S. 2003. Tabletop exercises. Presented at the Public Health Technical Network (PHTN) Annual Distance Learning Summit. http://www.rand.org/pubs/technical_reports/2006/RAND_TR319.pdf

Chapter 6

Developing a Prevention and Control Program with an Accompanying Simulation

J. Eric Dietz, Alok R. Chaturvedi, David R. Black, Julie E. Shaffner, Chih-hui Hsieh, Steven Dunlop, Kara E. Leonard, and John F. Burr

Contents

Abstract

Pandemic preparedness training for schools* is an evidence-based influenza prevention program. The purpose of this project was to provide an assessment of how policies, behaviors, and the environment might affect transmission of an influenza virus within a school. Following a thorough assessment of the school, specific recommendations for improvement are provided. The results of the assessment are enhanced by a "game-like" simulation of the spread of the virus through the school, providing a visual representation of how students and staff might be affected by an influenza virus. This preparedness exercise has many potential benefits for schools, such as providing knowledge to mitigate the impact of the flu, keeping students and staff healthy, building social capital by implementing programs directly related to the safety of the students, and reinforcing policy and preventive health training which reduces disease transmission. The simulation applied for this program can model the relevant geographic areas with all the relevant features (schools, hospitals, railways, airports, lakes, rivers, and business districts) to create an artificial virtual community. These virtual geographies can be customized to mimic real geographies from outbreaks to pandemics.

Keywords: Influenza, Preparedness, Simulation Modeling, Synthetic Environment, Analysis and Simulation

Developing a Prevention and Control Program with an Accompanying Simulation

In the last century, the United States has faced three distinct influenza pandemics: the 1918-1919 Spanish flu, the 1956-1958 Asian flu, and the 1968-1969 Hong Kong flu (US Department of Health and Human Services 2009). The 1918 pandemic was extremely deadly, killing approximately 675,000 Americans in just eight months,

---

* Note: The pandemic preparedness training for schools (PTS) project was developed in collaboration by the Purdue Homeland Security Institute (PHSI), the Synthetic Environment for Analysis and Simulation lab (SEAS), the Envision Center for Data Perceptualization at Purdue University, and members of the Department of Health and Kinesiology's Public Health program. Input from the Indiana Department of Education and the Tippecanoe County School Corporation also was invaluable in the development of this project.

and was ultimately responsible for an estimated 50 to 100 million deaths worldwide (Taubenberger and Morens 2006). According to Potter (2001), the Spanish flu is considered the "greatest medical holocaust in history" (p. 572). The Department of Health and Human Services (2009) indicated that Asian flu was responsible for nearly 70,000 deaths in the US and more than one million worldwide. A vaccine was developed in 1957 that helped limit the impact of the virus. The Hong Kong flu killed approximately one million people worldwide and more than 33,000 in the US (Department of Health and Human Services 2009). Improvements in detection mechanisms, vaccination development, and treatments are responsible for some of the differences in fatality rates between these pandemics. Distinct characteristics of each influenza strain also affect the spread and severity of the disease.

Though progress has been made in terms of detection, prevention, and treatment of influenza over the past century, the emergence of a novel strain of influenza could still be extremely unpredictable. Projections about the nature of future pandemics include estimates of 79,000 to 207,000 deaths in the US, with a projected economic burden anywhere from $71 to $166 billion (Haber et al. 2007). Which segments of the population will be most affected (in terms of age group), specific symptoms, and the geographic spread of an influenza virus cannot be predicted with great certainty until the virus has already emerged (Brundage 2006; Taubenberger and Morens 2006). Uncertainty about the specifics of a potential pandemic should not be viewed as a reason to forego planning. In fact, the opposite is true: Because there is such a high degree of uncertainty, this calls for considering and preparing for a variety of situations.

Seasonal influenza infects approximately 5 to 20% of the US population, and is responsible for 30,000 to 40,000 deaths annually, according to the Centers for Disease Control and Prevention (2009a,b). On average, according to the CDC, more than 200,000 individuals a year are admitted to the hospital for complications related to influenza in the United States. In addition, Benson and Marano (1998) estimated that seasonal flu is responsible for 200 million days of diminished productivity, 100 million days of bed disability, and 75 million days of work absence in the US alone. The author also noted that the total economic burden related to seasonal influenza is estimated to be more than $87 billion.

As a respiratory illness, the flu is primarily spread through aerosol droplets (expelled during a cough or sneeze), and by transmission of those droplets by the hand to the mouth or nose (Collignon and Carnie 2006). Heymann (2004) noted that because seasonal influenza has the most severe impact on the very old and very young, these tend to be the age groups that are a priority for receipt of a vaccination. Further, he noted that pandemic influenza differs because the infection rate among different age groups depends on the particular strain of influenza.

In the spring of 2009, McNeil (2009) noted the emergence of a unique strain of influenza type A/H1N1 (often referred to as swine flu) captured the attention of the world. The author reported that the initial outbreak occurred in Mexico and quickly spread to the US, though some experts suspect that the first human case may have occurred in Asia. According to Masterson (2009), the virus contains genetic material from the human influenza virus (which peaks in the US annually in the late fall and winter months), a North American avian virus, and a virus that occurs in pigs. It is likely that this novel strain was circulating among humans, unrecognized as a novel influenza, since late 2008 (Knox 2009). The possibility of a genetic link between the influenza strain that caused the 1918-1919 pandemic and the 2009 H1N1 influenza was initially a source of great concern. Fortunately, the fatality rates associated with the 2009 H1N1 influenza did not approach those recorded in 1918-1919. The decreases in fatality rates can be attributed not only to differences in the disease itself, but also to the prevention, control, and treatment options that have developed over the last century.

According to the CDC vaccination recommendation (Centers for Disease Control and Prevention 2009c), some adults over 60 may have had immunity to the 2009 H1N1 virus, due to exposure to a similar strain earlier in their lifetime. Those under 60, however, have likely never been exposed to that particular virus and therefore, had no immunity. World Health Organization (WHO) *Disease Outbreak News* (2009) noted that though fatalities from the novel A/H1N1 influenza remained relatively low worldwide, the lack of immunity in the world's population led to a large number of cases. By mid-October of 2009, there were more than 400,000 laboratory-confirmed cases and more than 5,000 deaths worldwide attributed to 2009 H1N1. However, these numbers are vastly lower than the actual number of cases and deaths, as many countries (including the US) ceased to conduct laboratory testing on suspected cases as the frequency increased exponentially. For example, according to the CDC and Prevention (2009a), between May and June of 2009, the US alone experienced more than one million cases of the novel influenza (this estimate includes those who became ill, but did not seek medical treatment). A report issued by the President's Council of Advisors on Science and Technology (2009) estimated that between 20 and 40% of the US population would ultimately contract the 2009 H1N1 influenza during the fall of 2009 and winter of 2010. By mid-November of 2009, an estimated 22 million Americans had been infected with the 2009 H1N1 influenza virus (World Health Organization: Disease Outbreak News 2009).

The costs associated with influenza are not merely the effects on the health of those infected. There are numerous social and economic costs associated with influenza. The recognition of these costs has led to an emphasis on prevention and control measures for influenza, including improvements in personal hygiene, increased social distancing, and the development and distribution of vaccinations (Mossad 2009). Focusing prevention and control efforts on elementary school-aged children as a method for decreasing transmission of influenza throughout an entire community is warranted. Although children comprise approximately 28% of the population, they are responsible for 46 to 47% of all infections, as represented through modeling work completed by Cauchemez et al. (2008). It has been estimated that between 70 and 164 million school days are lost annually due to absenteeism from communicable illnesses (Vessy et al. 2007). The effectiveness of alcohol-free hand sanitizer availability, and hand washing programs on decreasing both illness rates and illness-related absences among elementary students also has been measured and shown in multiple studies (Dyer, Shinder, and Shinder 2000; Guinan, McGuckin, and Ali 2002; Luby et al. 2005; Rabie and Curtis 2006).

The purpose of the pandemic preparedness training for schools (PTS) project was to develop a tool to assist schools in recognizing how their current behaviors and physical environment might affect the health of their students and staff, to develop a simulation of disease transmission, and to provide specific recommendations for improvements in order to decrease influenza transmission.

Method

Evaluation Instrument

An extensive literature review was conducted in order to develop an evaluation tool. By creating a program based in the scientific literature available regarding influenza transmission and prevention, the goal of PTS was to provide proven, efficient, and specific recommendations to schools in order to decrease morbidity rates among staff, teachers, and students. The evaluation tool was designed to assess the environment and behaviors of staff and students at participating schools. In its final form, the evaluation consists of six major topic areas: student behaviors, teacher behaviors, custodial staff behaviors, bathroom environment, cleaning supplies availability, and reminders for hand washing.

Procedures

Ways to provide feedback to the participating schools (based upon their responses to the evaluation questions) were developed and tested with review from subject-area experts. In addition to providing specific recommendations on procedures for improving the physical environment and behaviors that are related to flu transmission, it was determined that providing a computer simulation or model would illustrate the spread of the influenza virus for participants and increase their understanding of the risks of inaction. Ultimately, the results of the evaluation (as represented by the computer simulation of influenza spreading throughout the school) could be used to inform school policy in a variety of areas, from the decision to close a school to the cleaning practices of the janitorial staff.

Development of Simulation Model

Synthetic environment for analysis and simulation (SEAS) platform was used to develop the simulation model. SEAS is an agent-based modeling environment that mimics the dynamics of the real world (Anderson, Chaturvedi, and Cibulskis 2007; Chaturvedi, Mehta, and Drnevich 2004). Developed with the support of the National Science Foundation, Department of Defense, Indiana Department of Homeland Security, Indiana State Department of Health, and Fortune 500 companies, SEAS provides a test bed for decision makers to formulate, test, and analyze alternative courses of action under different bioterrorism scenarios (Chaturvedi et al. 2007; Drnevich et al. 2009).

The modeling life cycle for SEAS begins with a process of requirements gathering and analysis, which results in a definition of the system and its objectives. SEAS simulation supports "human-in-the-loop" capabilities so that analysts and/ or decision makers can interact with the artificial agents in any of the following three ways:

1. Multiple human players, synchronous mode: Sometimes called war-gaming, teams of human players convene in a single location to compete and/or cooperate with one another to meet specified performance goals within specified scenarios.
2. Multiple human players, asynchronous mode: Similar to synchronous, except human players are geographically distributed and the game is played remotely via the Web, often over extended time periods compared to synchronous mode.
3. Single human player, standalone mode: This is similar to the various computer games such as SimCity and its descendants wherein there is only one human player. Roles played by other human players in either of the above modes also must be simulated in addition to the artificial agents.

The model formulation and representation process converts the requirements specification into a conceptual model, the representation of which should be intelligible to both end users and analysts. Conceptual models for conventional operations research/management science models exist in many forms, including structured modeling (Geoffrion 1987), meta-models influence diagrams (Basu and Blanning 1998), system dynamics (Forrester 1961), and graph grammars (Jones 1995). Although these techniques are powerful for depicting the structure of mathematical models in terms of entities, attributes, and relationships, they are less effective in capturing the semantics of agents' behaviors that tend to be rule-based rather than mathematically driven.

The development process converts the conceptual models into actual software code to implement the model phase of the life cycle. This is done using any number of general-purpose programming languages. SEAS was developed to scale easily to support multiple classes of agents with large numbers of instances of each (typically from a few to a million) in a Web-based environment. SEAS societies are implemented in JavaSpace, a descendant of the Linda system developed at Yale University (Carriero and Gelernter 1987).

Description of the Environment

An agent is able to represent the activity of a human through a combination of learned variables and interactions. Research has shown that these agents act as the vertices of a societal network, and that their interactions comprise the edges of the network (Kelton et al. 2000; Wasserman and Faust 1994). Like living beings, each agent has different interactions and experiences, and thus acts differently when faced with a situation. While these *evolving* differences are essential for a useful simulation, certain *predefined* traits are necessary. As an example, though all students in a class may be exposed to a flu virus, certain members will be more susceptible, and case severity will differ among those who contract the illness. For this reason, parameters must be assigned that define the susceptibility of an agent to a given pathogen. The high number of relevant attributes for each agent serves to differentiate each agent from its peers. However, as the artificial agents grow in complexity, they also must grow in number, in order to maintain the characteristics of the society they seek to describe. Once the society has been sufficiently populated, the artificial agents begin to interact with and learn from each other, forming an environment well suited for analysis and interaction by human agents. A more complete description of artificial agent parameters follows.

The simulation created was originally designed to model geographic areas to include key features such as schools, hospitals, railways, airports, lakes, rivers, business districts, and the population in order to create virtual communities. These virtual geographies can be customized to represent any real geography, such as a county within the state of Indiana, as was the case with PTS. The virtual geography may be further divided into high population density residential areas, low population density residential areas, commercial areas, as well as uninhabitable areas. There can be various geographic levels to represent different communities as needed for the scenario (from international, national, state, district, county, city, to city-block levels).

Artificial Agent Definition

Artificial agents inhabit a virtual community. An artificial agent is able to represent the activity of a human through a combination of learned behaviors and interactions. Research has shown that these artificial agents and their interactions with one another create an emergent social network (Wasserman and Faust 1994). Like human beings, each artificial agent has different interactions and experiences, and thus acts differently when faced with a situation. While these evolving differences are essential for a useful simulation, certain predefined traits also are necessary. As an example, though all students in a class may be exposed to a flu virus, certain members will be more susceptible, and case severity will differ among those who contract the illness. For this reason, parameters must be assigned that define the susceptibility of an artificial agent to a given pathogen. The high number of relevant attributes for each artificial agent serves to differentiate each artificial agent from its peers. However, as the artificial agents grow in complexity, they also must grow in number, in order to maintain the characteristics of the community or society they seek to describe. Once the virtual community or society has been sufficiently populated, the artificial agents begin to interact with and learn from each other, forming an environment well suited for analysis. Computational models of artificial agents' attributes (such as age, gender, health status, location, infection susceptibility, and state of well-being), and behaviors (like mobility and social networking) were created.

While human beings can engage in any number of activities, the encoding of each would be impractical for the simulation. As such, we employ a carefully selected behavior set that fully satisfies the requirements for learning and understanding. Below is a partial list of behaviors in which each agent can engage, and a list of some that are not allowed by the simulation:

Can:

■ Move from one location to another
■ Interact with other agents → in some cases becoming infected, in others not
■ Discuss with other agents → serves to pass information throughout the society
■ Consume resources
■ Follow simple instructions

Cannot:

■ Heal themselves if infected by a pathogen

Characteristics

In addition to these behaviors, each agent is endowed with certain characteristics that help to differentiate the population. These attributes help to model the variability in human response to a situation. As an example, an obedient individual may be more likely to follow a teacher's instruction. The following is a partial list of characteristics that serve to differentiate one artificial agent from another:

■ Age
■ Sex
■ Income
■ Location
■ Education
■ Health

Problem-Solving Parameters

When faced with a decision, humans consider numerous variables. Using a combination of intuition, experience, and logic, one selects the alternative that leads to a certain goal; usually happiness (Law and Kelton 2000; Newell and Simon 1972). While different decisions vary in magnitude, the underlying cognitive model remains relatively constant. As such, while different physical or psychological needs take precedence in different situations, the human problem-solving process can be modeled by considering each need in a hierarchical manner. To illustrate, scholarship has shown that, when presented with a threatening environment, the primary focus of a living being shifts to ensuring its own survival (Maslow 1968). The list that follows partially describes the variables that an artificial agent considers before making a decision:

- Security
- Basic necessities
- Information level
- Health
- Mobility and freedom
- Financial capability

The possible values for each of these variables are from minus three to plus three, in increments of one. Each agent desires a higher value for the parameters, as a higher value reflects a superior condition for that variable.

Computational Epidemiology

The epidemiological model consists of two components: (a) emergent social networks based on the locality, mobility, and the interactions of the artificial agent, and (b) the epidemiology of influenza that spreads through the social network (Rvachev and Longini 1985). The artificial population is segregated into different groups representing the different stages of the disease: susceptible, exposed, infected, recovered, and deceased. The susceptible population includes those that have no natural or acquired immunity and can therefore contract the disease. In modeling the 2009 H1N1 influenza, all elementary school-aged children were classified as susceptible to the illness, at the outset of the simulation. The exposed group consists of the population that has encountered the pathogen, but is not showing any signs or symptoms yet. The infected population includes all the individuals who have become infected with the disease to the extent that they are showing symptoms. Both exposed and infected individuals are capable of infecting others, for this simulation. The recovered population cannot become infected with the disease either by consequence of cure, or acquired or natural immunity. Those unable to recover from the disease will eventually fall in the deceased group of

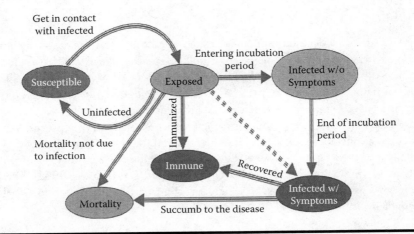

Figure 6.1 An example of the model that represents the propagation of a pathogen.

the population. The propagation of the disease may be affected via artificial agent isolation or artificial agent behavior. The model that describes the propagation of a pathogen can be seen in Figure 6.1.

To demonstrate the manner in which an agent evaluates these criteria, we elaborate on the security variable. The decision an agent makes depends in part on the risk level of that particular agent. The risk level of an agent varies over time, and is classified according to four levels:

- **None:** The agent is immune, is not susceptible to infection, or there is no carrier in the region
- **Low:** A low-risk level is associated with healthy adults
- **Medium:** Consists of unhealthy adults, healthy children, or healthy elderly
- **High:** An unhealthy child or an unhealthy elderly citizen

Although the agents seek to minimize their exposure to a pathogen, circumstances prevent everyone from doing so successfully. As such, the simulation must repeatedly update the health status of each agent. The health of an agent depends on several criteria, including epidemic attributes, such as population density and pathogen-specific capabilities. These variables interact with agent-level attributes to form a probability of infection. Some of the interacting variables are listed below:

- Resistance level of an agent
- Risk level of an agent
- Population density of the entire population of a region
- Population density of the infected population of a region

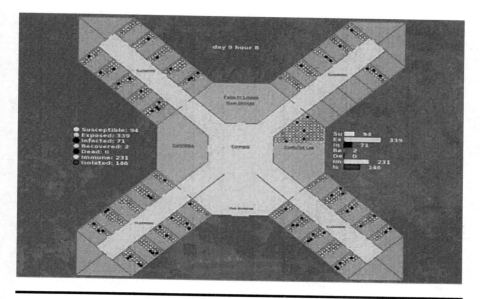

Figure 6.2 Represents a static example of an actual simulation according to the parameters described earlier.

Results and Discussion

The simulation applied modeled the relevant geographic areas with all the relevant features to create an artificial virtual community for participating schools. Virtual geographies were customized to mimic real geographies. The epidemiological model utilized consists of two components: the emergent social network based on the locality, mobility, and the interactions of the artificial agent and the epidemiology of influenza that spread through a social network (Rvachev and Longini 1985). The propagation of the disease may be affected via artificial agent isolation or artificial agent behavior.

The virtual community created in the simulation will have a virtual population represented by artificial agents. An artificial agent is able to represent the activity of a human through a combination of learned variables and interactions. Related research has shown that these artificial agents and their interactions with one another create an emergent social network (Wasserman and Faust 1994). Like living beings, each artificial agent has different interactions and experiences, and thus acts differently when faced with a situation. Computational models of artificial agents' attributes (e.g., age, gender, health status, location, infection susceptibility, and state of well-being) and behaviors (e.g., mobility and social networking) were created, in this instance, to reinforce policy and preventive health training to reduce disease transmission.

While the safety of the artificial agents takes highest precedence, school administration and government officials must consider the overall spirit of the population when making decisions. To illustrate, although safety may be maximized by closing the school in every instance of potential outbreak (Kaplan, Craft, and Wein 2002), such restrictive measures may not be tolerated by the population. To enhance the level of learning they can achieve through the simulation, the human agents must consider the impact on public sentiment that each of their decisions may have. As in real life, each artificial agent determines his or her happiness level using a combination of variables to include in this project health status, perceived security, information level, current health, basic necessities and whether or not they are being met, and freedom of mobility so as not to unjustly constrain civil liberties. The public sentiment of the entire population is computed based on the mean of the total agent happiness level.

The simulation environment for this preparedness exercise was customized. A virtual geography was created to mimic a simple school layout with rooms such as cafeteria and classrooms (see Figure 6.2). With a small amount of information about a school, specifically the layout and population size, a simulation could be customized to that specific school.

Artificial agents representing students and teachers in the school were created and populated within this virtual geography. Each agent was able to move between rooms and be in contact with other agents with a certain probability. Once an agent is in contact with an infected agent, there is a probability that he or she will be exposed to the disease. Those agents who were exposed then had a certain probability of becoming an infected agent and infecting others before recovering.

We implemented various intervention strategies, such as teachers being able to recognize students with flu symptoms and removing them from the classroom; and requiring students to wash their hands after recess, after using the restroom, and before eating. The impact of those interventions on the disease propagation within the school is emergent. Figure 6.3 shows the results of comparing those intervention scenarios with the baseline scenario where no intervention was taken.

By illustrating the decrease in the number of agents exposed and infected as a result of two fairly simple interventions (recognizing and removing sick students from the classroom, and requiring thorough and frequent hand washing) this simulation has the potential to affect decision making and preparedness policy at the school and school district level. For example, the effect of teacher or staff recognition (and subsequent removal from the classroom) of symptomatic students has clear implications for necessary training and education. First, staff must be trained to recognize the early symptoms of influenza in students. Second, they must be encouraged to utilize these recognition skills and be on alert for symptomatic students. Last, the school would have to provide an area for the sick students to remain until they could go home to recover.

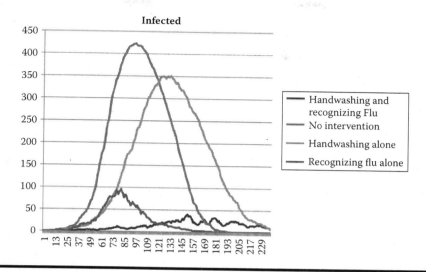

Figure 6.3 Graph showing when, compared to a no-intervention scenario, the number of infected agents reduced if hand washing and other intervention strategies were practiced in school.

Likewise, the positive effect of thorough and frequent hand washing also was evident. In order for this simple intervention to be successful, students and staff alike need to be educated on what constitutes "thorough and frequent" hand washing. The physical environment of the school must support this behavior as well: sinks, hand soap, and paper towels (preferably) should be available in as many locations as possible, and sanitizer pumps installed in areas where soap and water cannot be reached. As a pilot project, just the two interventions previously discussed were included in the simulation. Dietz et al. (2010) also showed that this approach can provide financial incentives for developing and implementing robust policies. Further research and development could estimate the likelihood of effectiveness of other interventions, allowing greater complexity for the simulation. Model simulations for outbreaks to pandemics related to disease transmission could be an efficacious method to mitigate the impact of the disease, keep the population healthy, build social capital by implementing programs directly related to human safety, reinforce policy, and provide preventive health training that reduces disease transmission.

References

Anderson, J., Chaturvedi, A., and M. Cibulskis. 2007. Simulation tools for developing policies for complex systems: Modeling the health and safety of refugee communities. *Healthcare Management Science* 10: 331-339.

Basu, A. and R. W. Blanning. 1998. The analysis of assumptions in model bases using metagraphs. *Management Science* 44: 982-995.

Benson V. and M. Marano. 1998. Current estimates from the National Health Interview Survey, 1995. *Vital Health and Health Statistics (National Center for Health Statistics; Hyattsville, MD)* 199:1-428.

Brundage, J. F. 2006. Cases and deaths during influenza pandemics in the United States. *American Journal of Preventive Medicine* 3:, 252-256.

Carriero, N. and D. Gelernter. 1987. How to write parallel programs: A guide to the perplexed. *ACM Computing Surveys* 21: 323-357.

Cauchemez, S., Valleron, A. J., Boelle, P. Y., Flahault, A., and N. M. Ferguson. 2008. Estimating the impact of school closure on influenza transmission from sentinel data. *Nature* 452: 750-755.

Centers for Disease Control and Prevention. 2009a. *Influenza: The disease.* http://www.cdc.gov/flu/about/disease/index.htm (accessed January 15, 2011).

Centers for Disease Control and Prevention. 2009b. *Seasonal influenza-associated hospitalizations in the United States.* http://www.cdc.gov/flu/about/qa/hospital.htm (accessed January 15, 2011).

Centers for Disease Control and Prevention. 2009c. *Vaccination recommendations.* http://www.cdc.gov/h1n1flu/vaccination/vaccine_safety_qa.htm (accessed January 15, 2011).

Chaturvedi, A., Mehta, S., and P. Drnevich. 2004. Computational and live experimentation in bio-terrorism response. In *Dynamic data driven applications systems,* ed. F. Darema, 1-16. Boston, MA: Kluwer Publications.

Chaturvedi, A., Mellema, A., Hsieh, C., Bhatt, T., Cheng, M., Dietz, E., and S. Stearns. 2007. Decision support for security: A mixed reality approach to bio-terror preparedness and response. In *Handbook on decision support systems,* ed. F. Burstein and C. Holsapple, 463-482. New York: Springer-Verlag.

Collignon, P. J. and J. A. Carnie. 2006. Infection control and pandemic influenza. *Medical Journal of Australia* 185: S54-S57.

Dietz, J. E., Drifmeyer, J., Leonard, K., Hsieh, C., Dunlop, S., Burr, J., Chaturvedi, A. and D. R. Black. 2010. *Pandemic preparedness training for schools.* Computer Games, Multimedia and Allied Technology, Singapore (pp. 362-371).

Drnevich, P., Chaturvedi, A., Mehta, S., and R. Ramanujam. 2009. Affiliation or situation: What drives strategic decision making in crisis response? *Journal of Managerial Issues* 18: 216-231.

Dyer, D. L., Shinder, A., and F. Shinder. 2000. Alcohol-free instant hand sanitizer reduces elementary school illness absenteeism. *Clinical Research and Methods* 32: 633-638.

Forrester, J. W. 1961. *Industrial dynamics.* Waltham, MA: Pegasus Communications.

Geoffrion, A. M. 1987. Introduction to structured modeling. *Management Science* 33: 547-588.

Guinan, M., McGuckin, M., and Y. Ali. 2002. The effect of a comprehensive handwashing program on absenteeism in elementary schools. *American Journal of Infection Control* 30: 217-220.

Haber, M. J., Shay, D. K., Davis, X. M., Patel, R., Jin, X., Weintrabuc, E., Orenstein, E., and W. W. Thompson. 2007. Effectiveness of interventions to reduce contact rates during a simulated influenza pandemic. *Emerging Infectious Diseases* 13: 581-589.

Heymann, D.L., ed. 2004. *Control of communicable diseases manual.* Washington, DC: American Public Health Association.

Jones, C. V. 1995. Developments in graph-based modeling for decision support. *Decision Support Systems* 13: 61-74.

Kaplan, E. H., Craft, D. L., and L. M. Wein. 2002. Emergency response to a smallpox attack: The case for mass vaccination. *Proceedings of the National Academy of Sciences* 6: 10935-10940.

Kelton, W. D., Sadowski, R. P., Sadowski, D. A., and D. Kelton. 2000. *Simulation with arena with CD-ROM*. 2nd ed. New York: McGraw-Hill Science/Engineering/Math.

Knox, R. 2009. *Inside the new flu virus*. http://www.npr.org/templates/story/story. php?storyId=103858702 (accessed January 15, 2011).

Law, A. and W. Kelton. 2000. *Simulation modeling and analysis*. New York: McGraw Hill.

Luby, S. P., Agboatwalla, M., Feikin, D. R., Billhimer, W., Altaf., A., and R. M. Hoekstra. 2005. Effect of handwashing on child health: A randomized controlled trial. *Lancet* 366: 225-233.

Maslow, A. H. 1968. *The farther reaches of human nature*. New York: Viking Press.

Masterson, K. 2009. *What is swine flu, or the new H1N1 virus?* http://www.npr.org/templates/story/story.php?storyId=112683634 (accessed January 15, 2011).

McNeil, Jr., D. G. 2009. In new theory, swine flu started in Asia, not Mexico, *New York Times*, June 23, 2009. http://www.nytimes.com/2009/06/24/health/24flu.html?_r=1 (accessed January 15, 2011).

Mossad, S.F. 2009. The resurgence of swine-origin influenza A. *Cleveland Clinic Journal of Medicine* 76: 337-343.

Newell, A. and H. Simon. 1972. *Human problem solving*. New York: Prentice Hall.

Potter, C.W. 2001. A history of influenza. *Journal of Applied Microbiology* 91: 572-579.

President's Council of Advisors on Science and Technology (PCAST). 2009. http://www. whitehouse.gov/the_press_office/Presidents-Council-of-Advisors-on-Science-and-Technology-PCAST-releases-report-assessing-H1N1-preparations/ (accessed January 15, 2011).

Rabie, T. and V. Curtis. 2006. Handwashing and risk of respiratory infections: A quantitative systematic review. *Tropical Medicine and International Health* 11: 258-267.

Rvachev, L. A. and I. M. Longini.1985. A mathematical model for the global spread of influenza. *Mathematical Biosciences* 75: 3-22.

Taubenberger, J. K. and D. M. Morens. 2006. 1918 influenza: The mother of all pandemics. *Emerging Infectious Diseases* 12: 13-22.

Taubenberger, J. K. Morens, D. M., and A. S. Fauci. 2007. The next influenza pandemic: Can it be predicted? *Journal of the American Medical Association* 297: 2025-2027.

US Department of Health and Human Services. 2009. Flu.gov: Pandemics and pandemic threats since 1900. http://www.pandemicflu.gov/general/historicaloverview.html (accessed January 15, 2011).

Vessey, J. A., Sherwood, J. J., Warner, D., and D. Clark. 2007. Comparing handwashing to hand sanitizers in reducing elementary school students' absenteeism. *Pediatric Nursing* 33: 368-372.

Wasserman, S. and K. Faust. 1994. *Social network analysis*. Cambridge: Cambridge University Press.

World Health Organization: Disease Outbreak News. 2009. *Pandemic (H1N1) 2009*. http:// www.who.int/csr/disease/swineflu/en/index.html (accessed January 15, 2011).

Chapter 7

Engaging Volunteer Organizations to Prepare for Pandemics

Steven Cain, Virginia Morgan, and Abby Lillpop

Contents

Abstract

Disaster preparedness, response, and recovery require large numbers of dedicated, knowledgeable, and skilled personnel. The term "volunteer" is defined and roles and types of volunteer groups are delineated. The Federal Emergency Management Agency national response framework recognizes volunteers and their critical role in all functions of a disaster: preparedness, response, relief, recovery, and mitigation. This chapter outlines the organizational and training needs of volunteer groups to effectively reduce the impact of major disasters. It also recognizes the growth of and the importance of the national voluntary organizations active in disaster (National VOAD) movement. A community collaborative effort is proposed for disaster preparedness, response, and recovery. Volunteer agencies need to be included in exercises as planners, role players, and be on the analysis team. Volunteers can contribute and play larger roles. Volunteer groups promote efficiency and reduce duplication of efforts in training and response. An examination of two key existing groups (the American Red Cross and the Salvation Army) is also provided. Free online training and evaluation is available for volunteers, and certification tests also can be taken online or administered locally. Every trained and educated person is needed during a pandemic and volunteer agencies play a critical and often unrecognized role.

Keywords: Disaster Preparedness, Disaster Recovery, Disaster Volunteers, Volunteerism, Community Organizations

Engaging Volunteer Organizations to Prepare for a Pandemic

Most of the authors' experiences are with volunteer workers and weather-related or geological disasters, such as floods and earthquakes. This chapter will show the commonalities among disasters because of reliance on volunteers and the benefits that they provided. According to the US Census Bureau (2010), from July 1, 2010 to July 1, 2011, the world's population has grown by almost 76 million people and the US population is now nearly 312 million people. Over-population is especially a concern in specific locations, such as localities where there are not enough physicians for the population, because it is a complicating factor for many other public health issues related to morbidity and mortality (Audibert 2006). According to the US Department of Health and Human Services (2009), there is a possibility of a pandemic having the devastating impact of 50 Hurricane Katrinas, especially in the absence of "herd immunity," rapid transmission of a virus, high incidence rates, high case fatality rates (cf. Black, Smock, and Ardaugh 2011). Increases in population make prevention, protection, and control a major challenge, which will increase as the population increases.

Increased population increases the threat of pandemics because more people are susceptible. Enlisting the support of trained and knowledgeable volunteers is necessary because demand for services outweighs supply. It is impossible for federal, state, and local emergency responders to meet all the demands of a pandemic, even with the assistance from agencies such as private insurance, other companies, and volunteer agencies. Unaffiliated volunteers can be indistinguishable from the employed professionals assigned and paid by federal, state, and local first responders. Organized volunteers are often unrecognized for their gallant efforts. Volunteers contribute in many ways, including working to reduce duplication and encourage coordination of services. Volunteers make important and critical differences.

Definition of Volunteers

A volunteer is an individual who, beyond the confines of paid employment and normal responsibilities, contributes time and service to assist in the accomplishment of a mission (Federal Emergency Management Association 2010a). People volunteer for as many reasons as there are people. But for study, FEMA puts volunteers into four categories: professional, unskilled, spontaneous, and affiliated.

- Professional. These are licensed or have a special skill. They can include medical, technical, as well as clergy and accountants.
- Unskilled. In this chapter, they are volunteers who do not have skills immediately useful to an emergency manager or health official. But they do have time and can be trained.
- Spontaneous. They show up at or immediately after the disaster. They may or may not have skills immediately helpful for disaster response or recovery. According to FEMA, "Channeling spontaneous volunteers—especially if they present in large numbers as they did in New York City following September 11—presents special management challenges."
- Affiliated. Volunteers who represent and are acknowledged by an agency or organizations recognized for disaster work are affiliated. They usually are ready to contribute immediately to the response or recovery efforts.

Because volunteers will be as diverse as the population, any analyses of volunteer efforts will involve a matrix of attributes. Volunteers can include:

- Trained volunteers to untrained volunteers
- Affiliated volunteers to unaffiliated volunteers
- Equipped volunteers to unequipped volunteers

- National volunteers to local volunteers
- Funded volunteers to unfunded volunteers

One could read this list and assume that the groups closest to the bullet points have higher value than those to the right. This assumption may have validity. However, during an epidemic, volunteers may be welcomed under any circumstance. Therefore, planners and community leaders should be prepared to work with anyone who volunteers. That is not to say that volunteers who show up and immediately take up limited resources, such as food, water, and management time, are not a problem. Unexpected volunteers may be a resource if a community has a plan for unsolicited volunteers. In the United States, volunteer agencies play and have a role in disasters. The American Red Cross and Salvation Army, for example, have well-defined roles compared to those of the unexpected volunteers. Volunteers, from those marshaled by the national volunteer organizations to individuals who will volunteer at the office, will act in a great range of efforts, including staying informed and leading a team to make that office more pandemic-resistant.

12 ROLES OF VOLUNTEERS

1. Develop plans, train, and exercise
2. Alleviate suffering
3. Coordinate human services
4. Provide case management
5. Manage donations
6. Educate
7. Advocate
8. Provide spiritual care
9. Provide mass care
10. Provide mental healthcare
11. Inform and refer
12. Organize recovery groups

Assumptions

The first assumption based on the authors' cumulative experiences over more than three decades is that US disaster preparedness is better than at any other time in history, but improvements must be ongoing. The second assumption is that pandemics will affect 30 to 40% of the population, absenteeism percentages will be equivalent, and they will occur in waves over several months (US Department of Health and Human Services 2006). A related assumption is that absenteeism will affect volunteer agencies as well as private, public, and government-operated businesses. Volunteers will be in demand and unsolicited volunteers will be accepted, trained, and integrated into the disaster process from beginning to end.

The third assumption is that a pandemic, defined as observed cases being greater than expected cases (endemic state) and engulfing a large geographic region such as the United States, a continent, or the world, is catastrophic (Black, Smock and Ardaugh 2011). The large geographic area, susceptibility, and quickness of transmission of disease add to the complexity of a pandemic. The complexities are exacerbated by intercontinental travel, migration, diagnostic uncertainties and inaccuracies, logistics and location of supply centers, adequate supplies, and availability of curative medicines (Cain 2005). In a world of multiple structures of government and operations of world organizations, and misinformation or misreporting by communication sources, many will cling to the belief that a global response to a pandemic will provide prevention, protection, and control for their communities and families. Experience indicates the following truisms: All disasters are local and the larger the disaster, the more local is the response and not all will receive aid as quickly as it is needed.

Federal and worldwide resources will quickly deplete in a pandemic (Cain 2005). Examples of recent disasters pale in comparison to the potential impact of a worldwide pandemic. Hurricane Ike, which made landfall in September of 2008, provides a heuristic example of an epidemic in the US. While dozens of volunteer agencies helped in the coastal and inland areas, there were insufficient numbers of affiliated volunteers to help with the needs of flood and storm victims across the South and Midwest that suffered aftermath effects of Ike (www.nvoad.org). In Indiana alone, 16 long-term recovery committees formed to provide recovery to the tens of thousands of flood and storm victims. While unaffiliated volunteer groups provided help, local volunteers responded when there were insufficient numbers of regional and national volunteer groups because of other disasters across the nation in 2008 and 2009. Even if these other disasters had not occurred, there may not have been enough help to provide the aid necessary. The major response to Hurricane Ike was local, while recovery was enhanced by national and even international assistance from volunteer agencies.

TYPES OF VOLUNTEER GROUPS

- Community and civic organizations
- Faith-based organizations
- Voluntary organizations
- Social service agencies
- Local businesses and unions
- Emergency management
- Educational institutions
- Governmental agencies
- Medical organizations
- General public feeling compelled to help their neighbors

Exotic Newcastle Disease (END) is another example of a disease threat. END may provide more proof that a community will be on its own. END is a fatal, contagious virus that affects all species of birds. While it does not directly affect humans, it is a disease that was epidemic (Husband and Cain 2008). END occurred in California in 2003. It stressed the federal response system's ability to contain the disease. Yet it occurred in only a few states, including Arizona, California, and Nevada. What if it had been confirmed in 20, 30, or 50 states? State agencies would have been without total federal support and increasingly on their own (Husband and Cain 2008).

What do END and pandemic have in common? It is the amount of federal resources required to contain or reduce disease transmission. While methods used for bird transmission of END will be different than those for humans who contract the flu, it is the response capabilities that must be compared. The sobering conclusion is that the larger the geographic area, the more response and recovery will become a local responsibility because of competition for state, federal, and global resources. As with Hurricane Ike and END, a pandemic and epidemic will necessitate that states and communities provide the bulk of the recovery or perish. Mortality also would decrease volunteer efforts because of not being immune from infection and the prospect of death (Husband and Cain 2008).

A history-changing response and recovery will require volunteer agencies to identify, plan, and exercise for the next disaster. Planning at the local level would help to limit morbidity and mortality of a smaller area. Kevin Cox, CEO of Hope Crisis Response Network, said:

> "While no exercise would be adequate preparation for a pandemic, it is better to train and practice than not. A significant aspect of preparedness is including volunteer organizations in planning and inclusion in exercises, which has not always been the norm," (K. Cox, personal communication, July 6, 2011).

National Voluntary Organizations Active in Disasters (VOAD)

Much has happened to advance volunteer capabilities in the US. Volunteer organizations strive to increase preparedness and recovery and decrease duplication. One very important historical change in volunteer preparedness at the local, state, and national level is forming agency partnerships. According to the National Voluntary Organizations Active in Disaster (2010), VOAD was founded in 1970 in response to the challenges many disaster organizations experienced following Hurricane Camille. The National VOAD provides common ground for volunteer organizations. National VOAD provides training and a culture of sharing information that helps national volunteer agencies better understand their roles in disaster.

Prior to the founding of National VOAD, numerous organizations independently served disaster victims sometimes competing for the privilege. These included agencies in government and the private, nonprofit sectors. Consequently, haphazard help was provided as various organizations assisted in specific as well as countless ways. Unnecessary duplication of effort occurred while other needs were unmet. The number and variety of organizations frustrated people who wanted to volunteer. Furthermore, there was only limited access to volunteer training. Information about services available to victims during disasters was woefully inadequate. Likewise, communication among voluntary disaster agencies was limited and coordination of services was negligible (VOAD 2010).

The seven founding organizations of National VOAD committed to fostering communication, coordination, collaboration, and cooperation (also known as the 4 Cs) to effectively serve disaster victims. Today, National VOAD is a leader and voice for the nonprofit organizations and volunteers that work in all phases of disaster: preparedness, response, relief, recovery, and mitigation. National VOAD is the primary point of contact for voluntary organizations in the National Response Coordination Center (at FEMA headquarters) and is a signatory to the National Response Plan (National Voluntary Organizations Active in Disaster 2010).

Today, National VOAD is composed of members with varied skill sets that assist in all types of disasters. A volunteer can become familiar with the member organizations to understand his/her role in reducing duplication and increasing cooperation, and consider affiliating with an organization that best fits his/her volunteer goals. The National VOAD membership list is in flux. The list was developed for weather or geological disasters, but many of the functions likely exist for epidemic and pandemic morbidity disasters.

State VOAD and Local VOAD or Community Organizations Active in Disasters (COAD)

At state levels, VOAD and/or their members are organized to participate in planning, preparedness, and exercises for disasters including outbreaks, epidemics, and pandemics. In this chapter we use COAD instead of VOAD because both terms are used at a local level and we opt to use the one that looks at using the community as a whole, and not just voluntary organizations. At the local level, community organizations active in disasters (COADs) are as varied as the geography of the US. Active COADs enhance the local preparedness and potential response from volunteer agencies. The most important message of this chapter is if a local community does not have an active COAD, local volunteers should take steps immediately to form one.

Epidemic and outbreak preparedness for the volunteer community depends on the 4 Cs at the local level. To contact a VOAD in your state, visit the members section of the National VOAD website or contact your local or state emergency management agency or health department. Emergency management and health department involvement in COADs are vital to how well the volunteer agencies perform in an incident command system (ICS). For more on ICS, visit the FEMA website, www.fema.gov, and see Chapters 2 and 3.

Some response personnel may not understand the value that a COAD can offer to outbreak, epidemic, and pandemic preparedness. The value of a COAD is evident when put into perspective with the emergency support functions (ESF). Emergency managers or health department officials are typically assigned to address the responsibilities of each of the 15 ESFs, and find value in utilizing the support of local COADs as advocates for emergency management and public health preparedness. They enhance local communication and provide the backbone for ESF 6 (mass care), ESF 8 (public health and medical services), and ESF 14 (long-term recovery). Enhancement of volunteer agencies' roles will occur when organized in a way that allows them to plan, prepare, respond, and recover while fully engaged in the ICS. Usually, the COAD does not deploy in a disaster; it is the members that deploy, largely composed of the volunteer/not-for-profit community. If volunteers train in the ICS system and understand the ESF, then they can more easily work together with federal, state, and local responders. A volunteer will have the responder's attention if she/he can show how a COAD can advocate for disaster preparedness and enhance ESF 6 and ESF 14.

If all disasters are local, then local institutions will be vital to response and recovery. Those local institutions will include (a) government, law enforcement, and military organizations; (b) medical and hospital organizations; (c) faith-based organizations; (d) schools; (e) businesses; (f) civic and other organizations; and (g) individuals. Groups (a) through (e) will not necessarily be paid, but will fulfill important volunteer roles. It is important to note that though governmental and medical organizations will have paid functions, they, too, will provide a significant number of volunteers. Volunteers will be doctors, nurses, and trained individuals who will be first responders. Enhanced abilities would be anticipated, if volunteers are part of an organized and trained volunteer group. The Medical Reserve Corps (2010) will have a role in a disaster. According to the MRC website, the mission of the MRC is to engage volunteers to strengthen public health, emergency response, and community resiliency.

Federal Emergency Management Agency Administrator Craig Fugate understands the role of the volunteer community (Federal Emergency Management Agency 2010e). In August 2010, on the fifth anniversary of Hurricane Katrina, he said,

> "The bottom line is, FEMA is not the team, FEMA is only part of the team. I was reminded of this as I toured recovery projects across the Gulf Coast this week. Everywhere I went, whether it was a school in St. Bernard Parish, a hospital in New Orleans, or a firehouse in Bay St. Louis, Mississippi, I met people determined to rebuild not just their own lives, but their communities. Numerous nonprofit and faith organizations, individual volunteers, and survivors have and continue to play the most significant role in the region's recovery. I was struck by their strength and resiliency this week, as I am every time I visit the Gulf Coast."

Emergency Management Functions

It is important to understand how volunteers are central to the five main functions of emergency management and might be integrated to help with specific functions. The examples below are from the incident command system (Federal Emergency Management Agency 2010a). Mitigation is a primary prevention action that prevents or reduces the impact of a disaster. For example, insurance is a mitigation action that reduces the personal cost of a disaster. Prevention in this case refers to a primary prevention action to avoid a disaster. Primary prevention often equates to terror-type events and includes such examples as screening methods to detect bombs, diseased plants, or food products. Preparedness is a primary prevention action taken in anticipation of the event. For example, getting a flu shot is a preparedness action. Response is a secondary prevention action directly applied to the event. Response can start before the event, and can include actions such as stockpiling food for sheltering-in-place and door-to-door searches for victims of the pandemic who cannot care for themselves. Recovery is a secondary prevention action that starts shortly after the disaster. Recovery is a tertiary prevention attempt to return the situation to pre-event conditions and volunteers help with reconstruction of homes, transportation, locating loved ones, and finding keepsakes as well as pets.

The point is that these roles and responsibilities are unconfined to those of paid local, state, or federal agencies and employees. Volunteer agencies have been involved in mitigation and prevention activities, such as educating the public about proper hygiene and safe distancing practices in public and workplaces. Free information for volunteers at school, at work, or anywhere in the community is available at www.flu.gov. Online courses are available, too (Cain 2005; Husband and Cain 2008).

Preparedness Is Key

The United States has a great capacity to communicate and educate about personal responsibilities and prevention procedures to help individuals prepare for a disaster.

> Georg W. F. Hegel (Hegel 1902) said: "We learn from history that we do not learn from history." Maybe Hegel can be proven wrong. The larger the pandemic, hopefully, the more it will change history. It is necessary to learn from history and expand knowledge and act on lessons learned. Pandemics have the capability of affecting hundreds of millions of people and killing as many if not more. A worldwide pandemic will require the services of millions of volunteers who will apply aid, comfort sick, and help in the recovery process to reestablish normalcy.

In many state and federal exercises, the American Red Cross (2009), Salvation Army (2010), and volunteer organizations are invited to "exercise" their ability by delivering lunches to those involved in the exercise. Instead of participating as pretend victims or lunch providers for the response agencies in the exercises, volunteer agencies need to be included in exercises as planners, role players, and be on analyses teams.

Volunteer organizations may form, perform well, and grow while poorly prepared volunteer organizations often do not respond well and fail to flourish. Disaster history also demonstrates that countries with multiple public ways to communicate and a free government will likely have populations, including volunteers and survivors, who are informed about the proper methods to contain or reduce morbidity and mortality and what is involved in the recovery process.

Good communication enhances prevention methods. Communication will help the public build trust and confidence in the volunteer agencies, which will in turn affect the agencies' ability to help with recovery. Kathleen Sebelius, secretary of the US Department of Health and Human Services, emphasized that communities and faith-based organizations (which include volunteer organizations) can ensure information is communicated (US Department of Health and Human Services 2009). FEMA emphasizes whole-of-community-response planning. Its goal is to improve the nation's preparedness through more effective collaboration with all members of the community. This reflects a shift from a government-centric approach to the concept that communities are capable of providing self-help. These principles depend on a public that is viewed as a resource, not a liability;

engaging atypical partners and collaborators; and developing training and exercises that involve all types of partners. Entire community planning may mean response agencies need to obtain regulatory waivers and change policy; focus on outcome-related objectives, especially increasing the number of people who survive; recognize response is an outward event and recovery is an internal event; and develop pre-scripts.

Volunteers tend to know their communities well and are trusted leaders. As trusted leaders, volunteers can encourage reading accurate information in an effective and motivating manner. Vital to a historical change in response and recovery is a volunteer agency's abilities to identify, plan, and exercise. Volunteer agencies increase their preparedness by selecting leaders and teams who are informed about the various aspects of training. In turn, those teams can help others prepare by distributing appropriate information, or by filling volunteer jobs in programs led by the volunteer organization. For example, many faith-based organizations may provide care and sheltering and/or assistance for people with functional needs. FEMA's "Guidance on Planning for Integration of Functional Needs Support Services in General Population Shelters" defines functional needs as those required by individuals to maintain their independence in a general population. Children and adults requiring assistance with functional needs may have physical, sensory, mental health, and cognitive and/or intellectual disabilities affecting their ability to function independently without assistance. Others that may benefit from functional needs support services (FNSS) include late-term, expectant mothers, elders, and people needing specialized medical equipment. Examples of FNSS include modification to policies, practices, and procedures; durable medical equipment; consumable medical supplies; personal assistance services; and other goods and services as needed.

Mitigation and Prevention

Like preparedness, mitigation and prevention help reduce the impact of an outbreak, epidemic, or a pandemic. Volunteer agencies mitigate by circulating accurate information. Educated populations will likely experience a reduced pandemic impact. Volunteer agencies have already been involved in helping people understand the threat of pandemic and proper actions to reduce the impact (Cain 2005). Mitigation efforts also might include proper medical and life insurance. Volunteer agencies can mitigate by advocating proper community planning for a disaster, including plans to shelter not only the core population, but also people with functional needs.

Response

Media coverage of people helping people in the immediate aftermath of a disaster usually represents volunteer agencies in action. The "spotlight" is often on the American Red Cross and Salvation Army. They are key providers of mass care during and after a disaster. Victims, along with first responders, work cooperatively, often in church basements, to provide for the basic needs, such as warm meals and drinks. Shelters with trained volunteer operations are critical to mass care in major disasters. Trained and untrained volunteers are invaluable when government, state, and local resources are overwhelmed.

American Red Cross

Red Cross chapters are the backbone of local preparedness and recovery. Red Cross was a volunteer organization involved in saving lives during the influenza pandemic of 1918 (American Red Cross 2009). The Red Cross, a humanitarian organization led by volunteers and guided by its congressional charter and the fundamental principles of the International Red Cross, provides relief to victims of disasters and helps people prevent, prepare, and respond to emergencies. It organizes people wanting to help their neighbors down the street, across the country, and around the world. The American Red Cross remains active in pandemic preparedness across the nation.

Salvation Army

Federal, state, and local governments officially recognize the Salvation Army as a disaster relief and assistance organization (The Salvation Army 2010). The Salvation Army was involved in the development of the Federal Emergency Management Agency's national response framework and is recognized within this framework.

The Salvation Army provides relief services to communities impacted by natural and man-made disasters until they are no longer needed (The Salvation Army 2010). When initiating a disaster relief operation, the first aim is to meet the basic needs of those affected, survivors and first responders. The Salvation Army's primary goals are to offer medical, physical, spiritual, and emotional comfort.

In the response phase, the Salvation Army provides numerous disaster relief services. Each disaster creates its own unique circumstances and the Salvation Army's response varies depending on the location, the community's needs, and the magnitude of the disaster (The Salvation Army 2010). Emergency response services are activated on short notice according to an agreed-upon notification procedure coordinated with federal, state, and local governments. Typically, Salvation Army personnel will congregate at predetermined staging areas and enter the impacted area only once government first responders have provided clearance indicating it is safe and constructive to be on-site.

Recovery

It is important to understand that resources will be limited. Therefore, volunteer agencies identify a means to apply recovery aid equitably. A logical model for non-medical recovery might resemble an established sequence of aid delivery for disasters. Federal Emergency Management Agency individual assistance and sequence of delivery and voluntary organizations created the timeline together. Federal agencies and volunteer organizations have applied this document to floods and earthquakes. It may require modification for morbidity disasters. However, the principles of sequencing of delivery of services should help local, long-term recovery groups apply aid after the response phase, when immediate medical, emotional, and spiritual care are needed (Federal Emergency Management Agency 2010b).

Private means, such as insurance or personal resources, receive priority in the recovery process. The next level in the individual assistance sequence of delivery model is federal and state resources allocated for property damage. The final section acknowledges there is an "unmet need" population in a disaster. This group is made up of individuals who have greater needs than state or federal authorities can provide. For example, an individual may be without income after the disaster. When personal, state, and federal resources are inadequate, communities may consider ways to help individuals recover; thus, helping the community to recover. Recovery is not limited to individuals, but may involve holistic community recovery. Figure 7.1 provides a graphic of individual assistance during a disaster, when it will be available, and from what provider.

Volunteers may help rebuild community property that has an intrinsic value beyond the cost of the construction materials and labor. In the aftermath of a disaster, recovery may include emotional, spiritual, and physical support even for property damage not due to the disaster.

Emergency Support Functions (ESF)

Community volunteers should examine the FEMA's ESFs and ICS to understand community emergency and disaster issues. Learning these systems helps volunteers understand how to assist in response to federal and state disasters. ICS and the ESFs provide for local flexibility to assign resources according to community capabilities to support the response (Federal Emergency Management Agency 2010a). The Joint Field Office (JFO) will likely establish federal and state responses when a response is more collaborative. Responders will operate within an ESF. To learn more about ICS, JFOs, and ESFs, volunteers are encouraged to take free ICS courses. Two basic courses are ICS-100 and National Incident Management System (NIMS) 700. A few hours are required to complete the courses. Some tests can be administered in a local setting. Consult your local emergency manager about availability in your area.

Individual Assistance Sequence of Delivery

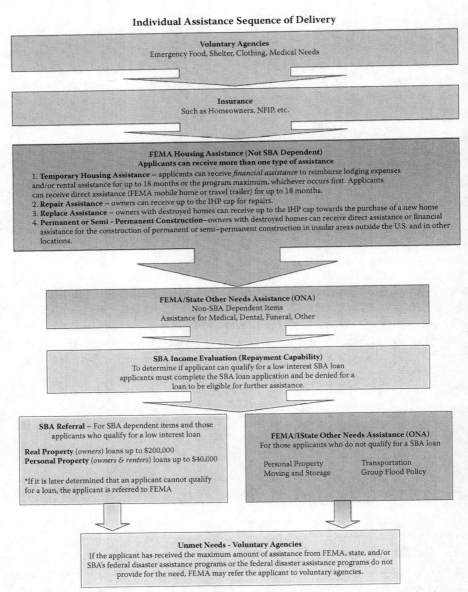

Voluntary Agencies
Emergency Food, Shelter, Clothing, Medical Needs

Insurance
Such as Homeowners, NFIP, etc.

FEMA Housing Assistance (Not SBA Dependent)
Applicants can receive more than one type of assistance
1. **Temporary Housing Assistance** – applicants can receive *financial assistance* to reimburse lodging expenses and/or rental assistance for up to 18 months or the program maximum, whichever occurs first. Applicants can receive direct assistance (FEMA mobile home or travel trailer) for up to 18 months.
2. **Repair Assistance** – owners can receive up to the IHP cap for repairs.
3. **Replace Assistance** – owners with destroyed homes can receive up to the IHP cap towards the purchase of a new home
4. **Permanent or Semi - Permanent Construction**–owners with destroyed homes can receive direct assistance or financial assistance for the construction of permanent or semi–permanent construction in insular areas outside the U.S. and in other locations.

FEMA/State Other Needs Assistance (ONA)
Non-SBA Dependent Items
Assistance for Medical, Dental, Funeral, Other

SBA Income Evaluation (Repayment Capability)
To determine if applicant can qualify for a low interest SBA loan applicants must complete the SBA loan application and be denied for a loan to be eligible for further assistance.

SBA Referral – For SBA dependent items and those applicants who qualify for a low interest loan

Real Property (*owners*) loans up to $200,000
Personal Property (*owners & renters*) loans up to $40,000

*If it is later determined that an applicant cannot qualify for a loan, the applicant is referred to FEMA

FEMA/IState Other Needs Assistance (ONA)
For those applicants who do not qualify for a SBA loan

Personal Property   Transportation
Moving and Storage   Group Flood Policy

Unmet Needs - Voluntary Agencies
If the applicant has received the maximum amount of assistance from FEMA, state, and/or SBA's federal disaster assistance programs or the federal disaster assistance programs do not provide for the need, FEMA may refer the applicant to voluntary agencies.

NOTE: Eligibility is based on a FEMA inspection conducted on the damaged property. Max amount of Individuals and Households Assistance (IHP) is adjusted annually according to the CPI index. The maximum amount for FY08 is $28,800.

Figure 7.1   Individual assistance sequence of delivery.

Conclusions

Undoubtedly, volunteer agencies play a critical role in a disaster. Volunteers require training and can provide important skills. There is variability in the amount of time they can volunteer. Some will be able to donate substantial amounts of time and others only a few spare hours per week. Some will have transportation, and others will not. Some volunteers will work at the companies where they are employed in order to first help their co-workers. They may voluntarily work extended hours to help their company economically survive or to supply needed critical services. Some may leave retirement to help their company. Others will work within the communities at shelters or help plan for recovery.

In every case, communities with collaborative groups working together to plan for disaster response and recovery will be more effective. The COAD model is designed to aid community collaboration. COADs are not difficult to start or maintain. They require a few meetings per year. Immediate benefits of community volunteer organizations include resource savings; reduced duplication; and understanding of national standards for training, exercising, preparing, response, and recovery.

The federal government alone cannot meet all disaster challenges. It takes everyone—community and faith-based organizations, government, state, and local agencies, businesses, and schools. The goal has to be to work cooperatively together, respect authority, deliver what is promised, follow through, honor commitment, and demonstrate willingness to put the needs of others before self. Communities must develop strategies to reduce the impact of the next disaster.

Acknowledgments

The authors wish to thank the following people for reviewing this manuscript: Brooklynne Slabaugh, Purdue University student for research assistance; and Chris Gilbert, emergency preparedness, and response manager of the American Red Cross of Greater Indianapolis.

Correspondence concerning this book chapter should be addressed to Steve Cain, Purdue University, 615 West State Street, West Lafayette, IN 47907, 765-494-8410, cain@purdue.edu.

References

American Red Cross. 2009. http://www.redcross.org/ (accessed June 29, 2011).

Audibert, M. 2006. Fighting poverty and disease in an integrated approach. *Bulletin of the World Health Organization* 84: 151-152.

Black, D. R., Smock, J. A., and B. Ardaugh. 2011. *The foundations of epidemiology.* 5th ed. Oshtemo, MI: Center for Social Problem-Solving Measurement.

Cain, S. 2005. *EDEN extension disaster education network: Reducing the impact of disaster through education. Pandemic preparedness for business.* http://eden.lsu.edu/EDENCourses/Pandemic/Pages/CourseMaterials.aspx (accessed June 29, 2011).

Exotic Newcastle Disease (END): Frequently Asked Questions. http://agr.wa.gov/FoodAnimal/AvianHealth/Docs/ExoticNewcastleDisease-website.pdf (accessed June 27, 2011).

Federal Emergency Management Agency. 2010a. *Developing and managing volunteers .*http://training.fema.gov/EMIWeb/IS/IS244A.pdf (accessed December 9, 2010).

Federal Emergency Management Agency. 2010b *Guidance on planning for integration of functional needs support services in general population shelters.* http://www.fema.gov/pdf/about/odic/fnss_guidance.pdf (accessed December 10, 2010).

Federal Emergency Management Agency. 2010c. Incident command system. http://www.fema.gov/emergency/nims/IncidentCommandSystem.shtm (accessed December 9, 2010).

Federal Emergency Management Agency. 2010d. Individual assistance and sequence of delivery. http://www.fema.gov/pdf/about/regions/regioni/sequence2008.pdf (accessed June 29, 2011).

Federal Emergency Management Agency. 2010e. Statement from the FEMA Administrator Craig Fugate on the 5th anniversary of Hurricane Katrina. www.fema.gov/news/newsrelease.fema?id=52497 (accessed June 29, 2011).

Hegel, G. 1902. *Lectures on the philosophy of history.* London, UK: George Bell and Sons.

Husband, A. and S. Cain. 2008. EDEN extension disaster education network: Reducing the impact of disaster through education. Animal agrosecurity and emergency management course. http://eden.lsu.edu/EDENCourses/AnimalAgrosecurity/Pages/default.aspx (accessed July 29, 2011).

Medical Reserve Corps. 2010. *About the Medical Reserve Corps.* http://www.medicalreservecorps.gov/About (accessed December 10, 2010).

National Voluntary Organizations Active in Disaster (VOAD). 2010. *Visit national VOAD partner organizations.* http://nvoad.org/partners/partner-organizations (accessed June 29, 2011).

The Salvation Army. 2010. *Our disaster relief program.* http://www.salvationarmyusa.org/usn/www_usn_2.nsf/vw-text-dynamic-arrays/3C5471700B61E262802573DF0063B7C8?openDocument (accessed June 29, 2010).

US Census Bureau. 2010. US and world population clocks. http://www.census.gov/main/www/popclock.html (accessed July 26, 2011).

US Department of Health and Human Services. 2006. For individuals and families. http://www.flu.gov/individualfamily (accessed December 10, 2010).

US Department of Health and Human Services 2009. *Faith-based & community organization pandemic influenza preparedness checklist.* http://permanent.access.gpo.gov/lps68930/faithbasedCommunityChecklist.pdf (accessed December 9, 2010).

Chapter 8

Lessons Learned from H1N1: Use of the Incident Command System in the Public Health Response

Connor D. Scott

Contents

Abstract

The H1N1 pandemic response in 2009 and early 2010 required a massive coordination effort between local health departments and partners within and outside of the public health community. The majority of these health departments used the incident command system (ICS) as the tool by which to organize the emergency response efforts. As public health is relatively new to ICS—a system predominantly used by fire and emergency medical services agencies—it is important to gather lessons learned from the H1N1 response, and incorporate these items into future responses. By capturing successes and identifying areas requiring improvement, organizations in the public health sector can learn from each other and implement best practices and corrective actions into existing plans before the next public health crisis emerges.

The majority of the conclusions in this chapter have been derived from a review of H1N1 after action reports written by local health departments across the United States. To protect anonymity, agency names have not been included, and the reports have not been cited, as many are protected documents.

Keywords: H1N1, Incident Command System, Public Health, National Incident Management System, Target Capabilities List, Emergency Response

Introduction

In 2003, the national incident management system (NIMS) designated the incident command system (ICS) as the means for coordinating emergency response activities within the US (The White House 2003). NIMS is the framework by which federal, state, and local governments prepare for, respond to, and recover from emergencies. While NIMS and ICS mandate management by objectives, individual responsibility, and time-sensitive decision making, the professional public health community emphasizes deliberation, collaboration, and thorough research and analysis when faced with a decision (Qureshi et al. 2006). Although the latter approach is reasonable and proven in traditional public health practice, recent world events have quickly thrown public health into the preparedness spotlight. A field designed to conduct long-term health planning and community assistance has been forced to operate in terms of emergency response (US Department of Health and Human Services 2007). Due to these fundamental differences in organization, the public health community has struggled at times to meet NIMS compliance objectives and implement ICS (Sergienko 2006).

ICS and the Target Capabilities List

The target capabilities list (TCL) is an implementation guideline published by the Federal Emergency Management Agency designed to direct preparedness efforts by guiding the development of 37 specific capabilities (US Department of Homeland Security 2007). The TCL identifies on-scene incident management as the "capability to effectively direct and control incident activities by using the Incident Command System (ICS) consistent with the National Incident Management System" (TCL, p. 197)." The TCL is the standard by which local health departments (LHDs) should be basing their capabilities and comparing their efforts. Many of the capabilities identified in this analysis are reflective of TCL priorities within on-scene incident management, if not stand-alone TCL priorities. The preferred outcome of effective on-scene incident management, according to the TCL, is a "safely, effectively and efficiently managed incident" (US Department of Homeland Security 2007).

ICS and H1N1 Response

ICS is designed to respond to small crises that last less than an hour, to a large-scale event that lasts months or years. The importance of using ICS throughout response operations became more evident during the 2009-2010 H1N1 response. The extended response period required a massive coordination effort from local health departments (LHDs), including collaboration with multiple agencies and organizations outside of public health. Most LHDs nationwide used an ICS structure in their response to H1N1, and in doing so, had to tailor the system to the needs of their organization and operation (NACCHO 2010). Emergency management begins at the local level and LHDs are the frontline of public health response in the US. More than 12,000 individuals died from the H1N1 virus in the US (Centers for Disease Control and Prevention 2010). Despite this tragedy, the incident allowed LHDs to assume their public health role and employ human and material resources during an actual event, resulting in a dynamic test of the public health response system. Therefore, the opportunity exists to conduct a thorough analysis of the LHDs' experiences with NIMS and ICS. The resources in this chapter are from open sources and unclassified after action reports, but are for official use only; therefore, specific agency names have been omitted.

Choosing to Implement ICS

ICS has a wide range of applicability. Originally developed by the State of California in response to massive wild-land fires, ICS has been evolving since the 1970s (State of California Office of Emergency Services 2006). ICS is used every day in the US, in response to events large and small. The fire service is particularly familiar with ICS, and federal law requires ICS for all hazardous materials events (Irwin 2009). However useful and adaptable, choosing to implement ICS during a public health emergency may not be intuitive to some local jurisdictions. ICS is relatively new to public health and many agencies had not responded to an emergency under ICS prior to H1N1 because it did not fit their typical response paradigm (Qureshi 2006).

Activation of ICS

Activation of ICS can look different depending on the agency and the type of event. Activation of ICS refers to the point in time when an agency begins operating under an ICS structure, rather than operating under normal operations and lines of authority. This may or may not mean operating under a continuity of operations plan. During H1N1, responding agencies learned the importance of early activation of ICS. ICS provides a highly structured and efficient planning process and it is imperative to establish functional roles before the pre-response planning begins. This allows individuals to approach planning from their position as it relates to the response, rather than everyday responsibilities. Establishing a formal ICS structure early in the response can help to avoid operational gaps that may not be considered until later, such as data collection and financial tracking. In the layout of an ICS chart, all potential roles and responsibilities can be reviewed and their applicability to the event can be determined. ICS provides clarity in the transition from planning to response and to ensure timely activation, some agencies recommended setting thresholds that would trigger the activation of ICS elements. Thresholds in public health can be the number of diagnosed cases of a disease within a given timeframe, World Health Organization alert levels, or any other threshold specific to the agency and the incident in question.

Staff Roles in ICS Structure

Differentiating between everyday job descriptions and roles during a response is key for the development of capable personnel and the ability for personnel to transition smoothly into a role within an ICS structure. Many agencies have developed incident management teams (IMTs), which consist of personnel with pre-designated roles during an emergency response. These individuals are generally high-level staff with decision-making authority, but also can include individuals with subject-matter expertise in emergency response or other desirable capabilities, depending on the type of response. Many agencies noted the importance of position-specific training and continuing education for IMT members. Training must be mandated to ensure each individual has the required knowledge, skills, and abilities to fulfill the duties of the assigned position. It also is important to consider continuity of operations while building and training an IMT. Ideally, each position would have at least two additional individuals capable of staffing the IMT role, should the primary person be unable to respond. It is important to note that IMT roles may not necessarily overlap into the ICS structure. For some individuals, such as the health director, it may make more sense for that person to remain outside of the response structure to ensure continuity of normal operations. When determining staff for ICS activation, many agencies noted that policies should be set prior to the incident to determine maximum work hours and rest periods; difficult policy decisions should be made well before an actual activation.

Staff and Volunteer Knowledge of ICS

IMT staff must have an intimate knowledge of ICS, but also it is critical that all staff and volunteers have a basic understanding of how ICS works and how they could and would incorporate it into a response. Training requirements differ by agency; however, the Federal Emergency Management Agency independent study programs IS-100 and IS-700 remain the bare minimum training for all staff and volunteers of many LHDs. Most agencies recommended additional training courses and exercises, in which ICS is used to further drive ICS principles. ICS-100, Introduction to the Incident Command System, and ICS-700, National Incident Management System: An Introduction, are considered the minimum for many agencies. Visit FEMA.gov for more information. The chain of command and span of control should be emphasized throughout training activities, and individuals should be reminded to know their task, where they are geographically assigned, and to whom to report. Some agencies decided to implement more training prior to an event to educate staff on potential roles and task forces to which they may be assigned as well as resource typing. Resource typing is a concept of NIMS that is used to standardize the use of personnel, facilities, equipment, and supplies in emergencies by assigning numbers to specific resources to ensure clarity and congruence in logistic management (FEMA 2009). Most jurisdictions found it useful to have a pre-operational briefing to reinforce ICS concepts and ensure staff members were aware of their roles. Some agencies involved the entire general staff and other supervisory positions in planning meetings before the event. Special consideration should be made when incorporating reserve staff (personnel waiting to be assigned work) into the response. Some reserve staff were asked to fill vacant positions without receiving the appropriate role briefing, adding to confusion. Agencies working with private sector companies during the response (such as nurse staffing companies) also noted that some staff members were not familiar with ICS. Private sector companies assisting with a response in the future should be encouraged to train their employees in ICS prior to the next emergency. LHDs and emergency management should conduct outreach and ICS education for emergency response stakeholders in the community. Health departments also should consider developing ICS just-in-time training (JITT) for unaffiliated volunteers and staff, or incorporating ICS into current JITT curricula.

Communication

Many agencies found that the use of ICS improved the flow of information, particularly when multiple agencies were involved. Communication along lines of authority proved to be critical in ascertaining situational awareness and confusion arose when the chain of command was broken. When working within an ICS structure, the temptation is to work laterally and communicate without relaying information to supervisors; not to be insubordinate, but simply because it is more intuitive to ask individuals working operationally. For example, if a member of a medical screening group needs chairs in the screening area, it may make more sense to ask a member of the screening team to find chairs instead of going through the proper chains of resource requests with the logistics section.

The use of situation reports (SitReps) helped all individuals and agencies maintain awareness of the overall operation. Many agencies developed and distributed SitReps with current vaccination numbers, ongoing clinic information, contact information of supervisors, and other critical information on a daily basis, if not more frequently. Some agencies distributed SitReps as frequently as every hour during highly active operational periods. These reports were distributed through e-mail or posted in a visible location. SitRep format varies, and agencies tailored each to their specific needs and capabilities. Meeting notes, updates, and incident action plans also were made available for review at all times. Some agencies used radios during clinic operations, but found that staff and volunteers were undertrained to use such equipment. Health departments should consider developing training programs for all staff and volunteers that may be issued a radio during an emergency.

Emergency Operations Center (EOC) Management

Many agencies realized the importance of an emergency operations center (EOC) in the response effort, either by establishing an EOC at the health department or at the county or city EOC. When agencies operated without a single point for information sharing and resource ordering, operations became more difficult and efforts duplicated. Many agencies found that logistics needed to be coordinated from the EOC, and single point ordering was crucial to help reduce wasted resources. One agency did not communicate effectively through the EOC and ordered supplies already on hand. Resource ordering procedures should focus on eliminating this confusion and increasing awareness of and adherence to agency procurement policies, and planning for the use of the emergency management assistance compact (EMAC). EMAC is the system by which all states structure personnel and resource sharing that crosses state borders. Depending on the type of activation, health departments may have varying levels of EOC staffing, and it is important that these levels, as well as roles and responsibilities, are determined well in advance of an actual activation.

Emergency Public Information and Warning

Public information is a critical part of the planning and response, and the ability to deliver accurate and timely information is enhanced by the ICS structure. The collection and dissemination of incident-related information is the responsibility of one individual (public information officer, PIO), but the actual process may be executed by multiple people and agencies, including coordination with other organizations and the news media. The organization of the information process is nearly impossible outside of an ICS structure. The PIO requires a specialized skill set, and depending on the agency, the person best equipped for the position may not even have ICS experience or training. For example, one agency found that a member of the Community Outreach team had experience working with the media and previously worked at a local television station. Although experienced in communicating with the public, this individual had no ICS training or experience. Agencies should work to pre-identify potential PIOs and ensure they have appropriate training to operate in the ICS structure.

Difficulty Implementing ICS

Some jurisdictions experienced difficulty adapting ICS to their response operation. The feeling among these agencies is that ICS should be modified to fit public health incidents. For example, some agencies experienced difficulty in assigning position titles when multiple operations were happening concurrently. Each clinic could have an individual commanding the response, but to be true to ICS, there can only be one incident commander. The same was felt in regards to the length of an incident utilizing ICS. Many jurisdictions felt that ICS only worked for a short duration, and did not translate to the long-term response. These potential inadequacies have been documented during H1N1 and other large-scale responses, and will need to be addressed on the policy level of the federal government (McKay 2010).

Hospital ICS

While public health has struggled at times to implement ICS, hospitals have not had such difficulties. In response to Homeland Security Presidential Directive-5, a workgroup of 20 hospital subject-matter experts, designed the hospital incident command system (California Emergency Medical Services Authority 2006). HICS is an ICS specific to hospital emergency management, used to better integrate ICS into a hospital emergency response program. The HICS sets a framework for hospital-specific incidents, such as evacuation, medication dispensing, relocation, and planning for medical surge. The HICS was preceded by the hospital emergency ICS, which had been in place since the 1980s (Taylor et al. 1998), and HICS was developed in an effort to integrate the two systems. It has been successful in boosting the preparedness efforts of hospitals nationwide, and a recent survey found that 100 percent of US hospitals follow the HICS guidelines (Deatley 2010). Various grant awards on the state and federal level are contingent on use of HICS, which incentivizes hospitals to comply. If a public health-specific ICS is created, the success of the HICS model should be considered as a reference point and best practice.

Conclusion

The public health community must continue to prepare for emergencies that will impact the health of the nation. Significant coordination efforts will be necessary to successfully integrate public health into the overall response structure, and the most effective tool to accomplish this is ICS. The onus is on health directors and emergency planners nationwide to learn from H1N1 and other real-life events. Although tragic, the H1N1 response was a useful exercise of the public health system's ability to respond to a major health emergency. As the public health community continues to integrate with traditional response agencies, it is important to ensure preparedness efforts are enhanced through incorporating lessons learned and best practices into future plans. ICS not only gives public health an effective incident management tool, but it allows public health preparedness officials to speak the same language as the other agencies involved with the response. In future emergencies, public health may either be the lead or play a supporting role, but regardless of the level of involvement, public health practitioners have learned that ICS is the tool to use to keep the public safe.

References

California Emergency Medical Services Authority. 2006. *The hospital incident command system guidebook.* Sacramento, CA: California Emergency Medical Services Authority.
Centers for Disease Control and Prevention. 2010. *2009 H1N1-related deaths, hospitalizations and cases:Details of extrapolations and ranges: United States emerging infections program (EIP) data.* Atlanta: CDC.
Deatley, C. 2010. *FEMA and business roundtable team up to discuss private sector's role in strengthening resilience.* www.domesticpreparedness.com (accessed October 29, 2010).

Eack, K. D. 2010. Fusion centers and public safety. In *Homeland Security: Best practices for local government,* ed. R. L. Kemp, 46-50. Washington, DC: ICMA Press.

Federal Emergency Management Agency. nd. *FEMA resource management.* http://www.fema.gov/emergency/nims/ResourceMngmnt.shtm (accessed March 6, 2011).

FEMA. 2009. *National infrastructure protection plan.* Washington, DC: Department of Homeland Security.

Implementing the 9/11 Commission Recommendations Act of 2007. 2007.

Irwin, R. L. 2009. Disaster response: Principals of preparedness and coordination. In R. L. Irwin, *Disaster response: Principals of preparedness and coordination* (p. Chapter 7: The Incident Command System (ICS).

Keim, M. 2010. O2C3: A unified model for emergency operations planning. *American Journal of Disaster Medicine* 169-179.

McKay, J. 2010. *Gulf of Mexico oil spill prompts debate on NIMS, unified response.* Emergencyanagement.com. http://www.emergencymgmt.com/disaster/Gulf-Oil-Spill-Debate-NIMS-Unified-Response.html (accessed October 1, 2010).

National Association of County and City Health Officials (NACCHO). 2010. *H1N1 policy workshop report.* Washington, DC: NACCHO.

Qureshi, K. G. 2006. *Public health incident command system.* New York: Mailman School of Public Health, Columbia University.

Qureshi, K., Gebbie, K., and E. Gebbie. 2006. *Public health incident command system.* New York: Mailman School of Public Health.

Sergienko, E. M. 2006. Public health and the incident command system. In *Public health in disasters.*

State of California, Office of Emergency Services. 2006. *Standardized emergency management system (SEMS): Guidelines.* http://www.oes.ca.gov/Operational/OESHome.nsf/Content/B49435352108954488256C2A0071E038 (accessed November 5, 2010).

Stoneking, D. 2010. Building public-private partnerships. *Continuity Insights.* http://www.continuityinsights.com/articles/building-public-private-partnerships (accessed September 21, 2011).

Taylor, M., Pletz, B., Cheu, D., Russell, P., and E. Nave. 1998. *The hospital emergency management system.* San Mateo, California: San Mateo County Department of Health Services.

The 9/11 Commission. 2004. *The 9/11 Commission Report.* Washington, DC: The National Commission on Terrorist Attacks Upon the United States.

The White House. 2003. *Homeland Security Presidential Directive 5—Management of domestic incidents.* Washington, DC: The White House.

The White House. 2006. *The federal response to Hurricane Katrina: Lessons learned.* Washington, DC: The White House.

Tumin, Z. 2007. *Closing the information gap in biosecurity readiness.* Cambridge, MA: Harvard University, John F. Kennedy School of Government.

US Congress. 2004. *Intelligence Reform and Terrorism Prevention Act.* Washington, DC: Congress.

US Congress. 2007. *Implementing Recommendations of the 9/11 Commission Act.* Washington, DC: Congress.

US Department of Health and Human Services. 2007. *Medical surge capacity handbook.* http://www.phe.gov/Preparedness/planning/mscc/handbook/Pages/default.aspx (accessed November 1, 2010).

US Department of Homeland Security. 2007). *The target capabilities list.* http://www.fema.gov/pdf/government/training/tcl.pdf (accessed November 3, 2010).

US Department of Homeland Security. 2008. *DHS information sharing strategy*. Washington, DC: Department of Homeland Security.

US Department of Justice. 2006. *Fusion center guidelines*. Washington, DC: The US Department of Justice's Global Justice Information Sharing Initiative.

US Government Accountability Office. 2010. *DHS could better define how it plans to meet its state and local mission and improve performace accountability*. Washington, DC: Government Accountability Office.

Chapter 9

All-Hazard Public Health: Business as Usual

Anne L. Drabczyk and Paul Etkind

Contents

Abstract

Public health has reached a higher level of recognition in the past decade as one of the necessary components of a comprehensive national security plan. In order to merge its skills and talents with those of more traditional public safety organizations, public health has had to alter its traditional concerns and practices by incorporating public safety strategies and practices, such as the national incident management system (NIMS) and the incident command system (ICS). While few, if any, debate whether public health has a legitimate role in assuring national security and public safety, public safety techniques have been seen by many as new or additional for public health. The authors contend that, throughout its history, public health has been very adaptable to new situations and tools. In fact, the practices and responsibilities of public safety are actually business as usual for public health. The vitality of public health, however, should not be viewed through a public safety lens. A robust public health system is a worthy and necessary goal in its own right, and will improve our nation's capacity to respond to emergencies of any origin.

Keywords: Public Health, Emergency Preparedness, All-Hazard Preparation and Response, Emergency Service Function Eight (ESF8)

Introduction

The Institute of Medicine (2003) and Mangold and Goldberg (1999) report that public health in America began receiving renewed interest in the 1990s as federal policy makers became increasingly concerned with the potential for biologic attacks on civilian populations. Public health has achieved a higher profile since the 9/11 attacks, as it became evident that security emergencies could involve health dimensions. Since that time, public health budgets increased with funds aimed initially at bioterrorism (Public Health Security and Bioterrorism Preparedness and Response Act 2002). This funding was renewed under a more general label of "emergency preparedness." (US Department of Health and Human Services 2006). This placed demands on public health to alter its traditional concerns and routine practices. The Pandemic and All-Hazards Preparedness Act (PAHPA) recommended the standard of practice be maintained through such activities as trainings, and certifications in public safety strategies, such as the incident command system (ICS) and the national incident management system (NIMS) were mandated. Public health professionals needed to be trained in public safety techniques and theories so they could work more closely and seamlessly with public safety organizations. This emphasis on public safety raised the questions as to the relationship between public health and emergency preparedness/public safety. Is there a set of theories and practices for traditional public health activities and a different set of public health theories and practices for safety issues?

This chapter contends that public health has a legitimate place at the public safety table, but the concepts and strategies it employs are the same regardless of whether it is promoting health or responding to an emergency. The "new" (to public health professionals) strategies such as ICS or NIMS should not be seen as "add-ons" to the traditional public health skill set. The role of public health in an emergency is essentially business as usual. What public health tries to accomplish on a daily basis in terms of surveillance, early disease recognition and response, disease prevention, engaging with community, and professional groups, etc., is the same as what they are tasked to accomplish in responding to and mitigating an emergency. Basing public health funding through an emphasis on public safety, which is where a significant portion of federal money for public health has come from in the past decade, does not recognize the value of what the profession does for the health and well-being of the nation on a daily basis. A robust public health system is a worthy goal in its own right. This will not only improve our nation's health, well-being, and resilience on a daily basis, but will also improve our nation's capacity to respond to emergencies, natural or man-made in origin, concurrently.

Brief History and Significance of Public Health

Lemuel Shattuck's *Report of the Sanitary Commission of Massachusetts* (Shattuck 1948), first published in 1850, was the initial blueprint for an organized state health department in the United States. The report outlined five recommendations: (a) a system consisting of state and local health departments, (b) a systematic collection of vital statistics, (c) sanitation inspections, (d) school health programs, and (e) controlling mental illness, alcohol abuse, and tuberculosis (TB). An influencing element at the time was the need to routinely conduct a census of the population, along with a careful recording of the population's vital statistics (as defined by each life event connected with a certificate: [a] birth, [b] marriage, separation, divorce, and death). In addition, there were recommendations regarding environmental sanitation, controlling infectious diseases, and regulating the purity and safety of food and drugs. There was very little publicity about the report after it was issued, although a synopsis of it was published 11 months later in *The Boston Medical and Surgical Journal* where it received favorable editorial comment (Winklestein 1999). However, the Massachusetts legislature did not act on the recommendations for almost 20 years.

The Civil War may also have diverted attention from the recommendations outlined in the Shattuck Report. The war also served as another "teachable moment" for the connection between public health and national security. The U. S. Surgeon General's Office (1870-1888) and Lee (1880-1902) list that approximately 600,000 soldiers died during the war. However, records show deaths were often due to disease (often measles and pneumonia) and poor sanitary conditions in the camps and in the field hospitals, and not due to battlefield fatalities or wounds (Adams 1952; Woodward 1863). Pneumonia and measles were two of the major killers of the Union soldiers. The War Department recognized the importance of health, leading to its ability to field functional armies, and it allowed members of a voluntary US Sanitary Commission to visit and inspect army camps, to provide nursing care to the wounded, and to be a source of health information to the soldiers and their commanding officers (Lewis 2011).

After the war and perhaps because of some of the lessons learned during the war, more attention was paid to the public's health. The first organized and functional state health department, based on the Shattuck Report, was created in Massachusetts in 1869. According to Patterson (1939), this was followed by others in California in 1870, the District of Columbia in 1871, Virginia and Minnesota in 1872, and subsequently in other states. From the beginning, however, one pattern that has remained true through the present was established: The state health departments had broad responsibilities, but were very poorly funded. Abbot (1900) notes that by 1900, only three states (Massachusetts, Rhode Island, and Florida) spent more than two cents per person per year for public health services.

The federal investment in public health dates back to 1798, when Congress passed the Act for the Relief of Sick and Disabled Seamen (Mullen 1989) to pay for constructing public hospitals in the port cities. Over the course of almost a century, the hospitals expanded their mission of providing care to sailors and the poor and, in 1887, established the first hygienic laboratory in order to improve the understanding of infectious diseases. This mission was then expanded in 1912, when the Marine Hospital Service became the US Public Health Service (USPHS). The USPHS was charged with investigating the causes and spread of infectious diseases and to be a source of health education and materials to the public.

The connections between public health and national security were evident during the US global expansion into a world commercial and military power in the Spanish-American War. The importance of health and sanitation was clear as the US suffered 968 battle fatalities, but 5,438 died from infectious diseases (Sternberg 1912). Sternberg also notes that when a yellow fever epidemic in 1900 threatened the American troops in Cuba, army physicians, who were sent to study the situation, determined that the disease was spread by mosquitoes. Subsequent drainage and sanitation measures ended the threat. As the US began competing for foreign markets, national defense began including provisions for controlling trade routes, and establishing bases in strategic places overseas. This expansion also created an increased emphasis on supporting public health measures. Overcoming the challenges of malaria and yellow fever to build the Panama Canal and establish American military and economic primacy in the Western Hemisphere was one of the great triumphs of public health (Gorgas 1915).

Mobilizing manpower is always an issue in the run-up to and during a war. Public health is vital in helping to fill the ranks of the armed forces as well as supporting industrial production with healthy and vital workers (Mustard 1941; Simmons 1943). The US had to establish special hospitals dedicated to treating syphilis and gonorrhea before and during both world wars (Padgett 1963). In World War II, Perrott (1944, 1946) reported that up to 40% of the manpower was not suitable due to a variety of diseases and conditions. Industrial production demand required increases in workers to move to industrial areas and those places where military bases were expanding. The USPHS increased its grants to states and local communities in 1940 to support health programs in such communities (Williams 1951; Furman 1973).

While the profile of public health rose along with the increasing prominence of the United States as a world power, public health within the US was developing along unscripted and uncoordinated lines. The professionalism of the early state and local practitioners was not valued, and public health departments were often staffed by recipients of political patronage with no training in public health. Policies were often dictated by political or economic, rather than health, considerations based in science. The Social Security Act of 1935 provided a major impetus for professionalizing the public health workforce (Social Security Administration 2011). Along with its grants to states under Title VI were requirements to establish standards and minimal qualifications for public health personnel hired with such funds. Professional public health training became the expectation. An increasingly professional workforce, increasing salaries, and well-publicized successes all helped to make the profession more attractive (Schiesl 1980).

Some larger city health departments began organizing as early as the eighteenth century. State health departments began to be organized after the Civil War. County- or locally based health departments began to form in the early twentieth century. Surveys conducted by the American Public Health Association's committee on administrative practices (CAP) showed a steady growth in their numbers: 83 local health departments by 1913 (Knowles 1913); 178 by 1923 (US Public Health Service 1923); and 1,197 by 1943 (Kratz 1945). Today, there are an estimated 2,800 local health departments in the US (National Association of County and City Health Officials 2009).

The 1945 CAP survey identified six core public health activities that would be expected of a local health department: communicable disease control, health education, laboratory services, maternal and child health services, sanitation, and vital statistics. The 1949 survey documented a shift from preventive services to therapeutic and diagnostic services. There also was an increasing link between local health departments and hospitals, with the health department often being a source of clinical care and frequently being administratively linked to and housed within a hospital (Corwin 1949).

This clinical focus began to change in the 1960s as private medicine became increasingly competitive with public clinical services. Federal and state legislation created health programs such as Medicare, Medicaid, and the Hill-Burton Act, each of which is a significant investment in acute care and restorative medicine. No similar investment was made in the prevention programs of public health. In addition, the traditional public health role in environmental health was altered with the creation of the federal Environmental Protection Agency. Thus, much of the regulatory authority once exercised by public health agencies was now housed in an agency that had less focus on health impact. Public health clinical programs were reduced to "safety net" programs that others did not want to perform (e.g., sexually transmitted disease clinics) or were not revenue-producing (e.g., tuberculosis).

In 1988, the Institute of Medicine (IOM) produced its report on "The Future of Public Health" (Institute of Medicine 1988). This landmark report spoke of three major goals of health functions: assessment, assurance, and policy development. The emphasis was on data collection in order to enable proper assessment

Table 9.1 Ten essential functions of public health

Essential Functions	Core Function
Monitor health status to identify and solve community health problems	Assessment
Diagnose and investigate health problems and health hazards in the community	Assessment
Inform, educate, and empower people about health issues	Policy Development
Mobilize community partnerships and action to identify and solve health problems	Policy Development
Develop policies and plans that support individual and community health efforts	Policy Development
Enforce laws and regulations that protect health and ensure safety	Assurance
Link people to needed personal health services and assure the provision of healthcare when otherwise unavailable	Assurance
Assure a competent public and personal healthcare workforce	Assurance
Evaluate effectiveness, accessibility, and quality of personal and population-based health services	Assurance
Research new insights and innovative solutions in health problems	Assurance

of health status and program impact; on assuring that all people were being equitably served; and, policies were based in science. In addition, the Centers for Disease Control and Prevention (2010), enumerated the 10 core functions of public health (see Table 9.1). While nothing was explicitly stated about the public health role in emergencies, these core and essential functions were all amenable to the goals of emergency preparedness. However, a clear link between public health and the public safety organizations that usually responded to emergencies was not specifically described.

Public health has moved into an expanded role in national security considerations since the attacks of September 11, 2001 (hereafter referred to as 9/11). This status has been building from within the profession, externally from policy makers, and from our national security partners (Ullman 1983; Buzan 1991; Price-Smith 2002; Garrett 2000). Public health has a history of being adaptable, although it is questionable if public health responsibilities require any adjustments, since the tools of public safety are routine public health practice by other names. Public health and public safety are two sides of the same coin, and we need to recognize that this is not a new or unprecedented relationship. The past decade of planning and training together has improved the understanding of the synergy offered by a seamless interaction of health and safety.

Public Health and All-Hazards: Old Concepts Become New

In the aftermath of 9/11, the roles and responsibilities of public health were viewed in a broader light: as a part of national security. The core public health practices of assessment, policy development, and assurance acquired a new and expanded meaning post-9/11. The routine emphasis on managing such traditional public health services as well baby clinics, immunizations, health education, and restaurant inspections is now competing with demands for planning for mass clinics, points of dispensing (PODs), medical surge, evacuations, mass pharmaceutical dispensing, community resilience, and any number of disaster or other emergency responses.

In December 2006, Congress passed and President George W. Bush signed the Pandemic and All-Hazards Preparedness Act (PAHPA), (Department of Health and Human Services 2010). The Act amended the Public Health Service Act and established within the Department of Health and Human Services (DHHS) a new assistant secretary for preparedness and response (ASPR). PAHPA provided new authorities for a number of programs, including the advanced development and acquisitions of medical countermeasures, and called for the establishment of a quadrennial national health security strategy. A few of the tangible outcomes of ASPR initiatives include formation of the medical reserve corps (a pool of trained volunteers who assist health professionals during hazards), increased training and exercising of incident command models, and development of continuity of operations plans for local health jurisdictions.

Following PAHPA, a number of homeland security presidential directives (HSPD) were issued by the president. The HSPD 21 Directive—Public Health and Medical Preparedness (Department of Homeland Security 2008)—established a national strategy to enable a level of public health and medical preparedness sufficient to address possible disasters. The HSPD led the Federal Emergency Management Agency (2008a) to further define emergency support function (ESF) annexes as the mechanism for coordinated federal assistance during a developing potential health or medical emergency. The specific annex for medical and public health functions is ESF8, and it is administered through the Secretary of Health and Human Services and the Office of the Assistant Secretary for Preparedness and Response. Public health and medical functions are both listed under ESF8; however, Table 9.2 highlights core functional areas considered specific to public health.

Table 9.2   ESF8—Core public health functional areas

Functions
Agriculture safety and security
All-hazard public health and medical consultation, technical assistance, and support
Assessment of public health/medical needs
Food safety and security
Health surveillance
Health/medical/veterinary equipment and supplies
Mass fatality management, victim identification, and decontaminating remains
Medical care personnel
Patient evacuation
Potable water/wastewater and solid waste disposal
Public health and medical information
Vector control

The IOM's 10 essential public health functions did not identify a role for public health during all-hazards, but ESF8 began to operationalize functions more specifically (see Table 9.1). As a result, health practitioners began to visualize their potential roles during all stages or cycles of an emergency.

The Federal Emergency Management Agency (2008b) recognizes four cycles of disaster management: mitigation, preparedness, response, and recovery. Mitigation is the first phase of all-hazard management and establishes practices and safeguards, which may lessen the devastation when a catastrophe occurs. Preparedness is the second phase of the cycle and stresses a heightened readiness to cope with a disaster, should one occur. Response is the third cycle of all-hazard management and entails taking action to bring the crisis under control, and serve the safety and medical needs of victims. The fourth and final disaster management phase is recovery and can be summed up as an effort to return to normalcy. An analysis of public health roles at each cycle will likely improve understanding of how the discipline incorporates disaster management into its everyday functions.

An example of mitigation is clearing brush away from the foundation of a home in order to reduce the potential for increased damage. A vital public health mitigation function is the ability to track trends, predict events, and strategize plans to reduce negative outcomes. All of these activities also have to be conducted across systems of multiple agencies. In the mitigation cycle, public health works in tandem with emergency responding partners and municipal stakeholders to gauge potential problems and to strive to reduce or eliminate them.

Preparedness might include an example such as having food and fuel stockpiles in order to weather a snowstorm. Public health prepares through surveillance of data. The CDC (2004) provides several online databases that support surveillance activities from outbreak detection, to verification and notification, and post-event tracking. The rapid syndrome validation project (RSVP) examines symptoms and trends that may predict potential outbreaks. The possibility of outbreaks can then be further clarified through a program called biological spatiotemporal outbreak reasoning module (BioSTORM). Once validation of an imminent outbreak is guaranteed, a program called the electronic surveillance system for early notification of community-based epidemics or (ESSENCE) is activated. These systems represent just a few public health business advancements post 9/11.

During the response cycle, an incident command system (ICS) is essential. Public health has demonstrated commitment to ensuring that preparedness personnel obtain ICS training and apply the knowledge through design and execution of exercises, and completion of after action reports. These trainings have allowed public health to work in tandem with community response partners. According to the US Department of Health and Human Services (2010), without this ICS foundation, it will become increasingly difficult for public health and medicine to maximize their roles in incident response.

For public health officials and emergency responder partners alike, the concluding disaster management cycle of recovery provides an opportunity to examine performance and plan for the next incident. Recovery affects the victims of the trauma, the professionals who responded to the incident, community stakeholders, and support agencies. All entities benefit from ongoing review of needs assessments, job performance, and support system status checks.

Post 9/11, and with each subsequent disaster from Katrina to the Gulf Oil Spill, another all-hazard phase is emergent: resilience. To define resilience has been a challenging undertaking for members of the all-hazard community. Kahan, Allen, and George (2009) suggest salient elements of a definition of resilience might include inherent strengths of systems to absorb a blow and rebound from an incident, and initiating the restoration process as quickly as possible. The H1N1 pandemic demonstrated the resilience of the public health system to be accountable to the challenge, absorb extra demands, and move back into a normal pattern as the crisis subsided. One reason public health was able to demonstrate a vital and visible role during the pandemic was the attention directed toward building a preparedness workforce infrastructure over the last decade. In 2002, the CDC received congressional funding to develop the public health emergency preparedness (PHEP) cooperative agreements across America (Centers for Disease Control and Prevention 2009). An essential intent of the PHEP was to provide public health emergency response (PHER) grants to local health jurisdictions to improve capacity and capability to respond to the public health consequences of not only terrorist threats, but also infectious disease epidemics/pandemics; natural disasters; and biological, chemical, nuclear, and radiological emergencies. The funding from PHER grants directly supported incident command systems (ICS) training for health practitioners, and made ICS a job requirement, and linked the training certificates to merit increases. The need to facilitate exercises and complete after action reports also required public health to build relationships with non-traditional community partners.

Based on the history of public health as a discipline, it was likely that it expanded its role in national defense. The functions embedded in prevention, mitigation, response, and recovery were not new to public health. Building infrastructure through ICS training and exercise functions is just one example of how public health reinvented itself once more.

Public Health All-Hazards: As Usual

A robust public health system has the capacity to seamlessly incorporate the responsibilities of ESF8 and the ICS model of emergency response organizations. Table 9.3 juxtaposes public health functions against all-hazards operations, and it is clear that monitoring health status is a necessary element in each of the following:

- Diagnosing and investigating health problems and hazards is a routine public health function.
- Information for and education of the public is a part of public health assurance and emergency operations.
- Developing community partnerships by local health departments is key to responding, mitigating, and recovering from emergency situations.
- Developing policies and plans to support community health efforts is a routine public health practice and helps to prepare for emergencies.
- Enforcing laws and regulations that protect health and safety are critical to aid assurance activities, emergency operations, and logistics concerns.
- Linking people to needed personal health services and assuring such services are available is a necessary component of any emergency response.
- Assuring a competent workforce is a part of the planning, policy making, and educational activities.
- Research for new insights is part of routine program evaluation, which is analogous to the after action report evaluation of an emergency response.
- Finance is the one component of ICS that is not mentioned directly but is surely understood as an essential function.

According to Cuellar (2006, 2009), the current attempt to marry public health with homeland security is simply an example of history coming full circle. In 1939, President Roosevelt created the Federal Security Agency (FSA), a very large agency

Table 9.3   Ten essential public health services, ESF8, and ICS

Essential Functions	Core Functions	ESF8	ICS
Monitor health status to identify and solve community health problems	Assessment	Assessment of public health and medical needs, health surveillance	Planning
Diagnose and investigate health problems and health hazards in the community	Assessment	Health and medical consultation, technical assistance, support	Operations
Inform, educate, and empower people about health issues	Policy development	Public health and medical information	Operations
Mobilize community partnerships and action to identify and solve health problems	Policy development	Vector control	Planning; operations
Develop policies and plans that support individual and community health efforts	Policy development	The planning that creates emergency response plans and relationships necessary for such plans is no different from what is needed to deal with any public health issue	Planning
Enforce laws and regulations that protect health and ensure safety	Assurance	Food safety and security; agriculture safety and security; potable water; wastewater and solid waste disposal	Operations; logistics
Link people to needed personal health services and assure the provision of healthcare when otherwise unavailable	Assurance	Patient evacuation	Planning; operations

(continued)

Table 9.3   Ten essential public health services, ESF8, and ICS (*continued*)

Essential Functions	Core Functions	ESF8	ICS
Assure a competent public and personal healthcare workforce	Assurance	Medical care personnel; health/medical/veterinary equipment and supplies; mass fatality management, victim identification, and decontaminating remains	Operations; logistics
Evaluate effectiveness, accessibility, and quality of personal and population-based health services	Assurance	Part of the after action report of an emergency response, which is essentially a standard program evaluation tool routinely used for "normal" public health practice	Command; planning
Research for new insights and innovative solutions in health problems	Assurance	Each after action report or program evaluation report is done to identify strategies or tactics that will need to be altered for the next opportunity	Command; planning

that had responsibility for public health, social security, drug regulation, protecting the food supply, civil defense preparedness, and others. It was an expression of a very broad definition of the elements of national security to include social well-being. The FSA existed until 1953, when the functions were separated into independent agencies within the federal government (Cuellar 2006, 2009). This model from the middle of the twentieth century is yet another lesson among a string of similar learning moments over the past two centuries that we have not learned: Public health is a seamless partner for national security.

National security is not restricted to issues related to destruction of property or infrastructure and the associated loss of lives. Price-Smith (2009) and Garrett (1995, 2000) have argued that pathogens, regardless of whether their distribution within the population is natural or man-made, can have a profound and unsettling impact on national security in different and interconnected ways. These can include altering the demographics of a nation; create widespread fear that threatens social institutions and structure; significantly affect the economy; diminish governance; and/or weaken a society's resilience and ability to rapidly adapt and respond to new situations. Examples of these can be found in Table 9.4.

Destruction of elements of a population's physical infrastructure can similarly have a negative impact on the public's health. Foul air, or contaminated food or water will pose obvious threats to health. If transportation is hobbled or power supplies are destroyed or diminished, then health effects are possible and likely.

Table 9.4 Possible societal impact of disease

Impact	Danger	Example(s)
Alter demographics	Weaken social structure	HIV; pandemic influenza (1918)
Fear from widespread disease	Weaken social structure	Yellow fever 1795; polio 1955; SARS 2003; pandemic influenza (1918, 2009); tuberculosis
Economic damage	Affect creation and distribution of necessary goods and services	Hookworm (early 20th century); BSE; salmonellosis outbreaks
Diminished faith in authority	Diminished social cohesion	HIV; MDR-TB (NYC); drug-resistant infections
Overwhelming disruption of society	Diminished ability to cope as a group	Smallpox and measles in Amerindians

Like the impact of physical destruction, pathogens can similarly affect society's economic well-being, its ability to govern, and can diminish the sense of legitimacy, capacity, or power of the government. Each of these can have an impact on the health of the population.

Destruction or impairment of the availability and/or delivery of necessary services highlights the importance of social justice and social equity, which are key concepts of public health philosophy and practice. These concepts point to the importance of assuring that everyone shares the risks equally and that services are equally available to everyone. This sense of inclusion and shared risks/rewards produces a greater degree of societal cohesion. Resilience will be positively affected if the entire population feels it has a stake in the response and individuals understand their role in response and recovery.

A robust public health system is a necessary element to society's ability to prevent emergencies, mitigate them if they occur, or shorten the recovery (thus diminishing the associated costs of any needed measures) from any kind of emergency. The Roosevelt-era Federal Security Agency incorporated the lessons of history into this sense of mission, and presents a model for current and future public health practice. The role of public health capacity is more expansive than being a government service that has certain tools for daily needs and a separate set of tools for emergencies. The disease monitoring, prevention/protection and control interventions, regulatory measures, health education, connections and planning with the public and medical communities, that public health works on each day, are exactly what would be expected of the service during an emergency or threat to national security. Consistency between daily plans and disaster plans will produce an effective merge of health and safety responsibilities. Daily activities, even when small in scale, serve as exercise or practice for larger-scale responses that would be created in an emergency. Preparing for the usual is the same as preparing for the unusual.

References

Abbott, S. W. 1900. *The past and present conditions of public hygiene and state medicine in the United States.* Boston, MA: Wright and Potter.

Adams, G. W. 1952. *Doctors in blue.* New York: Henry Schuman.

Buzan, B. 1991. *People, states, and fear: An agenda for international security studies in the post Cold War era.* Boulder, CO: Lynne Rienner Publishers.

Centers for Disease Control and Prevention. 2004. *Syndromic surveillance information system* http://www.cdc.gov/epo/dphsi/syndromic/websites.htm#manual (accessed February 4, 2004).

Centers for Disease Control and Prevention. 2009. *Emergency preparedness and response.* http://emergency.cdc.gov/cdcpreparedness/coopagreement/index.asp (accessed April 12, 2010).

Centers for Disease Control and Prevention. 2010. *National public health performance standards program: Ten essential public health services.* www.cdc.gov/od/ocphp/nphpsp/EssentialPHServices.htm (accessed December 9, 2010).

Corwin, E. H. L. 1949. *Ecology of health.* New York: The Commonwealth Fund.

Cuellar, M. F. 2006. Securing the bureaucracy: The Federal Security Agency and the political design of legal mandates, 1939-1953. Stanford Public Law Working Paper No. 943084.

Cuellar, M. F. 2009. Securing the nation: Law, politics, and organization at the Federal Security Agency, 1939-1953. *University of Chicago Law Review* 76: 87-717.

Department of Health and Human Services. 2010. *Pandemic and All-Hazards Preparedness Act.* http://www.phe.gov/preparedness/legal/pahpa/pages/default.aspx (accessed September 8, 2010).

Department of Homeland Security. 2008. *Homeland Security Presidential Directive 21: Public health and medical preparedness.*

Federal Emergency Management Agency. 2008a. *Emergency support function #8—public health and medical services annex.* www.fema.gov/pdf/emergency/nrf/nrf-esf-08.pdf (accessed February 6, 2010).

Federal Emergency Management Agency. 2008b. *Guide to emergency management and related terms.* http://www.training.fema.gov/EMIWeb/edu/docs/terms%20and%20defini-tions/Terms%20and%20Definitions.pdf (accessed April 16, 2009).

Furman, B. 1973. *A profile of the Public Health Service, 1798-1948.* Bethesda, MD: National Institutes of Health.

Garrett, L. 1995. *The coming plague: Newly emerging diseases in a world out of balance.* New York: Penguin Books.

Garrett, L. 2000. *Betrayal of trust: The collapse of global public health.* New York: Hyperion Press.

Gorgas, W. C. 1915. *Sanitation in Panama.* London: Appleton.

Institute of Medicine. 1988. *The future of public health.* Washington, DC: National Academy Press.

Institute of Medicine. 2003. *Microbial threats to health emergency, detection and response.* Washington DC: National Academies Press.

Kahan, J., Allen, A., and J. George. 2009. An operational framework for resilience. *Journal of Homeland Security and Emergency Management* 6, 1: 1-48.

Knowles, M. 1913. Public health service is not a medical monopoly. *American Journal of Public Health* 3: 111-122.

Kratz, F. K. 1943. Status of full-time local health organizations at the end of the fiscal year 1941-42. *Public Health Reports* 58: 345-351.

Lee, R. E. 1880-1902. *The war of the rebellion: A compilation of the official records of the Union and Confederate Armies.* Washington, DC: Government Printing Office.

Lewis, J. J. 2011. Sanitary Commission (USSC). http://womenshistory.about.com/od/civilwar/p/ussc_civil_war.htm (accessed February 20, 2011).

Mangold, T. and J. Goldberg. 1999. *Plague wars: The terrifying reality of biological warfare.* New York: St. Martin's Griffin.

Mullan, F. 1989. *Plagues and politics: The story of the United States Marine Hospital Service.* New York: Basic Books.

Mustard, H. S., ed. 1941. Yesterday's school children are examined by the Army. *American Journal of Public Health* 31:1207.

National Association of County and City Health Officials. 2009. *National profile of local health departments.* Washington, DC, pp. 1-85.

Padgett, P. 1963. Diagnosis and treatment of the venereal diseases. In, *Internal Medicine in World War II*, eds. J. Boyd, J. Coates, and W. P. Havens. Washington, DC: US Army Medical Department, Office of Medical History, pp. 410-435.

Patterson, R. G. 1939. *Historical directory of the state health departments in the United States of America.* Columbus, OH: Public Health Association.

Perrott G. S. 1944. Findings of selective service examinations. *Millbank Quarterly* 22: 358-366.

Perrott, G. S. 1946. Selective service rejection statistics and some of their implications. *American Journal of Public Health* 36: 336-342.

Price-Smith, A. T. 2002. *The health of nations: Infectious disease, environmental change and their effects on national security and development.* Cambridge, MA: MIT Press.

Price-Smith, A. T. 2009. *Contagion and chaos: Disease, ecology, and national security in the era of globalization.* Cambridge, MA: MIT Press.

Schiesl, M. J. 1980. *The politics of efficiency: Municipal administration and reform in America, 1880-1920.* Berkeley: University of California Press.

Shattuck L. 1948. *Report of a general plan for the promotion of public and personal health, devised, prepared, and recommended by the commissioners appointed under a resolve of the legislature of the state.* Cambridge, MA: Harvard University Press.

Simmons, J. S. 1943. The preventive medicine program of the United States Army. *American Journal of Public Health* 33: 931-940.

Social Security Administration. 2011. Social Security Act of 1935. http://www.ssa.gov/history/35actinx.html (accessed March , 2011).

Sternberg, G. M. 1912. Sanitary lessons of the war. In *Sanitary Lessons of the War and Other Papers.* Washington, DC: Beaufort Books.

Ullman, R. 1983. Redefining security. *International Security* 8(1): 129-153.

United States Public Health Service. 1923. Report of the Committee on Municipal Health Department Practice of the American Public Health Association, in cooperation with the United States Public Health Service. Washington, DC: US Government Printing Office.

US Department of Health and Human Services. 2002. Public Health Security and Bioterrorism Act. PL 107-188. http://www.fda.gov/RegulatoryInformation/Legislation/ucm148797.htm (accessed February 28, 2011).

US Department of Health and Human Services. 2006. Pandemic and All Hazards Preparedness Act 2006. PL 109-417. http://www.phe.gov/preparedness/legal/pahpa/pages/default.aspx6 (accessed February 28, 2011).

US Department of Health and Human Services. 2010. *Incident command system primer for public health and medical professionals.* http://www.phe.gov/Preparedness/planning/mscc/handbook/Pages/appendixb.aspx (accessed November 29, 2010).

US Surgeon General, Office of Medicine, Department of Medical History. 1870-1888.

Williams, R. C. 1951. *The United States Public Health Service, 1798-1950.* Washington, DC: The Commissioned Officers Association of the United States Public Health Service, 612-768.

Winklestein, W. 1999. The development of American public health, a commentary: Three documents that made an impact. *Journal of Public Health Policy* 30: 40-48.

Woodward, J. J. 1863. *Chief camp diseases of the United States Armies.* Philadelphia, PA: J. B. Lippincott & Company.

Chapter 10

The Future of Survey-Based Research: Exploring University Students' Vaccination Decisions

Julia E. Shaffner, David R. Black, and J. Eric Dietz

Contents

Abstract

This study was undertaken to compare university students who received the 2009 H1N1 influenza vaccination versus those who did not. This was prompted by the Centers for Disease Control and Prevention's declaration that individuals under the age of 24 were at risk for contracting this novel strain of influenza. The comparison between the immunized and non-immunized students was made in terms of gender, academic year, academic department, nationality, and the six constructs of the health belief model: perceived susceptibility, perceived severity, perceived benefits, perceived barriers, cues to action, and self efficacy. An e-mail with a hyperlink to an online survey was sent to 4,000 university students. The online influenza vaccination questionnaire was based on adapted questions from two earlier surveys. Construct validity was established through expert review of the survey items. Response bias, clarity, and readability were assessed by review and feedback from 30 individuals. Reading ease and grade level were assessed by the Flesch and Flesch-Kincaid tests. Principal components analysis was used to reduce the items used for further analyses, and to ensure that any survey items used loaded on just one theoretical construct. Backward stepwise logistic regression analyses showed the following variables were significantly related ($p < 0.05$) to immunization: cues to action, perceived barriers, and perceived benefits. Characteristics of the vaccination played a role in the decision, while the characteristics of the disease itself did not. This finding has implications for the development and implementation of future vaccination campaigns targeted at specific segments of the population.

Keywords: Pandemic Preparedness, Survey-Based Research, Influenza Vaccination, Health Belief Model

Introduction

Future of Survey-Based Research: Exploring University Students' Vaccination Decisions

This chapter focuses on the public health preparations for a pandemic influenza. The cornerstone of public health is epidemiology. The structure of public health also contains components of behavioral, social, natural, physical, and applied sciences, as well as homeland security. Because of its comprehensive nature, a variety of research and analytical tools are useful to public health scientists, including everything from comprehensive literature reviews to case studies. This chapter provides a detailed description of the development and delivery of a survey instrument designed to understand the public's reaction to a non-mandatory vaccination during a pandemic. The purposes of this chapter are fivefold. The intention is to accomplish the following: to describe (a) the development of a survey instrument, (b) the results of the survey, (c) information for future researchers or practitioners to replicate the steps undertaken for this project, (d) the inherent strengths and weaknesses of survey-based research, and (e) lessons learned from this project.

Background

In the spring of 2009, the emergence of a unique strain of influenza Type A/H1N1 (often referred to as swine flu) captured the attention of the world (US Department of Health and Human Services 2010). The initial epidemic occurred in Mexico and quickly spread to the United States, though experts suspected the first human case may have occurred in Asia (McNeil 2009). The virus contained genetic information from a human influenza virus (which normally peaks in the US in the late fall and winter months), a North American avian virus, and a virus that occurs in pigs (Masterson 2009). It is likely that the novel strain was circulating among humans, unrecognized as a novel influenza, since late 2008 (Knox 2009). The possible genetic link between the influenza strain, which caused the 1918-1919 pandemic, and the 2009 H1N1 influenza strain was a source of concern during the early stages of the 2009 pandemic.

Fortunately, even though the 2009 H1N1 flu was (and remains, at the time of this writing) a health concern; the case fatality rates associated with the illness did not approach those recorded in 1918 and 1919 (Taubenberger and Morens 2006). The difference in the case fatality rates between the two pandemics can be attributed to differences in the disease itself, and to advances in prevention, control, and intervention options developed over the last century (Haber et al. 2007).

According to the Centers for Disease Control and Prevention (2009), some adults over the age of 60 may have had immunity to the virus, due to exposure to a similar strain earlier in their lifetime. Those under 60 however, likely had no exposure to this virus and thus, were not immune (Centers for Disease Control and Prevention 2009). Though mortalities attributed to the 2009 H1N1 influenza fortunately remained below expectations worldwide, the lack of immunity in the world's population led to high incidence rates. As of January 10, 2010, there were more than 600,000 laboratory-confirmed cases (though the World Health Organization stopped reporting cases in late November of 2009) and more than 13,000 deaths worldwide attributed to 2009 H1N1, as reported by the World Health Organization (WHO Disease Outbreak News 2009). However, the number of reported cases was likely vastly lower than the actual number of cases, as many countries (including the US) ceased to carry out laboratory testing on suspected cases as the frequency increased exponentially. For example, according to the CDC, between May and June of 2009, the US experienced more than one million cases of the novel influenza (this estimate includes those who became ill, but did not seek medical treatment). A report issued by the President's Council of Advisors on Science and Technology (PCAST) estimated that between 20% to 40% of the US population would ultimately contract the 2009 H1N1 influenza over the fall of 2009 and winter of 2010 (The White House PCAST, 2009). By mid-November, an estimated 22 million Americans were infected with the 2009 H1N1 influenza virus (WHO Disease Outbreak News 2009).

According to Mossad (2009), the costs associated with influenza have led to a public health emphasis on prevention and control, including improvements in personal hygiene, increased social distancing, and the development and distribution of vaccinations. He also noted that a discussion about the development and distribution of a vaccine began as soon as health officials recognized the presence of a novel strain of influenza in the spring of 2009. Even in instances when an effective and safe vaccine could be developed, the production of a sufficient amount of vaccine and the logistical issues surrounding delivery can cause further delays, resulting in increased morbidity, mortality, and injury. Vaccines were available for public distribution during the 2009 H1N1 pandemic initially as a live attenuated influenza vaccine in the form of a nasal spray, and later as an inactivated vaccine delivered by injection (Centers for Disease Control and Prevention 2009).

The CDC 2009 Report on Vaccination Recommendations identified five major at-risk groups: (a) pregnant women, (b) people who live with or care for babies under 6 months old, (c) healthcare professionals and emergency services personnel, (d) all people 6 months to 24 years old, and (e) those over 24 who are immunocompromised or at high risk of developing medical complications from influenza. It was hypothesized that segments of the population with varying demographic characteristics (as was the case with the five major risk groups identified by the CDC) might respond in unique ways to the recommendation to receive a vaccine. In order for any population-based public health campaign to be successful, the message must be developed explicitly for the intended audience. Consequently, if the messages are developed for distinct portions of the population, the values, beliefs, and expectations of each group must be taken into account. For example, in the case of the 2009 influenza, a campaign developed to convince pregnant women to receive the vaccine would not necessarily be relevant or effective for healthcare professionals and emergency personnel. Likewise, the factors affecting the vaccination decision for those who live with or care for babies under 6 months old are not necessarily the same factors that might affect the decisions of college-age individuals.

The sample population for the study consisted of students at a large midwestern university who were 18 to 24 years old. The rationale supporting the CDC's recommendation for those less than 24 years old to receive the vaccine (at the time of guideline development) was that many cases of the 2009 H1N1 influenza had been seen in "...healthy young adults [because] they often live, work, and study in close proximity, and they are a frequently mobile population."

Public health uses a variety of strategies for surveillance and to assess problems. One procedure frequently used for which there is a long history is surveys. Presented below is the preferred way to develop a survey for analytical epidemiology. The survey often is based on a theoretical framework, which is the preferred way to develop a survey (McKenzie, Neiger, and Thackeray 2005).

Theoretical Framework

Public health behavioral epidemiologic interventions are frequently based upon behavioral theories (Glanz, Rimer and Viswanath 2008). The theory chosen for this study was the health belief model (HBM) (Bandura 1977; Rosenstock 1974). There were six constructs evaluated: perceived susceptibility, perceived severity, perceived benefits, perceived barriers, cues to action, and self-efficacy. Perceived severity encompasses the negative impacts or consequences the illness would have on the individual's life. Perceived benefits are any positive outcomes associated with a health action to reduce the likelihood of developing the illness. Any factors that might inhibit an individual's ability to take this health action, or any negative aspects associated with the action are the individual's perceived barriers. The cues to action construct accounts for any events, whether interpersonal, intrapersonal, or environmental, that might impede an individual from intention toward action. Last, is the construct of self-efficacy. Self-efficacy is "the conviction that one can successfully execute the behavior required to produce the outcomes" (Bandura 1977, p. 193).

The relationships between these constructs and behavior are represented in Figure 10.1.

The HBM has been used in the past to model a variety of health behaviors, including the choice in a population of college students to receive an immunization for measles (Pielak and Hilton 2003) and within the general population to receive the vaccine during the swine flu threat of the mid-1970s (Brock 1983; Cummings et al. 1979).

Problem Statement and Purpose

Though the illness had relatively low fatality rates, the costs to an individual contracting the disease may have been significant in terms of ability to work and function (Greenbaum 2006). It was previously unknown how these cohorts, college-age adults, would respond to non-mandatory immunization recommendations during a pandemic. In past research focusing on healthcare workers (Weingarten et al. 1989) and students in healthcare-related fields, Pennie et al. (1991) perceived that severity, susceptibility, and barriers influenced the vaccination decision.

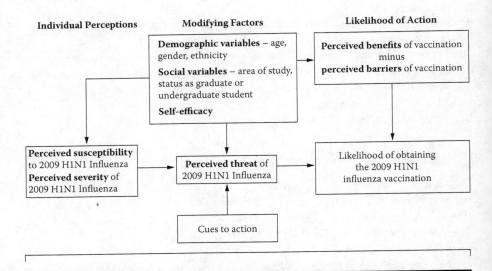

Individual Perceptions | Modifying Factors | Likelihood of Action

Demographic variables – age, gender, ethnicity
Social variables – area of study, status as graduate or undergraduate student
Self-efficacy

Perceived benefits of vaccination
minus
perceived barriers of vaccination

Perceived susceptibility to 2009 H1N1 Influenza
Perceived severity of 2009 H1N1 Influenza

Perceived threat of 2009 H1N1 Influenza

Likelihood of obtaining the 2009 H1N1 influenza vaccination

Cues to action

Figure 10.1   Relationship among HBM constructs and vaccine choice. Adapted from Becker et al. 1977.

The purpose of this study was to compare students who chose to attain the 2009 H1N1 vaccine versus those who did not. Areas of comparison consist of the constructs of the HBM: perceived susceptibility, severity, benefits, barriers, cues to action, and self-efficacy.

Methods

Research Design and Sample

The study design was cross-sectional. The HBM, and previously used instruments based on the HBM (Champion 1984, 1993; Pielak 1999), provided a framework for the design of the survey instrument used in this study to compare those students who decided to receive the 2009 H1N1 vaccine versus those students who did not get the vaccine. The institutional review board of the university approved procedures of this study. An electronic survey (Qualtrics 2005) was distributed via e-mail to 4,000 randomly selected university students between 18 and 24 years old.

Instrument Development

Dr. Victoria Champion gave permission (personal communication, November 14, 2009) for the revision of her 1993 "Breast Self Examination-Related Health Belief Model Scales." This instrument had been previously revised and used to assess immunization decision making in college students toward measles vaccination (Pielak 1999; Pielak and Hilton 2003). The influenza vaccination questionnaire (IVQ), the survey instrument for the study, was developed using these Champion and Pielak surveys as guides.

Construct validity of the IVQ was established using a review process previously employed by Champion (1984). A panel of seven experts familiar with the HBM individually reviewed potential items, which were presented in random order and were not labeled by construct. The subject area experts indicated which survey item aligned with each HBM construct. Items not receiving agreement from the panel of experts were modified until complete agreement upon the measured construct was reached.

Readability of the survey was assessed using the reading grade level function of Microsoft Office, which employs the Flesch-Kincaid test. A cognitive interview process was conducted with five individuals in order to assess the following: (a) comprehension of the questions, (b) retrieval from memory of relevant information, (c) the decision process, and (d) the response process (Tourangeau 1984). Response bias, readability, and item clarity were assessed, with input from 30 undergraduate student volunteers. Minor revisions (to improve clarification) to four of the survey items occurred after reviewing the results of this preliminary testing.

Data were analyzed using SPSS (statistical packages for the social sciences, v.17.0). Principal component analyses (PCA) with varimax rotation were conducted in order to determine how each individual survey item loaded on the constructs. Items were eliminated from further analyses if they loaded on multiple components with loading values of 0.4 or more. After eliminating co-loading items, the PCA were repeated until all co-loading items were eliminated. The remaining items were considered to be loading on a particular component if the loading factor corresponding with that component was 0.4 or greater. Components with eigenvalues of 1.0 or greater remained in the analyses.

Five rotations of the principal component analysis (PCA) were completed, with co-loading items (cutoff value of 0.40) being eliminated from further analysis. The final PCA resulted in six distinct components, reflecting the six constructs of the HBM.

A composite score for each of the identified components was created using a weighted sum (as determined by the PCA) of the items that loaded on that component. Internal consistencies of the components identified by the PCA were calculated using Cronbach alpha. Overall reliability of the IVQ instrument also was calculated using Cronbach alpha.

All reliabilities indicated moderate to moderately high reliability. The minimum value was for perceived susceptibility (0.58) and the maximum was for the self-efficacy (0.87). Overall, the IVQ had a Cronbach alpha of 0.66. This is an acceptable value, but the higher and closer to 1.0, the better.

Instrument Administration

A hyperlink to the IVQ was distributed to 4,000 randomly selected students via electronic mail. The link to the survey remained active for 10 days. The electronic survey (and its distribution through e-mail) allowed the respondents to remain completely anonymous. A reminder e-mail was sent to all 4,000 students one week after the initial e-mail. The intention behind this reminder, in addition to an incentive to participate, was to achieve a response rate of 50% or higher (Dillman 2000; Dillman, Smyth, and Christian 2009). Those who completed the survey were entered into a drawing to win a $10 gift certificate to on-campus dining establishments. University policy states that the "[s]ample may not exceed 4,000 students" and that "[o]nly one follow-up message is permitted" (see instructions for research study e-mails to students in the following box). The detrimental effects of this policy will be discussed further in the "Lessons Learned for Future Research" section.

INSTRUCTIONS FOR RESEARCH STUDY E-MAILS TO STUDENTS

Note that policy is different for surveys for university business.

In conjunction with the Graduate School, the Office of the Registrar provides a mass e-mail serve for student researchers conducting studies and surveys. To request a mass e-mailing, you must do the following:

Studies by graduate students require permission from the Associate Dean of the Graduate School [name and e-mail address redacted]. We must receive permission from [name redacted] before we will accept a request for sending an e-mail. Any requests received before we are authorized to go forward with this will be cancelled and you will be forced to resubmit your request. This is not required for studies conducted by faculty or university administrators.

Studies intended for publication or presentation must have approval by the IRB. A copy of the IRB approval should be dropped off to the attention of [name redacted] at the Office of the Registrar.

Once you have approval from the Graduate School and IRB if necessary, send the following information to [name redacted].

- The name of your major professor and his or her e-mail address. The message will go out in your major professor's name but your e-mail address should be used for a reply address.
- The e-mail address that you want as the reply to: address. The Header Line of the e-mail message. This should be designed to catch the attention of the student.

- The text body of the message.
- The date you wish the e-mail message to be sent. Note that messages will be sent when this does not interfere with routine functioning of the Registrar's Office and may be delayed to meet business needs. The Office of the Registrar reserves the right to disapprove any message it deems inappropriate.

One follow-up-reminder e-mail may be sent to the same population. This should be requested one to two weeks after the date set for the original message. This should be sent to the e-mail address above. Only two messages will be sent per survey or project, even if you do not get enough responses to be statistically valid. There will be NO exceptions to this policy.

No e-mails will be approved for dates where [the University] is not in session. All e-mail populations will be of those of the current session. No e-mails will be approved from the beginning of Dead Week through the end of session in Spring and Fall. This includes follow-up messages, so plan accordingly.

RESTRICTIONS ON SAMPLES:

1. Only currently enrolled [University] students on the [main] campus.
2. No students who elected to restrict their directory information.
3. Sample may not exceed 4,000 students.
4. Message may not contain graphics.
5. Only one follow-up message is permitted.

Data Analyses

Descriptive statistics, including mean and standard deviation, were used to analyze the ages of the respondents. Frequencies of responses were analyzed for the following variables: gender, status as an international student, academic class, academic department, and 2009 H1N1 vaccination choice. The demographic variables selected for inclusion were based on prior research conducted by Pielak (1999).

Backwards stepwise logistic regression was computed to determine the probability that students made their vaccination decision based on age, gender, status as an international student, academic class, and on the basis of the six constructs of the HBM. Backwards stepwise logistic regression also was computed to determine whether the demographic variables and which HBM constructs (perceived susceptibility, perceived severity, perceived benefits, perceived barriers, cues to action, and self-efficacy) could be utilized to answer the outcome question: "Did you receive the 2009 H1N1 vaccination?"

Results

The hyperlink to the IVQ, along with a short explanation (see enclosure 2), was e-mailed to 4,000 students. Five of these (0.13%) were returned undeliverable. Of the 3,995 e-mails received by students, 565 (14.1%) completed the survey.

E-MAIL TO STUDENTS

Dear [University] Student,

You are invited to take part in an anonymous research survey aimed at understanding what factors affected your decision about whether or not to get the H1N1 influenza vaccination, entitled the Influenza Vaccination Questionnaire (IVQ).

The information you provide will be a valuable contribution to helping us better understand what factors affect students' decisions. You must be 18 or older to participate in the research study. It should take approximately 10 minutes to complete the research survey.

By choosing to complete the IVQ, you will be offered a chance to win one of ten $ [student union] gift certificates.** To be entered in this random drawing, simply provide your e-mail address after you have completed the research survey. The e-mail address you provide will not be associated with your responses and will be deleted once the gift certificates are distributed.

Please note, you only have 10 days to complete the research survey before the link becomes invalid. Only those completing the research survey during the allotted time period will be eligible for the drawing.

This research study is IRB-approved. Your responses will be voluntary and you can choose to quit taking the research survey at any time. Should you have questions or concerns, you can contact [name redacted].

If you agree to participate, please use the URL below:

Thank you for your time and consideration.

**The odds of winning a gift certificate are dependent on the number of individuals who complete the survey. If all 4,000 recipients of the initial e-mail complete the survey and choose to enter the drawing, the odds of winning a gift certificate are one winner for every 400 students. However the average response rate for e-mail surveys is approximately 25%, increasing the odds to one winner for every 100 students.

Table 10.1 summarizes the demographic data, H1N1 vaccination status of the sample, and demographics of the student population as a whole, where available.

The best logistic regression model, accounting for the most variance, included the following variables: gender, perceived severity, perceived benefits, perceived barriers, and cues to action. Of these five variables, cues to action, perceived benefits, and perceived barriers were significant ($p < 0.05$). Table 10.2 displays the non-standardized regression coefficients (B), the Wald statistic (W), the standardized regression coefficients (β), the statistical significance for each component, and the 95% confidence interval for the standardized regression coefficients.

This model had a specificity of 94.2%, and sensitivity of 75.5%, leading to an overall accuracy rate of 88.4%. For those that reported that they did not receive the vaccine, the model would accurately predict this (based upon the five variables remaining in the model) 94.2% of the time. Conversely, of those who did get the vaccine, the model would accurately predict this action 75.5% of the time. This was determined by creating a classification table within the logistic regression. Any result above chance (50%) is considered a useful finding. The prediction model was applied to each respondent's answers, and then the predicted outcome was compared with the actual outcome.

Discussion

Major Findings

The purpose of this study was to ascertain which demographic variables and HBM constructs would be most useful to predict an individual's vaccination decision. Backwards stepwise logistic regression led to the acceptance of a model that included perceived benefits, perceived barriers, and cues to action for prediction of the vaccination decision outcome.

Most interesting are the differences between those HBM constructs that were significant contributors to the model (perceived benefits, perceived barriers, and cues to action) as opposed to those that were not significant contributors (perceived susceptibility, perceived severity, and self-efficacy) (see Table 10.3). It seems to follow logically that self-efficacy would not be a significant predictor of vaccination behavior. In comparison with health behaviors requiring a long-term commitment or several steps to change behavior (such as improving diet, increasing physical activity levels, or quitting smoking), acquiring a vaccination requires just one action: to get an injection. Once the decision to be vaccinated is made, the individual is a passive participant.

Perceived susceptibility and perceived severity did not play a significant role in the final prediction model. These constructs, when combined, created perceived

Table 10.1 Sample characteristics

Demographic Characteristics			
Variable	**Response**	**% of Sample**	**% of Population**[a]
Sex	Male	32.3	57.9
	Female	67.7	42.1
International Student Status	International Student	8.3	13.9
	American Student	91.7	86.1
Academic Class	Undergraduate	87.4	79.5
	Graduate	12.6	21.5
Age	**Mean**	**Standard Deviation**	**Variance**
	20.73	1.65	2.72
Department of Study		**% of Sample**	**% of Population**[a]
College of Agriculture		9.1	7.9
College of Consumer and Family Sciences		8.0	5.2
College of Education		3.4	3.2
College of Engineering		17.9	23.4
College of Liberal Arts		20.9	19.1
Krannert School of Management		5.3	8.6
College of Pharmacy, Nursing, & Health Sciences		12.9	6.5
College of Science		11.6	10.4
H1N1 Vaccination Status			
Response		**% of Sample**	**% of Population**[b]
Yes, received vaccine		36.2	9.7
No, did not receive vaccine		63.8	91.3

[a] "% of Population" in the demographic characteristics was based upon the University's Office of Enrollment (as of Sept. 2009).

[b] "% of Population" in the H1N1 vaccination status question refers to the percentage of the student body that received the vaccination from the university's health center. It is likely that many students received the vaccine from other healthcare providers.

Table 10.2 Logistic regression of variables on immunization status

	B	SE	W	df	Sig.	β	95% C.I.for β	
							Lower	Upper
Gender	-.674	.365	3.407	1	.065	.509	.249	1.043
Perceived Severity	.302	.165	3.336	1	.068	1.352	.978	1.869
Cues to Action	1.395	.190	54.031	1	.000	4.035	2.781	5.852
Perceived Barriers	-1.834	.223	67.887	1	.000	.160	.103	.247
Perceived Benefits	.640	.171	14.055	1	.000	1.896	1.357	2.648
Constant	-1.144	.206	30.841	1	.000	.319		

Note. Variable(s) entered on step 1: Gender, academic class, academic major, status as an international student, self-efficacy, perceived severity, perceived susceptibility, perceived benefits, perceived barriers, and cues to action

Table 10.3 Health belief model constructs' role in the predictor model

Significantly contributed to the prediction model	Constructs that did not significantly contribute to the predictive capabilities of the model
Cues to Action	Self Efficacy
Perceived Barriers	Perceived Susceptibility
Perceived Benefits	Perceived Severity

threat. Because the H1N1 influenza was not perceived as a particularly likely or serious threat, these constructs did not contribute to the predictor model. However, the perceived benefits and barriers to receiving the vaccination were significant contributors. In other words, in this instance, it was perceptions about the characteristics of the action (receiving the vaccine), as well as cues toward that action, as opposed to the respondents' perceptions about characteristics of the threat (H1N1), that affected the respondents' decision. The HBM in total, may not be an appropriate model for predicting college students' vaccination decision. Nevertheless, half the items were beneficial and focus should be on those constructs in future research.

Though it is unwise to draw too broad conclusions from a single study, it also is important to consider what the findings of this study imply for future health promotion programs, specifically vaccination campaigns aimed at college students. According to the analyses, respondents did not view themselves as extremely susceptible to the H1N1 virus, and this construct did not affect their vaccination decision. There was some recognition that the H1N1 had the potential to cause many adverse side effects. Of the questions associated with perceived severity, the majority of respondents indicated that they either "agree" or "strongly agree" with the items presented. However, this construct was not a statistically significant contributor to the model predicting the vaccination decision ($p = 0.07$).

The fact that the respondents' perceptions of the barriers and benefits to vaccination did affect their decision is important. In terms of future vaccination campaigns, emphasis should be placed on addressing any concerns or reducing potential barriers to receiving the vaccination, and emphasizing the benefits of vaccination. Cues to action also had a significant effect on the respondents' vaccination choice. According to the findings, simple reminders and encouragement from a trustworthy source, such as a family member or healthcare professional, can significantly affect behavior.

The development of future vaccination campaigns could benefit by considering the unique characteristics of the intended population. While, in the current study, it was found that characteristics of the vaccination (as opposed to the disease itself) affected the vaccination decision, this may not necessarily be the case for all segments of the population. A "one size fits all" approach is not appropriate for health campaign development, whether the target action is improving nutritional intake, increasing physical activity, or receiving a vaccine.

The results of this study, as well as past research on related topics (Li and Taylor 1993; Pennie et al. 1991; Pielak 1999; Roberts et al. 1995; Weingarten et al. 1989) have shown that the HBM, when taken as a complete model, is an unsatisfactory explanatory or predictor model for understanding the decision to receive (or not) a voluntary immunization. However, the constructs of the Health Belief Model, when considered individually have received mixed support for their utility to explain or predict the vaccination decision. This is an area open for future research, especially when considering the development of vaccination campaigns for specific populations. Campaign methods that adhere to Occam's razor might be public service announcements through the university's public radio station or other radio stations, newspaper articles in campus newspapers, letters, posters, flyers, intercept interviewing methods to talk with students, and open forums. Various evaluation methods would be used to test and change each method to make it more efficacious.

Lessons Learned for Future Research

The crux of this chapter is low response rate. Although the survey was based on theory, developed according to standards, and accepted methods of survey development and appropriate psychometric methods of survey evaluation were used, the response rate was only 14% despite best efforts and hopes for external validity. A 14% response rate might lead to erroneous conclusions. A better response rate would have been 50% as mentioned early in the chapter. Even this%age is not ideal. Presumably, if all the remaining non-respondents responded, the conclusions might change dramatically or be totally different. The issue can be mitigated if it is possible to interview or convince a randomly selected subgroup to respond and their responses align with those initially surveyed. In this case, it is unknown whether the responses of the 14% are representative of the total number of possible respondents. The low response rate is a threat to external validity of the total group evaluated and the campus at large. Further examination of these two important issues, their causes and potential solutions, is warranted.

There are a number of potential reasons for the low return rate (14.1%). The university at which the survey was distributed limits researchers to two e-mail contacts: one for the survey and a second for a reminder. Though it has been shown (Dillman 2000; Dillman, Smyth, and Christian 2009) that a "pre-contact" letter from a trustworthy source to inform potential respondents that they will receive a survey in the coming days can increase return rates, the regulations of the university made this pre-contact impossible. While it is commendable that the university policy protects the privacy of students, its effect on research outcomes cannot be ignored. Another possible impact is the relatively low incentive ($10 to 10 individuals) provided by the researcher. It is possible that many students did not deem this incentive amount worthy of the time it would take them to complete the survey. Survey and topic fatigue also may have played a role in the low response rate.

Another is the regularity that groups are asked to respond to surveys. Taking an online survey is not a novel experience and may be regarded as a nuisance or intrusive. It is clear that 86% in this study responded by pressing the delete button. The 2009 H1N1 influenza was in the news for many months, though it is no longer the priority it once was within the collective mindset of the culture (Henrich and Holmes 2009). Perhaps upon seeing this topic, students decided not to take the survey because the topic is no longer interesting or important to them.

In addition to the low response rate, the characteristics of the respondents did not reflect the population of the university as a whole (as seen in Table 10.1), reflecting poor external validity. The largest area of difference was seen in the breakdown between the sexes. While males comprise nearly 58% of the student body at the university, just over 32% of the respondents to the survey were male, $c^2 = 148.6$, $p < .05$. Though it is possible that the proportion of males to females in the whole

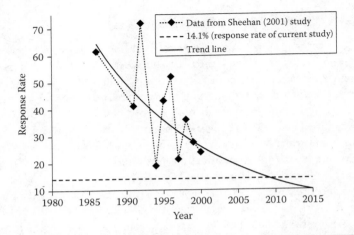

Figure 10.2   Decrease in response rates to e-mailed surveys over time.

sample (as opposed to simply focusing on the respondents) is more reflective of the population as a whole, this information was not accessible to the investigators due to university policy. Again, the protection of students' privacy is commendable, though the effect on research is devastating.

The low response rate and lack of external validity led to a deeper review of the potential usefulness of Internet-based surveys for health-related research in the future. The merits of Internet-based surveys are many: They are simple and inexpensive to administer, they allow for easy transition between data collection and analyses, and they allow for greater anonymity than mail, telephone, or face-to-face surveys. However, if institutional policies and cultural changes lead to unacceptably low response rates and a lack of external validity, social scientists may find themselves in need of finding alternative ways to collect real-time data. Relative new and better methods are reported in the next chapter. Survey research in the future may become extinct.

According to Sheehan (2001), response rates to e-mail surveys have shown a decreasing trend from 1986 until 2000. Interestingly, projecting an exponential trend line generated from Sheehan's data to the year 2010 would nearly exactly predict the response rate of the current study (14.1%). These data and trend line are shown in Figure 10.2. Clearly, there are more factors at play here than ineffective distribution of the survey. Electronic surveys may have outlived their usefulness as a way to collect data, at least given the policy restrictions of this particular institution. It is time to concentrate on a variety of other means of data collection and modify the over-reliance by public health and other disciplines in which they are the mainstay. It may be that surveys have outlived the useful in providing reliable, valid, and meaningful data. Future research will tell, perhaps where there are less restrictions.

References

Bandura, A. 1977. Self-efficacy: Toward a unifying theory of behavioral change. *Psychological Review* 84: 191-215.

Becker, M. H., Haefner, D. P., Kasl, S.V., Kirscht, J.P., Maiman, L.A., and I. M. Rosenstock. 1977. Selected psychosocial models and correlates of individual health-related behaviours. *Medical Care* 15: 27-46.

Brock, B. M. 1983. *Factors influencing intentions and behavior toward swine flu vaccine: Prevention and vaccination.* Ann Arbor, MI: University of Michigan.

Centers for Disease Control and Prevention. 2009. CDC vaccination recommendations. http://www.cd c.gov/h1n1flu /vaccination/ vaccine_safe ty_qa.htm.

Champion, V. L. 1984. Instrument development for health belief model constructs. *Advances in Nursing Science* 6(3): 73-85.

Champion, V. L. 1993. Instrument refinement for breast cancer screening behaviors. *Nursing Research* 42: 139-142.

Cummings, K. M., Jette, A. M., Brock, B. M., and D. P. Haefner. 1979. Psychosocial determinants of immunization behavior in a swine influenza campaign. *Medical Care* 17: 639-649.

Dillman, D. A. 2000. *Mail and Internet surveys: The tailored design method.* 2nd ed. New York: John Wiley & Sons, Inc.

Dillman, D. A., Smyth, J. D., and L. M. Christian. 2009. *Internet, mail and mixed-mode surveys: The tailored design method.* 3rd ed. Hoboken, NJ: John Wiley & Sons, Inc.

Glanz, K., Rimer, B. K., and K. Viswanath. 2008. *Health behavior and health education: Theory, research, and practice.* San Francisco: Jossey-Bass Inc.

Greenbaum, E. 2006. Seasonal influenza: The economics of vaccination. *Center for Prevention and Health Services.* Issue Brief.

Haber, M. J., Shay, D. K., Davis, X. M., Patel, R., Jin, X., Weintrabuc, E., Orenstein, E., and W. W. Thompson. 2007. Effectiveness of interventions to reduce contact rates during a simulated influenza pandemic. *Emerging Infectious Diseases* 13(4): 581-589.

Henrich, N. and B. J. Holmes. 2009. The public's acceptance of novel vaccines during a pandemic: A focus group study and its application to H1N1. *Emerging Health Threats Journal* 2: 2-10.

Knox, R. 2009. Inside the new flu virus. http://www.npr. org/templates/s tory/story. php?storyId=103858702 (accessed November 25, 2009).

Li, J. and B. Taylor. 1993. Factors affecting uptake of measles, mumps, and rubella immunization. *British Medical Journal* 307: 168-171.

Masterson, K. 2009. Q&A: Where did the swine flu come from? http://www.npr. org/template s/story/story.php?storyId= 112683634 (accessed November 24, 2009).

McKenzie, J. F., Neiger, B. L., and R. Thackery. 2005. *Planning, implementing, and evaluating health promotion programs: A primer.* 5th ed. San Francisco, CA: Benjamin Cummings.

McNeil, D. G. 2009. New theory, swine flu started in Asia, not Mexico. *New York Times,* June 23.

Mossad, S. F. 2009. The resurgence of swine-origin influenza A. *Cleveland Clinic Journal of Medicine* 76(6): 337-343.

Pennie, R. A., O'Connor, A. M., Garvock, M. J., and E. R. Drake.1991. Factors influencing the acceptance of hepatitis B vaccine by students in health disciplines in Ottawa. *Canadian Journal of Public Health* 82: 12-15.

Pielak, K. L. 1999. University students immunized and not immunized for measles: A comparison of beliefs, attitudes, and perceived barriers and benefits. Thesis, University of British Columbia.

Pielak, K. L. and A. Hilton. 2003. University students immunized and not immunized for measles. *Canadian Journal of Public Health* 94(3): 193-196.

Purdue University, Office of Enrollment. 2009. Purdue system's total enrollment is on the rise.: http://www.pur due.edu/uns /x/2009b/090911CordovaEnrollment.html (accessed April 15, 2010).

Qualtrics. 2005, version 12.018. Developed by Qualtrics Labs, Inc, Provo UT.

Roberts, R. J., Sandifer, Q. D., Evans, M. R., Nolan-Farrell, M. Z., and P. M. Davis. 1995. Reasons for non-uptake of measles, mumps, and rubella catch-up immunization in a measles epidemic and side effects of the vaccine. *British Medical Journal* 310: 1629-1632.

Rosenstock, I. M. 1974. The health belief model and preventive health behaviors. *Health Education Monographs* 2: 354-386.

Sheehan, K. 2001. E-mail survey response rates: A review. *Journal of Computer Mediated Communication* 6: 1-5.

Taubenberger, J. K. and D. M. Morens. 2006. 1918 influenza: The mother of all pandemics. *Emerging Infectious Diseases* 12(1): 13-22.

Tourangeau, R. 1984. Cognitive sciences and survey methods. In *Cognitive aspects of survey methodology: Building a bridge between disciplines*, eds. T. Jabine, M. Straf, J. Tanur, and R. Tourangeau. pp. 73-100. Washington, DC: National Academy Press.

United States Department of Health and Human Services. 2010. Flu.gov: H1N1 (swine flu). http://www.flu.gov/individu alfamily/about/h1n1/in dex.html (accessed January 17, 2010).

The White House, Office of the Press Secretary. 2009. President's Council of Advisors on Science and Technology (PCAST) releases report assessing H1N1 preparations. http://www.whitehouse.gov/th e_press_office/Presidents-Council-of-Advisors-on-Science-and-Technology-PCAST-releases-report-assessing-H1N1-preparations/ (accessed November 20, 2009).

Weingarten, S., Riedinger, M., Burnes, B.L., Miles, P., and M. Ault. 1989. Barriers to influenza acceptance: A survey of physicians and nurses. *American Journal of Infection Control* 17(4): 202-207.

World Health Organization. 2009. *Disease Outbreak News*. http://www.who. int/csr/don/en/.

Chapter 11

A Demonstration of Social Media Research Methods: Investigating the Public Opinion of the Flu Shot during the H1N1 Pandemic

Jennifer A. Smock, David R. Black, and J. Eric Dietz,

Contents

Abstract

This chapter is a demonstration of novel research methods used to investigate the public opinion through analysis of Twitter mentions on health topics. This study presents an alternative to current research methods of assimilating focus groups, constructing survey instruments, and disseminating surveys in order to evaluate the public opinion. The methods proposed drastically decrease the lag time of the several months recommended between news media coverage on a specific topic and a survey to gain the public opinion relating to that topic (Eyal 1979; Eyal 1981; Stone and McCombs 1981). The robust marketing technology, Radian[6], was used to gather Internet mentions and perform automated sentiment analyses to the health topic mentions. This automated monitoring and analyses of topic mentions greatly reduces non-response bias, response bias, survey instrumentation error, and biased analyses by investigators. Although this technology has not yet been applied to public health research, it is currently being utilized by multiple *Fortune* 500 companies (e.g., Pepsi, IBM, Microsoft, General Electric, and Johnson & Johnson). By using Radian[6] and the novel research methods, the public opinion can be observed and analyzed in real time.

Keywords: H1N1, Pandemic Influenza, Twitter, Social Media, Radian[6], Agenda-Setting Theory, Heuristic Demonstration of Social Media Research Methods: Investigating Public Opinion of the Flu Shot during the H1N1 Pandemic

2009 H1N1 Vaccination Campaign

The 2009 influenza vaccination campaign promoted vaccinations as best practices for not contracting seasonal influenza and avoiding the H1N1 (swine flu) pandemic (Centers for Disease Control and Prevention, CDC 2010). Although the federal government budgeted an estimated $1.4 billion for this public health campaign (Morgan 2010), there was a low rate of compliance. According to the CDC, only

22.7% of adults and 40.5% of children were administered the H1N1 influenza vaccination between October 2009 and May 2010 (CDC 2010). The government consumed large sums of money for the 2009 influenza vaccination campaign and yet compliance rates were low.

Pandemic Epidemiology

In 2009, H1N1 flu gained national and international attention. According to a CDC report, approximately 57 million people contracted the H1N1 virus, resulting in 257,000 hospitalizations and 11,690 pandemic flu-related deaths in the US from April 2009 to January 2010 (CDC, 2010). Although the 2009 H1N1 pandemic was considered "mild," it is paramount to increase the influenza vaccination compliance rate in order to prepare for seasonal influenza and possible future pandemics.

Scientists continue to believe that the avian influenza virus (AIV) pandemic will occur and should not be forgotten (CDC 2007). As of March 2010, the mortality rate for AIV cases was an astounding 59% (WHO 2008). If these figures incorporated the population for the rest of the world, there would be an average of approximately 1 billion cases of flu, around 3 to 5 million cases of severe illness, and 300,000 to 500,000 deaths (Flu Facts 2009). Therefore, it is important, independent of mortality rate and whether it is pandemic or epidemic, to understand the effectiveness of health messages in communication to increase influenza vaccination compliance during future pandemics.

Theory

The agenda-setting theory is used to evaluate the effects of the news media on the public agenda and public opinion (McCombs and Shaw 1972, 1993). The growth of Internet accessibility, the increase in social media engagement, and a decrease in popularity in several forms of the news media may have altered how the public accesses health information (Schwitzer 2009). This transition may affect how the public agenda is set and public opinion is shaped. Having a greater understanding of how the population is influenced may improve influenza vaccination campaign strategies in order to prevent morbidity and mortality during normal influenza seasons and future pandemics. Therefore, this research combines novel information technology research methods and the use of the agenda-setting theory to help with explanation and the analyses of health issues.

The agenda-setting theory proposes that the more a topic is broadcast by news media, the more salient the topic is from the public's perspective (McCombs and

Shaw 1972). The salience of an issue is related to the degree of importance perceived by the public. There has been a vast amount of research on the effectiveness of news media's influence on "what to think about" (Dearing and Rogers 1996). This agenda-setting mechanism of the news media also has shown to alter "how we think" about a topic, by highlighting certain aspects and quickly passing over others (McCombs and Shaw 1993).

The Chapel Hill Study (McCombs and Shaw 1972) set the foundation of the agenda-setting theory. The research involved surveying 100 undecided voters three weeks prior to the 1968 election. The survey focused on what participants personally considered the important issues that the government should address. This research found an almost perfect correlation ($r = 0.98$) between the top five issues mentioned by those surveyed and the top five topics mentioned in the mainstream news media. From the findings, it was apparent that the news media "set" the agenda for the viewing population.

In a recent study by T.H. Freely and D. Vincent (2007), news articles on organ donation were gathered over one year and were analyzed by sentiment. Sentiment analyses distinguish the positive, negative, or neutral content within the news articles. Out of the 702 articles found, organ donation was portrayed with mostly positive (57%) or neutral sentiment (29%). This confirmed an overall positive view toward organ donation in a study by Morgan and Miller (2001). This research further strengthened the agenda-setting function of the news media in influencing how we think about certain topics.

According to Schwitzer (2009), the exponential growth in social media engagement may have caused a transformation in how individuals seek news information, and thus altered the agenda-setting function of the mainstream news media. As indicated by Schwitzer, the popularity of social media is thought to be the cause for the decrease in the popularity in such news outlets as newspapers and news broadcasts. By monitoring what is being said regarding two different health topics, influenza vaccination as the main area of interest and monitoring organ donation on Twitter as the control, the effects of the agenda-setting function of the mainstream news media on the public's opinion can be analyzed.

Social Media

Launched in October 2006, Twitter is a micro-blogging site where users can post a message of up to 140 characters. By "tweeting," members can share their ideas, get reviews and advice on products, and updates on their status, and Twitter can be used as a source to receive news information. In the fall of 2009, it was found that one in five Internet users access Twitter or another service to share updates or to see updates about others, which grew astoundingly from one in 10 in April 2009 (Fox, Smith, and Zickuhr 2009). There has been recent Twitter growth from two million Twitter accounts in December of 2008 to 17 million in May 2009, a 700% increase (comScore 2009). Those who use demographic status to update social media sites find a relatively even spread according to gender, race, and income (Fox, Smith and Zickuhr 2009). The rising popularity and the spread across these demographics ensure representation of the US population.

According to the Pew Internet and American Life Project 2009 Fall Update, the drastic increase in Twitter usage has been attributed to the increase in mobile Internet accessibility (laptop or cell phone). The study reports 54% of all Internet users have a wireless connection, and of those that have a wireless connection, 25% use Twitter or another status updating service (e.g.., Facebook, Myspace). This increase rose from 14% in December of 2008. The growing popularity of these devices will make Twitter analyses useful in gathering real-time information about what the population feels and thinks.

Additionally, the Pew Internet and American Life Project found the younger generation to be one of the fastest growing users. It was reported that 37% of Americans between the ages of 18 and 24 years old used Twitter or another status updating service, which had increased from 19% in December 2008. In a CDC webinar in 2009 titled "CDC's Communication Response to 2009 H1N1: Examples of Strategic Integration of Social Media," it was noted that only 34% of the 25-and-under generation daily accesses news media of any type. On the other hand, 55% use social media sites on a daily basis. Over time, it will be more important for public health to utilize these outlets to both listen to what people are saying about health messages and as a way to communicate with this audience.

Research Goals

The goals of this research are threefold: (a) to verify if Radian[6] has utility for health issues, (b) to ascertain whether a significant correlation exists between the frequency of news media articles disseminated to the population and the frequency of comments on Twitter regarding influenza vaccination, and (c) to find whether the sentiment of news media is similar to the sentiment of the public opinion voiced through Twitter toward both influenza vaccination and organ donation campaigns.

Radian⁶ Research Method

Data Collection

The Radian⁶ marketing software was available for the first time in 2006. Radian⁶ is an exceptionally robust marketing analyses platform built to monitor "product" mentions in various social and news media outlets (Weinberg 2009). Several Fortune 500 companies, like Pepsi, Dell, General Electric, Johnson & Johnson, and Microsoft, utilize this software platform to monitor mentions of their products (Radian⁶ 2010). Among the numerous capabilities of this program, this research focuses on gathering topic mentions on Twitter and mainstream news media over time, and performing Radian⁶ automated sentiment analyses on influenza vaccination and organ donations. Mentions of influenza vaccination and organ donation were gathered between the dates of December 7, 2009, and March 7, 2010, within Twitter and mainstream news media sources.

Exclusion and inclusion keywords were chosen by using the keyword generators Wordtracker and Google's Key Word Sandbox to help determine "what is a case." Based upon the keywords generated by these programs, exclusion and inclusion criteria were established to ensure the results would capture relevant mentions (see Table 11.1).

Procedure

Trend analyses. The frequency of mainstream news articles and Twitter mentions regarding influenza vaccination were gathered over time. Pearson coefficient is used to analyze the correlation between the daily fluctuations within mainstream news articles and Twitter comments throughout this time period. This assumes individuals who tweet about the influenza vaccination believe it is an important topic to share among the Twitter community. Therefore, a significant correlation between Twitter and mainstream news media may further authenticate the agenda-setting ability of the news media to establish the importance of the influenza vaccination within the agenda of the population.

Sentiment analyses. Freely and Vincent (2007) used multiple coders to assign themes and sentiment to articles regarding organ donation in the news media, which ultimately resulted in lower reliability coefficient than is generally scientifically accepted ($r = 0.68$). By using an automated sentiment analyses system provided by Radian⁶ software, it eliminates the potential bias of experts assigning sentiment to Twitter comments and news media articles. It also eliminates the need for intercoder reliability estimates and eliminates response bias.

The Radian⁶ automated sentiment analyses system was utilized to evaluate the positive, negative, neutral, and mixed mentions in the following sources: (a) news media articles regarding influenza vaccination, (b) Twitter comments regarding

Table 11.1   Exclusion and inclusion selection terms defining what is a case

Influenza Vaccination		Organ Donation	
Exclusion Criteria	Inclusion Criteria	Exclusion Criteria	Inclusion Criteria
No Mention of: shot, vaccine, vaccination, mist, and no mention of: immunization, flu, H1N1, or influenza	Mention of: influenza vaccination, flu shot, flu vaccine, flu mist, flu immunization, H1N1 shot, H1N1 vaccination, H1N1 vaccine, H1N1 mist, H1N1 immunization, influenza shot, influenza vaccination, influenza vaccine, influenza mist, or influenza immunization	No Mention of: donation, donor, donated, and no mention of: organ, or tissue	Mention of: organ donation, organ donor, organ and donated*, tissue donation, tissue donor, or tissue and donated*

* Both terms are contained within the text.

influenza vaccination, (c) mainstream news articles regarding organ donation, and (d) Twitter comments regarding organ donation.

Neutral Twitter comments were eliminated from the sentiment analyses to remove neutral news messages and those comments submitted by the population that are non-directional. For instance, Twitter messages that contain hyperlinks to news articles are not important to the rationale of this study, and therefore are eliminated. This allows for a direct comparison between the positive, negative, and mixed comments regarding each topic. It gives a better glimpse of whether the opinions of the population are more in favor of or against these health topics.

Chi-squared was used to evaluate if the difference between the sentiment categories was significant or not.

Results

From December 7, 2009, to March 7, 2010, Radian[6] acquired 11,656 mainstream news articles and 73,944 Twitter comments involving the influenza vaccination and 908 mainstream news articles and 2,456 Twitter comments regarding organ donation (see Table 11.2).

The Pearson coefficient suggests there is a significant correlation between the mentions of the influenza vaccination in news media and Twitter over time, $r(89) = 0.82$, $p < 0.001$. This implies that the more the influenza vaccination was mentioned in the mainstream news media, the more the population was commenting on the topic on Twitter (see Figure 11.1).

The proportion of sentiment within the mainstream news is significantly neutral in regards to the topics of organ donation (96.4%), $\chi^2(2, N = 908)$, $p < 0.001$, and the influenza vaccination (97.4%), $\chi^2(2, N=11,656)<0.001$, $p < 0.001$. The news media shows slightly more positive than negative sentiment for both organ donation (2.2%, 1.3%, respectively) and influenza vaccination (1.2%, 1.2%, respectively). However, Twitter posts regarding influenza vaccination are significantly

Table 11.2 Sentiment of influenza vaccination and organ donation mentions

Topic	Mainstream News (%)	Twitter (%)	Non-Neutral Twitter (%)
Influenza Vaccination Total	11,656 (100.0)	73,944 (100.0)	13,539 (100.0)
Positive	141 (1.2)	5,183 (7.0)	(38.2)
Negative	143 (1.2)	8,331 (11.2)	(61.6)
Neutral	11,391 (97.4)	61,616 (81.8)	—
Mixed	15 (0.1)	25 (0.0)	(0.2)
Organ Donation Total	908 (100.0)	2,456 (100.0)	369 (100.0)
Positive	20 (2.2)	312 (12.4)	(80.8)
Negative	12 (1.3)	73 (3.0)	(19.0)
Neutral	875 (96.4)	2,070 (84.6)	—
Mixed	1 (0.1)	1 (0.0)	(0.3)

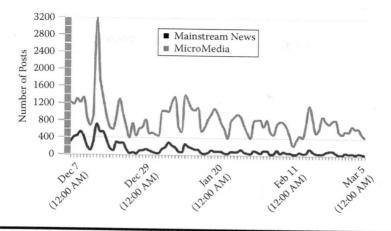

Figure 11.1 Influenza vaccination of posts over time.

more negative (61.6%) than positive (38.2%), $\chi^2(2, N=13,539)<0.001$, $p<0.001$, and Twitter posts regarding organ donation are significantly more positive (80.8%) than negative (19.0%), $\chi^2(1, N=385)<0.001$, $p<0.001$.

Discussion

This study extends a novel way of exploring public opinions without focus groups, survey instrument development, and survey participants. This study was successful in using relatively new information technology to analyze public health campaigns in real time. The study sought to find a correlation between mainstream news articles and Twitter mentions regarding influenza vaccination over time. This study assumes the individuals commenting on Twitter about the influenza vaccination feel this specific topic is important enough to share with the other 17 million Twitter members (Fox, Smith, and Zickuhr 2009). Therefore, the significant correlation of news and Twitter comments may show the agenda-setting function of the media in influencing the salience of a topic. In other words, the news media may have the power of setting our personal agenda by focusing on certain topics and not others (McCombs and Shaw 1993). This finding is consistent with previous research on the agenda-setting effects of the news media (McCombs and Shaw 1972). Although there is a decrease in newspaper sales and news broadcast audiences (Schwitzer 2009), it is important to understand the population is still affected by the mainstream news topics.

Contrary to previous thought, mainstream news media may not always be able to alter how society thinks about a topic. The majority of mainstream news mentions about the influenza vaccination were neutral (97.4%) and only 1.2% of all news stories were negative and 1.2% of all news stories were positive. After adjusting data to remove neutral sentiment, 61.6% of Twitter comments are negative (only 38.2% are positive). Similarly, 77.3% of adults in the US did not receive the H1N1 shot (CDC 2010) and therefore, were not compliant with public health messages. On the other hand, 80.8% of all comments on Twitter were positive (19.0% negative). Correspondingly, a national poll found 78% of Americans are very likely to be organ donors (Gallup Organization 2005). Although the salience of a topic is affected by the frequency of mainstream news media mentions, news may not always be able to change how we feel about a certain topic. This function of the news media is important to understand. For example, if mainstream news media were the chosen channel to resolve miscommunication and rumors involving a health behavior, there is no guarantee their message would change the thoughts and opinions of the viewing audience.

The negativity toward the influenza vaccination is consistent with the general distrust in vaccinations (Cooper, Larson, and Katz 2008; Senier 2008; Wilson et al. 2008). A report by Cooper, Larson, and Katz titled, *Protecting Public Trust in Immunizations,* analyzed the reasons for the modern distrust in vaccinations. The authors discussed numerous reasons for this change since the creation of the vaccine in 1955. First of all, vaccinations are meant to prevent diseases that are not a modern day problem. Many individuals have no personal experiences with many vaccine preventable diseases. Therefore, individuals have greater fear of vaccinations than the diseases they may prevent. Furthermore, being in the information era, more people are apt to research diseases online than solely taking the advice of their physician. Although the Internet can be a wonderful resource, it also is a tool that can provide misinformation (Bonnar-Kidd et al. 2009). The population is thus easily exposed to incorrect information. Scientifically proven research takes a profoundly longer time to publish than rumors. The population's acceptance of these rumors may be due to society's exposure to deceptive government politics, large corporations, and media. This type of distrust is not a new phenomenon, but has occurred several times throughout history (Alcabes 2009).

These research findings may be a result of a change in how people obtain health and news information. Radian[6] performs analyses of "key influencers" by pre-set equalizer (EQ) ratings of websites evaluating the amount of on-topic posts (i.e., Internet articles), comment count, average engagement, among other measures of user engagement. The three top-rated influencers on the influenza vaccination include: The Big Picture, www.h1n1vaccinerisks.net, and Infowars. Among the first news media to be mentioned were CBC News-Health News and Today's News ranked 13th and 14th, respectively. There are many key influencers that are not under the control of the news media. The frequent and consistent negative comments regarding influenza vaccination may be a result of Americans transitioning from mainstream news to non-news media to access health information.

Theoretical Implications

In 1972, when the agenda-setting theory was first developed, society developed an understanding of current events solely through personal experiences and news media (Dearing and Rogers 1996). Through the increase in Internet capability, capacity, and accessibility, people are now able to obtain more information and misinformation through news and non-news media. Although this has not affected the salience power of the news media, society is now able to develop broad degrees of opinion based on how they receive information. Additionally, people may be more likely to trust the recommendations of virtual friendships made through social networking sites than the recommendations made by the news media. More research needs to be conducted to gain a better understanding of these Internet relationships in order to more efficiently and accurately inform the population on important health issues.

Practical Implications

This research presents an alternative to developing and disseminating surveys to the population. It is crucial for major health organizations to understand public opinion regarding health messages. Apart from understanding the general positive or negative feelings toward health topics, Radian[6] also provides a means for finding the common themes at any point in time by using a word cloud widget—the more a word is mentioned within the designated media channel, the larger it appears in the "word cloud." In Figure 11.2, a word cloud was taken from the peak of the trend of flu shot mentions in Twitter (also known as micromedia). This word cloud includes such terms as "recalled," "H1N1," and "vaccine." To further analyze the data, a trend line of the "recalled" mentions within the already established flu shot parameters can be observed. With this evidence, it appears the H1N1 flu shot was recalled at 10:00 a.m. on December 15, 2010. Radian[6] makes it quick and easy for investigators to view themes used within these media outlets. Receiving this information in a timely manner is especially critical during such emergencies as a pandemic. With real-time analyses of social media networks, health messages can rapidly evolve in response to common misconceptions and rumors.

Limitations

Although the attitudes expressed are similar using automated sentiment analyses and previous research findings regarding the influenza vaccination and organ donation, the reliability of the Radian[6] sentiment analyses software has not been thoroughly tested. For example, slang terms and abbreviations are not recognized

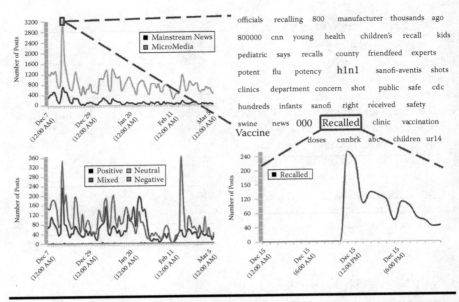

Figure 11.2 Word cloud taken from peak of the trend of flu shot mentions in Twitter.

by automated sentiment analyses process which could create additional bias. However, this system consistently and efficiently codes entries without the bias or error of human coders. The large number of articles and comments also would help to reduce error as well as reveal general trends. Additionally, it is not known if the thoughts and opinions of the Twitter community represent the thoughts and opinions of the population as a whole. However, prior research finds the usage of Twitter is evenly distributed among demographic variables to include gender, race, and income categories (Fox, Smith, and Zickuhr 2009). Additionally, even though a significant correlation was found between mainstream news and Twitter, $r(89) = 0.82$, $p < 0.001$, a stronger correlation might have been found if data were gathered during the height of the pandemic instead of the tail end. Lastly, the majority of news and Twitter mentions were labeled neutral by the Radian[6] automated sentiment analyses system. However, the accuracy and consistency of the findings to previous research supports the use of these methods. Similarly, Google Flu Trends uses the Google search engine query data involving influenza and influenza-like symptoms to accurately estimate influenza cases three weeks prior to the CDC reports (Brammer et al. 2009). Even though not all influenza-related search queries performed through Google are by those infected with the influenza, and not everyone who is ill with influenza uses Google to research their symptoms, it still provides important information through online data gathering and analyses.

Suggestions for Future Research

Future research is necessary to further express the research capabilities of the Radian[6] platform regarding important health topics. Some of the most significant contributions of this protocol and software could include the following: (a) What individuals have the greatest influence and what are their agendas?, (b) What media outlets are the most influential and what is their relationship to each other?, (c) What are the common positive and negative themes regarding vaccinations?, (d) What are the most influential positive and negative themes?, (e) Does the population react to events in a predictable manner?, and (f) Is it important to further delineate the neutral sentiment into true neutral mentions and false neutral mentions?

By organizing the data under the agenda-setting theory, this study has helped identify the relationships between mainstream news and the public opinion. Studies of the modernization of how the population is influenced in the salience of and how to think about topics are important to understand. Future research will need to be performed on how society forms its opinions in order to formulate a highly successful and effective health communication campaign.

The success of this study in obtaining consistent findings using novel technological methods may revolutionize the discipline of public health and health communication by incorporating these new methods of collecting and analyzing data.

References

Alcabes, P. 2009. *Dread: How fear and fantasy have fueled epidemics from the Black Death to Avian Flu*. New York: Public Affairs Books.

Bonnar-Kidd, K .K., Black, D. R., Mattson, M., and D. Coster. 2009. Online physical activity information: Will typical users find quality information? *Health Communication* 24: 165-175.

Centers for Disease Control and Prevention. 2009a. Questions and answers about avian influenza (bird flu) and avian influenza A (H5N1) virus. http://www.cdc.gov/flu/avian/gen-info/qa.htm

Centers for Disease Control and Prevention. 2010. Final estimates for 2009-10 seasonal influenza an influenza A (H1N1) 2009 monovalent vaccination coverage–United States, August 2009 through May, 2010. http://www.cdc.gov/flu/professionals/vaccination/coverage_0910estimates.htm

comScore. 2009. Twitter traffic explodes…And not being driven by the usual suspects. http://blog.comscore.com/2009/04/

Cooper, L. Z., Larson, H .J., and S. K. Katz. 2008. Protecting public trust in immunization. *Pediatrics* 122:149-153.

Dearing, J. W. and E. M. Rogers. 1996. *Communication concepts 6: Agenda-setting.* Thousand Oaks, CA: SAGE Publications, Inc.

Eyal, C.H. 1979. Time-frame in agenda setting research: A study of the conceptual and methodological factors affecting the time frame context of the agenda-setting process. PhD diss., Syracuse Univ.

Eyal, C.H. 1981. The roles of newspapers and television in agenda-setting. In *Mass Communication Review Yearbook 2,* eds. G.C. Wilhoit and H. DeBock, 225-234. Beverly Hills, CA: Sage.

Feeley, T.H. and Vincent, D. 2007. How organ donation is represented in newspaper articles in the United States. *Health Communication* 21(2): 125-131.

Flu Facts. 2009. Impact of the flu: Influenza statistics. http://www.flufacts.com/impact/statistics. Accessed Dec. 15, 2000.

Fox, S., Smith, A., and K. Zickuhr. 2009. Twitter and status updating, fall 2009. Pew Internet & American life project. http://www.pewinternet.org/Reports/2009/17-Twitter-and-Status-Updating-Fall-2009

Langer, G. 2009. Supply problems and safety concerns continue to hamper swine flu program. *ABC News/Washington Post Poll: Swine Flu.*

McCombs, M. E. and D. L. Shaw. 1972. The agenda-setting function of the mass media. *Public Opinion Quarterly* 36: 176-187.

McCombs, M. E. and D. L. Shaw. 1993. The evolution of agenda-setting research: Twenty-five years in the marketplace. *Journal of Communication* 43(2): 58-67.

Morgan, D. 2010. US H1N1 flu vaccination program gets under way. http://www.reuters.com/article/idUSN06437135. Accessed Dec. 15, 2010.

Morgan, S. E. and J. K. Miller. 2001. Beyond the organ donor card: The effect of knowledge, attitudes, and values on willingness to communicate about organ. *Health Communication* 14(1): 121-134.

Radian6. 2010. Some of the leading companies working with Radian6. http://www.radian6.com/community/our-customers. Accessed Dec. 15, 2010.

Schwitzer, G. 2009. *The state of health journalism in the U.S: A report to the Kaiser Family Foundation.* Menlo Park, CA: University of Minnesota.

Senier, L. 2008. It's your most precious thing: Worst-case thinking, trust, and parental decision making about vaccinations. *Sociological Inquiry* 78(2): 207-229.N

The Gallup Organization, Inc. 2005. National survey of organ and tissue donation attitudes and behaviors, Washington, DC. ftp:ftp.hrsa.gov/organdonnor/survey2005.pdf. Accessed Nov. 25, 2001.

Weinberg, T. 2009. The new community rules: Marketing on the social web. O'Reilly Media, Inc.

Wilson, K., Barakat, M., Vohra, S., Ritvo, P., and H. Boon. 2008. Parental views on pediatric vaccination: The impact of competing advocacy coalitions. *Public Understanding of Science* 17(2): 231-243.

Zhang, W., Johnson, T. J., Seltzer, T., and S. L. Bichard. 2010. The revolution will be networked: The influence of social networking sites on political attitudes and behavior. *Social Science Computer Review* 28(1): 75-92.

Chapter 12

Developing a Mission-Ready Influenza Epidemic Preparedness Strategy for Campus Public Safety Responders

Jefferson F. Howells, Kevin Ply, and William Newgent

Contents

Abstract

In developing a mission-ready influenza epidemic preparedness strategy, myriad preexisting mechanisms must be used and capitalized upon. With planning and preparedness as our primary focus, our chapter will look at methods to reduce risk while preparing for a threat that we may have no control over. In doing so, campus public safety responder (CPSR) action-oriented occupational bias and esprit de corps for the perpetuation of greater mission-readiness capabilities during an epidemic on campus will be highly regarded and relied upon. This bias for action approach is also paramount in the cultivation of sustainable relationships and collaboration across all campus public safety, academic, student, and operations stakeholders. While this practice is all too important in any successful campus operation, it becomes even more so during an epidemic given that complete prevention of virus transmission will be a less realistic scenario than the disease running a natural course. This concept was given further credence when our team accepted this fundamental assumption: A person infected with the H1N1 influenza virus was contagious for at least 24 hours before exhibiting signs or symptoms and seven days after signs and symptoms subsided. Therefore, with those assumptions firmly in place, along with our highly social demographic with an already elevated susceptibility, it was accepted that the virus would be quickly and easily spread to large numbers of our campus population. All of these considerations proved to synergistically fuel our development, implementation, and recovery actions in response to the epidemic and subsequently serve as the foundation for our paper.

Keywords: Emergency Management, Public Safety, Responders, Campus Police Department, Campus Fire Department

The predominant physical and demographical situational assumptions evident throughout this chapter are that a "campus" consists of those geographic areas, facilities, and critical infrastructure directly associated with or controlled by higher education institutions (HEI). However, because certain industrial, military, and private sector related entities may represent applicable concepts and compositions of typical HEI's, at the reader's discretion, they also may be included in the overall definition of a "campus."

For the purposes of this chapter, campus public safety responders will consist of any in-house, contracted, or pre-designated mutual aid departments providing integrated emergency services for the campus (see Figure 12.1).

Typically, ancillary service providers offering redundant/supplemental capacities to campus public safety responders should also be included, where applicable, in the planning process at the discretion of campus pandemic preparedness planners. These may include such services as: student health services, rescue squads, and call centers.

Figure 12.1   Campus public safety responders (CPSR).

As a foundational framework for this chapter we will explore and evaluate the mission-readiness of CPSR pandemic preparedness by utilizing FEMA's four-phase approach to emergency management, as shown in Figure 12.2.

As one can see by the brief definitions in Figure 12.2, "action" is the lead characteristic in each phase. With this bias for action in mind, we will explore many plausible actions, their desired outcomes, strengths, and weaknesses. As with all public safety initiatives, life-safety will be the overarching theme and direction for actions, not only for the responder, but for all campus stakeholders—from the sick patient to executive leadership and administration.

Additional recommendations and references have been derived from on-campus operations and established planning resources, specifically, NFPA-1600 *Standard on Disaster/Emergency Management and Business Continuity Programs* 2010 version

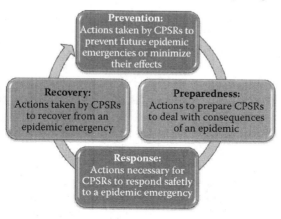

Figure 12.2   CPSR action cycle.

and the FEMA *Comprehensive Preparedness Guide* (CPG) 101. In addition to the planning guidance previously listed, having in practice the national incident management system (NIMS) components of preparedness, communication and information management, resource management, command and management, plus ongoing management and maintenance, in conjunction with tenets of the national response framework (NRF), will prove to be critical to the coordination of efforts across campus stakeholders. These guidance documents and practices will also be bolstered and substantiated by our own planning and preparedness efforts and activities at the Purdue University-Main Campus Emergency Preparedness and Planning Office.

Public Safety Prevention

An action taken by CPSRs to prevent future emergencies or minimize their effects.

In order to proactively understand and better attenuate the threats to CPSRs associated with an influenza epidemic or an influenza pandemic, we must first develop a conceptual, functional, and practical definition of what constitutes an epidemic or pandemic and then cultivate strategies to react appropriately.

As far as the concept of a pandemic goes, a simple path of logic would indicate that a specific pandemic is nothing more than a local epidemic propagated on a global scale. So with this in mind, the prevention strategies utilized should be best suited for your local population rather than attempting to accommodate global strategies that may be ineffective for your campus situation. For example, during the 2009 H1N1 pandemic, we as CPSRs were keenly aware that the pandemic would have a greater impact on our campus population due to our narrow demographics and the apparently increased level of susceptibility associated with those demographics. With this in mind, it was determined that prevention efforts would need to be in tune with other higher education institutions as our local populations would be consistent and subsequently facilitate proactive peer modeling well.

Another approach vital to the success of a pandemic prevention strategy is the exploration of relevant historical perspectives from past pandemics. One web resource useful in gaining functional historical perspective, www.flu.gov, offers numerous links and subject matter expert guidance across many disciplines. While the efficacy of this research will depend on many variables, most notably, how long ago and where did the pandemic first emerge, the interpretation of data and insights gained from multiple sources is essential in order to form a functional historical perspective. An example of this approach, albeit dated, would be the information gained from the 1918 influenza pandemic. Information concerning the speed at which the pandemic spread across the country and how easily the disease was contracted proved to be a foundational element in many of our campus pandemic preparedness planning efforts effecting triggers, thresholds, and other metrics used to prompt additional actions and initiatives. Surprisingly, however, we soon realized that the H1N1 pandemic did not fit well into our previously established models.

With this in mind, our responders and administrators reacted swiftly by adopting a more practical and rudimentary approach to our campus situation. With a "what do we know now?" approach, it was determined that adults 18 to 24 years of age were disproportionally predisposed to an elevated level of susceptibility to the H1N1 virus. As this demographic represents the primary campus population, our prevention activities would need to be accelerated compared to those areas of the world not represented as such.

A foundational element vital to the success of any epidemic planning effort is the effective utilization of essential campus stakeholders. It has been a regularly accepted practice that when an unfamiliar or potentially damaging situation presents itself on campus, a committee is convened for the purpose of solving or assessing the threat. While this model is an effective tool to reach resolution, it is also a fundamental tool to be used in the mitigation phase of a pandemic as well. Moreover, it is imperative that it is developed, populated, and exercised before that actual threat or emergency occurs on the campus. As for the development of a campus pandemic preparedness committee, it is recommended that the committee should include representatives from all essential departments on campus. One way to make this easier is to utilize FEMA's emergency support functions (ESF) model, whereby, all areas of campus operations fall within an operational group of like services, or ESFs, for more effective coordination and communication between related campus departments with similar operational responsibilities. For example, ESF8, "Public Health and Medical Services," is comprised of such subgroups as public health, medical, mental health services, and mass fatality management. As one can see, these groups relate cross functionally normally and even more so during an acute medical emergency like a pandemic. Furthermore, the individuals associated with ESF8 will most likely mold and/or define public safety actions during multiple phases of operation. An often overlooked function that should be included in the epidemic preparedness committee is that of public safety. As the pointy end of the pandemic response spear, they will be looked at by the greater campus population as those individuals "in-control" and should be kept informed with increasing frequency as the pandemic grows. Their keen insight and real-time reporting capabilities should also be harnessed regularly to deliver a timely operating picture of the campus.

Once the committee has developed into a fully functional multidiscipline synergistic working group, products can be accurately produced and endorsed by the committee for layered dissemination to the campus community as deemed most effective and in accordance with established media release practices. Three examples of possible committee products are:

■ Frequently Asked Questions (FAQs) for specific elements of the pandemic

- Homepage status—a central electronic platform for information and direction
- Situation reports (campus/local, national, and international)—to show what the pandemic is doing here and elsewhere

These products also should include additional media, such as webinars and podcasts to promote understanding or to provide population-specific instructions on procedures related to the pandemic. Another consideration for the group would be to identify and practice using technology to facilitate remote (virtual) meeting sites or the use of "calling bridges" to adhere to social distancing practices without compromising the mission of the group by elevating their susceptibility to the illness.

Finally, as a way of supporting and vetting the information being pushed out to the campus community by the committee, special consideration should be given to using peer institution situation reports and national/international organization supporting documentation. This strategy can also be useful for CPSRs' discipline-specific national organizations and accreditation agencies, as they will be producing information and guidance as well.

However, even with the best prevention strategies in mind or in operation elsewhere, priority should be given to those strategies deemed most effective not only to the campus population but to the public safety infrastructure currently in existence. This strategy also extends to the campus international student population as well. It is strongly suggested that campus international student services, and departments specializing in all represented cultures and languages on campus, be solicited in advance for consultation and application of services in order to avoid language and/ or cultural barriers that could compromise the performance of needed pandemic procedures and treatments for those cultures represented. While new technologies, thoughts, and processes inundate us daily, we must remain cognizant of our current situation and grow additional capabilities and capacities by metered doses whenever possible. These capabilities will need to be vetted in application, prior to implementation, for the entire campus population with thorough attention given to all identified and implied at-risk populations. Further assistance with these capabilities can be achieved by the early involvement of campus disability resource centers, human resource services. Therefore, competent and committed early representation from CPSR leadership and pre-identified campus departments in the identification and application of mitigation practices and strategy is essential. Through this sustainable and engaging partnership, a prudent course for further pandemic preparedness planning success will develop.

Public Safety Preparedness

An action that will help prepare CPSRs to deal with the consequences of a pandemic.

Effective campus public safety response efforts are centered on a life-safety approach. An integral and expanding element of that approach is that life-safety preparedness for emergencies is even more important and attainable than prevention actions alone. As the operational picture of responders is predominantly driven by the emergent needs of the campus they serve, having the ability and support to cultivate preparedness efforts for their "customers" prior to an emergency need is not only valuable to the campus community but also to the responders themselves. While dealing with the not-so-pleasant aspects of campus fire, EMS, and law enforcement incidents is an accepted reality among the responders, it is a common belief that this awareness should be an opportunity to effect change by exposing the campus population to metered doses of reality in the form of campus emergency awareness training initiatives. This type of awareness training should be adopted for campus emergency responders when a novel or different threat to the population they serve emerges. Therefore, as before, we must assert and perpetuate thoroughness in understanding to our situational baseline (see Figure 12.3).

The responders, in and among their strongest tendencies, are problem solvers and planners. They are vigilant not only to the threat itself and how it affects their campus populations, but also how the threat affects them personally. This is evidenced when questions and concerns from CPSRs arise as to the possible carryover into their off-duty lives, and what potential effects it could or will have on significant person(s) within their life. Proper attention, support, and guidance will need to be provided for the CPSR—a holistic approach in order to best capture or ease on-duty to off-duty concerns.

As routine public safety threats go, typically they are not taken home at the end of the shift. The fires will be extinguished, the high-risk traffic stops will be

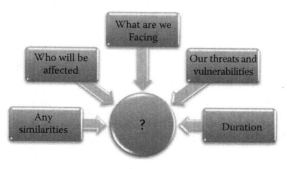

Figure 12.3   Questions to be answered in awareness training.

safety executed, and all with little significant carryover into off-duty life. Infectious diseases however, are far from routine and do pose an increased threat-risk to the CPSRs and their off-duty lives due to the specific way in which they inflict harm on individuals in a largely undetected and unseen method. This is why, once the infectious disease has been determined and prevention strategies are examined, the next logical step is preparation of our responders and their families for the response phase of an epidemic. By doing so, we are not "giving-up" on prevention, but rather setting a realistic expectation by accepting the possibility of an epidemic and preparing the CPSR, plus their personal support structure(s), for the epidemic emergence on campus.

In doing so, campus public safety administrators should review and reevaluate their department's personal protective equipment (PPE) and body substance isolation (BSI) policies and procedures currently in practice as they relate to the specific impending infectious disease pandemic. Certain plans and policies may be deemed ineffective or insufficient to fully protect the responder and patients. It is recommended that equipment used, both durable and disposable, be evaluated in order to avoid any possible contraindications in use. One example, would be if a piece of durable equipment was not able to be fully decontaminated from exposure to the specific infectious disease in question, that a suitable disposable or single-use alternative be sought prior to the immediate need. This is where consultation with suppliers and company representatives will prove to be valuable. Also, campus environmental managers, such as industrial hygienists, should be involved in the development and reinforcement of new and existing decontamination/sanitation procedures for equipment and facilities. As staffing resources dictate, these individuals would also be effective in education and training initiatives as well.

As a direct result of an impending pandemic, the stockpiling or advanced ordering of PPE/BSI items will become prevalent and only increase in ferocity as the pandemic progresses. Decisions on exactly what will work for your campus stakeholders are just as important as what will not. Considerations such as shelf life (storage), interoperability, availability, and necessary responder/user training should occur early. Supplier relationships are a key element in this process as well. In many cases, bulk-order agreements between multiple organizations or departments on campus should be coordinated. Also, campus purchasing/materials management departments should have representation on the planning committee with public safety in order to minimize the possibility of "suitable-alternative" interpretation errors. Additionally, it provides better leveraging for purchasing relationships and forecasting supply/material needs effectively. As a final note on PPE/BSI acquisitions, attention should also be given to any alternative uses for pandemic-specific items purchased to evaluate if the device is safe and effective in uses or applications other than those directly related to the prevention of exposure from the pandemic.

Our next topic in public safety preparedness is staffing. Even though a campus possesses all the best projections and robust pre-pandemic planning initiatives, staffing will be the force multiplier between success and failure during a pandemic crisis. When acceptable staffing levels are established, they should be calculated with the minimum levels or "worst-case scenarios" in mind. The reasons for this are twofold. By understanding the relationship between available responders and the services they provide, performance thresholds can be determined in advance and alternative care provider solutions put in place as needed. Whereas if staffing levels decrease 30% due to illness and call volumes are increased exponentially, either additional (ancillary care) personnel will have to be added or radical augmentation to patient care models will need to be initiated. As these scenarios are not too often utilized, they will need to be defined, established, and prepared for prior to need. One example of this would be to utilize ancillary care personnel to administer antivirals, vaccines (when available), palliative care where appropriate, and support for those who are directed or self-isolated.

An additional element to public safety staffing is that because an infectious disease pandemic is primarily a medical emergency, considerations for possible reductions in other public safety staff and essential functions capabilities not associated with direct patient care will need to be anticipated and planned for as well. Much like effective disaster emergency medical triage and treatment will define the overall success of an incident, so too will the public safety responder's ability to provide essential services aside from those associated with patient care. Buildings will still burn, vehicles will still crash, and crimes of all natures will not cease just because people are sick. These services also should be prepared for by the utilization of alternative personnel as ancillary responders should the need arise to supplement and/or support CPSRs. Also, the inclusion of civilian preparedness training initiatives, such as the Community Emergency Response Team (CERT), if available, may be a great resource to be utilized on your campus in support of not only response functions, but prevention and preparedness activities as well.

In addition to the proper setting for public safety responder staffing, additional elements will need to be prepared for, such as those seen in Table 12.1.

These elements will need to be prepared and practiced due mostly to the fact that they inherently require operational paradigm shifts or changes in established behaviors for most public safety responders. All of these elements will require additional training for the responders and associated campus staff, but also proactive and applicable educational initiatives to the campus community will be essential. One

Table 12.1 Impacts of isolation practices

Impacts of Isolation Practices	
Personal	*Environmental*
New decontamination procedures	Ventilation /Air exchange
Social distancing recommendations	Mass prophylaxis operations
Information sharing	Alternative uses of structures

example of this is hand washing. Often overlooked as an intuitive process, hand washing was not performed correctly. Therefore, FAQs, posters, and even videos were circulated in order to promote change and cultural acceptance of proper hand washing practices well in advance of the pandemic emergency on our own campus.

One of the most complex preparedness activities our campus emergency managers, student health services providers, and public safety responders participated in was the establishment of procedures and practices for implementation of points of dispensing (POD) locations for the mass prophylaxis of the campus community. This involved extensive consultation and guidance from all facets of campus public safety, pandemic preparedness committee members, and the local health department.

Considerations were given logically, to establish campus situation. Our primary situation was the served and associated campus populations such as students, staff, faculty, and their families. With a campus of approximately 40,000 students and 15,000 staff and faculty members, it became evident very quickly that for the purpose of a POD, only large venue facilities or those capable of supporting high-traffic loads would need to be identified. It was also determined that progressive and sustainable relationships with a broad cross-section of on- and off-campus public health stakeholders would be prudent to our overall success. This served as the basis for the core POD planning team consisting of campus emergency planners, county health department emergency managers, and CPSRs. The team was charged with finding a workable solution(s) to carry out multiple mass prophylaxis campaigns on campus with minimal impact on campus operations. This was accomplished by utilizing the POD planning team in all phases of the design, staffing, and logistical support requirements for pre-designated sites/structures on campus. Site designs and patient flow paths were developed collaboratively with tremendous attention to detail given to the safety, security, and efficiency of each process to be performed within the POD. By doing so, we maximized the use of existing features within each site to accommodate multiple lines of inoculation stations, perform in-process restocking of stations, expedite data collection, real-time modification of staffing functions, all while maintaining the greatest level of patient privacy possible. Site and staffing assessments were reviewed and evaluated based on estimated populations to be served, estimated time needed to do so, and re-staffing needs for POD workers. We were fortunate to effectively and efficiently operate two separate POD locations successfully. The most rewarding benefit to CPSRs, campus emergency planners, and student health staff was the sustainable and collaborative relationship cultivated with our local health department. This benefit is directly associated with the proactive involvement of campus public safety professionals early in the process in order to accurately perform safety, security, and response assessments for each location as an act of preparedness.

Public Safety Response

An action necessary for CPSRs to respond safely during a pandemic emergency.

The transition trigger from the preparedness phase to the response phase will begin for most campuses when the first suspected case is reported either on or within close proximity to campus. It is important to assert that even though the incident has shifted to a response strategy; all previous phase-based activities should be continued as applicable. Responders should augment the previous activities by accepting a pandemic response-bias mindset, utilizing lessons-learned guidance and considerations developed in the previous phases in concert with mission-ready tactical and strategic response operation practices.

As the majority of campuses utilize a 911-based emergency telephone system, we will use that as the baseline in-crisis emergency notification system on campus. It is also important to note and prepare for the civilian utilization of any and all means to summon assistance, not only 911. Therefore, during the response phase of a pandemic emergency, the CPSR should be prepared to receive notice of an ill individual(s) by victims themselves, a support or second party, or even a third party that is not located with the victim (geo-detached). Geo-detached notification is most often demonstrated by the parent of a student calling the CPSRs directly in order to summon assistance for their children (students). It is also not uncommon for walk-in patients and walk-in notifications to increase dramatically, especially during times of higher than normal call volumes as a result of an increased campus population's restlessness and worry.

It is during these times that call takers either of 911, direct line, or other methods, should utilize a series of pre-scripted questions as a guideline in order to facilitate a more accurate and efficient response. These questions will be based on signs and symptoms that the patient may have as they relate to pandemic-specific criteria. These guidance questions should be posted over CPSR direct-line phones, carried with the responders in a pocket form, and as a computer aided dispatch (CAD) note if applicable. It is further suggested that a call log be in place for any and all calls where the questions are used. This will serve to further assess the total numbers of ill on campus in addition to those who are "worried-well." It is important to note, that with a population as predisposed to sharing information as college campuses are, the efficacy of these guidance questions for prioritization may be compromised as the pandemic response continues. This however, can be used to the CPSR's advantage. If the signs and symptoms of your specific pandemic are distributed in a Frequently Asked Questions (FAQ) format, with explicated direction given as to where to go when these symptoms are present, it is possible that calls for assistance would be lessened by providing the ill with pre-need guidance and direction.

If isolation, either self-directed or mandatory, is determined to be effective, responders must strictly adhere to the guidance and/or policies associated with the specific type of isolation deemed necessary. This isolation awareness must also include the responder's family and or dependents and how either the responder or their family would be affected by possible isolation practices.

An effective precursor to isolation is prevention by the use of social distancing practices. These not only will include CPSRs and co-workers, but also the general public and even the CPSR's family. Social distancing practices can include a number of mechanical and environmental controls, but one of the more common techniques is the use of spatial-awareness distancing, such as "an arm's length" away or even a simple measure like "no closer than 10 feet." These are easy to understand and communicate for a broad campus population.

Perpetual and proactive decontamination practices for the responders are a critical response strategy, not only for the responders, but for all campus stakeholders to employ. This strategy will be much more effective if approached in a holistic mind-set, in that the CPSR's decontamination efforts should include any item that comes in direct contact with them or others.

That includes CPSRs themselves, patient care supplies, emergency apparatus and equipment, and their duty station. Specific attention should also be given to areas shared by multiple CPSRs and where foodstuffs are being stored or prepared.

Normal operations response functions should be performed with the 1-2-3 considerations seen in Table 12.2 in mind.

Response efforts will be commanded and coordinated as necessary by utilizing the US Department of Homeland Security, the Federal Emergency Management Agency (2008), the National Incident Management System (NIMS), and the incident command system (ICS) model and will be supported by a campus emergency operations center (EOC) in keeping with the US Department of Homeland Security and Federal Emergency Management Agency (2008). National Response Framework (FEMA Publication P-682) as dictated by the scope and severity of responses. One fundamentally important mission-ready function of ICS and EOC personnel should be to proactively monitor staffing levels and develop alternate staffing strategies as far

Table 12.2 1-2-3 Considerations

1	Use the most appropriate level of emergency medical services to meet the needs of the incident.
2	Use the least amount and most appropriate type of response for the needs of your patient(s). If possible, coordinate and consolidate your response to a central location, such as a triage facility or field clinic.
3	Use the minimum amount of support personnel (engine crew, law enforcement, ancillary healthcare providers) to facilitate patient treatment.

in advance of need as possible. These considerations are important not only to the current situational picture of an incident, but to the developing operational picture as well. Alternative strategies should include the utilization of volunteers, mutual-aid responders, and ancillary campus staff where appropriate.

One often overlooked response function is the recognition of those individuals and groups necessary for the care of domesticated animals. Personal pets, service animals, livestock, and commodity animals are often kept and cared for by CPSRs during their off-duty hours. Proper considerations must be given for the care and safety of these animals during any extended CPSR deployments outside of their scheduled shifts on campus. Strategies include the use of agricultural extension services, veterinarian teaching hospital staff, clubs/organizations, and rescue groups. These groups usually are eager to assist in the pandemic response by tending to or facilitating the care of the CPSR's animals.

If deemed necessary, a campus point of dispensing (POD) location for mass prophylaxis of the campus community will be initiated. These locations should be staffed accordingly by campus emergency medical personnel either remotely or co-located within the POD. Campus law enforcement and security responders will effectively maintain site security and site access as the situation determines.

An additional element in support of CPSR's pandemic response will be to secure, promote, and utilize a multitude of counseling/emotional support mechanisms for the responders. These may include campus counselors visiting duty stations, critical incident stress debriefing sessions, and preparations to support the possible effects of post traumatic stress disorder on responders. Often too, supporting the responder by the departmental facilitation of contact between them and their personal support structures, such as web-cam enabled communications, station visits (if not contra-indicated for exposure prevention), will also serve to support the responders' emotional well-being. Proactive collaboration between campus counseling and public safety administrators will be essential early on. The tendency for responders will be to care for others rather than themselves. Therefore, having CPSRs comfortable and familiar with counseling resources and personnel can have a significant impact on the responders' utilization of available services during the pandemic response phase.

Public Safety Recovery

An action taken to recover from a pandemic emergency on campus.

Once the pandemic threat has been eliminated from your campus, those actions taken during the previous three phases must be captured quickly and accurately in order to effectively and completely cultivate lessons learned in documents and improvement plans, which will in turn serve as a roadmap for the campus during the recovery process. As situational awareness has been a constant theme in this chapter, we will continue by applying it to the recovery phase. To do so, we'll need to implement department-wide damage and needs assessment initiatives. These will serve as the baseline for where your campus public safety presence is post-pandemic as it relates to the following:

- Personnel
- Facilities/infrastructure
- Equipment/materials
- Apparatus

After each of these has been assessed, that information is then used in the construction of formal after action review (AAR) and lessons learned (LL) documents so that future guidance can be established for preparedness, response, recovery, and mitigation phases should a similar pandemic re-emerge. An additional document, the improvement plan, will also prove to be a valuable post-pandemic document due largely to the chronological and quantifiable metrics established.

It also is imperative that the public safety departments review and revise as needed their standard operating guidelines (SOGs) and standard operating procedures (SOPs), or reinstate them if they were temporarily suspended during the response phase of the pandemic. Continued collaboration with and inclusion in the pandemic preparedness committee will prove a must to effectively move forward. While the composition of this committee may be reduced, it should remain a functional central force in setting the direction for campus recovery. This could be further substantiated by having this group gather and consolidate individual departmental plans into the form of an integrated pandemic emergency plan with revised triggers, metrics, and assumptions as needed.

For a final review, CPSRs should solicit and review feedback from internal and external stakeholders as it pertains to their response to the campus pandemic. This should include focused questions to establish the campus community's expectations and or capabilities of campus public safety as they relate to the reality of those operations in the further propagation of learning and moving forward.

Conclusion

By developing a mission-ready epidemic preparedness strategy as a product of sustained, synergistic, and collaborative planning efforts, a campus better positions itself with the appropriate and adaptable capabilities to best weather the far-reaching and devastating effects of a campus influenza epidemic. In order to be effective, these planning strategies and assumptions must be rooted in established all-hazard methodologies using solid bias for action and attention to situational details. Also, strategies will need to consider all stakeholders involved for each (emergency management) phase of an influenza epidemic. As validated in our experience and exercise, these strategies have held true. However, by utilizing a science-of-alternatives approach and situational vigilance, we also assert that effective mission-ready epidemic preparedness is a perpetual process and must be dynamic and long lived to be truly successful.

References

National Fire Protection Agency. 2010. Standard on Disaster/Emergency Management and Business Continuity Programs (NFPA-1600).

US Department of Homeland Security, Federal Emergency Management Agency. 2008. National Incident Management System.

US Department of Homeland Security, Federal Emergency Management Agency. 2008. National Response Framework (FEMA Publication P-682).

US Department of Homeland Security, Federal Emergency Management Agency. 2010. Comprehensive Preparedness Guide (CPG 101, version 2.0).

Chapter 13

Lessons Learned from Tabletop Exercises

David Hankins, Marti Burns, Pat Kuhlman,
Tim Baldwin, Jennifer A. Smock, Andrew Bynum,
Julie E. Shaffner, J. Eric Dietz, and David R. Black

Contents

Abstract

This chapter provides information regarding development and delivery of pandemic influenza preparedness exercises for Indiana rural hospitals and their partner stakeholders between 2008 and 2010. In 2008, functional exercises were delivered across the state using a web-based system that was supported by video, e-mail, phone, and fax. This approach allowed us to remain at Purdue University, yet communicate with and deliver the exercise to players who largely remained at their respective work stations within their counties to participate in the exercise. Worksheets were included with each inject with more than half required to be returned. Returned worksheets allowed us to ensure that participants were engaged and helped measure their success or identify areas that needed improvement. In 2009 and 2010, we developed tabletop exercises that were delivered on-site to nine counties in five of the Indiana homeland security districts. Again, these were primarily aimed at rural hospitals and their stakeholders. In this series of exercises, the spotlight was aimed at identifying those essential services that hospitals/communities wanted to retain despite the challenges of an influenza pandemic. In other words, it required players to determine what they would stop or alter in order to continue providing what they had identified as their "essential services." The chapter concludes with some tips that may be valuable for those new to exercise planning.

Keywords: Pandemic Influenza, Essential Services, Exercise Planning, Tabletop Exercises, Functional Exercises

Pandemic Influenza 2008 Emergency Preparedness Exercises

Background

Since 2008, the Purdue Homeland Security Institute (PHSI) has been active in developing and then conducting pandemic influenza emergency preparedness exercises across the state of Indiana. Our primary partner in this effort was Purdue's Healthcare Technical Assistance Program (HTAP), which received grant funding from the Centers for Disease Control and Prevention via the Indiana State Department of Health. The 2008 exercises were accomplished long distance, meaning that they were planned and executed from Purdue University without actually being physically present at the exercise sites. This approach had inherent challenges to be reviewed later, but the benefit was being able to reach large populations over a relatively short time period. These exercises concentrated on myriad challenges our communities face when trying to care for the large numbers of ill patients that would be presenting to healthcare facilities during an influenza pandemic. The discussion below concentrates on the 10 functional exercises conducted for the 10 Indiana homeland security districts.

Indiana is a midwestern state with the fifteenth largest population in the nation. Known as the crossroads of America, there are significant rural areas, along with several population areas that exceed 100,000. As well, there are numerous smaller cities and towns, many with established industries. Indiana is home also to a number of professional sporting events and well-known universities, including Purdue University.

Exercise Organization

The functional exercises were organized for Indiana's 10 public health/homeland security* districts (state homeland security districts were suggested by the US Department of Homeland Security, [USDHS], and US Department of Health [US DH]) but delivered to and played by individual counties. In all, 68 counties (of the 92 counties in the state) participated, with 790 registered participants. Most counties played the exercise from a centralized location, but some participated from multiple locations, which provided more realism and increased communication and coordination challenges. The exercise participants were from a broad range of emergency management specialties, including public health, hospitals,

---

* Note: The USDHS and USDH asked all 50 states to create homeland security areas that combine counties. Indiana created its 10 districts common to the Indiana Department of Homeland Security (IDHS) and the Indiana State Department of Health (ISDH), and that simplified planning and exercise delivery.

emergency management agencies (EMA), law enforcement, emergency medical services (EMS), fire departments, volunteer agencies, and more. A few of the counties had elected officials and members of the media present as well.

Exercise Objectives

The functional exercise scenario focused on the following objectives that were published in the Exercise Situation Manual:

- Participants will identify an appropriate incident command structure (ICS) to support their community's response to an influenza pandemic (Branum, Dietz, and Black 2010).
- Participants will establish local Departmental Operations Centers (DOCs)/ County Emergency Operations Center (EOC) in order to respond to an influenza pandemic.
- Participants will identify an order of command succession (backup personnel) for local DOCs/County EOC.
- Participants (county public information officers, PIOs) will develop, coordinate, disseminate, and manage public information during an influenza pandemic.
- Participants will demonstrate the ability to manage strategic national stockpile (SNS) pandemic countermeasures, including receipt, storage, security, and distribution.
- Participants will determine their county's existing medical surge capacity and identify alternate means of providing care for those ill with influenza.

Exercise Delivery Methods

To provide this number of exercises in a very compressed period to potentially all 92 counties in Indiana, Purdue Homeland Security Institute (PHSI) and partners (including the School of Nursing, Regenstrief Center for Healthcare Engineering, School of Health Sciences, Purdue University Regional Visualization and Analytics Center-PURVAC, Biomedical Engineering, and Department of Health and Kinesiology) developed web-based exercises that were supported by e-mail, phone, and fax. In total, 32 scenario injects were delivered to exercise participants (a scenario inject provides exercise information to which players respond). The first four scenario injects were delivered to the local health departments (LHDs) prior to the exercise day. Each inject included a scenario, task, worksheet, and return instructions. As well, the exercises used PowerPoint to instruct the participants and videos to enhance the presentations.

The injects were distributed over a four-hour period and were intended to simulate various complex problems that community stakeholders would potentially face during a pandemic emergency. The large number of task-oriented injects added a sense of urgency to simulate a stressful environment and required players to prioritize and re-balance workloads. The participants were asked to perform various tasks, such as developing press releases, determining antiviral distribution, and requesting security assistance from the Indiana National Guard. Return of inject worksheets, e-mail, fax, and telephone interactions, as well as county participant feedback, contributed to the information we collected, which is presented here.

Inject Review Summary

This section provides a summation of the returned exercise worksheets and e-mail/phone exchanges between the county and the simulation cell (SIM cell). While all 32 scenario injects required some type of action, there were 14 of these injects during the exercise that were required to be returned. These were evaluated by the project team for appropriate decision making and a review of the actions taken. Inject topics were considered "strengths" if a majority of the counties could clearly and accurately complete the inject task. Topics were considered "improvement needed" subject areas if more than half the counties in a district responded incorrectly or appeared to not understand an issue after discussion. Table 13.1 provides a "big picture" view of the districts' success in completing a worksheet task. The check marks indicate that the majority of the counties in the district successfully completed the worksheet task. The Xs indicate that the majority of the counties in the district did not successfully complete the worksheet task. A question mark (?) indicates we couldn't determine whether a response was a strength or weakness. Evaluation group consensus was used in determining a district's success or the lack thereof.

Based on the inject worksheets, common strengths appeared to be:

- Awareness of county's language diversity
- Ability to identify backup personnel for key county response positions
- Understanding of media access (filming) regarding strategic national stockpile site

The following deficiencies were observed and are listed in the order of most occurrences to least:

- Triage plans (majority of counties either did not have or are not aware of a written plan or haven't exercised the plan)
- SNS allocation plans (majority of counties did not have a written plan on who would receive allocations and/or the amount they would receive)
- Majority of counties were not aware of who had appropriate authority to sign for their county SNS pandemic countermeasures shipment
- Inconsistent county PIO messages

Table 13.1 Functional exercise inject responses

Functional Exercise (May/June 2008) Inject Responses											
		INDIANA DISTRICTS									
Inject #	Inject Topic	1	2	3	4	5	6	7	8	9	10
5	Initial actions	✓	✓	✓	✓	✓	✓	✓	✓	✓	✓
6	Draft a press release (English & Spanish): SNS release	✓	✓	✓	✓	✓	✓	✓	✓	✓	✓
7	Decision on filming in local delivery site	✓	✓	✓	✓	✓	✓	✓	✓	✓	✓
9	Receipt, storage, & security of SNS	✓	X	X	X	X	✓	X	X	X	X
10	Healthcare surge capacity	✓	✓	✓	✓	✓	?	✓	?	✓	✓
11	LHD PIO communication on sustained transmission	✓	X	✓	✓	X	✓	X	✓	✓	✓
13	Identify major languages/ communication strategies	✓	✓	✓	✓	✓	✓	✓	✓	✓	✓
14	SNS allocation quantities determined	X	X	X	✓	X	X	X	X	✓	X
17	Exercise scenario awareness	✓	X	✓	✓	✓	✓	✓	X	✓	✓
23	Elected officials prepared for interview	X*	X	✓	✓	✓	✓	✓	✓	✓	✓
24	County triage plan	X	X	X	X	X	?	X	X	X	?
IN NG	Assistance needed from National Guard	✓	✓	✓	✓	✓	✓	✓	✓	✓	✓
27	Replacements for absent employees	✓	✓	✓	✓	✓	✓	✓	✓	✓	✓
30	Backup generator for SNS	✓	X	✓	✓	X	✓	✓	✓	✓	✓
TABLE KEY ✓ = Successful completion X = Gaps in completion ? = Inconclusive		* Return not required for 1st exercise									

We also identified two improvement areas based on participant discussion (not included in the prior table):

- Improve knowledge of SNS antiviral usage guidelines and personal protective equipment
- Improve knowledge of incident command systems (ICS) and the difference between the functions/responsibilities of ICS and EOC/DOC organizations*

Strengths and Areas for Improvement

As the exercise closed, the participants were asked to assess what they perceived as their top three strengths and top three areas for improvement. As expected, the responses were diverse. Some counties' participants noted they have good basic plans and communicated and coordinated well together with their community stakeholders. Others would list those same issues as areas for needed improvement. In Figure 13.1, subject areas that were identified by each county as either a "strength" or an "area for improvement" are tallied. Note that the responses indicated are out of a potential total of 68 (the number of counties that participated in the functional exercises). These data are compelling evidence of the need for a more consistent training program(s) for all local public health departments, as well as their community stakeholders.

Exercise Delivery Lessons Learned

Upon completing the exercises with each district, the PHSI PanFlu2008 exercise team asked the project team members for their insights into the strengths and improvement areas of the exercise project. As each team member held different roles in the project, the ideas and perspectives differed for each of them. Following is an account of what was mentioned as the strengths as well as possible recommendations for future exercises.

One of the first efforts was to develop a website that would provide information about the project. That website was called PanFlu2008 and was available for both the tabletop exercises (TTXs) and the functional exercises (FEs). The site contained general exercise information as well as information regarding technical guidance/requirements, suggested participants, event registration, and PHSI contact information for participants regarding issues/questions. The site included a calendar of all the exercises and gave district-specific information regarding location of the

---

* Note: ICS is simply a systematic tool used for the command, control, and coordination of emergency response, while the EOC/DOC is typically a facility that supports and coordinates response and recovery actions as requested by the incident commander(s).

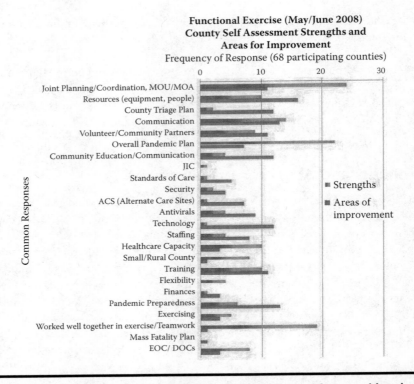

Figure 13.1 Tally by countries of subject areas that are either considered as a strength or as needing improvement.

county exercises and their points-of-contact. The website also contained links to a variety of pandemic documents for use as references. Overall, the site was intended to be the focal point for educating and informing participants about upcoming exercises. We believe this worked well, but in many cases, found that participants were not aware of the site and/or did not take time to review it. That said, we believe development and advertisement of an informational website is an excellent tool and the right approach in trying to provide information to exercise participants. Recall, these exercises were completed long distance and we didn't have face-to-face meetings.

Two pre-exercise conference calls were held for the county points-of-contact as preparation for the functional exercises. In addition to overall exercise structure and details, technology needs and information about how to view the videos were discussed during these calls. A variety of technological methods (phone, fax, e-mail, webcast) were used for the exercise delivery. Technology support was provided prior to and throughout each exercise. Even with these measures in place, some counties still had technical problems during the exercise. This was primarily attributed to their lack of attendance on the pre-exercise conference calls. Their participation was crucial in the understanding of the exercise as well as the technology needed to keep the exercise flowing. A recommendation to increase the participation on the pre-exercise conference calls is to make attendance a mandatory part of the grant requirements.

One repeated technical problem was with viewing videos. The technical difficulties with the videos came from two sources. First, we found that Adobe Connect does not buffer the videos very efficiently. Adobe Connect is software that allows presentations to be delivered over the Internet to multiple locations. This software was used to host the PowerPoint presentation as well as video injects that were given to participants throughout the exercise. Second, the Internet connection speeds at many participant locations were too slow or too variable for the videos to be viewed without interruption. These problems were compounded by the lack of technical preparedness at many sites before the exercise. Many computers were not tested to make sure they met the prerequisites of the exercise. While some counties tested one site, they used another during the actual exercise, leaving many unprepared and in a conference room that was unfamiliar to them. Also, many counties did not have IT staff present at the beginning of the exercise, so problems could not be quickly fixed. Future exercises could have even more "walk through" procedures to make sure each county site's technologies are adequate and working correctly prior to the start of each exercise.

During the exercise, conference-calling technology and speaker phones were used as a way for the facilitator to describe the exercise activities and allow participants to offer feedback. It was imperative to mute speaker phones at the participating sites to avoid unnecessary background noise during the exercise. While many of the participants complied with this request, some locations were unable to mute their phones. This could have been due to the fact that the participants did not have an understanding of how to mute the phones, phones did not include a mute function, or some participants did not attend the pre-exercise conference calls in which this request was given and were not able to hear the request once the exercise was under way.

For the functional exercises, ISDH agreed to participate in the SIM cell from their duty stations in Indianapolis. The ability to contact ISDH directly was beneficial to the local health departments as they found it reassuring to know ISDH was involved in the exercise. It also benefited ISDH personnel by increasing and/or reinforcing awareness of various local health departments' issues that may be confusing. Involvement by the sponsor (ISDH) added to the success of the exercises because the counties could turn to them for immediate assistance and it reinforced the importance of participation.

While 74 percent of the Indiana counties participated in the functional exercises, the remaining non-participating counties missed an opportunity to test their plans, get their local community stakeholders more involved, and to take another step forward in their day-to-day preparedness. In future exercises, it may be advantageous to investigate methods to get everyone involved, including more community stakeholders.

Conclusions

Evidence in this report indicates the project was very successful in several ways. First, the functional exercises provided training for 790 participants and 68 counties across the state of Indiana. The participants included a wide array of specialties, including public health, hospitals, EMAs, EMS, law enforcement personnel, and even some elected officials and members of the media. Second, the surveys from these same participants showed that 93% of the respondents believed the exercise would improve their day-to-day operations. Third, positive strides occurred for many of the health departments and community stakeholders in their pandemic influenza planning and preparedness from our work with them over the past two years. Throughout the recent exercises, we identified various strengths, including a strong spirit of cooperation among emergency management agencies, a growing awareness of the issues confronting our communities in the event of an influenza pandemic, and an overall commitment to improve their preparedness planning processes.

We also identified several areas for improvement to include the following:

- For triage planning and SNS allocation plans (processes for distributing and for determining allocation amounts): suggest ISDH emphasize that counties need to complete these plans and perhaps tie them to deliverables at the next opportunity. This also might be helped if ISDH could provide a template for developing the plans or perhaps some counties would be willing to share their plans with others.
- For appropriate signing authority for SNS pandemic countermeasures: suggest written guidance be redistributed to all counties specifically identifying this authority.
- For the issue of misunderstood antiviral usage guidelines and protective equipment measures: this has not been easily overcome, but we made solid progress between the tabletop and functional exercises. During the last three or four pre-exercise conference calls, we stressed the CDC and ISDH guidance. Further, the ISDH article entitled "Crisis Standards of Patient Care Guidance with an Emphasis on Pandemic Influenza: Triage and Ventilator Allocation Guidelines" helped greatly. We recommend that this issue continue to be stressed in conference calls and papers.
- For the issue of non-standardized PIO releases from county LHDs: the issue is that seemingly every county PIO was providing somewhat different information to the public. It appears this could be largely overcome with standardized messages from ISDH PIOs to the county PIOs. Our concept would be that ISDH PIOs provide a skeleton message, stating the basic information for everyone and then county PIOs could add to that for county specific information that needed to be included.

- For the issue of incident command structures: many LHDs don't understand ICS and need additional training regarding its application during a pandemic. Some also confused ICS with EOC/DOC responsibilities. We suggest ISDH continue to encourage LHDs to receive ICS training and then to continue discussing the issue of how ICS would be applied in a pandemic situation.

Finally, we would recommend a training program concentrating on:

- Recurring training for existing LHD employees that would include subject areas identified as needing improvement from this series of exercises (including the TTXs)
- Training for new hires that would provide a minimum level of knowledge to be determined by ISDH
- On-demand training that would provide educational opportunities for all LHD employees on newly released documents such as CDC antiviral guidance or pre-pandemic vaccines (our recent exercise experience indicates that this kind of standardized education is very much needed)
- Continue to conduct challenging exercises; ultimately, individuals and organizations will "play like they practice" and exercises are a cost-effective tool to pre-determine their capabilities and identify needed improvements before the next disaster strikes

Pandemic Influenza 2009–10 Emergency Preparedness Exercises

Background

In 2009 and 2010, we again worked with HTAP and ISDH to present four tabletop exercises regarding pandemic influenza. This time, the focus was on rural hospitals, with participants concentrating on how they would maintain their strategic plan for delivery of essential healthcare services despite the pressures of pandemic influenza. This exercise was funded by the Centers for Disease Control and Prevention through the Indiana State Department of Health. Accordingly, this series of exercises was developed to explore and measure the capabilities of hospitals and healthcare systems to sustain essential healthcare services that were identified in their plans (plans were accomplished with the aid of HTAP prior to the exercises).

The exercise planning team consisted of individuals from diverse backgrounds at Purdue University, including PHSI and the healthcare technical assistance program (HTAP), with helpful advice and recommendations from local planning committees, and staff members at the Indiana State Department of Health. Several video clips depicting potential real-world situations enhanced the exercise. Assumptions for severity of the exercise pandemic were derived with help from ISDH and were similar to those occurring in the 1918 influenza pandemic. Additionally, methods from the CDC flu surge models were combined with county populations to predict numbers of those who would be sick, those needing hospitalization, and expected death rates.

Exercise Objectives

Two of the four tabletop exercises used all of the objectives below. However, when there were three counties participating in an exercise, the objectives relating to communication were deleted due to time constraints.

- Participants will identify appropriate trigger points for both surge triage set-up and surge triage implementation. Participants will then discuss how surge triage will be implemented and sustained.
- Participants will discuss, then draft appropriate messages and identify media methods to convey public information regarding access to healthcare services.
- Participants will describe their communication plan detailing how they will keep local healthcare system providers informed.
- Participants will identify the minimum essential staffing and appropriate support needed by the staff to continue essential healthcare services.
- Participants will discuss the strategies necessary to provide essential supplies and outline how they will be stockpiled, stored, reordered, and potentially reused.
- Participants will identify security issues at locations delivering healthcare services and propose solutions to these issues.
- Participants will identify the triggers and/or events that need to occur for each healthcare system provider to alter healthcare services and describe how each altered service will change.

Exercise Organization

Unlike 2008, these exercises were played by individual counties with the exercise conducted on-site and with one to three counties participating. In all, nine counties participated, with representation from five of Indiana's 10 homeland security districts.

To emphasize that participants remain vigilant in maintaining essential healthcare services, participants were asked during each exercise module to identify those essential healthcare services that would be continued, discontinued, or altered. They did this in response to ever-increasing patient loads as the three exercise modules moved forward into weeks one, three, and five of a model 12-week influenza pandemic wave.

There were two pre-exercise scenario injects. The first inject, given 10 days prior to the exercise start date, provided a scenario and asked the hospitals/county participants to identify an appropriate ICS structure with qualified personnel and back-ups. The second inject, seven days prior, increased the seriousness of the scenario and asked participants to review their plan(s) and share their plan(s) with appropriate healthcare service providers and community stakeholders.

Three Exercise Modules and a Working Lunch

Module 1

On exercise day, the module 1 scenario introduced confirmed cases of a novel virus in Indiana with a World Health Organization (WHO) alert phase of 5, and a significant number of worried well and sick reporting to the hospital emergency departments (EDs) and healthcare providers. Participants were faced with discussing surge triage triggers and implementation, traffic issues and security needs, and then based on these factors, the resulting impact on continuation of their essential healthcare services.

Working Lunch

After Module 1, the participants took part in a working lunch where they considered ethical issues surrounding three different scenarios. The scenarios focused on hospital visitation policies, staffing absenteeism, and ventilator allocation. Participants identified the primary ethical issues to be considered in arriving at a recommended solution(s) and various other issues, including who the decision makers would be and how decisions would be communicated to affected parties. As well, laws, policies, and regulations surrounding the ethical issues were identified, allowing the participants to recommend potentially beneficial changes.

Module 2

The second module introduced a large increase in patients needing triage and hospitalization, an escalation of security concerns, and significant absenteeism among nursing staff; and WHO has increased the pandemic alert level to phase 6.[*]

Participants were asked to determine their nursing staff demands/needs by completing an Excel spreadsheet that would reveal staffing requirements based on bed counts, patient:nurse ratios, work shifts, and the assumptions about the virus itself, as provided by the ISDH (see Table 13.2). Participants were also asked to identify supply strategies to include ordering, storing, reusing, and responding to security issues in triage lines. Finally, they were asked to determine the impact of

---

[*] Note: The World Health Organization (WHO) uses a six-phased system to express the seriousness of a disease outbreak. Phases 1–3 correlate with preparedness, including capacity development and response planning activities, while phases 4–6 signal the need for response and mitigation efforts.

Table 13.2 Spreadsheet used to determine staffing needs and hospital bed availability during a pandemic influenza

Inputs (Calculate Total Nurses Needed / Shift)		
Flu Patient:Nurse Ratio	4	:1 Ratio
Flu Beds	100	Beds
Non-Flu Patient:Nurse Ratio	4	:1 Ratio
Non-Flu Beds	25	Beds
Critical Care Patient:Nurse Ratio	1	:1 Ratio
Critical Care Beds	15	Beds
Triage Nurses Needed	5	Nurses / Shift
Inputs (Calculate Total Nurses Needed / Week)		
Shift Length	12	Hours / Shift
Days Worked / Nurse / Week	3	Days
Total FTE Nursing Available	200	Nurses / Week
Total Indirect and Administrative Nursing Staff	30	Nurses / Week

Note: Pandemic Influenza Nurse Staffing. This spreadsheet was developed to project the nurses required to attend beds and provide triage during an influenza pandemic.

the scenario events on their essential healthcare services and to identify what they would continue, discontinue, or alter.

Module 3

The third module continued to increase patient loads exacerbating bed and staffing shortfalls, contributing to "community panic." Staff availability was reduced by 30% to account for staff members who were either sick or absent to take care of sick family members. Participants were asked to review their ICS structure from the pre-exercise injects, and replace members as controllers removed them from the exercise. Participants also identified community stakeholders and agencies that would provide assistance during pandemic efforts. Most importantly, participants again discussed what essential services they would keep unchanged, discontinue, or alter.

To help participants work through the staffing and bed availability aspects of the exercise quickly in Modules 2 and 3, we developed an Excel spreadsheet for them to use. As they updated the information on the spreadsheet (see Table 13.2) we then input that data into bar charts (see Figure 13.2 and Figure 13.3) so they could visually see the impact(s) of their staffing decisions and whether or not they had sufficient capability to meet the needed workload. This not only allowed the staff working group to see their decisions visually, but it allowed all exercise participants to view their decisions and see their results.

We used this spreadsheet and the corresponding charts in both Modules 2 and 3. Participants could also see the results of increasing the number of available hospital beds (surge beds) versus the number of patients who required hospitalization. Shortfalls of registered nurses (RNs) or beds could then be analyzed and many times, numerous ethical issues were raised and then discussed regarding courses of

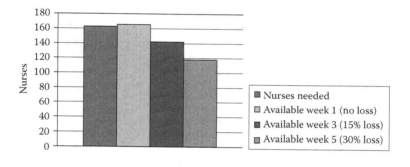

Figure 13.2   Nurse staffing projections.

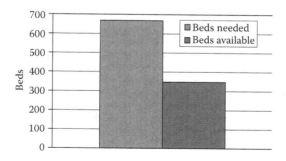

Figure 13.3   Bed status projections.

action that participants suggested to help resolve these problems. While this exercise looked specifically at RNs and respiratory therapists, any of the hospital staff positions could be analyzed in the same way.

The importance of sharing information is evident from this quote in a US Department of Homeland Security document:

> "A public-private partnership across all levels of government and the private sector is critical to preparing for and responding to all types of catastrophic events. The effects of a pandemic cross all sectors of infrastructure and government. Effective preparedness and timely response to and recovery from disasters of this scale necessitate fundamentally integrated partnerships between Federal, State, local, and tribal government agencies and private sector...owners and operators." (Pandemic Influenza Guide: Preparedness, Response, and Recovery. Guide for Critical Infrastructure and Key Resources; page 66.)

Accordingly, we would like to share the exercise evaluator comments that provide feedback on what they saw as the exercise major strengths and suggested areas for improvement:

Strengths:

- Strong understanding of security issues
- Strong community commitment
- Good discussions on staffing and essential services issues

Areas for improvement:

- Identify clear trigger points for surge triage and altering services
- Identify and prioritize essential healthcare services in plan
- Review staffing sustainment and capabilities
- Poll staffs to determine their buy-in and support needs
- Increase staff training on the plan contents (as well as training for community stakeholders that your plan depends on for success)

Participant Lessons Learned

At the conclusion of each exercise, we asked participants for their top three "lessons learned" based on participating in the exercise. Their major responses are summarized below:

Planning

- Importance of good leadership and direction
- All community partners should be involved with planning
- Develop plan for community with Spanish-speaking population

- Assess plans and policy impacts with an ethics committee(s) (for instance, "Are you willing to alter standards of care or would you ever 'close' the hospital to new admissions if beds are full?")
- [The Plan] is a living, breathing document that always needs evaluation

EMS

- Need defined and agreed-upon altered standards of care for EMS
- EMS needs transport protocols (impacted by standards of care above)

Communication

- Need to keep medical staff (employees and their families) informed along with all other stakeholders
- Critical to have cooperation within communities/districts

Security

- Need work with security staff and [police departments]...or civilian agencies
- Issues to consider are traffic and crowd control
- Security needs increase during a pandemic

Staffing

- Train staff on the plan
- Identify staffing strategies and altered services strategies
- Anticipate staffing losses due to illness or other reasons
- Poll staff members for their inputs...willingness to work extra hours/identify support needs

Supplies

- Need a reuse policy...when to start and how to do it
- Criteria for allocating care and resources needs to be equitable and transparent
- Know what SNS quantities you will receive
- Ethically altered standards of care cannot be instituted until all other options are exhausted

Other

- Elected officials and upper administration must be invited
- At some point each hospital will only be able to rely on its own resources/capabilities
- It will be a 24-hour operation, 7 days a week

Conclusions

The exercises were very successful with regard to increasing hospital and community preparedness. Many county hospital and healthcare providers, as well as emergency management personnel, with key decision makers were in attendance to work through various challenging scenarios that ultimately overwhelmed the individual hospital's capacity to admit and care for the ill patient load. Participants could then see the number of patients that would be turned away from local hospitals and were then asked the question: "Where will these ill patients go?" Overall, the answer was that the "overflow" of ill patients would be in their homes. While the exercise did not specifically address the myriad issues surrounding that outcome, it is an area that merits a much closer look. In fact, in the majority of cases, by week 5 of the pandemic, the number of patients that were turned away from receiving a hospital bed, exceeded those that were admitted because there simply were more patients than beds.

Members from state agencies, particularly the Indiana State Department of Health, were present and contributed immensely to the overall success with their inputs and observations. We were also fortunate to have two members from the Centers for Disease Control and Prevention (CDC) observing one of the exercises. To the survey question of "How satisfied were you with the TTX overall?," the average respondent indicated a score of 4.7 out of 5.

We believe that the findings from these exercises are applicable to surrounding states and perhaps nationally. Simply said, plan for patient loads that will ultimately exceed availability of patient care. These exercises only went to week 5 of a 12-week pandemic period, where week 7 would have the highest number of patients. In week 5, available health resources were depleted and/or exhausted. By week 5, hospital staffs were also significantly depleted. This means that many patients will not have a hospital bed, and likely are at home trying to "get well." With this in mind, communities should consider how they would support those patients and their caregivers. For instance, they will need resources such as food, water, medicines, heat/cooling, and working sanitation systems.

Tabletop Exercise Tips

- Start early.
- Identify a planning staff member who has expertise in the exercise area. If possible, use members from the community where the exercise will be held and get their buy-in.
- Identify exercise objectives early and apply the SMART acronym in writing them.
- Keep them simple, measureable, achievable, realistic, and task-oriented.

- From the objectives, write the scenario and necessary exercise injects that will drive the scenario and the accomplishment of the stated objectives.
- Identify knowledgeable and credible evaluators early in the process. Use one of those evaluators as your lead evaluator to help write the evaluator guides and provide evaluator training as needed.
- Identify a venue that has ample room to hold the expected audience. If lunch or snacks are to be served, consider extra tables, kitchen area, servers, etc. Also, the venue needs to have an excellent sound system. This is an area that can be easily overlooked or you may end up with a room with poor acoustics. If the players can't clearly hear, the exercise delivery becomes difficult and frustrating.
- Identify at least two evaluators for each objective and encourage them to take lots of notes.
- Conduct an evaluator debriefing to review their findings.
- Write the Exercise Evaluation and Improvement Guides using the evaluator notes.
- Hold an after action review (AAR) within 30 days so that the exercise is still fresh in everyone's mind and review the draft evaluation report.
- Use the AAR comments to finalize the evaluation reports and provide copies of those to the players.

References

Branum, A., Dietz, J. E., and D. Black. 2010. An evaluation of local incident command system personnel in a pandemic influenza. *Journal of Emergency Management* 8(5): 39–46.

FEMA Homeland Security Exercise and Evaluation Program. https://hseep.dhs.gov/pages/1001_HSEEP7.aspx. Accessed Dec. (2011).

Indiana State Department of Health Draft document. Dec. 2011. "Crisis Standards of Patient Care Guidance with an Emphasis on Pandemic Influenza: Triage and Ventilator Allocation Guidelines."

US Department of Homeland Security. Sept. 19, 2006. Pandemic influenza guide: Preparedness, response, and recovery. Guide for critical infrastructure and key resources, p. 66.

Chapter 14

Preparedness Planning: Five Motivating Dimensions

John F. Burr

Contents

Abstract

Like many events, planning is an important part of minimizing disruption. A pandemic is no exception. The public health sector has made reasonable progress. Attention to the likelihood of a pandemic flu has increased the attention to planning in order to minimize the spread of disease. The progression of events, such as the 2009 H1N1 outbreak, has allowed those in public health to see this planning in action and has informed the planning process. The private sector appears to lag behind public health in planning and at the individual level, planning is minimal. Yet this is an important part of minimizing negative effects.

To motivate planning, it is important to understand the utility parties place on the planning process. In this chapter, five motivational factors are used to express the utility function. These are: (a) probability, (b) impact, (c) duration, (d) timing, and (e) individual risk tolerance. Each of these variables acts independently, yet is theorized to have explanatory power for the motivation to plan. At a level of abstraction, the utility of planning for an event must simply outweigh the cost of not planning.

Keywords: Preparedness, Planning, Risk

Introduction

Within the public health community, there is little current concern about the spread of infectious disease such as cholera, typhoid fever, tuberculosis, measles, etc., because the etiology is well known. Yet, these pandemics have claimed hundreds of millions of lives (Conlon 2010; Encyclopaedia Britannica 2010; Lees 1996; Time 1940). Even tuberculosis, though fairly well understood, annually infects nine million people and two million people die worldwide (Centers for Disease Control and Prevention 2010b). Influenza pandemics have occurred roughly three times each century for the last 300 years, with the most recent in 2009 with nearly 30,000 confirmed cases in 74 countries (Chan 2009; Nicholls 2006). A recent analysis showed that the influenza pandemic of 1918 and 1919 killed 50 million to 100 million people worldwide (Johnson and Mueller 2002), and although its severity is often considered anomalous, the pandemic of 1830 through 1832 was similarly severe, but occurred when the world population was only roughly a billion people. Today, with a world population of 7 billion, even a relatively "mild" pandemic could kill many millions of people. Sobering to realize is when roughly one million people were killed worldwide in the 1968 Hong Kong flu pandemic, the virus emerged in China that had 790 million people, a pig population of 5.2 million, and a poultry population of 12.3 million. These are much smaller populations than the current numbers of 1.3 billion, 508 million, and 13 billion, respectively (Osterholm 2005).

Through time, the spread of disease has been managed by identifying the organism, mode of transmission, and creating some mechanism or set of behaviors for control (Heymann 2008). From the standpoint of detection and monitoring, we live in a fortunate period. With the H1N1 pandemic, no other outbreak has been detected so early with surveillance indicating migration trends or where the observed number of cases were greater than expected (Chan 2009). Today, we have better monitoring, investigation techniques, mathematical modeling, and the necessary frank reporting from other countries. These advances probably contributed to the official end of the global pandemic being declared on June 23, 2010. Early detection does not mean there is no risk. The 2009 H1N1 virus will probably continue to spread for many years (Centers for Disease Control and Prevention 2010a). Severe acute respiratory syndrome (SARS), avian flu, swine flu, and Nipah virus outbreaks have all occurred within the last few years. Our ability and propensity to travel simply adds to the transmission risk (Colizza et al. 2007). A sneeze in Penn Station in Philadelphia can be railed to Union Station in New York in 70 minutes. A cough in seat 2B can appear in Hong Kong in a matter of hours. Transmission of disease can occur rapidly. If a disease such as influenza is transmitted globally, mutations are apt to increase its lethality (Morens et al. 2010). Manufacturing the 300 million doses of influenza vaccine needed annually worldwide requires more than 350 million chicken eggs and six or more months (cit). A cell-culture approach may produce higher antigen yields and be faster, but the process is not yet developed. If a process was developed, assured industrial capacity would be required to produce sufficient vaccine for the world's population during the earliest days of a pandemic (Osterholm 2005).

This is not meant to be a shallow warning from a book central to the issue of pandemics, but a simple recognition that things have changed in a manner that favors the spread of disease or simple illnesses. Hopefully this is balanced with improved methods of detection, reporting, and wisdom regarding the disease and its progression. One question that arises is whether the general public is prepared for a pandemic and to what degree? If the public is unprepared, what is missing and what are the ways to motivate it?

Presented below are two scenarios focusing on two different circumstances. Scenario 1 concentrates on college students. For example, college students might think about what minimal food is needed. Regarding medical supplies, the student might think about aspirin, Band-Aids®, Alka Selzer®, Pepto Bismol,® and other medical remedies. The students might consider how far away they are from their parents and what friends have transportation for re-supply. From these supplies we could infer that these are the items with the highest marginal utility for the person and exceed the cost of planning and associated inventory.

Scenario 2, might be parents with a baby. The medical supplies might include pediatric medicines including Imodium, children's acetaminophen, ibuprofen, a thermometer, etc. Parents prepare for a fever, gastrointestinal distress, and other maladies which have the highest utility to them. Even if their preparation were optimum, it is unlikely that they have engaged in equivalent planning for themselves. In fact, recent studies show the odds ratio of preparing for a pandemic with something such as a flu vaccine is almost twice as likely when worried about one's child versus yourself (Rubin, Potts, and Michie 2010).

With all the discussion about another likely pandemic flu, the presumption would be there would be better preparation. At its height, H1N1 was receiving significant media attention, which we know is associated with individuals' perception of risk of being infected (Rubin, Potts, and Michie 2010). How is it that the WHO declaration of a worldwide pandemic, communications from schools and other institutions, and (sensationalist) journalism did not inspire preparation? In fact, in the Rubin study of swine flu preparation, the effect of risk was only associated with media coverage during the first wave of flu (Rubin, Potts, and Michie 2010). Perhaps this is a function as in Aesop's fable, "The Boy Who Cried Wolf" (Aesop 1990). If the concern is not validated, then future motivators of concern are discounted. The pending doom seemed remote or unlikely. Most worry if the disease were impacting their local community and if the event was exceptional and noteworthy.

For a pandemic, guidance sounds like any other flu season: wash your hands, cover your mouth and nose when you cough and sneeze, and follow public health advice avoiding crowds and other social distancing measures (US Department of Health and Human Services 2010). In large part, planning is left to individuals and whether they think it is best to purchase a case of water, flu masks, or a pound of Braunschweiger.

Institutions are not guided by the same principles and beliefs that guide the individual. Individuals are concerned about themselves and family before work (Maslow 1954). This follows Maslow's hierarchy of physiological needs prior to addressing other needs (Maslow 1943). Institutions, though composed of individuals, do not follow the same hierarchy of needs, which was originally designed around individuals. Institutions are concerned with avoiding work disruption in the event of a pandemic.

Conceptually, the chief concern of both public and private institutions and businesses is adequate resources to operate during disruptions. Adequate resources may include, but not be limited to, staffing, stocks of materials, access to spot labor, or general funds. Schools have a budget for substitute teachers and spot labor, which is built around a historical average of absences of instructors (Ng et al. 2008). Over the years, these absences have a pattern, which is statistically predictable with some known variance. The predictability of the pattern allows planning around these events so they do not become disruptive.

Problems arise only when patterns are disrupted (Ng et al. 2008). As an example, multinational firms quickly learn that the months of July and August are when the majority of vacation is taken in Western Europe. We learn to plan around Asian holidays like Golden Week(s) and the US businesses are ghost towns during the Christmas and New Year's holiday. Because of the predictability of these events and the historical impact these have had on business and continuity of operations, adaption occurred quickly. Once the new pattern is understood and behavior adapted to the new pattern, disruptions are reduced. This is not at all unlike planning for the standard flu season. Once the pattern of flu migration and timing is understood, the supply chain for vaccination operates more efficiently. We know the rate and probability of occurrence as well as the strain. This allows planning for the right amount and right type of vaccination.

If the goal is to minimize disruption, whether personal or institutional, what are the motivating factors which will cause a person or institution to allocate attention and resources to planning? The answer probably lies in rational human behavior. Planning has a cost. Planning allocates attention away from other activities that may be more immediate or of higher probability of occurrence. Planning may have a cost in accumulation and storage of resources. Yet, if we look closely enough as to why people plan for events, it would appear there are some observable common factors that lead to planning.

Five-Factor Planning Model

For the purposes of understanding planning motivation, it is posited that there are five motivational factors that appear to correlate to willingness to plan for an event. These five factors are as follows: (a) probability, (b) impact, (c) duration, (d) timing, and (e) individual risk tolerance. Each of these factors interacts with the others to form a utility function for planning. At a level of abstraction, the utility of planning for an event must simply outweigh the cost of not planning. The five factors influence the *perceived* cost of planning, as real costs are not truly known. Also, as we have seen from the work done by Rubin (2010), perception of things, like probability of events, is up to individual interpretation. Further, utility cannot be directly measured but only inferred by the outward phenomenon of action (Marshall 1920). In this case, the action is allocating time and resources toward planning.

$$u\left\{\frac{E[I \times D]}{(1+r)^t}\right\} \geq C_p$$

Where:

"I" is the impact measured conceptually in unit cost or inconvenience per time unit;

"D" is the duration of the event;

"E" is the expected probability that the event will happen with parameters I and D;

"$(1+r)^t$" is the standard form for discount rate; and

"u" is a factor to account for personal utility for risk.

Each of these factors operates independently, yet forms a collective utility. For explanation of the equation we can build from the center out. Impact would be something such as a local school district closing its schools for a day. Duration would be the number of days closed. For illustration, assume five days. The numerator is then schools closed for five days times the probability that the event will occur. In financial terms, this would be the cost of the school being closed for five days times the probability, or expected cost. The higher the numerator, the greater the utility for planning.

The denominator is a standard discount rate. The concept of applying this to the planning utility is to capture the temporal notion that planning for events years from now versus weeks from now bears a greater opportunity cost (the future value of time). Said another way, the farther an event is away in time, this number decreases the utility of planning, and thus less need to plan immediately. In addition, planning for events far in the future is subject to greater parameter uncertainty and ambiguity. While t in the discount rate is simply time, r is typically the discount rate meant to capture the cost of tying up capital at the prevailing rate of return. In the strictest definition in an industrial setting, r would be the employees' time planning and cost of tying up other resources as well as their opportunity cost. In the case of an individual, r may only be the opportunity cost of a person's time. The last variable is an adjustment for an individual's/organization's willingness to take risk.

This chapter progresses by trying to observe human behavior and draw parallels to how this behavior may translate into planning for pandemic flu. In fact, planning as a behavior, may be fairly agnostic to the typology of the event. It may help inform the issue of how to motivate individuals to plan for the flu by stepping back from strict flu planning and make certain we can understand the behavior as a whole. It should be expected that there may be some idiosyncratic or deeply rooted values motivating behavior when it comes to health and safety following Maslow's hierarchy. However, these deeper rooted needs for health and safety should simply serve to increase the utility of planning versus examples unrelated to health and safety.

Probability

All methods appear to be flawed in predicting the occurrence of rare events (Goodwin and Wright 2010). It may be planning for rare events is appropriate when it either (a) provides protection for the organization against the occurrence of negatively valenced events while allowing the organization to benefit from the occurrence of positively valenced events, or (b) provides conditions to challenge one's own thinking and hence improve anticipation.

In this instance, event probability might be the most dominant factor that drives planning. Event probability is not just the actual mathematical probability that an event will occur but the person's perception of the likelihood that an event will occur. It is to some extent subjective and thus subject to individual interpretation and human rationality. While there may be actual parameters around the probability that an event will occur, an individual's interpretation may be influenced by his/her own biases. This is one cause of some variance in the response function of planning.

Take for example, traffic. For the past year, it has taken 30 minutes to drive to and from work to accommodate an 8-to-5 work day. Because traffic has not varied, the commuter plans for a 30-minute commute. Without traffic, the commute actually takes 20 minutes, but traffic has been unvarying. Planning is important because the same amount of traffic flow has occurred with high probability. Leaving later will result in tardiness and leaving earlier may not significantly reduce commute time. The probability of a 30-minute commute is almost 100%, so we plan on a 30-minute buffer on each side. Once it is built into the routine, no mental energy is used to plan the commute, as it becomes routine.

Casual observation suggests that individuals add their own bias and filter to the probability that an event will occur or for the impact that it may have. Commuters begin to think they can arrive at work in 25 minutes on a day where they would like to get in at 7:30 versus 8:00 a.m. It is raining, so they add a little more time to their schedule. If there is construction, plans are altered for duration of the construction. Upon commencement of the construction, delays will be difficult to estimate as no routine has yet been tested. Those who are risk-averse to being tardy may leave for work significantly earlier than those with less risk aversion.

The idea that probability dictates whether and how we plan can also be seen when we look at low probability events. Even though tornadoes occur in all 50 states, it is less likely that families in Maine have a family disaster plan for tornadoes versus families in Texas. Should the tornado siren go off in Norman, Oklahoma, it is likely that students in K-12 would know precisely what to do and where to report. The same drill in K-12 classes in Schenectady, New York, is probably regarded by students as break rather than preparing for an emergency. The kids in Norman have mentally prepared, while the kids in Schenectady probably believe they will never see a tornado.

Take the Federal Emergency Management Association (FEMA) as an example of planning for low-probability events. FEMA had not updated its flood plain maps in the New Orleans area since 1985 (Insure.com 2010). It was only in 2008, following the impact of Hurricane Katrina in 2005, that it added the classification of "zone X protected by levee" as well as coastal areas, which had "velocity hazards," and could be flooded by high waves (Insure.com 2010). These areas can now participate in the National Flood Insurance Program (NFIP), which administers flood insurance policies for homeowners. Interestingly, FEMA now calls for all levee owners to certify that their levees will protect the surrounding area during severe flooding. Failure to do so immediately results in a high-risk insurance rate. FEMA has now updated maps after 23 years to address the possibility that another event such as Katrina could happen. Planning for such an event also should include planning for rebuilding as the economic health of the surrounding area relies on continuity of businesses and the associated workforce. In the event of a catastrophic failure, there is a contingency plan for economic loss and planning needed at all levels.

The occurrence of a devastating event such as September 11, 2001, also serves to adjust our assessment of event probability. The Lloyds of London payout (before receiving reinsurance payouts) for September 11 and the associated losses was approximately £5 billion. However, this proved in the future to be an excellent business opportunity for Lloyds of London because it significantly increased the number of policies about insuring against terrorism (The Economist 2004). September 11 also showed many businesses how vulnerable their infrastructure was as many data centers were centralized. Following this, many information technology processes changed to accommodate a distributed environment for data so that no one localized event would cripple the infrastructure.

The parallel of probability with a pandemic is fairly apparent. Planning for a pandemic occurs if individuals or institutions feel that there is a reasonable probability for a pandemic. At the extremes of probability of occurrence, 100% and 0%, precautionary measures are almost certain to happen if people believe they will be exposed to an impending pandemic spread. Even if the probability is known, those in public health should be prepared to take into account the discounting of information which appears to happen following the concern of an initial outbreak. Should a second wave of a pandemic become likely, it may be important to overemphasize the risk of exposure (Rubin, Potts, and Michie 2010).

Impact

Impact is not one-dimensional but can take several forms. For example, consider what happens in a pandemic when businesses need to shut down due to the need for social distancing. In this case, there would be a direct economic impact of the business incurring loss of operations during a short period. There is also likely to be some systemic disruption of things like supply chain, customer orders, backlogs, etc. Finally, there is a probability that there will be some psychological impact due to prolonged anxiety or other psychological distress. While some of these are more easily monetized than others, a holistic approach is recommended. Each is expressed separately below.

Economic Impact

Planning for an event is related to the impact the event will have on the individual or institution. Even though the probability of an event may be low, if the impact is high, then it increases the probability of preparation due to the expected impact (E[impact]). People and institutions plan for events they cannot easily absorb financially. An example of this would be a house fire. Homeowners' insurance is a necessary part of a contingency plan. The likelihood of a house fire is rare, yet the impact on the individual can be devastating financially (as well as emotionally). The purchase of insurance allows for mitigation of the financial devastation involved with losing a home and possessions to fire. Because the impact is high, other measures are taken, such as fire extinguishers and smoke detectors. These are other planning instruments to reduce the risk of financial devastation due to a fire. Similarly, auto insurance is a mechanism to protect from loss and potentially the second largest expense incurred, but also protects from costs associated with other property or personal injury.

There is little planning for events that are easily absorbed. Contingency plans usually are not written for a DVD player which stops working because the loss is of minimal impact. Recovering from this loss involves roughly $75. The same lack of need for planning would apply to a cell phone. The cost of a contingency plan compared to marginal benefit does not support planning for low-impact events.

If we were to apply this logic to a pandemic, the severity of the virus would have an impact on the probability that persons and institutions would allocate attention toward planning. If the workforce is likely disrupted, it provides economic motivation for businesses to have contingency plans. If the population was broadly affected, it raises many issues in the public health sector all the way down the financial chain to the insurance companies. Pandemics are by nature relatively unique. Fortunately, with current reporting and monitoring systems, we can get much better at understanding the severity and breadth with which the general population will be affected.

Systemic Disruption

Impact and planning have a few subsets. While the previous paragraphs dealt with monetary loss following an event, there are other impacts. One of these subsets is disruption of a system or planned chain of events. Consider planning for a business trip. A business trip has a chain of events that are predictive. The chain may consist of the trip to the airport, the flights, meetings, and whatever is scheduled on the itinerary. If the trip is domestic or to a location similar to American culture and infrastructure, less mental energy is invested in the planning process. The itinerary is planned because we know the chain of events that will occur. Allowance of extra time is considered for flight time uncertainty. It is expected upon arrival that a pre-booked rental vehicle will be available, meetings will operate as scheduled with some variance. Variance is planned because schedule adjustments like flight maintenance or traffic or conference equipment may not operate properly. The planning allows for minimal disruption in the chain of events. While the example above is at the individual level, consider the impact on an airline of a cancelled flight, or bad weather in a particular region. Fog in the New York metropolitan area may delay flights in LaGuardia, JFK, and Newark and may have a cascading effect on the rest of the system. One study suggested that the number of passengers delayed due to the delay ripple effect was 27 times greater than the initial number delayed (AhmadBeygi et al. 2008; Dearmon and Breitler 1992; Hartman 1993). While augmentation in flights translates into monetary impact because of altered or rebooked passenger transport, there is an obvious second dimension of systemic disruption that airlines would likely plan or try to avoid. This is not a new phenomenon. System mitigation for systemic disruption has been reviewed by the airline industry as well as absorbing the impact of any type of delay including weather and unplanned maintenance (AhmadBeygi, Cohn, and Weir 2009), optimal maintenance scheduling (Papakostas et al. 2010), and routing and crew scheduling (Weide, Ryan, and Ehrgott 2010). Planning has taken place because maintenance, weather, and crew problems are random events, but with reasonably high probability.

With respect to a pandemic incident, many of the disruptions may be difficult to monetize a priori, such as the impact of social distancing or school closings. School closings have a ripple effect on teachers, students, parents, parents' places of employment, etc. Consideration of this ripple effect needs to be given in the planning process. While there may be issues of bounded rationality and monetizing system disruptions, they are an important part of preparation.

Psychological Impact

A third dimension of impact is psychological. If mental anguish is at issue, planning may be an excellent remedy. Worrying about loss of control and the associated preparation has limits. The amount of worry may be difficult to simulate until actual occurrence of an event. The prospects of cascading events also are difficult to predict. However, if the future becomes so riddled with uncertainty and possibilities, it limits feelings of control and the ability to plan. Worry also may be influenced by the infrequency and uniqueness of some events. Similarly, we can worry about giving a public speech and we can plan for the anxiety we might feel, but in all likelihood the effort we spend in preparation may reduce, but not fully eliminate, the anxiety we anticipated. In fact, the total mental energy exerted during the process may be worsened as the very act of trying to suppress the feeling or thought may actually magnify the problem (Najmi and Wegner 2009).

Worrying and the mental time it wastes, depends on context. If an event is of no consequence, there is likely no worry. The strength of the concern from a perceived threat or event is influenced by the perceived probability and cost of an undesirable future outcome, along with danger/risk salience (Berenbaum 2010). Simply put, greater worry is associated with higher probability and "cost" estimates of the event (Berenbaum, Thompson, and Pomerantz 2007) supporting inseparability of probability and impact.

Worry relates to planning and also is positively associated with negative health issues, such as coronary heart disease and general somatic health complaints (Brosschot and van der Doef 2006; Kubzansky et al. 1997). Anyone who has experienced a major life event involving uncertainty, such as family health matters, knows the immediate and long-term impact. Social and work lives are impacted. It is the allocation of attention to negative and costly outcomes that are uncertain, which has a negative effect, versus a negative and certain event which is not associated with worrying.

Worry is replaying negative or uncertain mental scenarios; a virtual Monte Carlo analysis of outcomes. It is the outcome of these scenarios that is the impetus to plan for a particular event. However, planning in itself does not eliminate the worry as the construct of worry is more complex. If we posit why people worry, it is because it has personal utility. However, worry may have positive benefits if a person can talk to a confidant as many times as needed until he/she reaches equilibrium. Worry appears to equate to two factors. The first is the acceptance of the uncertainty (Berenbaum 2010). And it is uncertainty which is the most dominant issue of why people worry (Buhr and Dugas 2002). The second factor is when they have a sense of their own role in trying to prevent or plan for an event (Berenbaum 2010). Should people feel an event is totally out of their own control, it is more uncomfortable than if they feel they have some degree of control. Control means either being able to prevent an event or being able to plan and have some role in mitigating negative consequences of the event.

While worry plays a role in planning before an event, there is also the psychological impact post event. A pandemic would likely result in some emotional distress, especially if the virus is severe. Both pre- and post-event psychological impact increase the need for planning. Planning can also mitigate issues with feelings of control over the event. From an organization leadership standpoint, this is an issue to consider if people appear to be distracted by concern over an impending problem, including pandemic flu. The planning process itself may be a means to refocus individuals or the organization at large. The same logic applies to the community level.

Duration

Duration Known

The duration of an event also plays a critical role in willingness to plan and prepare for an event. For example, a trip planned for one evening receives less mental investment than a trip planned for a week. If we have a water line break, we may call the plumber to come fix the problem. If we know the water will be off for a week, then we need to make additional arrangements. Yet the duration of the event may not be separable from the nature of the event. It may be acceptable to drive an extra five minutes to work to accommodate construction for a month. Yet, it would be unacceptable to allow your infant to be sick for a month.

To motivate planning, the duration of the event and waves of the event, if known, can be an effective means to communicate the need for preparation. Yet even today, the event horizon for the normal flu season is something the public at large observes ex post. Should the duration of risk be known, it should be communicated. Unfortunately long before the event, the duration is likely unknown. As the event becomes more defined and more observation points become available, hopefully there will be sufficient time to prepare.

Duration Unknown

In many cases, the event duration may be unknown. This causes a different set of complications and a different kind of planning. An example is a continuous operation in a chemical plant, which has added complexity due to procedures in the stopping and restarting operations. If there is a disruption of the workforce or a critical input that causes the line to stop, there are a series of steps that need to occur for safety or to avoid ruining critical assets. There is considerable planning to establish procedures for shutting down. Starting a continuous chemical line requires critical care. Reactors need to rise to the proper temperature, the proper amount of intermediate chemicals need to be produced, etc. In this example, the planning was for an event of unknown duration. This may cause additional contingencies, which need to be included in the planning. Shutting down for three weeks may be very different than shutting down for one day. The planning for unknown duration has to incorporate various "what-if" scenarios increasing the cost and complexity of the plan.

Consider a flight with an hour maintenance delay. To fix the plane, it will take one hour with 95% certainty. Because unexpected maintenance of short duration has been built into the system, this delay will be easily absorbed. Even if connections are missed, the flight manifest is known. Those passengers who missed their connection may be easily re-routed.

However, if the flight is removed from service, this creates a new set of cascading events and need for a plan. In this example, there are multiple iterations of planning as the delay gets longer. The reason for multiple iterations of plans is because of uncertainty of locating a replacement aircraft and the air time required for the plane to arrive. Passengers are in limbo because they are unsure whether a replacement aircraft can be located or the flight will be cancelled. Planning in this case is much more difficult because operational parameters are unknown. Planning for events such as pandemics with unknown duration may require the need to take into account varying or multiple time periods where applicable. For the purposes of building the concept of utility for planning, boundaries of time should be established. This would allow planning and perhaps motivate those especially when the duration impact is non-linear.

Duration with Interaction Effects

Duration makes planning more challenging because it typically happens in a dynamic environment. If the event is short, planning is unnecessary. If the duration is lengthy, contingencies or secondary effects must be taken into account. For example, the longer the public health infrastructure is disrupted following a natural disaster, the greater the spread of infectious disease (Aghababian and Teuscher 1992; Murthy and Christian 2010).

Timing

The Value of Time and Delaying Planning

Planning is related to event timing. If an event is far in the future, willingness to invest in planning is relatively low. There is no sense of immediacy or motivation to plan for a trip that is one year away. Planning involves the allocation of time, attention, and preparation for the event. Time has intrinsic value to individuals and firms and represents an opportunity cost of doing an alternate activity (Jacoby, Szybillo, and Berning 1976).

Temporal distance and the ability to plan are supported psychological constructs. First, research suggests that individuals often place higher value on immediate rewards than distal rewards. Distal rewards can be influenced by large payoffs (Mischel, Grusec, and Masters 1969; Mischel, Shoda, and Rodriguez 1989; Read and Loewenstein 2000).

Second, temporal distance influences responses to future events by systematically changing the way events are construed (Trope and Liberman 2003). Individuals form more abstract representations, or high-level constructs of distal events rather than immediate or near-term events. High-level constructs consist of general, decontextualized features that convey the essence of information but without finite granular detail (Trope and Liberman 2003). The implication for a future event is that the higher-level decontexturalization makes planning for future events a challenge. Focusing on the "big picture" implications may be sufficient. However, preparation and planning in detail abstractly about a future event, misses details that would increase planning accuracy.

From an economic viewpoint, the notion of value in delaying planning is fairly simple and can be represented by looking at the equation for net present value or NPV, where NPV for a future discounted cash flow is calculated by = $Rt/(1+i)^t$ (Brealey and Myers 1988). R represents the net cash flow, i is the interest rate or the rate of return earned through an investment with similar risk, and t is the time. This equation answers the question whether $100 today is preferable to $100 five years from now? For any positive value of i and t, the present value is greater than the future value. This also applies to time since time is not without value (Mincer 1963). If the time it takes to plan for an event is two days, whether planning occurs now for an event long in the future or immediately prior to the event, then there is no benefit to planning early because it is more "costly."

A Real Options Perspective on Delaying

When the cost of planning in the future is increased, then the consumer has to weigh the cost of planning now versus later. Delaying may have value because it may resolve uncertainties (McDonald and Siegel 1986). To illustrate, we can use the dynamic pricing models of airline tickets. At present a one-week roundtrip ticket from O'Hare (ORD) to Los Angeles (LAX) costs $420 when purchased the day before the flight. For flights two weeks in advance, the price drops to $402. However, if we can plan three months in advance, the cost drops to $245. Uncertainty increases the necessity of the ticket. This can be due to exogenous or endogenous factors. In this example, supply and demand are trying to balance. The airlines have an incentive to know their loading factors. Ticket buyers have an incentive to buy in advance in order to secure lower fares.

Since time has value, it is best to delay or wait to book the flight. Both the value of time and the resolution of uncertainty drive the process of delaying. Delaying is balanced against the cost of delaying. In the airline ticket example, the more the consumer delays for planning time or resolution of uncertainty, the greater the cost.

The process of trying to balance delay with cost of delay works in other markets and situations as well. However, it is restricted to situations where the supply is finite. For example, if there is a hurricane that may approach your area, the cost of plywood steadily rises with demand. As the uncertainty is resolved regarding the path of the hurricane over time, demand in the path increases while demand in the areas unaffected returns to the original cost. Knowing the parameters of time, probability, and cost increases, we could optimize the function. Knowing an optimum time to purchase plywood, based on probability of occurrence, would influence the cost of plywood once uncertainty is resolved. However, in many cases, the parameters are unknown (such as how much plywood costs will increase) or the computation becomes too complex.

Though the cost of delaying applies only if the resource is finite, it is not limited to physical assets. Application can be made to physical space. Waiting to arrive a short time before a major sporting event can cause time delays in parking. Tornado shelters fill up as certainty about tornadoes in the area increases. If critical resources are centralized, there can be constraints on physical distribution resources. For example, if everyone affected by Katrina had access to clean water from only one point, it would pose certain inefficiencies. Similarly, if bottled water existed in one location, the demands of distribution could exceed the resources available.

The public health implications are somewhat obvious. There is an inherent bias to waiting until the event is near and uncertainty is resolved. The problem with doing this is with supply and demand. As uncertainty is resolved and the event draws near, demand pushes prices up for necessary supplies when supply is finite or mobility is sticky. Those most affected will be those of lower socioeconomic status as they will, in theory, be the least prepared to deal with increased cost of supplies.

Mental Bias on Time Estimation

Diagnosing plus mental bias may influence planning horizon. People are willing to impose deadlines, but often they are not optimal to their schedule. There is inherent bias to underestimate the amount of time a task will require even if the person is good at time management. Judgment is based on prior similar tasks and the time required to complete those tasks. Issues occur when there is a lack of attention to time passing and the deadline nearing (Buehler, Griffin, and Peetz 2010; Francis-Smythe and Robertson 1999). In retrospect, we may think the task took several days when it took a week or more, which is known as "the planning fallacy" (Tversky and Kahneman 1974). If the deadline is critical and inflexible, then planning needs built-in time to absorb estimation bias. Distributing work to employees, including pandemic planning, without consideration of time bias may lead to frustration and poorer product. Rushing often reduces attention to detail and quality.

Time Compression Diseconomies

Assume it is necessary to build a road between two towns. A crew is hired and equipment and other resources are procured. The time it takes to build the road is, in part, a function of the resources deployed, such as the number of crew or bulldozers, and whatever else is necessary. If it is important to reduce time in half, it may simply be a function of doubling the resources. If we double the crew and rent more earthmoving equipment, they can build the road faster. Two people versus one mowing the yard, laying bricks, making cupcakes, etc., may speed up the time to complete the task. Similarly, there are situations where doubling resources for pandemic planning may reduce the amount of planning time commensurately.

The learning curve is a concept that is used widely in strategy, economics, and operations management. The concept of accumulated experience increases speed and reduces cost (Spence 1981). The millionth semiconductor made costs less to fabricate than the thousandth. Yield is increased as failures are diagnosed and employees improve and greater efficiency occurs.

However, there are some situations where adding resources does not yield an advantage or there are natural rate limiting steps (Abernath and Wayne 1974). In trying to decrease time for a process by adding resources, the additional resources may add no value and therefore are wasted. If we are laying a concrete foundation, the addition of people will not affect the time it takes for the concrete to cure.

Certain contaminants in food processing depend on cell culturing for detection. This happens at a fixed rate, regardless of resources added. This is one issue with diagnosing strains of infections and developing vaccinations, including flu, where time cannot be compressed.

Other rate-limiting factors may include organizational or individual learning (Hatch and Dyer 2004). Planning and preparation may involve learning new organizational behaviors. For example, first responders must learn prior to an emergency about chemical hazards and how to handle them. The process of teaching and absorbing the knowledge about different hazards involves a fixed amount of time. Operating room theater staff members have spent countless hours to learn the equipment, processes, and procedures. They also have gained efficiency as an operating team. Similarly, a group of people off the street could not assemble to manage a business because it takes time to establish a common syntax. The learning time must be factored into the process of planning and preparation. The language they deal with may be new, the processes unknown, and the parameters not well defined.

Individual/Organizational Risk Adjustment

Risk Tolerance

The process of planning for an event with potential negative consequences also would be associated with risk tolerance. Individuals have their own utility for worry and amount of risk they are willing to accept. In many cases, the risk accepted is a function of the benefit derived. For example, many people ride motorcycles despite the additional risk they are taking in the event of an accident. Some motorcyclists ride without a helmet, while others wear full protective gear. Some ride conservatively, some weave in and out of traffic at high speeds.

Despite the statistics on smoking and the correlation to heart disease and cancer, there are still smokers. Others have weighed the benefits and costs. Spouses of motorcyclists who do not ride, generally discourage the behavior. Friends and family of smokers would likely prefer the cessation of smoke. They bear risks emotionally and physically (effect of secondary smoke, spouse dying prematurely, etc.) and yield no benefit. Another example is prevention of HIV or other sexually transmitted diseases and the use of condoms. Some take the risk of sex without a condom while others practice safer sex.

If personal tolerance for risk is associated with the willingness to plan, then a closer examination of benefits derived may be warranted. Understanding of the benefits may provide motivation to use planning and preparation to alter the behavior. It would then appear that the benefits (or costs) can be of different natures. One typology is to group anticipated gains (or benefits) and the anticipated losses (or costs) into four major types of consequences: (a) utilitarian gains or losses for self, (b) utilitarian gains or losses for significant others, (c) approval or disapproval from significant others, and (d) self-approval or self-disapproval (Janis and Mann 1977). The implication is that planning can be motivated by such factors as social pressure.

The four categories of gains and losses help in describing the nature of benefits. In essence, they are ordinal, but they lack a measure of magnitude. Risk acceptance also needs magnitude for explanatory power of the continuum, which exists within a given population. There is an implicit assumption that the public interprets risk information in a logical fashion and adopts logical behavioral changes to reduce risk. The reduction could be to a ratio of the balance between risk and reward to (risk/reward). As this ratio increases, the chance that the behavior will change to favor a reduction in risk increases. The higher the perceived risk, the more likely the adoption of practices or behaviors to reduce perceived risk. It is not the actual risk and knowledge of this risk which is important, but the perception of the risk. Those who tend to overestimate risk, tend to engage in less risky behavior. While those who underestimate risk (both voluntary and involuntary) tend to engage in risky behavior (Brewer et al. 2004; Cook and Bellis 2001).

Perception of Risk

Lab research on risk assessment and basic perceptions has shown that difficulties in understanding basic probabilistic processes, biased media coverage, misleading personal experiences, and anxieties generated by life's gambles cause uncertainty to be denied, risks to be misjudged (over and under), and judgments of fact to be held with unwarranted confidence. Experts' judgment appear to be prone to many of the same biases as those in the general public and they tend to rely on intuition when not relying on available data (Henrion and Fischhoff 1986; Kahneman, Slovik, and Tversky 1982)

One hypothesis that appears true is that lay citizens undergo a significant change in the manner in which they formulate judgments about risk to new hazards as they are exposed to a stream of information and feedback about risks over time (Gomez, Jenkens-Smith, and Miller 1992). At the earlier stages, individuals have only rudimentary means to attach perceptions of risk to other, more familiar constructs that typically form the basis of risk judgment. This is exacerbated by unfamiliarity with the topic. For example, individuals have a grasp on the risks and prevention strategies for the common cold, because colds are common. When it comes to something like the SARS pandemic, both the impact of the infection and the magnitude of the issue are unknowns and framing the problem becomes difficult. In a relative information vacuum, people have little systematic means to organize and make sense of new hazards. In the absence of more specific cues regarding how to fit the new hazard and associated risk into their lives, an individual will rely on other, perhaps more simplified, situations in making a judgment about risks. This situation changes as new bits and streams of information are encountered. Statements by various identifiable parties of authority help place the issue into more familiar conceptual terrain. For many people, interactions with friends or coworkers may serve to provide further coherence to the issue (Mackuen and Brown 1987) or be a primary determinant of behavioral change as the friends or coworkers attach social acceptance to risk behaviors (Kunreuther 1978). In this process, context is important. The judgment of risk will be linked to general constructs and beliefs. This linkage becomes stronger, and perceptions of risk more tightly nested within broader political orientations, as policy debate occurs (Gomez, Jenkens-Smith, and Miller 1992).

Research further indicates that perceptions of risk should not be expected to change significantly in short periods, even in the presence of evidence. Strong initial views are resistant to change because they influence the way subsequent information is processed and interpreted. New evidence appears more credible if it is confirmatory to our existing beliefs. Evidence contrary to existing beliefs is discounted and may be thought to be erroneous or unrepresentative (Nisbett and Ross 1980).

Care must be taken in order to accurately convey the risks. Appropriate channels should be used to generate the appropriate amount of fear. Further research may indicate an appropriate rate with which to raise public concern or the frequency by which to convey the message.

Planning for a Pandemic

It is in everyone's best interest to plan for events with negative consequences in order to mitigate the negative effects. Motivating the planning process for a pandemic is not necessarily a complex task. However, motivating planning for a pandemic when the probability of an outbreak is low is a challenge. Discussion of the topic and trying to motivate planning and accumulation of necessities in the event of a pandemic, without a foreseeable problem with reasonable impact, may be somewhat unproductive. Because of already held beliefs about risk, compliance may be limited at best. Simply observing hurricane evacuation data shows lack of full compliance even when the probability is high, and the impact, duration, and timing are known. What actually happens versus what is likely to happen are two different things. In the Appalachee Bay region of Florida, three advisory evacuations occurred in 1985. Two were from Hurricane Elena and one from Hurricane Kate. People in the area who were later polled failed to comply with more than one out of the three advisory evacuations (Army Corps of Engineers 1997).

Each of these hurricane events had the proper elements of motivation. The probability was high. The potential impact with some variance was foreseeable. Duration and timing were known and risk was perceived differently by each individual. Multiple realities operated. Review indicated the perceived benefit of evacuation was simply not worth the cost for most individuals. Two key factors with Hurricane Katrina put a large population at risk. First, the impact was miscalculated or discounted by most. The flooding due to storm surge and levees breaking was not predicted. Second, the cost of evacuation for the people who stayed was higher than the risk. Unfortunately, this cost was socioeconomically skewed, and those who could afford to evacuate were probably those with better preparation and ability to recover. What these events may indicate is compliance for preparedness may be weak if the parameters discussed above are not well understood.

A 2005 national survey of companies of various industries and sizes reported that businesses were beginning to recognize pandemic influenza as a threat, but were uncertain of the appropriate actions to take to ensure business continuity (Watkins, Barnett, and Links 2008c). Most were completely unprepared with respect to planning regardless of acknowledgment of the threat to their ongoing business.

However, after the flurry of official guidelines and preparedness plans in 2006, public awareness and media attention decreased in 2007. This could be attributed to fewer cases and fatalities being reported in 2007 or to a natural slowing of media momentum as new information decreased and/or did not pertain to the broadcast audience. A national poll from July 2007 indicated that as news coverage declined during the year, so did Americans' fear of an impending influenza pandemic (Watkins, Barnett, and Links 2008).

Properly communicating the parameters around the motivators is key to getting people to prepare for a pandemic. Geographic level of analysis makes comparing media attention between hurricane awareness and pandemic flu awareness difficult without primary research. Temporal differences and ex-post recall of awareness would further confound findings. Yet if we look at events and their level of attention and media coverage we can anecdotally see some differences. Hurricanes receive significant media attention because the event is fairly temporally compressed. We know there is impact and risk, but there is also news. Hurricane progress can be reported at some relative frequency because it is newsworthy due to change in the event. Information is continually updated as the event unfolds. In short, within a period of a few weeks, media coverage can be very heavy without being repetitive.

Pandemics, by comparison, are slow moving. Statistics are not updated on an hourly basis. The media attention is drawn out over time. The event is not as dynamic, so it almost becomes background information. Yet, compared to a hurricane, the impact can be exponentially higher.

In the wake of media coverage in 2006 and 2007 of the H5N1 spread, corporate preparedness was a concern. In Montgomery County, Maryland, 50 biotechnology and pharmaceutical companies were asked if they had a preparedness plan specific to pandemic influenza. Of those 50, 40 did not have any plan, three were drafting a plan, and six had a "general preparedness plan" which could be applied to pandemic influenza (Watkins, Barnett, and Links 2008b).

This information, taken at face value, would suggest that 12% of the companies polled were prepared as they could adopt their existing plan. Yet, this is questionable if we compare these findings to guidance from the US Department of Homeland Security and their *Guide to Critical Infrastructure* (US Department of Homeland Security 2006). The impact of a pandemic is an order of magnitude different than other disasters; including major hurricanes, earthquake or flood, localized terrorist conventional or bio-attack. The scenarios outlined in the continuity of operations include between 30% and 50% of key personnel being absent for weeks during the peak of a pandemic. Because of the differences in magnitude, it may not be that these firms can actually adopt a general plan. By definition, "general" would imply it applies to all or most catastrophic situations. In many ways it may be good that *only* 12% of those polled believe they are prepared. It may be better to know you are not prepared; much like it is better to know you don't know the answer to something so you can seek the correct answer versus believing you know the answer but being incorrect. The scale and scope of the impacts and possible outcomes demands a dedicated level of effort, investment, and planning beyond typical business continuity planning.

The biggest threat of a pandemic at the moment is the unknowns surrounding the relevant parameters. The unknowns (and unknowables) make it very challenging for both firms and individuals to be motivated to plan. Unknown parameters make the planning process itself challenging. In order to motivate planning for both firms and individuals, we need to understand the impact, probability, timing, and duration. We need to collectively understand issues, such as developing a vaccine will take six to nine months. We need to understand that adding more resources probably will not change this number. Teaching your organization what to do in various stages of a pandemic (such as media relations) is also subject to the same level of time compression diseconomies. We need to understand that schools may be closed for extended periods of time. Parents need to think through how they will deal with schools being closed for an indeterminate duration, responsibilities of employment, and directives toward social distancing in the event of a pandemic. These are almost mutually exclusive directives. Going to work violates social distancing. Schools being closed likely results in kids who still play in the neighborhood—just one of many second-order interaction effects. Impact of personal risk tolerance and perception on health guidance compliance is yet another variable.

The constructs outlined above suggest the parameters which will govern whether and when planning will occur. Key to the process will be communication of these elements and communicating them in a way which parameterizes the elements without sensationalizing them. Key also is paying attention to all of them simultaneously, yet discretely. While the constructs are related, they need to be dealt with and operationalized separately. For example, rational economic analysis of buying a lottery ticket accounts for payoff (impact) and probability separately.

Last, it is important to understand the difference between push and pull through marketing of the planning process. Media attention is critical for creating demand: the greater the media attention, the greater the demand for planning both at the individual and firm level. People need to be motivated to seek out information on how to plan. Yet this can result in scattered results. An Internet search can result in varying levels of quality and type of reference based on syntax. For example using Google® to search "how to plan for a pandemic," "pandemic planning," and "pandemic flu planning," all result in very different findings. The former takes me to a discussion forum on the topic, the latter takes me to flu.gov (as the first suggested site at time of writing).

This brings us to the push strategy. While the correct information needs to also be pushed to those who plan and/or those affected by an impending pandemic, it may be a challenge to figure out who or what agency should be doing so as well as who has jurisdiction. Further, it's important to communicate who really does have jurisdiction and expertise versus those who appear in authority. Delineation may not even be clear to those parties responsible. As in all situations of mass information, continuity of message is critical.

> "We don't know the timing of the next pandemic, how severe it will be. We don't know what drugs will work. We don't have a vaccine. Yet we are telling everyone to prepare for a pandemic. It's tricky...This is scary and we don't know...that's the message."—Dick Thompson of the World Health Organization, December 2005 (US Department of Homeland Security, 2006).

It appears obvious, when it comes to pandemics, it is significantly easier to be a historian versus a prognosticator.

References

Abernathy, W. J. and K. Wayne. 1974. Limits of the learning curve. *Harvard Business Review* 52(5): 109-119.

Aesop. 1990. *Aesop's Fables: A classic illustrated edition*, ed. B. Higton. San Francisco: Chronicle Books.

Aghababian, R. V. and J. Teuscher. 1992. Infectious-diseases following major disasters. *Annals of Emergency Medicine* 21(4): 362-367.

AhmadBeygi, S., Cohn, A., Guan, Y., and P. Belobaba. 2008. Analysis of the potential for delay propagation in passenger airline networks. *Journal of Air Transport Management* 14(5): 221-236.

AhmadBeygi, S., Cohn, A., and M. Weir. 2009. An integer programming approach to generating airline crew pairings. *Computers & Operations Research* 36(4): 1284-1298.

Army Corps of Engineers. 1997. *Apalachee Bay region hurricane evacuation study: Technical data report.*

Berenbaum, H. 2010. An initiation-termination two-phase model of worrying. *Clinical Psychology Review* 30(8): 962-975.

Berenbaum, H., Thompson, R. J., and E. M. Pomerantz. 2007. The relation between worrying and concerns: The importance of perceived probability and cost. *Behaviour Research and Therapy* 45(2): 301-311.

Brealey, R. A. and S. C. Myers. 1988. *Principles of corporate finance.* 3rd ed. New York: McGraw Hill.

Brewer, N. T., Weinstein, N. D., Cuite, C. L., and J. E. Herrington. 2004. Risk perceptions and their relation to risk behavior. *Annals of Behavioral Medicine* 27(2): 125-130.

Brosschot, J. F. and M. van der Doef. 2006. Daily worrying and somatic health complaints: Testing the effectiveness of a simple worry reduction intervention. *Psychology & Health* 21(1): 19-31.

Buehler, R., Griffin, D., and J. Peetz. 2010. The planning fallacy: Cognitive, motivational, and social origins. *Advances in Experimental Social Psychology* 43: 1-62. San Diego: Elsevier Academic Press, Inc.

Buhr, K. and J. J. Dugas. 2002. The intolerance of uncertainty scale: Psychometric properties of the English version. *Behaviour Research and Therapy* 40(8): 931-945.

Centers for Disease Control and Prevention. 2010a. 2009 H1N1 flu. (Accessed December 8, 2010).

Centers for Disease Control and Prevention. 2010b. Tuberculosis (TB) http://www.cdc.gov/tb/statistics/default.htm

Chan, M. 2009. World now at the start of 2009 influenza pandemic. http://www.who.int/mediacentre/news/statements/2009/h1n1_pandemic_phase6_20090611/en/index.html

Colizza, V., Barrat, A., Barthelemy, M., Valleron, A. J., and A. Vespignani. 2007. Modeling the worldwide spread of pandemic influenza: Baseline case and containment interventions. *PLoS Medicine* 4(1): 95-110.

Conlon, J. M. 2010. *The historical impact of epidemic typhus.* http://entomology.montana.edu/historybug/TYPHUS-Conlon.pdf

Cook, P. A. and M. A. Bellis. 2001. Knowing the risk: Relationships between risk behaviour and health knowledge. *Public Health* 115(1): 54-61.

Dearmon, J. S. and A. L. Breitler. 1992. Do air-traffic flow problems interact: A preliminary analysis. *First IEEE Conference on Control Applications, Proceedings,* Vols 1 and 2:531-538.

The Economist. 2004. Insuring for the future? *The Economist Online.*

Encyclopaedia Britannica. 2010. Cholera. (Accessed December 8, 2010).

Francis-Smythe, J. A. and I. T. Robertson.1999. On the relationship between time management and time estimation. *British Journal of Psychology* 90: 333-347.

Gomez, L. S., Jenkens-Smith, H. C., and K. W. Miller. 1992. *Changes in risk perception over time.*

Goodwin, P. and G. Wright. 2010. The limits of forecasting methods in anticipating rare events. *Technological Forecasting and Social Change* 77(3): 355-368.

Hartman, B. K. 1993. The future of head-up guidance. *IEEE Aerospace and Electronic Systems Magazine* 8: 31-33.

Hatch, N. W. and J. H. Dyer. 2004. Human capital and learning as a source of sustainable competitive advantage. *Strategic Management Journal* 25(12): 1155-1178.

Henrion, M. and B. Fischhoff. 1986. Assessing uncertainty in physical constants. *American Journal of Physics* 54(9): 791-798.

Heymann, D. 2008. "Emerging Infections: What Have We Learned After 15 Years?" *International Journal of Infectious Diseases* 12: E36-E36

Insure.com.Flood insurance: Are you in the zone? http://www.insure.com/articles/floodinsurance/flood-zone.html (accessed September 5, 2010).

Jacoby, J., Szybillo, G. J., and C. K. Berning. 1976. Time and consumer behavior: An interdisciplinary overview. *Journal of Consumer Research* 2(4): 320-339.

Janis, I. L. and L. Mann. 1977. *Decision making: A psychological analysis of conflict, choice, and commitment.* London: Cassel & Collier Macmillan.

Johnson, N. and J. Mueller. 2002. Updating the accounts: Global mortality of the 1918-1920 "Spanish" influenza pandemic. *Bulletin of the History of Medicine* 76(1): 105-115.

Kahneman, D., Slovik, P., and A. Tversky, eds. 1982. *Judgement under uncertainty: Heuristics and biases.* New York: Cambridge University Press.

Kubzansky, L. D., Kawachi, I., Spiro, A., Weiss, S. T., Vokonas, P. S., and D. Sparrow. 1997. Is worrying bad for your heart? A prospective study of worry and coronary heart disease in the normative aging study. *Circulation* 95(4): 818-824.

Kunreuther, H. 1978. Even Noah built an arc - why aren't you insured? *Wharton Magazine* 2(4): 28-35.

Lees, R. E. M. 1996. Epidemic disease in Glasgow during the 19th century. *Scottish Medical Journal* 41(1): 24-27.

Mackuen, M. and C. Brown. 1987. Political context and attitude change. *American Political Science Review* 81(2): 471-490.

Marshall, A. 1920. *Principles of economics. An introductory volume.* 8th ed. London: Macmillan.

Maslow, A. 1943. A theory of human motivation. *Psychological Review 50*: 370-396. http://psychclassics.yorku.ca/Maslow/motivation.htm

Maslow, A. 1954. *Motivation and personality.* New York: Harper.

McDonald, R. and D. Siegel.1986. The value of waiting to invest. *Quarterly Journal of Economics* 101(4): 707-727.

Mincer, J. 1963. Market prices, opportunity costs, and income effects. *Measurement in economics: Studies in mathematical economics and econometrics in memory of Yehuda Grunfeld* (pp. 67-82). Palo Alto, CA: Stanford University Press.

Mischel, W., Grusec, J., and J. C. Masters. 1969. Effects of expected delay time on subjective value of rewards and punishments. *Journal of Personality and Social Psychology* 11(4): 363.

Mischel, W., Shoda, Y., and M. L. Rodriguez. 1989. Delay of gratification in children. *Science* 244(4907): 933-938.

Morens, D. M., Taubenberger, J. K., Harvey, H. A., and M. J. Memoli. 2010. The 1918 influenza pandemic: Lessons for 2009 and the future. *Critical Care Medicine* 38(4):10-20.

Murthy, S. and M. D. Christian. 2010. Infectious diseases following disasters. *Disaster Medicine and Public Health Preparedness* 4(3): 232-238.

Najmi, S., and D. M. Wegner. 2009. Hidden complications of thought suppression. *International Journal of Cognitive Therapy* 2(3): 210-223.

Ng, T. S., Huang, H. C., Ng, J. Y., and IEEE. 2008. Human resource planning with worker attendance uncertainty *IEEM: 2008 International Conference on Industrial Engineering and Engineering Management* 1-3: 364-368). New York: IEEE.

Nicholls, H. 2006. Pandemic influenza: The inside story. *PLoS Biology* 4: 156-160.

Nisbett, R., and L. Ross. 1980. *Human Inference: Strategies and shortcomings of social judgement.* Englewood Cliffs, NJ: Prentice Hall.

Osterholm, M. T. 2005. Preparing for the next pandemic. *New England Journal of Medicine* 352(18): 1839-1842.

Papakostas, N., Papachatzakis, P., Xanthakis, V., Mourtzis, D., and G. Chryssolouris. 2010. An approach to operational aircraft maintenance planning. *Decision Support Systems* 48(4): 604-612.

Read, D., and G. Loewenstein. 2000. Time and decision: Introduction to the special issue. *Journal of Behavioral Decision Making* 13(2): 141-144.

Rubin, G. J., Potts, H. W. W., and S. Michie. 2010. The impact of communications about swine flu (influenza A H1N1v) on public responses to the outbreak: Results from 36 national telephone surveys in the UK. *Health Technology Assessment* 14(34): 195.

Spence, A. M. 1981. The learning curve and competition. *Bell Journal of Economics* 12(1): 49-70.

Time. 1940. Medicine: War and pestilence. *Time Online.* http://www.time.com/time/magazine/article/0,9171,794989-1,00.html

Trope, Y. and N. Liberman. 2003. Temporal construal. *Psychological Review* 110(3): 403-421.

Tversky, A. and D. Kahneman.1974. Judgment under uncertainty: Heuristics and biases. *Science* 185(4157): 1124-1131.

US Department of Health and Human Services. 2010. Flu.Gov: Prevention and Treatment. http://www.flu.gov/individualfamily/prevention/index.html (accessed December 9, 2010).

US Department of Homeland Security. 2006. *Pandemic influenza preparedness, response and recovery guide for critical infrastructure and key resources.* 1-79.

US Department of Homeland Security. (2006). *Pandemic influenza preparedness, response and recovery guide for critical infrastructure and key resources.* p. 22.

Watkins, R. J., Barnett, D. J., and J. M. Links. 2008. Corporate preparedness for pandemic influenza: A survey of pharmaceutical and biotechnology companies in Montgomery County, Maryland. *Biosecurity and Bioterrorism-Biodefense Strategy Practice and Science* 6(3): 219-226.

Weide, O., Ryan, D., and M. Ehrgott. 2010. An iterative approach to robust and integrated aircraft routing and crew scheduling. *Computers & Operations Research* 37(5): 833-844.

Chapter 15

Recovery Planning for Critical Pandemic-Associated Built Infrastructure

Randy R. Rapp

Contents

Abstract

The condition of the infrastructure of medical and other buildings and facilities plays a primary role in supporting the medical activities required to control pandemics. This chapter discusses some of the possible infrastructure damages and requirements that might erupt in conjunction with a pandemic to exacerbate its effect. It recommends planning techniques by which pandemic-associated built infrastructure recovery might be quicker and more thorough.

Keywords: Built Infrastructure, Disaster Restoration, Reconstruction, Contingency Planning

Introduction

It may be glib to admonish that failing to plan is planning to fail, and any experienced disaster recovery professional will confirm the truth of that warning. One understands that conditions assumed for planning purposes and those under which the plan is executed will usually be different in some ways. What matters most is a thorough planning process that educates and trains the people who must accomplish the plan's purpose. Among other benefits, they who participate in a planning process learn what assets are available when and from whom; what conditions help or hinder necessary coordination and implementation of actions; and they begin to understand the personalities and cultures of people and organizations with whom they must deal. A well-written plan communicates necessary action to those who must prepare to execute it or otherwise know its content.

This is so for owners and operators of the structures and facilities, which enable medical personnel to cure pandemic victims. Disastrous non-medical conditions can foster or exacerbate pandemics. Common practices and procedures to restore and reconstruct must be carefully considered in the context of the potential massive changes that could be wrought by a pandemic.

Infrastructure recovery is defined in this chapter to include restoration and reconstruction of the built environment. Restoration is possible if enough of a damaged structure remains that it can be repaired without wholesale replacement. Reconstruction occurs if the structure is so damaged that it must be totally demolished and the edifice constructed anew, assuming that doing so is economical. These distinctions may seem rather artificial and academic to some, but for public entities, funding might come from different accounts—different "colors of money"—and demand different authorities to proceed. Restoration and reconstruction are complementary parts of recovering the built infrastructure.

Recovery = Restoration + Reconstruction

Detailed recovery plans for the built environment should recognize the difference between these functions, although both have a similar objective: bring the infrastructure back to its pre-disaster functionality and capacity.

The recovery phase begins when the disaster emergency response and unsafe conditions stabilize sufficiently that restoration and reconstruction can commence without undue risk to contractor personnel or wasted effort from additional damage. The transition from the emergency response phase, which precludes further damage to things or harm to people, and the recovery phase to re-establish the infrastructure may not be perfectly distinct, since they can overlap for at least a few days at different locations in the affected area.

Conditions leading to a pandemic may not substantially affect the built environment. Then again, disastrous forces may damage or destroy elements of essential infrastructure to exacerbate the effects of a pandemic, or a disastrous event may set the conditions that permit a smaller infestation to flourish as a pandemic. Substandard or unserviceable infrastructural elements may delay transportation or communication essential for prompt and thorough treatment of patients sickened by invading pestilence. Responsible public and private sector organizations will plan for infrastructure restoration and reconstruction. This chapter recommends planning that will be helpful to prepare for effective recovery of treatment facilities in the event of a disaster that creates or aggravates a pandemic. It supplements the requirements of the national incident management system (NIMS) and the recommended procedures of the American Society for Healthcare Engineering (Richter 2008).

Recovery Is Not Quite Conventional Construction

Those who have limited experience with disaster recovery operations may view them to be no different from what is done for conventional construction. This lack of distinction could lead to difficulty, since nuances in understanding can noticeably affect the quality of decisions and planning. Three characteristics complicate recovery operations and make them somewhat different from conventional construction:

1. The speed of action that is required to reconstitute the infrastructure. Quick action can provide great value by restoring parts of structures and contents before they must be replaced at much higher cost. Public and political pressure to restore various infrastructural components can be very strong. Plans must rigorously focus on prompt response for all that is required.
2. The psychological dimension that affects people's behavior. The stressors to which survivors have been subjected must be considered by recovery professionals and laborers. Responding managers should also note that the stressors of disaster recovery, such as the long hours, unpleasant sights, and distraught victims, will affect their people. Planning must ensure that activities include consideration of the how the stressors should be moderated and controlled, if possible, emphasizing daily rest, a balanced diet, and multi-day periods away from the stricken region.
3. The unusually high, sudden demand for direct work crews and materials. Construction materials and supplies, skilled labor, equipment of all sorts, and whatever supports them, will be in short supply for recovery, at least temporarily, from any sizeable disaster. Planning must allow for these logistical and economical dislocations and moderate their impacts. Labor and material scarcity delays operations, increases their costs, and often compels acceptance of "good enough" instead of "ideal" technical specifications in the reconstructed facility.

Characteristics of a Responsive Infrastructure Recovery Plan

An effective plan of action derives from an analysis of natural or man-made risks expected for the infrastructure element and its location. In addition to pandemic preparations, the planner may contact local or state government emergency management offices to see what perils they anticipate and the probable level of damage that is forecasted by them to result from the disastrous event. Damaged buildings result from almost any common large catastrophe. The type and amount of expected general damage should then be related to the characteristics of the planner's facility in order to determine the restoration and reconstruction requirements to be satisfied by the plan. The critical damage assumptions are published in the first section of the infrastructure recovery plan, so that readers can place the subsequent details into proper context.

Besides assuming damages and other probable, significant conditions that would impact the performance of the plan, writing a clear, concise mission statement—who, what, when, where, why—is one of the most important tasks for the planner. The planner must therefore know the strengths and weaknesses of the organization for which the plan is composed, as well as the opportunities offered and constraints imposed by the assumed environment in which the organization will operate.

One of the most critical requirements for proper execution of any plan of action is establishing unambiguous lines of primary responsibility for each element of the plan. For any of a number of reasons, government organizations may routinely overlap or share duties with regard to various functions. That is not acceptable for assigning responsibility in plans. Redundancy in capabilities is desirable, but there must be no doubt in the mind of anyone associated with the plan as to the single office or manager who shall be responsible to perform any duty. With responsibility must come appropriate authority to direct and implement actions necessary to execute his or her part of the plan.

In the event of a pandemic, operational continuity for almost all organizations in the stricken region could be threatened by employee absenteeism, whether due directly to their illness, fear of illness, or death of their loved ones. This would impede the performance of other interacting businesses or agencies, too. Organizations should therefore plan to operate more autonomously than otherwise. Planning should include establishing and maintaining communication between each employee and employer. Employees might be grouped by residential neighborhoods and asked to stay in touch and assist each other to the extent possible with transportation, living essentials, and maybe even security.

Organization leaders should expect their people will try to operate during infrastructure recovery in a way similar to what their business culture normally encourages. If there is typically a good deal of trust and delegation of decision making in the organization, then fast-paced recovery operations are simpler to implement. If decision making is usually very centralized, then the plan might specifically reflect delegation or "power down" beyond normal control. Actual events will probably begin to compel changes in the plan of action from their very start. Managers should ensure that requirements imposed for decisions to be made at higher levels are essential, such as if subordinates would stand little chance of deciding matters as quickly and correctly as higher-level supervisors. However, the bias in planning should be to keep decision making at the lowest level competent to usually make an accurate decision.

Another critical criterion for a good recovery plan is that probable resources are matched to requirements, in priority.

First Things First

The preponderance of work to restore and reconstruct the infrastructure after a disaster strikes should be planned in detail by responsible public agencies or private owners. The main challenges for managers is determining how much restoration work and of what type will probably be encountered, so that they can decide effective work priorities, which are balanced with anticipated assets.

Debris Removal

The disposal of debris defines the effectiveness of early stages of disaster recovery. Access to work locations is reduced or prevented until the debris is cleared. The great volume of damaged materials strewn about the countryside after a disaster, which can vary from disaster to disaster, demands close and prompt attention (see Figure 15.1). If the debris is not removed, it draws the attention of many citizens and offices from whom those responsible for its disposal would prefer not to hear. Debris can thus become a public relations challenge; and those responsible for the work must recognize that it can draw much attention, if citizens think the work is not being done quickly or correctly. Some of the debris must be removed, if only to enable access to work sites so that recovery can begin for those owners. Even when promptly addressed, full debris removal and disposal is very time-consuming. The longer it sits, the more vermin nest in the haphazard mixture, and stench grows. To further complicate matters, burying disaster leftovers may pollute the water, and burning it contaminates the air. Proper disposal of many tons of medical biohazard waste from greatly increased numbers of a pandemic's sick and dying will burden existing systems and sites. Acceptable temporary storage, perhaps in drums, or expedient destruction requires that special assets be available. Federal and state environmental authorities will remain very attentive to their water and air regulatory duties, despite any pandemic.

Planning for debris removal requires that an event of some sort be assumed, so that the quantity and quality of work can be forecasted. Different disastrous events,

Peril	Damaged Buildings	Sediments	Green Waste	Personal Property	Ash and Charred Wood
Hurricanes	X	X	X	X	
Earthquakes	X	X	X	X	X
Tornadoes	X		X	X	
Floods	X	X	X	X	
Fires	X			X	X
Ice Storms	X		X	X	

Figure 15.1 **Types of debris commonly created by devastating events of various types. Earthquakes tend to create the greatest variety of debris, but floods and hurricanes are not far behind. It is reasonable to expect that a major disaster could contribute to the consequences of a pandemic. Restoring the built infrastructure might then be critical to eradicating the disease. (*Sources*: FEMA and US Army Corps of Engineers.)**

which might contribute to the harm done by an assumed pandemic, will create different debris types. Different types of debris may require different disposal sites and volume reduction methods, such as burning or chipping. Concerns with ground water contamination tend to involve federal authorities, while those about air pollution tend to be state matters. The scope of the debris removal effort is forecasted by ground measurement, aerial photography, geographical information systems (GIS), or a combination of techniques applied against previous damage experience for whatever disaster is expected. Similarly, some or all of those techniques, plus observation of actual damages, are applied by debris contractors to estimate the volumes that must be hauled and disposed from the region of mayhem.

The first priority for debris removal may include medical, law enforcement, and fire and rescue facilities. Surprisingly, residential areas may be a top priority, so victims can gather essentials for living and secure their property from further damage and thievery. Second priority usually goes to remaining municipal structures, such as schools, shelters, water and wastewater treatment plants, power generation plants, and transportation hubs. Plans must be adapted to the situation, of course, so priorities will vary from place to place and event to event.

The costs for debris operations can become a public relations nightmare if not handled correctly, even if the other aspects of debris management are proceeding fairly well. Owners, both private and public sector, prefer firm-fixed price contracts for debris management, so that they know what their costs will be. Such contracts are usually practicable. Where total quantities are less certain, a unit-price or cost-reimbursement contract might be better. A cost-reimbursement scheme requires much closer oversight of the contractor.

Electrical Power Restoration

Although some tools and equipment are directly powered by fossil fuels or by gasoline and diesel-powered electrical generators and air compressors, recovery is far more convenient with the widespread availability of electrical power. Any sense of return to normalcy demands that electricity be restored. Electrical generators may not satisfy all demands; they are costly to run in any case; and keeping them supplied with fuel can be challenging when many other demands are imposed on overtaxed logistical systems (see Figure 15.2). Circuits within a building or other facility are commonly the responsibility of the owner-operator.

Outside, the primary grid for the region and the secondary lines, which run from primary grid to buildings and facilities, are repaired in priority by the utility (see Figure 15.3). Those priorities are similar to what are established for debris

Figure 15.2 Some of the portable generators required to restore the Opryland Hotel after the Nashville flooding of 2010. The electrical demands for dehumidification and construction tools may exceed the normal capacity of a building's circuits. The cost of temporary power is significant, but there may be no alternative. Man-made and natural disasters can cause or increase the effect of a pandemic. Planners should ensure that backup electrical generators and fuel can satisfy all essential functions in the event of failure of the electrical power for a pandemic treatment facility. (Photo by author, courtesy of Rapid Restoration, LLC.)

Figure 15.3 These lines are a high priority for repair to restore power and keep the public safe from electrocution. (Photo by author.)

removal, except that residential areas may be among the last to have power restored. After the primary grid functions again, secondary lines to high-priority activities, such as medical facilities and emergency responders, are repaired and re-energized.

Since the volume of work often exceeds what they can expeditiously perform, local and regional utilities hire electrical repair crews from outside the affected region to supplement and speed restoration. Infrastructure recovery plans must prioritize the anticipated work and ensure that sufficient resources are available organically or covered by contracts or agreements for the effort.

Dry-In

This refers to restoring the building envelope, so that water cannot penetrate into the structure. No one should think that only hurricanes or flooding compel one to pay attention to water losses. Any disastrous event that violates the integrity of the envelope can expose the interior of the structure and its contents to subsequent precipitation that results in water damage. Roofs may be temporarily replaced by tarpaulins and other expeditious materials to weatherproof the facility. FEMA required contractors to provide a square-foot-unit price for temporary roofing after Hurricane Katrina, and that method of contracting worked acceptably well. There can be more to drying-in than roofs: new or repaired doors, windows, and siding are usually necessary.

Dry-Out

Once dry-in repairs are performed so that water cannot readily penetrate into the structure, or simultaneously with drying-in, the building is dried out. Speed of drying is essential, since mold often flourishes in damp environs offering food sources and mild temperatures. Mold readily consumes natural and engineered wood, drywall, and contents made of cellulosic and other naturally occurring materials. Temperatures from 40°-100°F permit fungi to grow. The combination of many food sources, a fairly wide allowable temperature range, and higher levels of moisture make the remediation of mold a tough challenge. Liquid water need not touch materials to stimulate fungal growth. Higher levels of water vapor in the air can be enough to nurture mold or spores that are already present in a building. Planners expecting water loss in their building must ensure quick extraction of liquid water and dehumidification of a damp atmosphere.

Information about recommended performance for dealing with water loss and mold are published by assorted organizations. Well-established standards for dry-out and mold remediation include those published by the Institute for Inspection, Cleaning, and Restoration Certification (IICRC) and endorsed by the American National Standards Institute (ANSI). IICRC S-500 is the *Standard and Reference Guide for Professional Water Damage Restoration*, and IICRC S-520 is the *Standard and Reference Guide for Professional Mold Remediation*. These documents embody the consensus of industry, so a contractor failing to adhere to S-500 or S-520 might be at legal disadvantage if a dispute about water loss restoration or mold remediation arises. Similarly, owners who hire contractors that do not apply these standards could be in legal jeopardy, if those who visit or work in their buildings become ill from poorly dried structures and possible mold contamination.

Some well-respected professionals state that S-520 alone is not a complete standard of care for mold remediation, so other documents should also be consulted (Pinto 2008, pp. 4-12). It is prudent for planners and other experts who specify pandemic-related work for their facilities to review publications about mold, other contaminants, and air quality by the Restoration Industry Association (RIA), the Indoor Air Quality Association (IAQA), the New York City Department of Health, the Occupational Safety and Health Administration (OSHA), and the Environmental Protection Agency (EPA). Planners should seek contracts or agreements with experienced water loss and mold remediation professionals who know and routinely apply the standards. Requiring that a recovery contractor include staff members or subcontractors who are duly certified by the IICRC, the RIA, the IAQA, or similar organizations associated with proven techniques of facility maintenance and recovery is wise.

Building Structural Condition Assessment

Owners planning for recovery from infrastructure damage should ensure that the information needed to inspect, restore, and reconstruct their facility will be available. One expects that a commercial, industrial, or institutional facility owner securely stores complete hard copy drawings and equipment specifications. Devices that read digital files may not be useful until power is fully restored. Recovery professionals will tap into the knowledge of the facility manager and maintenance personnel. The building's history may be relevant in order to accurately assess current damages.

The recovery contractor performs a walk-through site inspection to identify distressed areas. Architectural coverings are removed in order to observe underlying features. Necessary documentation includes photographs and measurements of distressed structural components. Of course, the engineering analysis should be performed by a duly licensed engineer who is well-versed in the local building code. A plan for recovery may need to consider obtaining this expertise. After earthquakes, explosive blasts, or other substantial events that might weaken a structure, no one should be allowed back into the facility until an engineer confirms that it is safe to do so.

Microbial Disinfection

Preparation for a pandemic requires realistic appraisal of the kinds of microbes that might contaminate the infrastructure to threaten human life. Molds, bacteria, and viruses of assorted types will have to be controlled and eliminated. In the case of more widespread contamination of facilities, the normal facility maintenance staff may not be adequate to deal with the contagion. Decontamination contractors will then be the primary agents to clean the facilities. However, regular maintenance staff should be trained and equipped to treat smaller infestations effectively. Planners should expect that pandemics can result in accidental and dangerous contamination that must be quickly sanitized. Medical waste will be abundant, so local and expedient incineration might be a viable alternative.

Microbial remediation is carefully controlled to prevent aerosolization of bacteria and mold spores. The zone of contamination is contained with polyethylene or other suitable sheeting and slight under-pressurization of the air relative to ambient conditions. High efficiency particulate air (HEPA) filters scrub the air inside the chamber and ensure that any exhausted air is filtered. Provision for personal protective equipment (PPE) and full decontamination of personnel is essential. Appropriate sterilizers, biocides, and sanitizers are essential. While not necessarily ideal for long-term solutions, encapsulants might supplement the array of tools to control infestations.

Documentation of the Facility Condition

Comprehensive and organized images of the facility can be especially valuable for accurate, irrefutable insurance claims for owners of pandemic infrastructure buildings. Videos with narration can be appropriate. Full documentation of the facility, before and after, should enable claims to be settled more quickly. This should speed payments and the physical plant recovery work that depends on the insurance cash flow and enables treatment of pandemic victims.

Possible Recovery Plan Outline

An office responsible for planning the recovery of critical infrastructure may have its own format for a written plan of action. If not, Table 15.1 is a long-proven format for effectively organizing and communicating a contingency plan of action (HQDA):

Table 15.1   Operational planning format

I. Situation
A. Threats and perils for which the plan is formulated. A few plans may adequately address required actions for a variety of disastrous circumstances.
B. Related organizations. Missions and locations of next higher, lateral "sister," and supporting (not formally subordinate) organizations essential to the planner's organization accomplishing its work.
C. Assets that shall be added to or taken from the organization. Contracts or pre-agreements with entities providing people or things for the response should be considered here. The labor skills and equipment, their numbers, and their time-phased availability or loss should be programmed.
D. Critical assumptions. The amount and type of damages assumed for the infrastructure elements should be stated here. Upon deciding to implement the plan, these assumptions are omitted as a separate section, and the actual conditions apply as much as possible to the published instructions. The offices included in the plan then implement their respective duties.
II. Mission (who, what, when, where, why)
III. Execution
A. General concept of the response activity.
1. Broad statement for entire organization.
2. Missions of subordinate organizations, divisions, and offices.
B. Details of what subordinate organizations or offices should do, but not so comprehensive as to needlessly curtail subordinate initiative to plan their own actions.
C. Coordinating instructions about necessary interactions in time and location for subordinate organizations, divisions, or offices.
IV. Administration and Logistics
A. Quantities, consumption rates, and sources and storage for supplies, materials, and equipment as organized by these groups.

Table 15.1 Operational planning format (continued)

1. Sustenance such as food and water.
2. Durable hand tools and implements other than medical.
3. Petroleum (gasoline, diesel, kerosene), oil, lubricants.
4. Construction materials, both bulks and installed equipment. These will be specified in appropriate contract or work directive documents after damages are known. Based on plan assumptions of damages, there are some construction materials that will almost certainly be required but probably be in short supply. Where shall they then be obtained to timely advance the work?
5. Explosives and ammunition. A common item in this section would be charges for nail drivers. Some organizations may have firearms for internal security personnel and require cartridges.
6. Personal demand items for hygiene and protective equipment (PPE).
7. Major items, such as generators, vehicles, and equipment other than medical. This does not include equipment that shall be permanently installed into the planned work.
8. Medicines and medical equipment and supplies of all sorts.
9. Repair parts and spares for major and other mechanical items.
10. Non-standard items to support victims and not included elsewhere.
B. Transportation.
  1. Assets available or to be obtained, such as prime movers, trailers, vans, recreation vehicles, pickup trucks, and automobiles.
  2. Routes of movement of people and things.
C. Medical evacuation personnel, equipment, locations, and routes.
D. Administrative and logistical staff in detail, names, positions, and functions.

V. Supervision and Communication A. Communication media, addresses (postal and e-mail), and telephone numbers. The planner is wise to anticipate that only satellite or face-to-face communication shall be available when the pandemic strikes, if the plan conservatively considers the possibility of concurrent, significant destruction of the infrastructure. (Communication has a tremendous impact on keeping people informed of threats and allowing efficient allocation of resources. It is imperative that planners look beyond internal contacts alone and obtain communication devices and media that will serve for all offices with whom they might need to be in touch. Interoperable communication capacity is critical throughout the area in which the planner has interest.) B. Planned face-to-face meeting or conference call times and locations. C. Supervisory personnel, principal functional staff, and their locations. Everyone who might have a need to communicate with functional decision makers should be given this information.

Pre-Pandemic Infrastructure Recovery Agreements

Even well-staffed and equipped organizations will often find themselves swamped with more to do than their organic assets enable them to accomplish. Outside support is essential. Based on the plans, outside support may be effectively, tentatively secured with pre-agreements about what a contract between the parties will include in its terms and conditions.

The committing contractors should, in turn, be required to draw pre-agreements with subcontractors and suppliers to provide people, equipment, and materials that the prime contractor cannot draw from its own organization. The labor skills and other items should be detailed in terms of whom and what is needed, in what numbers or amounts, and for how long. The agreements should include response time to mobilize the necessary assets to the locations needed.

To provide a fair idea of appropriate content for a formal agreement between any entities, the Federal Acquisition Regulation (FAR 2010, part 16) stipulates that agreements under its provisions may be used for negotiated fixed-price and cost-reimbursement contracts and shall require the following:

■ Clauses required by statute, ordinance, executive order, or the FAR, plus those routinely included by the organization.
■ Provision for discontinuing the agreement upon 30 days' written notice by either party.
■ A plan to review the document annually and modify it as required. The agreement itself must be modified and should not be changed by incorporation into a contract.
■ The agreement should not commit the issuing organization to obligate funds or seek the funds from specific appropriations. Neither should it in any way imply or state that the organization shall certainly place future orders or contracts with the entity subscribing to the agreement.

Once an event damages the infrastructure, the nature of requirements is determined using negotiated labor rates for assessing damage, quantifying repair requirements, and beginning the restoration of critical facility functions. After those immediate needs are satisfied, suitable contracts are made.

Contracts

Contracts are the legal "glue" that reduce risk to parties by compelling their performance according to the terms and conditions agreed. They generally assume one of three different forms: firm-fixed price, cost-reimbursement, or unit-price. The type of contract offered by the owner should hinge on establishing an equitable balance of risk between owner and contractor for the conditions under which the work shall be performed. Appropriate risk allocation between contracting entities requires that they analyze all aspects of the project conditions, which usually enables one party or the other to (a) derive more benefit from reducing the risk; (b) better control any aspect of risk; and (c) more easily bear the loss, if the undesired event occurs.

Firm-Fixed Price Contracts

If the infrastructure recovery work is readily discernable or already well defined in an agreement, then a firm-fixed price contract is probably appropriate. It provides the lowest risk for the owner by establishing the greatest monetary outlay required in order to accomplish the scope of work, provided contract change orders are not required. Contract change orders or modifications can be very costly. Economic dislocations are common for infrastructure construction materials and labor after disasters strike, so materials costs can impose great risk on contractors. Provisions can be incorporated in firm-fixed price contracts to reimburse the recovery contractor by an established formula, if material or labor costs drastically increase above some pre-determined level. Economic dislocations after major disasters can have great effect on the supply-demand relationship. Sharing of the risks associated with such dislocations will perhaps encourage more bidders to seek the economically risky pandemic-related work when they might otherwise decline. Progress payments are made on the basis of either a schedule of values or a cost-loaded critical path method work activity schedule—but not both, or confusion will result.

Cost-Reimbursement Contracts

On the other hand, if the quantity and type of work cannot be accurately determined by the time the contract is prepared, then a cost-reimbursement (cost-plus) contract might prove better. For cost-plus contracts, it is especially important that (a) the owner routinely and closely oversees the contractor to confirm the cost-effectiveness of the contractor's operations, and (b) the contractor has an accurate and timely cost accounting and control system to reliably apprise the owner of all allowable, allocable, and reasonable costs incurred. The cost-reimbursement contract may be of two types: term level-of-effort or completion of specified products. For the former, specified numbers of labor and equipment types perform assigned work for a set period or until funds run dry. For the latter, the contractor determines what crew effort she must have to timely deliver the required work.

Fees can be fixed or award, and award fees can include both base (fixed) and award (variable) components. A cost-reimbursement contract with a fixed fee, i.e., a certain amount for overheads and profit to be paid the contractor no matter the final reimbursed cost of the work, offers lowest risk to the contractor. In other cases, part or the entire earned fee can be determined at least partly by a formula that rewards the contractor for actual costs being under a pre-established target cost or penalizes him progressively more for the degree to which actual costs exceed the target. Besides cost control, matters of quality control and assurance, responsiveness, and overall project or program management might be evaluated to determine how much of the award fee the contractor shall earn. The owner should state in solicitation documents the objective criteria against which the contractor's performance shall be adjudged.

The United States government emphasized procedures for administration of cost-reimbursement with award fee contracts for disaster recovery work (DOD-IG 2008, 16) are:

1. Obtain cost estimates for all work performed. Stipulate that sufficient data must routinely be provided to enable determination of cost reasonableness.
2. Evaluate proposals and associated pricing and cost data, maybe comparing the estimates to other independent estimates.
3. Formally document the principal elements of the cost-related negotiations.
4. From its probable cost, determine the funding limit and award fee for the reimbursable work.
5. Closely track incurred costs to promptly adjust the funding limit as it can be forecasted. If overruns occur, increase the funding for reimbursable costs, but do not increase the available award fee.

Unit-Price Contracts

The risks imposed by unit-price contracts are balanced between firm-fixed price and cost-plus fixed fee contracts. If the quality of work can be specified, but the quantity required offers risk, then unit-price contracts might be useful. Work line items of unit-price contracts state the contractor's bidded cost for each unit of work, such as cost per cubic yard of soil excavated or cost per square yard of pavement placed. Owners commonly give bidders quantity estimates of all work items for which unit prices shall be tendered. As long as the actual quantities installed or performed are within an established range of the originally estimated quantity, usually 15 to 25%, the unit price is paid for measured quantities of performed work. Since the unit-price contract includes the contractor's overheads and profit, actual quantities substantially above the estimated amounts overpay the contractor and harm the owner, while actual amounts substantially below the estimates become undue enrichment for the owner and harm the contractor. Thus, unit-price contracts should be renegotiated when quantities vary much from original estimates.

In any case, the measurement of the work quantity must be accurate for a unit-price line item. Even if measurements for firm-fixed price contract progress payments are occasionally incorrect, it is not serious, since the owner's exposure is ultimately bounded by the contract price. This is not so for unit-price work. If emplaced unit-price work should be generally over- or underestimated, then one party would be unduly enriched and the other harmed. Therefore, an important requirement for unit-price contract administration is that quantities be measured very accurately.

Project Controls

Project controls often include the functions of cost estimating and budgeting, work activity scheduling, cost control (not financial accounting), and change management. These functions help ensure that the project or program is completed timely and within budget. Broad and tentative (order-of-magnitude) schedules and cost estimates can and should be developed for the possible reactions by which to recover the infrastructure, based on assumed damages and contamination, so that alternative courses-of-action might be compared for their timeliness and cost. Once the scope of work for restoration and reconstruction is known, better-defined schedules and cost estimates can be compiled.

Work Breakdown Structure

It is almost essential that potential restoration and reconstruction work be disaggregated into what is called a work breakdown structure (WBS). A project is divided into constituent parts that include all work elements, with no overlap or gaps among them. Owners sometimes develop and specify work based on their own organization's WBS, and they expect contractors to adopt that scheme for the recovery work. On the other hand, owners can allow the contractor to develop a WBS. Either way, the work item breakdown is the basis for creating activity schedules and budgets. They will be no more reliable and accurate than the quality of the WBS allows. Management information systems might depend on the WBS designations for efficient communications.

Scheduling

The owner typically requires a critical path method (CPM) network schedule prepared with scheduling software (MS Project, Primavera Project Planner, etc.) before the contractor gets a notice-to-proceed (NTP) and commences work at the job site. That is often impractical in the fast-moving project environment for infrastructure recovery. Experience shows that a thorough analysis of the required cost-reimbursed work for facility restoration efforts valued at tens of millions of dollars can take a month to six weeks, depending on task complexity. A detailed work activity schedule prepared prior to that point will probably be unsatisfactory and imply greater certitude of the schedule than would actually yet be achieved. However, an approximate or order-of-magnitude work schedule can probably be forecasted by planners, once damages are assumed. After the catastrophe, owners should expect such a conceptual schedule from their contractor within the first week of completing the initial "triage" of damages. That schedule should at least provide overall start and completion dates and some critical intermediate milestones, such as when critical offices or functions within a building shall recover. The contractor's detailed task schedule might come weeks after. Progress payments to the contractor should contractually hinge on submittal of required schedules: the contractor draws no payments until a suitable schedule is submitted.

Cost Estimating

A number of cost estimates are commonly prepared for projects involving larger scopes of work. Based on forecasted damages, the planner will wish to estimate the cost of necessary infrastructure recovery efforts. Only with such estimates in hand can the planner know with some certitude what his or her restoration and reconstruction costs may be, so that a budget can be established. Of course, insurance policies and their coverages come into play for most private owners, but public sector organizations will need funding for all of the expected work. Pre-disaster cost estimates enable cost-benefits to be established in prioritization of planned work effort and determination of feasibility.

After a disaster strikes, an order-of-magnitude (O/M) estimate is commonly performed to find out what the actual damages appear to be. The accuracy of O/M estimates places the final tabulated costs neither more than 50% above nor less than 30% below the stated estimate, 80% of the time. Planners should expect that cost estimates for damage recovery work performed within the infrastructure recovery plan will be developed hand-in-glove with the refinement of the work schedule: time and money are practically inseparable. As the work for the project is better understood and disaggregated into a more detailed WBS, the resultant estimate and schedule can be more detailed and, presumably, more accurate. It may take weeks for enough information about damages to be fully determined and a very accurate cost estimate to be determined.

Cost Control

Besides routine cost analysis and reporting administration, good field procedures must be required to ensure data accuracy and cost control for cost-reimbursed work. Costs incurred by the recovery contractor under firm-fixed price agreements are of little concern to the owner, as long as the contractor is not losing so much money as to risk bankruptcy and fail to finish the work. Cost-reimbursement work demands much more oversight if the owner or its agent is to exercise due fiduciary responsibility. The contractor's cost accounting system should be vetted for reliability, thoroughness, and accuracy. Besides vetting software and office cost control procedures, the owner should ensure adequate observation of contractor field operations and cost reporting procedures, especially if any time and materials (T&M) contracts apply. Any reimbursable costs must be allowable, allocable, and reasonable. Unit-price work requires careful attention to emplaced and paid quantities, since their number forms the basis for payment, and revenues vary with the count. For example, each compacted cubic yard of earthwork that is paid should be within carefully surveyed pay lines. Installed units should be specifically required by contract documents. These kinds of matters are checked after the disaster occurs, but planning should ensure that the owner has or can hire sufficient competent restoration and reconstruction professionals to oversee the work effort that is planned to be contracted.

The best time to control costs is before the infrastructure is damaged. Preliminary agreements with recovery contractors and their preliminary agreements, in turn, with subcontractors, suppliers, and vendors, serve to keep costs lower than ordering materials and hiring labor after major catastrophes, when demand and costs are much higher. Better preliminary planning usually leads to smarter spending of private insurance payments or public recovery funds.

Procurement, Logistics, and Material Management

If planners expect that conditions accompanying a pandemic at least include temporary but significant dislocations in the regional economy and damage to the constructed infrastructure, then procedures for obtaining, moving, and otherwise managing essential bulk commodities and individual items must be developed. Planners must anticipate the functions that will have to be performed and the work effort that will be essential to ensure their accomplishment.

Procurement

To the extent that shelf-life, space, and funds permit, organizations will want to store materials, supplies, and repair parts that will be critical for their operations for a number of weeks in the event of supply constraints. However, the preponderance of infrastructure restoration and reconstruction materials might be procured by contractors hired to do the recovery. Owners should include provisions that enable them to confirm that the contractors with whom they have standing agreements for disaster recovery have located sources for commonly required materials and supplies, especially from outside potentially stricken regions.

There might be a tendency to place more procurement authority in the hands of individuals lower in the hierarchy during recovery from infrastructure catastrophes. In principle, this is usually sound. However, not every aspect of procurement should be delegated too much into the hands of too few employees. To keep good people honest, those who purchase and pay for whatever is ordered should not be the same as those who receive and inventory the supplies and materials. Once a detailed cost estimate is performed, then a material control budget ought to be required. The material budget improves accountability for materials and helps ensure that they are installed as planned.

Logistics

Logistics may be defined as the system of people, vehicles and equipment, information, and procedures by which materials or supplies are optimally moved from their place of manufacture or production to their point of use or installation in a project. The challenge of logistical management in the event of a pandemic is that the immediate need for materials and supplies may be greatest when the capacity of the established system is most compromised, due to physical destruction of the infrastructure and the absence of logistical personnel. People may be ill; they may wish to care for family members and not report to work; or access to their place of work may be restricted.

Whenever disaster strikes, redundancy in services is valuable. That is especially true for logistical modes and routes, if prompt and effective recovery of infrastructure shall be possible. The planner should include options for movement of materials and supplies by multiple routes and transportation modes. Similarly, any contractors with which the planner's organization strikes agreements should plan to traverse different routes and employ different modes of transport.

Material Management

Storage may be difficult to find. If substantial parts of the infrastructure are damaged, then storage will be more limited and in higher demand. Just-in-time delivery can be difficult to coordinate under the best circumstances, so if much damage to the transportation infrastructure accompanies a pandemic, then the capacity to store materials on or near the site of their installation grows more important. If the owner can provide material storage space to its contractors, they can expect to save substantial costs. Erecting temporary structures to store the materials is expensive. Whatever is needed to restore and reconstruct an organization's facilities should be accessible by forklift or other necessary materials handling equipment and be protected from the elements, damage, and theft. One expects the threat of burglary to be greater in these circumstances.

An array of information must be maintained by those ordering materials for the infrastructure recovery effort, so that concerned managers know the availability status of the necessary materials: what and how much is on hand; what is ordered; when items are due in. Planners should anticipate this requirement by including information requirements—what, when, how, to whom—in pre-agreements and contracts. Materials and items stored by the organization or its contractors should be listed in a current inventory available to all who might need to know.

A material master log in spreadsheet or database format should be established to track information about purchases and installation for materials whose costs shall be reimbursed. Especially government owners may wish to audit the management and installation of materials, to ensure that they receive all for which they pay. The contents of the log might include the following, which were found to be useful entries for a spreadsheet log for Hurricane Wilma recovery work:

1. Item description
2. *Facility where installed*
3. *Quantity ordered*
4. Unit of issue
5. Total quantity required (from consolidated bills of materials)
6. *Cost of requisition or purchase order (adjust estimated to actual, if different)*
7. *Date ordered*
8. Transmittal number (if submittal required)
9. Ordering organization (if other than contractor orders for all parties to use)
10. *Ordering organization internal requisition or purchase order number*
11. *Supply source*
12. Initial date due-in
13. *Date of delivery*
14. Quantity received to date
15. Quantity on-hand in warehouse
16. *Remarks*

All stocked item types are listed on separate lines. The italicized bullets above sometimes carried multiple entries in cells. If a materials master log is deemed useful, then the planner should stipulate its inclusion in solicitation documents and designate the frequency of its submission during infrastructure restoration and reconstruction projects.

Quality Assurance and Quality Control

Good quality assurance and quality control (QA/QC) must be planned as thoroughly as other aspects of the recovery effort. Some post-disaster reconstruction quality standards might be safely and temporarily reduced, but pandemic-associated medical facilities will commonly have to meet rigorous quality standards despite such challenges. QA includes the systems that enable QC to be assured. For example, QA demands that the laboratories upon whose tests QC data and decisions depend shall employ only duly certified technicians and use only regularly calibrated and serviceable testing equipment. Recovery work solicitations should require necessary reconstruction quality despite the possibility of more challenging working conditions. A backup plan might be necessary in order to obtain essential testing services.

Health, Safety, Environment, and Security

The operational environment that characterizes recovery activities after a disaster strikes is more dangerous than the norm. The added risks must be recognized, and the plan of action should address them. The sense of urgency that typifies the actions of a good recovery contractor might lead to activity that is not as carefully considered as it would be under normal circumstances. The hectic conditions that typically exist shortly after recovery begins offer perils uncommon to normal work. A 12-7 schedule—12 hours per day, seven days per week—is common during early weeks of recovery, so a possible sleep deficit can compromise the awareness of risky surroundings. As examples, structures may be unstable, and trees or branches may be prone to fall when least expected. Severed or dangling electrical power lines pose a deadly hazard. Rough debris covering the landscape might penetrate personal protective equipment and clothing or vehicle tires.

There might be decomposing remains of people and animals, and vermin run rampant to spread pestilence. Water carries treacherous surface contaminants, so whatever it touches becomes a possible source of disease or chemical injury. Recovery personnel must be inoculated against all probable threats and pay special attention to hygiene. More than for common construction, disaster restoration and reconstruction work is not for medically compromised, physically weak, or emotionally frail people, no matter how motivated they may be to participate. Plans should ensure that responding organizations screen their employees appropriately. In the midst of a pandemic, these conditions would only serve to exacerbate the health threats to staff. For example, people whose immune systems are degraded by the effects of a pandemic will be more susceptible to harm from the by-products of active mold colonies.

Task hazard analyses should be required of and prepared by all contractors for their work activities and reviewed by a safety professional. These can be prepared in anticipation of direct work tasks that the infrastructure recovery plan lists or implies. Internal and contracted managers will then know what safety measures shall be implemented and can prepare their personnel, as required. Each task hazard analysis displays (THA) (a) the name of the task, (b) the task analyst, (c) the principal operational steps to perform the task, (d) any potential safety and health hazards, and (e) all recommended controls to reduce or eliminate the hazards. The recommended controls might include procedures to be added to or removed from normal crew activities, safety equipment to be worn, restrictions from some operational areas, specific supervisory actions, or focused training. The US Department of Labor's Occupational Safety and Health Administration (OSHA) promulgates construction industry safety and health standards in 29 CFR 1926/1910, so the requirements of the various subparts of the standards must be satisfied.

Personal protective equipment (PPE) requirements are commonly listed with each THA, if they might reduce risk of injury to work crew members. This is appropriate, but better risk reduction also results when engineering controls are included in the THA. For example, mold remediators don PPE, but the contaminated zone in which they work should be fully contained—segregated by impermeable membranes to preclude migration of mold spore-suspending air to unaffected zones in a structure. The containment plan should include negative air machines, to provide slight inward air pressure to hold contaminated air within the work area. HEPA air scrubbers remove mold spores from processed air, so the engineering safeguards enhance safety in a more comprehensive way than PPE. In any case, PPE should be viewed as the last resort, the final line of defense against some safety threat or adverse condition.

Thorough training in safety matters that commonly characterize infrastructure recovery environments should be ongoing and not postponed until a catastrophe. Planners should have a good idea of what safety knowledge and skill they can expect employees to have, if they are involved with recovery without prior notice. Contractor personnel must also arrive with adequate levels of safety skills and knowledge, and any such requirements should be stipulated in solicitation documents.

It is strongly recommended that safety requirements to which the planning organization wants contracted parties to adhere be stipulated by comprehensive citation in the contract, even if government agencies publish and enforce the same regulations. It is true, for example, that contractors who fail to adhere to OSHA or state safety regulations can be fined. This would likely happen after the agency is notified and sends an inspector to observe and document infractions. However, sending appropriate inspectors timely to the site could be problematic, especially during the early stages of infrastructure recovery and the disruptions of a pandemic. Getting unsafe contractors fully removed from the job is more difficult, if the requirements are only statutory and not contractual. Violation of safety requirements incorporated into a contract is a legal breach, so unsafe parties can be dismissed promptly from the work even if the state or OSHA imposes any penalties more slowly.

Security

One does not wish to be an alarmist, but along with the best in human behavior, pandemics might bring out some of the worst. Responsible plans for infrastructure recovery might need to include dedicated security personnel, equipment, and procedures for all who are involved with infrastructure recovery. The staffing level for security derives from the credible threat of wrongdoing under the generally assumed conditions. If they work with law enforcement, remain vigilant and aware of their surroundings, and know how to keep themselves and their equipment, materials, and supplies reasonably secure, then employees might remain safe from harm. Active security measures may be needed. Medical facilities may have the only dependable utilities and shelter in the area, but they should prevent all except staff and victims from migrating into their confines. Smaller construction contractors typically cannot afford to hire security services, so active security is usually more economically and effectively managed by the larger firms or agencies that hire them. However, personnel of all organizations must know and practice passive security measures.

Conclusion

Medical services for pandemics must be supported with a suitably functioning infrastructure to care for the ill and to move people, equipment, and materials in order to maintain life and the functions and activities that support it. If suitable plans are not developed before the event, then there will be greater risk of harm to the disease-afflicted regions. The approach to planning that is recommended in this chapter certainly can be further developed and amended to address expected conditions for which a responsible party may wish to prepare. The format by which essential activities are addressed might be different, as well. If planners have what they believe to be a better format and subject matter for planning, then they should use it. However, the underlying requirements and concerns about medical infrastructure recovery that are outlined herein should be distinctly addressed. Doing so will help ensure that the effects of a pandemic are better controlled through the advantages of a reliably functioning built infrastructure.

Acknowledgments

I hope my chapter and this work might spark improved preparedness for significant adverse contingencies, whether natural or man-made. If so, credit is due the US Army Corps of Engineers, Kellogg-Brown & Root, Purdue University, and many disaster restoration professionals who have generously shared their insights.

References

ANSI/IICRC. 2006. S-500 Standard and reference guide for professional water damage restoration. 3rd ed. Vancouver, WA: Institute for Inspection, Cleaning, and Restoration Certification.

ANSI/IICRC. 2008. S-520 Standard and reference guide for professional mold remediation. 2nd ed. Vancouver, WA: Institute for Inspection, Cleaning, and Restoration Certification.

Centers for Disease Control and Prevention (CDC). National Institute for Occupational Safety and Health. Appendix C: Moisture, mold, and mildew. http://www.cdc.gov/niosh/pdfs/appenc.pdf (accessed July 7, 2010).

Department of Defense-Inspector General (DOD-IG). 2008. Hurricane relief costs on the Navy construction capabilities contract. (Report D-2008-097).

Federal Acquisition Regulation. FAC 2009-37, October 14, 2009. https://www.acquisition. gov/far/current/pdf/FAR.pdf, (accessed June 10, 2010).

Pinto, Michael. 2008. Fungal contamination: A comprehensive guide for remediation. 2nd ed. Kalamazoo, MI: Wonder Makers Environmental.

Rapp, Randy. 2011. Disaster recovery project management: Bringing order from chaos. West Lafayette, IN: Purdue University Press.

Richter, Paul V. 2008. Hospital disaster preparedness. Chicago: American Society for Healthcare Engineering (ASHE).

Index